The Truth About Postmodernism

For my mother

The Truth About Postmodernism

Christopher Norris

BLACKWELL
Oxford UK & Cambridge USA

The right of Christopher Norris to be identified as author of this work has been asserted in accordance with the Copyright, Designs and Patents Act 1988.

First published 1993

Blackwell Publishers
108 Cowley Road
Oxford OX4 1JF
UK

238 Main Street, Suite 501
Cambridge, Massachusetts 02142
USA

British Library Cataloguing in Publication Data

A CIP catalogue record for this book is available from the British Library.

Library of Congress Cataloging-in-Publication Data

Norris, Christopher.
    The truth about postmodernism / Christopher Norris.
        p.   cm.
    Includes bibliographical references and index.
    ISBN 0-631-18717-0. – ISBN 0-631-18718-9 (pbk.)
    1. Postmodernism.   2. Kant, Immanuel, 1724–1804.   I. Title.
B831.2.N66   1993
149'.9 – dc20   92-33828
                                                                          CIP

Typeset in 10½ on 12 pt Garamond
by Best-set Typesetters Ltd., Hong Kong
Printed in Great Britain by T.J. Press Ltd, Padstow, Cornwall

This book is printed on acid-free paper

Contents

Acknowledgments

I have been lucky during the past few years to have had such a fine group of graduate students working with me in Cardiff. Individually they offered more ideas and constructive criticisms than I am able (or willing) to recollect in detail, while together they relieved the solitude of authorship and provided a real sense of shared intellectual purpose. All this despite the numerous discouragements placed in their way by a government 'policy' on higher education which seems bent upon reducing research (in the sciences and humanities alike) to a dead level of cost-efficiency and success as defined by the job-market indicators. Let me thank especially Taieb Belghazi, Clive Cazeaux, Gary Day, Arwel Evans, Kathy Kerr, Nigel Mapp, Kevin Mills, Marianna Papastephanou, Lynn Reynolds, David Roden, and Peter Sedgwick. When this book went to press I had not yet read *The Truth About Relativism* by my old friend and mentor, Joe Margolis. Sufficient to say that I owe him much more than an apology for the resemblance of titles. I am also grateful to Stephan Chambers of Blackwell Publishers for commissioning the book and for much expert help and advice along the way; to Cameron Laux for his exceptional thoroughness and care in editing the typescript; to Geoffrey Harpham, Janice Carlisle, Mike Kuszynski and y'all at Tulane for the welcome I received as Mellon visiting professor in Summer, 1992; to Wendy Lewis for her splendid work on the jacket illustration; to my colleagues in Cardiff (Terry Hawkes and David Skilton in particular) for their goodwill and patience over the years; and to Alison, Clare and Jenny for reasons too many to recount.

Cardiff, June 1992

Note: Modified versions of Chapters 1 and 2 will have appeared in (respectively) the journal *New Formations* and the *Cambridge Companion to Foucault*, edited by Gary Gutting. Both are printed here in their original, more expansive form. I am grateful to the publishers and editors concerned for permission to reproduce this material.

1

The 'End of Ideology' Again: Old Themes For 'New Times'

These essays were written over a period (1990–2) that witnessed, among other melancholy episodes, the return of the British Conservative government for a fourth consecutive term of office and the outbreak of a large-scale neo-colonialist war fought by the US and its coalition partners in the name of a New World Order equated with Western economic and geo-strategic interests. I left off work on the Foucault chapter to write another book which tried to explain how large sections of the erstwhile left or left-liberal intelligentsia had been won over to consensus-based doctrines of meaning and truth that left them unable to articulate any kind of reasoned or principled opposition.[1] Critical theory – or what passed itself off as such among postmodernists, post-structuralists, post-Marxists and kindred schools – amounted to a wholesale collapse of moral and intellectual nerve, a line of least resistance that effectively recycled the 'end-of-ideology' rhetoric current in the late 1950s. Francis Fukuyama achieved overnight celebrity on the lecture circuit with his announcement that history had likewise come to an end, since the entire world – or those parts of it that counted for anything – had converted to free-market capitalism and liberal democracy, thus rendering conflict (and the history of conflict) a thing of the past.[2] Of course there would continue to be trouble-spots, those unfortunate 'Iraqs and Ruritanias' (in Fukuyama's phrase) where the winds of change had yet to penetrate, and where 'crazed dictators' like Saddam Hussein could still create problems for the New World Order.[3] But these regions were beyond the civilized pale, their conflicts 'historical' (or ideological) in the bad old sense, and therefore to be treated – not without regret – as scarcely 'the kind of place that we should wish to make our home'.

The same applied to those internal dissidents and critics of US policy who persisted in raising awkward questions. They might point (for instance) to the record of Western involvement in the region, the CIA's role in the *coup d'etat* that first brought Saddam to power, the various efforts to destabilize his regime when the puppet started pulling (or breaking) the strings, the diplomatic intrigues and economic blackmail that created the alliance of 'Free

World' forces lined up against Iraq, the propaganda lies, re-writings of history, manipulated casualty-figures, urban mass-destruction covered up by talk of 'precision bombing', 'surgical strikes', 'hi-tech weaponry', etc., the cynical abuses or blatant disregard of UN Security Council resolutions, and other such – albeit contested – matters of record. But these critics merely signalled their own chronic failure to catch up with the current rules of the game, the fact that we had now (at last) moved on into a 'post-ideological' epoch where consensus values and beliefs held sway, and where nothing could count as valid grounds for dissent among those bred up on a decent respect for liberal democracy, market capitalism and the emergent New World Order. To suppose otherwise – to treat all this as just a cultural propaganda-line in the service of US hegemonic interests – was merely a sign of one's still being hooked on old-style (Marxist or Enlightenment) notions like truth, ideology or critique. Quite simply there was now *no difference* – no difference that made any difference – between what the majority could be brought to think and what was true for all practical purposes. The 'end of history' was also an end to those deluded self-aggrandizing notions on the part of critical intellectuals who had once defined their role in principled opposition to the ideological self-images of the age. Such ideas could no longer have any place in a liberal consensus – or postmodern polity – happily delivered from the conflicts thus induced by questioning one's fortunate role as a citizen in this best of all (presently-existing) worlds. To oppose the Gulf War or any other aspect of US foreign or domestic policy was a Canute-like gesture pretty much on a par with those futile revolts against the new dispensation which condemned the 'Iraqs and Ruritanias' of the world to their condition of chronic obsolescence.

In *Uncritical Theory* I described this picture as one whose 'sublime naivety and lack of historical perspective could only have exerted such widespread appeal at a time when many people (intellectuals and political analysts among them) were eager to substitute the reassuring placebos of consensus belief for the effort to criticize US policy in light of its real-world consequences and effects'.[4] And I argued that the same diagnosis should apply to postmodernism, neopragmatism, post-structuralism and kindred movements of thought which were busily engaged in reducing all truth-claims to a species of rhetorical imposition, assimilating history to the realm of narrative (or fictive) contrivance, and rubbishing 'enlightenment' values and beliefs in whatever residual form. Thus commentators in journals like *Marxism Today* – whose very title had by now become something of a standing joke – queued up to renounce any lingering attachment to such old-hat notions as truth, reason, critique, ideology, or false consciousness. Whatever their doubts with regard to Fukuyama and his end-of-history thesis, at least they were united in rejecting those ideas as having now been overtaken by the passage to a postmodern ('New Times') outlook that acknowledged the collapse of any hopes once vested in Marxism or other such delusory 'meta-narrative' creeds.[5] This realignment of theoretical positions on the left went along with a widespread tactical retreat from socialist principles among Labour Party politicians, policy-makers, and (more or less) well-disposed media and academic pundits. Such thinking was presented as a victory for the 'new realism', for a programme that sensibly adjusted its sights to the horizon of a broad-based popular appeal defined in accordance with the latest opinion-poll feedback. On a range of issues – nuclear disarmament, trade union law, privatization, public sector funding, etc. – it was thought to be in Labour's best electoral interests to adopt a more pragmatic line, or one more responsive to perceived changes in the currency of popular belief.

This involved a great deal of awkward (not to say devious and shuffling) argumentation, most of all with respect to Labour's erstwhile unilateralist stance, which had now to be presented, absurdly enough, as an option that somehow lacked credibility in the post-Cold War era. Better dump such commitments, it was felt, than carry on arguing a reasoned and principled case for this or that item of old-style socialist policy. For elections were no longer won or lost on the strength of valid arguments, appeals to moral justice, or even to enlightened self-interest on the part of a reasonably well-informed electorate. What counted now was the ability to seize the high ground of PR and public opinion management by adopting strategies that faithfully mirrored the perceived self-image of the times. No matter if this led to a series of policy climb-downs that inevitably left the Labour leadership exposed to charges of inconstancy, tergiversation or downright cynical opportunism. No matter if it rested on a *false* consensus, a devalued and distorted version of the pragmatist appeal to what is 'good in the way of belief', more aptly characterized (in this case) as what is 'good in the way of consensus ideology as determined by those with the power and influence to shape popular opinion'. For to raise such objections was merely to demonstrate one's failure to move with the times, or one's attachment to hopelessly outworn ideas of truth, right reason, or ethical accountability.

Of course there would always be socialist diehards who continued to think that way, to believe (for instance) that Labour should persist in arguing its case for unilateral disarmament as the best, most rational or enlightened policy both in principle *and* in view of current shifts in the global balance of power, or (again) that a sizable proportion of the electorate had nothing to gain – and a lot to lose – from a further period of Conservative rule, in which case surely the best line of argument *even on pragmatic grounds* was one that contrasted their real interests with the false image of those interests given back by the opinion polls, tabloid rhetoric, manipulated 'consensus' values and so forth. But these arguments were marginalized to the point of near-invisibility by a kind of tacit cross-party alliance – a virtual conspiracy of hush – which locked the whole 'debate' into a meaningless charade, a pseudo-contest where the main concern was how best to massage the various illusions and forms of false consciousness that effectively decided the outcome. For such techniques had long been the stock-in-trade of Conservative propaganda, depending as it did – then as always – on an appeal to the lowest common denominators of ignorance, prejudice and entrenched self-interest. The only thing different about this campaign was the extent to which Labour went along with the charade. Thus its strategists managed to back down on almost every issue of principle to the point where there was little to choose between the parties save a Tory rhetoric of 'incentives', 'self-help', 'free enterprise', 'market forces', etc. *versus* a Labour rhetoric that likewise took those values on board, but which shied away from their harsher implications through the adoption of various qualifying adjuncts ('social market' and suchlike).

Small wonder that the end of all this pragmatist adjustment was a situation where many perplexed voters opted for the dubious comfort of sticking with the devils they knew. And on the intellectual left – among the pundits in journals like *Marxism Today* – the same orthodox wisdom prevailed. Thus it was taken as read that Labour's only chance was to update its image by adopting a rhetoric more consonant with these new (postmodern, post-industrial or 'post-Fordist') times.[6] In the process it would need to dump old alliances, among them its close relationship with the unions, its traditional reliance on a strong base of working-class support, and its claims to represent or articulate such interests in the name of a better, more just and egalitarian social order. These principles no longer held much appeal, it was argued, for an increasingly *déclassé* electorate whose allegiances had more to do with social aspiration – with Conservative talk of 'upward mobility', the 'classless society' and so forth – than with facts like unemployment, urban deprivation, the run-down of public services, or the emergence of something like a two-tier system in health care and education. To harp on such facts about the Tory record in office was a mistake, so the pundits urged, since it ignored the extent to which voters could identify with an upbeat rhetoric (however remote from their present situation and real future prospects) which clearly struck a responsive chord among many of Labour's erstwhile or potential supporters. Only by abandoning the moral high ground, by attuning its message to those same hopes and aspirations, could the party hope to win back the confidence of voters in its crucial target groups. What this advice came down to was a domesticated version of the wider postmodernist outlook, that is to say, a line of argument that renounced all notions of truth, principle or genuine (as opposed to imaginary) interests, and which counselled that those values henceforth be replaced with a straightforward appeal to whatever seemed best in the way of short-term electoral advantage. More specifically, it involved the four major premises: 1) that for all practical purposes truth is synonymous with consensus belief; 2) that ideology (or 'false consciousness') is an outmoded concept along with other such Marxist/enlightenment doctrines; 3) that any talk of 'class' or 'class-interests' was likewise a chronic liability, given the changed (and immensely more complex) conditions of present-day social experience; and 4) that these conditions required a complete re-thinking of Labour's claims to 'represent' any actual or emergent community of interests. What might be left of 'socialism' at the end of this revisionist road was a question that the pundits preferred not to raise, unless by according it – as many now advised – the dignity of a decent burial.

When the results came through one might have expected some modification of this line, or at least some acknowledgment that pragmatism had not paid off, and that maybe it was time for a long hard look at matters of policy and principle. On the contrary: the first postmortem articles were off on exactly the same tack, arguing (as in a *New Statesman* piece by Stuart Hall) that Labour had betrayed its own best interests by *not going far enough* along the revisionst path.[7] The litmus-test here was the issue of tax reform and redistribution of wealth, since it offered the sole instance of an election pledge (higher taxes for those who could afford to pay) where Labour had, albeit very cautiously, ventured to challenge the consensus wisdom. Indeed there was heartening evidence from interviews and polls during the run-up campaign that this policy enjoyed support even among voters in the projected high-tax band who agreed ('in principle') that the extra burden would be more than offset by the wider benefits of improved health care, increased spending on education, investment in public transport, social services, welfare provision, etc.. In the event it appears that many people switched votes at the eleventh hour, or perhaps (more depressingly still) that they had intended to vote Conservative all along, but concealed the fact as simply too shameful to acknowledge. Anyway the post-election consensus was that this had been yet another great mistake on Labour's part, a piece of high-minded (but pragmatically disastrous) policy-making which once again revealed the widening gap between socialist principle – or principled politics in whatever form – and the 'realities' of life as currently perceived by voters in the crucial interest-groups. As Stuart Hall put it:

> the shadow budget's tax bands gave Labour the look of punitive vindictiveness. It drew the line where, realistically, it reckoned people could afford it, forgetting that in post-Thatcher Britain, people calculate their tax liabilities not on what they actually earn, but how much they hope, desire or aspire to earn in the very near future. Labour was playing the economics of realism and fiscal rectitude. The Tories played the 'sociology of aspirations'. (Hall, p. 14)

The language of this passage would repay close analysis in the style of Raymond Williams' *Keywords*, that is to say, a socio-cultural anatomy of the times based on the semantics (or the structures of compacted meaning) contained within certain ideologically loaded terms.[8] To be 'realist' in such matters, on Hall's account, was to abandon that other (more pragmatic or efficacious) kind of 'realism' which might have carried Labour to victory had its strategists only taken heed of the opinion-polls and not indulged their old, vote-losing fondness for values like truth, reason and principle. For such values count for little – so the argument runs – as compared with those 'hopes and aspirations' (however ill-founded) which the Conservatives were much better able to exploit by appealing to a highly seductive realm of imaginary wish-fulfilment.

Stuart Hall would most likely reject any comparison between this kind of hard-headed 'realist' assessment and Baudrillard's wholesale postmodernist espousal of a 'hyperreality' that negates all distinctions between truth and falsehood, fact and fiction, real human needs and their simulated counterparts as purveyed by the opinion-polls, market-research agencies, voter-group pro-files and so forth.[9] His essay is after all a serious contribution to debate, written from a standpoint of sobre diagnostic hindsight, and hence worlds apart from Baudrillard's style of puckish nihilist abandon. But this does seem to be where his arguments are headed, especially in view of the way that 'realism' shifts over, in the course of his article, from a usage that signifies something like 'old-fashioned socialist respect for the truth-telling virtues' to a sense much more within the Baudrillard range, that is, 'willingness to play the postmodern game and make the most of one's chances through a "realist" appeal to the current self-images of the age'. It is hard to know how else one should interpret passages like the following:

> Bland and colourless as he is, Mr. Major may indeed be finely tuned, as a political symbol, to these intricate (and perhaps self-deceiving) attempts to square the circle, and to the other underlying sociological and aspirational shifts in the electorate that have taken place. His meritocratic 'decency' registers with extraordinary precision exactly that balance between the desire for a more 'caring' self-image, which led committed Thatcherites, with heavy hearts, to ditch Mrs. Thatcher, and that deeply self-interested calculation, which remains her enduring contribution. (Hall, p. 14)

On the one hand this acknowledges the specious character of John Major's electoral appeal, his continuation of Thatcherite policies under a different (more 'caring' and 'decent') rhetorical guise, and the extent to which voters had been taken in by this superficial switch of style. On the other hand it veers away from any such realist judgement: 'realist', that is to say, in the strong sense of maintaining the distinction between truth and falsehood, or allowing that those electors were actually *wrong* (deceived by the rhetoric or their own 'aspirational' self-image) into voting as they did. What Hall cannot countenance is any hint of a return to notions like 'ideology' or 'false consciousness', terms that might provide at least the beginning of an answer to the questions posed by his article.

Thus Hall's talk of 'squaring the circle' applies most aptly to his own attempt to explain this phenomenon while denying himself recourse to the only adequate explanatory concepts. For on a postmodernist reading of the signs there is simply no escaping the closed circuit – the pseudo-logic of specular misrecognition – which accounts for John Major as a 'finely tuned' (albeit a 'bland and colourless') symbol of voter aspirations, while viewing the electorate as a passive reflector of those same imaginary interests. 'Imaginary', that is, for the majority of voters who would surely lose out (on any realist reckoning) once the Tories were returned to power. Of course there were a relative few whose 'real' (if selfish and short-term) interests John Major could plausibly claim to represent, and who thus had cause, if not justification, for welcoming the outcome. But Hall is in no position to remark such differences, resting as they do on a prior set of distinctions – real/imaginary, true/false, knowledge/ideology, and so forth – which he regards as simply obsolescent. Not that he wishes to dump the whole baggage of socialist aims and principles. Indeed he goes so far as to acknowledge that these are still 'decent' values, that Labour fought a 'decent' campaign, and that even its fiscal policy was justified – in real if not in 'realist' terms – by the existing maldistribution of wealth. Nor is the reader left in any doubt as to Hall's grim prognosis for the coming electoral term. Thus:

> under his [Major's] benign regime, Thatcherism as a model of social transforma-
> tion will continue to work its way through the system. By the time we are
> allowed to vote again, education, public transport and the welfare state will have
> been reconstructed along the two-track lines of the National Health Service, and
> broadcasting will have succumbed to the new brutalism. Everything in life will
> be 'private' ('I have, of course, no intention of privatising the NHS') – in the
> sense of privately owned, run, or managed, driven by the short-term model or
> powered by the self-interested, profit-motivated goals of British bosses, the most
> philistine and least successful ruling class in the Western world. In this sense,
> Mr. Major is child and heir of Thatcherism, smile and smile as he may. (Hall,
> p. 15)

One could hardly wish for a clearer, more forthright and impassioned statement of the social evils likely to follow from another four years of Conservative rule. Certainly Stuart Hall has no desire to line up with the chorus of ideologues, tabloid commentators, business analysts, captains of industry and the like, all of them greeting the election result as yet another chance to

proclaim the demise of socialism East and West. But they could well take
comfort from his other, more 'realist' line of argument concerning the need for
Labour to move with the times and adapt its image to current ideas of what is
good – pragmatically warranted – in terms of consensus belief. For in the end
this amounts to a vote of no confidence in any kind of reasoned or principled
socialist case that would counter the drift toward a politics based entirely on
the workings of (real or illusory) self-interest.

II

It seems to me that the lessons to be learned from Labour's defeat were
precisely the opposite of those proferred by Stuart Hall and other commentators
of a 'New Times'/postmodernist persuasion. One lesson has to do with the
inbuilt limits (or the self-defeating character) of a pragmatist approach that
goes all out for electoral appeal by abandoning even the most basic standards of
reason, consistency and truth. In this sense there was justice in the charge
against Labour – exploited to maximum effect in the Tory press – that its
turnabout on the issue of nuclear disarmament was merely a tactical ploy,
having nothing to do with any change of conviction or (still less) any realist
assessment of the altered geopolitical state of affairs. By taking the line of least
resistance (very much in accordance with 'New Times' wisdom) Labour
relinquished not only the moral high ground but its chance to argue a case
much strengthened by this turn in real-world events. For their policy shift was
all the more absurd when set against the obvious benefits to be gained by
sticking to the unilateralist case *on pragmatic as well as principled grounds* and
thus pointing a sensible way forward from the deadlock of entrenched Cold
War attitudes. On fiscal policy, by contrast, Labour came up with a justified
(fully workable and right-minded) set of arguments, despite all the sage
advice from opinion-poll watchers, media pundits, and those who counselled
a more 'pragmatic', 'realist' or consensus-based line of approach. Quite possibly this cost them dear in the election, though the case is by no means
proven. What seems more likely is that various things combined to sway
people's voting intentions at the last moment, among them the distorted press
coverage, the 'aspirational' factor (as Stuart Hall defines it), and no doubt a
measure of greed and self-interest on the part of those high-bracket earners who
wished only to protect their own pockets. But none of this touches the central
issue, that is to say, the question whether Labour was right to adopt such a
policy, or whether – on a more 'realistic' assessment – it should have switched
course and fine-tuned its message to the signals coming back with each new
opinion-poll or latest media sounding. For on this account what is right
(pragmatically effective) in any given context just *is* what produces the required

results by appealing to the widest possible range of in-place values and beliefs. That the voters might actually be wrong – and that a 'failed' policy might nonetheless be *justified* on reasoned and principled grounds – is simply inconceivable, along with all that old-style enlightenment talk of 'ideology', 'false consciousness' and the like.

Let me quote one further passage from Hall's article which exemplifies some of the moral and intellectual contortions produced by this effort to analyse Labour's defeat from a post-ideological standpoint.

> Choice, opportunity to rise, mobility within one's lifetime, the power to decide your own fate, where anyone, whatever his or her background, can become anything, provided they work hard enough; this is what Mr. Major means by 'classlessness' and 'a society at ease with itself'. The claim appears ludicrous to more egalitarian folk. But it is exactly the kind of 'accessible classlessness' that millions believe to be desirable and realistic, and exactly the kind of low-powered motor that takes Majorism beyond traditional Tory areas into a new arena where new constituencies are there to be won. This is the voice that was heard in Basildon and a thousand new 'classless' working-class and suburban communities across the country, the heartland of the new 'sociology of aspirations'. (Hall, p. 15)

Stuart Hall knows full well how bogus was this appeal to a 'classless' society that existed only as a figment of the social imaginary, projected on the one hand by shrewd Tory strategists with an eye to the electoral main chance, and on the other by those 'millions' who doubtless believed such a prospect to be both 'desirable' and 'realistic'. He also knows that there is a difference between wish and reality; that this gap is not closed (though it may be kept from view) by pragmatist talk of what is 'good in the way of belief'; that voter 'aspirations' were expertly played upon in the course of the election campaign; and that they bore no resemblance – outside this imaginary realm – to anything that might with reason be expected from a further term of Conservative rule. More precisely: Hall knows all this at the level of straightforward knowledge-by-acquaintance, or on the basis of certain hard-to-ignore facts (unemployment, social deprivation, high-income tax breaks, cutbacks in the health service, in public transport, education etc.) which gave the lie to those illusions so sedulously promoted by the Tory propaganda machine. But when it comes to drawing the relevant lessons there are things that Hall either chooses to ignore or somehow cannot bring himself to 'know'. Among them are the three most salient points: that many people voted against their own and the country's best interests; that they did so for ideological reasons; and, following from this, that despite being out of fashion as a concept among present-day critical theorists, 'false consciousness' still has some useful explanatory work to do.

Hall's reluctance to concede these facts gives rise to some curious argumentative and rhetorical shifts. The symptoms appear in those queasy quotemarks around phrases like 'accessible classlessness', 'sociology of aspirations', and 'a society at ease with itself'. For the passage simply won't let on as to whether we should take them at face value (that is, as both 'desirable' and 'realistic') or whether, on the contrary, they are best treated from a critical, diagnostic, or socio-pathological standpoint. To opt for the first and reject the second reading entirely would amount to a line of unresisting acquiescence in whatever the opinion-polls happened to say, or whatever people could be brought to accept through forms of manufactured consensus belief. It would thus mark the end of any socialist hopes for a better, more just or humane social order achieved by criticizing false beliefs and exposing their imaginary (ideological) character. But from a 'New Times' perspective this looks too much like the old Marxist or enlightenment line, the arrogant idea that intellectuals are somehow entitled to speak up for truth, reason or principle as against the current self-images of the age. Thus Hall has to occupy the odd position of recognizing 'Majorism' for the hollow fraud that it is – a re-run (so to speak) of Marx's *Eighteenth Brumaire*, with Thatcher and Major standing in for Napoleon and *Napoléon le petit* – while denying himself the conceptual and ethical resources to come straight out and acknowledge the fact. And this despite his often clear-eyed perception of the means by which voters were persuaded to endorse a mystified version of their own real interests as purveyed by the Tory media.

One could make the same point about Hall's passing nod to the standard 'left' analysis, his remark that such popular hopes and aspirations must appear ludicrous 'to more egalitarian folk'. For this prompts the obvious question: does Hall still count himself among their number, or has he now moved on with these postmodern times to the stage of abandoning all such high-toned (unrealistic) talk? Hence what comes across as the tonal insecurity, the sense of an irony that somehow misfires and hits the wrong target. For *either* Hall believes (as surely he does) that egalitarian and socialist principles are still worth upholding, *or* (to judge solely by the passage in hand) he has redefined 'socialism' in such a way as to sever its links with any principled commitment to notions of equality, social justice, or redistribution of wealth. This is the real irony of Hall's analysis: that in leaning so far toward consensus-values (or refusing to endorse a critique of those values in ideological terms) he effectively denies any prospect of escaping from the goldfish-bowl of imaginary misrecognition. And if the message is directed primarily at old-style left intellectuals – or 'egalitarians' who have failed to register the postmodern signs of the times – then it also rebounds on those other, more representative types for whom 'Majorism' exerted a genuine (if in some sense illusory) appeal. For theirs, as Hall reminds us, 'was the voice that was heard in Basildon and a thousand new "classless" working-class and suburban communities across the country'.

With a little decoding this last sentence has a good deal to say about the problems and perplexities that beset Hall's diagnosis. Again he resorts to quote-marks in order to soften that otherwise oxymoronic conjunction of terms (' "classless" working-class') required by an argument which in effect wants to have it both ways, conceding the reality of social class as a matter of everyday experience, while renouncing such ideas – from a 'New Times' perspective – as nominal definitions that no longer correspond to anything in the nature of current social trends. Then there is the reference to Basildon, a place-name that will surely be fixed in the memory of anyone who stayed up late on election night to see the results come in. For Basildon was a Conservative-held seat high on the list of Labour's looked-for gains if it was to stand much chance of forming the next government. What made this result even more crucial as an index of the way things were going was the fact that Basildon presented such a challenge to conventional (income- or class-based) demographic methods for predicting electoral trends. Situated in the border-zone between London and Essex, home to a great many upwardly mobile or hard-to-classify voters, representing as it did (and as Hall rightly notes) the very heartland of the 'new sociology of aspirations', Basildon was indeed a feather in the wind for psephologists and other watchers of the pre-election scene. In the event it was among the first results to be declared and marked the turn from predictions (however guarded) of a workable Labour majority to predictions (increasingly confident) that the Conservatives were back in power.

So Stuart Hall has good reason, on these grounds at least, for his choice of Basildon as something of a test-case in light of the election result. But again there is a crucial difference between analysing the factors (socio-economic, psychological, demographic etc.) which conspired to produce that result, and holding it out as an object-lesson, a model instance of the kinds of voter-appeal that Labour would have done well to cultivate. For in this case pragmatism (in its 'Majorite' form) would define the agenda of political debate not only for the Basildon electorate but also for those others – professing socialists or Labour campaign managers included – who sought to learn the lessons of electoral defeat and adapt more successfully the next time around. After all, according to Hall, John Major 'embodies the growing number of people who, though not mystified about their humble class origins, no longer believe they should remain, as he puts it, "boxed in" to them forever'. And moreover, 'he articulates this attitude, not in terms of the reality of, but the *aspiration to*, social mobility, and the ethic of personal achievement'. This passage would again bear a lot of conceptual unpacking, but a few salient points must suffice. What can it mean to be non-mystified about issues of class and social origin if this promotes a mind-set perfectly attuned to John Major's spurious *déclassé* rhetoric, or a groundswell of imaginary identification with class-interests so remote from those of even the most upwardly-mobile Basildon voter? How should we interpret such talk of an 'ethic of personal fulfilment' if not by realistically translating it back into the language of straightforward Thatcherite greed, self-interest, or acquisitive individualism? What remains of the socialist argument against these values if one adopts a new 'realism' (or a 'new sociology of aspirations') which models itself so closely on the style and techniques of Tory campaign management? And again: why assume that Basildon points a way forward to the only kind of future – or the only 'realistic' policy options – for a re-think of Labour strategy in light of its latest electoral defeat?

One might have thought, on the contrary, that any lessons to be learned from 'Basildon 1992' had to do not so much with Labour's need to back down on yet more of its socialist principles as with its need to stand by those principles, communicate them more effectively, and (above all) combat their malicious and distorted presentation in the organs of Tory propaganda. It would indeed be cause for depair if the 'voice of Basildon', as heard on election-night, were taken as a truly representative sample, an instance of those 'heartland' communities that Labour has to win by ditching its every last policy commitment and espousing a rhetoric of ' "classless" working-class' values. This message may perhaps carry credence with analysts – especially cultural critics of a post-Marxist 'New Times' persuasion – whose main interest is in seeking out evidence to support their reading of the signs. Otherwise there would seem little merit in resting one's case for policy review very largely on the vagaries of a localized melting-pot constituency where voting behaviour can better be analysed in causal–symptomatic than in rational terms. Stuart Hall of course draws the opposite conclusion, lamenting Labour's failure to press far enough with its revisionist line. Thus: 'the adaptation has been too shallow, painful without cutting deep. . . . More the kind of face-lift marketing men give an old product when launching it with a new package, less a shift of political culture and strategy rooted in the configurations of modern social change'. In effect this attempts to turn the tables on all those old-fashioned, high-toned moralists by suggesting that the *principled* course would have been for Labour to conduct such a wholesale policy review, as contrasted with a shifty compromise approach or a kind of halfway revisionism that lacked the courage of its own pragmatist convictions. Nothing could be further from the truth, at least to the extent that 'truth' is still in question (as distinct from its suasive or imaginary substitutes) for anyone adopting this line. What the election results bore home with painful clarity – and nowhere more so than in Basildon – was the fact that Labour could only lose out by playing the Tories at their own cynical game, or adjusting its image to whatever seemed currently good in the way of belief.

On Stuart Hall's account the best, most courageous (as well as effective) electoral strategy would have been one that pushed right through with this revisionist programme and denied itself the recourse to such old-style palliatives as 'ideology', 'false consciousness' and the like. Such is at any rate the message implicit in his call for a thoroughgoing 'shift of political culture and strategy' responsive to, or dictated by, the 'configurations of modern social change'. In fact Hall's phrase is 'rooted in', which suggests something more like a Gramscian organic relation, a quasi-naturalized elective affinity between socio-economic structures and their articulation at the level of cultural values and political beliefs. But there is no room here for the role that Gramsci attributes to 'critical' intellectuals, that is to say, those thinkers who challenge the dominant ideology from a dissident standpoint identified with interests that are marginalized by the current consensus.[10] For they could exercise this role only in so far as such interests achieved articulate expression *over and against* the prevailing set of values, beliefs, or cultural self-images. And this would in turn require a stronger (more adequately theorized) account of 'ideology' than anything allowed for by Hall's consensualist model, that is, his understanding of 'political culture and strategy' as a matter of finely-tuned feedback response, or rapid adjustment to the latest opinion-poll findings. What drops out of sight on this analysis is the difference (again) between real and imaginary interests, or the extent to which people can be swung into accepting a false or systematically distorted view of those interests through various well-tried suasive techniques.

Clearly there would be small hope of success for any future socialist strategy which ignored the 'Basildon factor', or which failed to take account of the demographic shifts – the new 'sociology of aspirations' – noted by observers like Hall. Such data provide the indispensable starting-point for a politics aware of the problems it confronts in overcoming those forms of imaginary investment (or ideological misrecognition) so effectively exploited by Conservative Central Office and its allies in the tabloid press. But this is far from saying that the only realistic way forward for Labour is to tailor its appeal to the image given back by those same (however accurate or in some sense representative) findings. For it is a counsel of despair, a no-win policy even in tactical terms, to adopt this pragmatist line of least resistance and thus offer nothing but a softened-up version of Tory electoral strategy. Given such a choice many voters will feel that they might as well opt for the genuine article – for a politics frankly wedded to the values of self-interest and acquisitive individualism – rather than one that concedes those values in a shamefaced or opportunist manner. This was how it appeared with Labour's climb-down on the unilateralist issue, and also (contrary to Hall's post-mortem) with its rush to abandon other such policies without the least show of reasoned or principled argument.

Of course there is the danger of arrogance, complacency or worse in the use of terms like 'ideology' and 'false consciousness', terms that may connote an offensively us-and-them attitude, a presumption of superior (undeluded) wisdom on the part of enlightened leftist intellectuals. In Terry Eagleton's words, 'I view things as they really are; you squint at them through a tunnel vision imposed by some extraneous system of doctrine'. Or again: 'His thought is red-neck, yours is doctrinal, and mine is deliciously supple'.[11] After all, as Eagleton bluntly remarks, 'nobody would claim that their own thinking was ideological, just as nobody would habitually refer to themselves as Fatso. . . . Ideology, like halitosis, is in this sense what the other person has'.[12] No doubt the desire not to strike such an attitude plays its part in current variations on the pragmatist, postmodernist or end-of-ideology theme. It is likewise a factor in commentaries on the British political scene which understandably back off from imputing 'false consciousness' to a sizable portion of the electorate, or from setting themselves up as somehow in possession of a truth denied to those other, more benighted types. But one should also bear in mind Stuart Hall's reference to the illusions suffered by well-meaning 'egalitarian folk' who continue to believe, despite all the signs, that socialism cannot or should not make terms with the reality of social injustice. For it is they, Hall implies, who must nowadays be seen as the real dupes of ideology, that is to say, of an attitude which vainly persists in distinguishing truth from its various 'imaginary' or 'ideological' surrogates. What thus starts out as a decent respect for the other person's viewpoint – or a dislike of high-handed moralizing talk – in the end becomes a kind of reverse discrimination, a refusal to conceive that anyone could have grounds (reasoned and principled grounds) for adopting such a dissident stance. And this would apply not only to left intellectuals hooked on notions like truth, critique, or ideology but also to those credulous old-guard types – among them the majority of Labour voters – who persist in the deluded belief that 'socialism' means something other (and more) than a shuffling adjustment to the signs of the times.

III

The essays in this book may appear far removed from the doldrums of present-day British and US politics. They address (among other things) the postmodern fashion for distorted aestheticist readings of Kant; the issue of truth-claims in literary criticism; the relation between truth and violence on a certain understanding of 'Western metaphysics' promulgated by Heidegger and others; and that strain of ultra-nominalist sceptical thought for which the sublime figures as a limit-point of language or representation, a point where (according to theorists like Lyotard) philosophy comes up against a salutary check to its truth-telling powers and prerogatives. These are specialized concerns, sure enough, and unlikely to rank very high on the list of anyone seeking a persuasive diagnosis of contemporary social and political ills. But the connection may appear less remote if one considers (for instance) some of Lyotard's claims with regard to the Kantian sublime, a topos whose extraordinary prestige and prominence in recent critical debate can hardly be explained without taking stock of that wider cultural context.[13] For what the sublime gives us to reflect upon, in Lyotard's account, is the absolute 'heterogeneity' of phrase-regimes, the gulf (or 'differend') that exists between judgments in the cognitive or epistemic mode and judgments of an ethical, political, or evaluative nature.[14] These latter cannot (should not) be subjected to the same kinds of validity-condition that standardly apply with phrases in the domain of factual or historical knowledge. That is to say, they belong to a realm quite apart from that of theoretical understanding, where the rule is that phenomenal intuitions must be 'brought under' concepts by way of ascertaining its operative powers and limits. For there is always the danger (so Kant warns us) that philosophy will overstep those limits, pursuing all manner of ideas which may be perfectly legitimate in themselves – that is, as bearing on the interests of reason in its pure or speculative modes – but which can have no basis in our knowledge of the world as given by the forms of sensuous cognition and adequate conceptual grasp.[15]

To confuse these realms is a mistake which leads on to some large and damaging consequences. On the one hand it exposes theoretical enquiry (science and the cognitive disciplines) to a range of bewildering distractions, projects that begin by aiming beyond their epistemological reach, and which end up, most often, by reactively adopting some posture of extravagant sceptical doubt. On the other it tends to annul the distinction, so vital for Kantian ethics, between *determinate* judgements (having to do with matters of causal consequence, factual truth or logical necessity) and *reflective* judgments that issue from the sphere of 'suprasensible' ideas or principles, and which thus secure a space for the exercise of freely-willed autonomous agency and choice. Any confusions here are apt to produce the worst of both worlds, an illusory freedom (or unrestrained speculative licence) in the realm of theoretical understanding and a bleakly reductive (determinist) outlook with regard to ethical issues. Hence the significance of the Kantian sublime as a name for that which somehow 'presents the unpresentable', or which calls forth an order of affective response beyond what is given us to think or understand at the level of cognitive judgment. Hence also its attraction for Lyotard and other revisionist readers of Kant, anxious as they are to play down his attachment to the philosophic discourse of modernity and to stress those aspects of his thinking which supposedly prefigure our current 'postmodern condition'. But the result of such readings, as I argue, is a perverse misconstrual of the Kantian project which elevates the sublime to absolute pride of place, and which does so solely in pursuit of its own irrationalist or counter-enlightenment aims.

This emerges most clearly in Lyotard's extreme version of the incommensurability-thesis, his idea that there exists a multiplicity of language-games (or 'phrase-regimes') each with its own *sui generis* criteria of meaning, validity or truth. From which it follows – again by analogy with the Kantian sublime, or Lyotard's reading thereof – that the cognitive phrase-regime not only has to yield up its privileged truth-telling role, but must also be seen as committing a form of speech-act injustice (a suppression of the narrative 'differend') whenever it presumes to arbitrate in matters of ethical or political justice. What this amounts to, in short, is a postmodern variant on the drastic dichotomy between fact and value standardly (though wrongly) attributed to Hume, allied to a strain of out-and-out nominalism which denies that statements can have any meaning – any truth-value, purport or operative force – aside from the manifold language-games that make up an ongoing cultural conversation. Only by seeking to maximize narrative differentials – by cultivating 'dissensus' or 'heterogeneity' – can thinking be sure to remain on guard against those kinds of coercive (and potentially totalitarian) phrase-regime that have so far exerted their malign hold upon the discourse of 'enlightened' reason.

Thus it is wrong, so Lyotard would argue, to adduce historical or factual considerations when assessing the significance of 'great events' like the French Revolution, the Nazi death-camps, or other such charged and evocative phrases whose meaning eludes cognitive criteria. For this is to confuse the two distinct orders of truth-claim, on the one hand those that properly have to do with issues of empirical warrant, eye-witness testimony, archival research, etc., and on the other hand those that can only find expression in a language whose evaluative character precludes any straightforward probative appeal to the facts of the case. The crucial point here is the way that certain *names* are taken up into a range of contending discourses which then set the terms, or establish their own criteria, for what should count as a truthful, relevant, or good-faith assertion. Those names would be 'rigid designators' (in Kripke's parlance) only to the extent that they served to pick out persons, places or dates whose reference – in some minimal sense of the word – could be taken pretty much for granted.[16] Beyond that they would evoke such deep-laid disagreement that the names would function more as surrogate descriptors, nominal points of intersection for a variety of language-games, narrative paradigms, imputed attributes, ethical judgements, and so forth, each of them assigning its own significance to the term in question. Such names might include (to mix some of Lyotard's examples with some of my own) 'Napoleon', 'Marx', 'Lenin', 'Hitler', 'Auschwitz', 'Leningrad', 'Dunkirk', 'October 1917', 'Berlin 1953', 'Prague 1968', 'Berlin 1990', 'Baghdad 1991' and others of a kindred character.[17] In every case, according to Lyotard, their utterance gives rise to a strictly irreducible conflict of interpretations, a dispute (or differend) between rival claims as to their 'true' historical meaning.

Least of all can such issues be resolved through an attempt to establish what actually occurred, or to offer more adequate (factual or evidential) grounds for ariving at a properly informed estimate. For on Lyotard's account there is simply no passage – no possible means of translation – from the phrase-regime of cognitive (or factual-documentary) truth to the phrase-regimes of ethics, political justice, or other such evaluative speech-act genres. And this rule must apply, he maintains, even when confronted with apparently outrageous instances, like Faurisson's right-wing 'revisionist' claim that for all we can know the gas-chambers never existed, since there survive no witnesses who can vouch for the fact on the basis of first-hand experience or knowledge-by-acquaintance. Of course it may be said that such arguments amount to nothing more than a vicious sophistry, an effort to obscure or deny the truth by adopting criteria grossly inappropriate to the case in hand. But this is to miss the point, according to Lyotard, since Faurisson has not the slightest interest in getting things right by the normative standards of responsible (truth-seeking) scholarly enquiry. Nor, for that matter, is Faurisson much concerned with issues of right and wrong as conceived by most historians of the Holocaust, those for whom the interests of factual truth are indissociable from questions of moral accountability or good-faith ethical judgment. On the contrary: 'the historian need not strive to convince Faurisson if Faurisson is "playing" another genre of discourse, one in which conviction, or the attainment of consensus over a defined reality, is not at stake'.[18] Opponents may have good reason – at least by their own disciplinary or moral lights – for denouncing Faurisson as a rabid ideologue, a sophistical perverter of the truth, or a pseudo-historian whose 'revisionist' project is a cover for the crudest kinds of anti-semitic propaganda. But they will be wrong so to argue, Lyotard thinks. For quite simply there is *no common ground* between Faurisson and those who reject his views, whether professional historians affronted by his cavalier way with the documentary evidence or non-specialists appalled by his indifference to the manifest evils of Nazism and the suffering of its victims.

To suppose otherwise – as by thinking to refute or discredit his bad scholarship – is according to Lyotard a temptation that Faurisson's critics would do well to resist. Such rejoinders will in any case be wholly ineffective, failing as they do to acknowledge the differend – the radical heterogeneity – that separates his discourse from theirs. But they will also run the risk of his turning the tables, accusing his accusers of practising a language-game (referential, cognitive, factual-documentary or whatever) that not only ignores but actively suppresses the crucial point at issue between them. In Lyotard's words: '[i]f the demand to have to establish the reality of the referent of a sentence is extended to any sentence . . . then that demand is totalitarian in its principle'.[19] So it is better to accept (as he thinks we must in the end) that there is nothing to be gained by disputing Faurisson's 'arguments' as if these were subject to the normal criteria or validity-conditions for statements of historical truth. Given such a downright clash of heterogeneous discourses – of beliefs, values, ideologies, 'phrase-regimes', or narrative paradigms – the best that one can do is renounce any prospect of engaging in reasoned argumentative debate. Thus 'Auschwitz' must figure as one of those names whose significance cannot be established by any amount of patient archival research, since it so far exceeds our powers of understanding – of adequate conceptual grasp – as to render such debate otiose.

This is where the sublime comes in, once again, as an index of the gulf between factual truth-claims and judgments of an evaluative or ethico-political order. For what the death-camps signify (according to Lyotard) is an event beyond all the capacities of rational thought, an event that stands as the ultimate rebuke to 'Enlightenment' aims and principles. At this point, he writes,

> something new has happened in history (which can only be a sign and not a fact) which is that the facts, the testimonies, which bore the traces of *heres* and *nows*, the documents which indicated the meaning or meanings of the facts, and the names, finally the possibility of diverse kinds of phrases whose conjunction makes reality, all this has been destroyed as much as possible.[20]

If 'reality' (or historical truth) were indeed just a matter of 'phrases' – a construct out of various descriptions, vocabularies, language-games, tropes, narratives etc. – then one might (just about) make tolerable sense of Lyotard's argument. And of course such ideas are pretty much *de rigueur* among the adepts of postmodern and post-structuralist theory, those for whom the referent is a fictive postulate, a redundant third term whose role has been eclipsed (since Saussure) by our knowledge of the 'arbitrary' relation between signifier and signified. Otherwise the passage will serve as an index – a cautionary reminder – of the sceptical extremes to which 'theory' may be driven when divorced from any sense of real-world cognitive and moral accountability. For it is a *fact* (not an 'idea' in Lyotard's quasi-Kantian usage of the term) that Auschwitz existed, that it became one of the sites for the Nazi programme of mass-extermination, that the gas-chambers functioned as a part of that programme, and moreover – as will surely be agreed by any but the most blinkered of 'revisionist' ideologues – that there exists an overwhelming mass of evidence to prove that case. Nor would Faurisson's lies (or Lyotard's scepticism) be in any way justified even if it were true that 'all this' (that is, all the documentary evidence) had in fact been 'destroyed as much as possible'. For witness to the event would still be borne by those material traces – relics of various kinds – that were not (or could not be) so destroyed, together with the archives, the depositions of death-camp survivors, the testimony of convicted war-crime defendants, and so forth.

Of course the sceptic may then wish to argue that such evidence is 'textual' in the sense of being open to various interpretations, one of which (Faurisson's) will reject it out of hand, while another (Lyotard's) will defend a form of principled agnosticism, a refusal to privilege any reading, any set of truth-claims or interpretive criteria, which seeks to have the last word.[21] And indeed there is no refuting this position, unless by various forms of *reductio ad absurdum* argument, like that whereby the sceptic is shown to inhabit a solipsistic world (or textualist prison-house) of his or her own devising. For they can still refuse to play by the commonsense, rational, good-faith or realist rules, declaring such rules to be simply irrelevant – no part of their chosen language-game – and preferring to stick with their position whatever its consequences. But it is important to be clear about those consequences, especially in view of Lyotard's claim that we can only do justice to the rival litigants in any given case by respecting the speech-act or narrative differend between them, and thus suspending all judgments of truth and falsehood or right and wrong. What this 'justice' means with regard to Faurisson is that the sceptic *has every right* to assert that the gas-chambers never existed, or were never put to the purpose of mass-extermination, just so long as he allows others the right to maintain a contrary opinion according to their own cognitive and ethical criteria.

Thus they might well respond by remarking, like Stephen Greenblatt in a recent essay, that the Nazis, so far from destroying all the evidence, in fact displayed an equal and opposite compulsion to amass huge amounts of it, including those collections of personal effects, bodily remains, hair, teeth-fillings and other such grim testimonials to the nature and scale of their atrocities.[22] Nor (presumably) would Lyotard deny the evidential force of such arguments or their claim upon the conscience of anyone committed to establishing the truth of what happened. All the same, 'positivist historians are at the mercy of a Faurisson if they imagine that justice consists solely in the application of cognitive rules in such cases'. And again: '[i]f history were merely a question of such rules, it is hard to know how Faurisson could be accused of injustice'.[23] For it is only through the exercise of interpretive freedom – a freedom unconstrained by cognitivist appeals to the known, reconstructed, or empirically warranted facts of the case – it is only on this condition, Lyotard asserts, that opponents can claim any ethical right to criticize Faurisson's arguments. And even then they will be placed in the wrong (subject to the charge of suppressing the differend or imposing their own criteria for debate) if they seek to discredit Faurisson by appeal to truth-claims or ethical values that he simply will not acknowledge. In such cases,

one side's legitimacy does not imply the other's lack of legitimacy. Applying a single rule of judgment to both in order to settle their differend ... would wrong (at least) one of them (and both of them if neither side accepts this rule). . . . A wrong results from the fact that the rules of the genre of discourse by which one judges are not those of the judged genre or genres of discourse.[24]

This passage shows just how far Lyotard is willing to go along the path to an ultra-nominalist position where language-games (or speech-act genres) go all the way down, and where issues of truth are wholly subsumed to issues of linguistic (or textual) representation. Like so much postmodern and post-structuralist theory it begins by setting up a straw-man opponent – the unreconstructed 'positivist' – and ends by renouncing any claim to adjudicate in questions of truth and right. That he is willing to apply such arguments to an instance like Auschwitz – and (in effect) accord Faurisson the benefit of the sceptical doubt – is a sign of the moral confusions brought about by this most extreme variant of the present-day 'linguistic turn'.

The same confusions are visible (albeit in less spectacular form) when Lyotard addresses political issues of class, ideology, and representation. Here again he falls back on the sublime as a kind of postmodernist shibboleth, a reminder – if any were needed – of the problems confronted by left intellectuals who still seek to make sense of history from a standpoint of class-based *Ideologiekritik*. His response to Terry Eagleton during a 1985 debate at the Institute of Contemporary Arts in London is a fair enough sample of Lyotard's reflections in this quasi-Kantian vein.

Nobody has ever seen a proletariat (Marx said this): you can observe working-classes, certainly, but they are only part of the observable society. It's impossible to argue that this part of society is the incarnation of the proletariat, because an Idea in general has no presentation, and *that is the question of the sublime*. . . . I'm sure we have to read and re-read Marx, but in a critical way: that is, we must say that the question of the proletariat is the question of knowing whether this word is to be understood in terms of the Hegelian dialectic (that is to say, in the end, in terms of science), expecting to find something experiential to correspond to the concept, and maybe to the concept itself; or is the term 'proletariat' the name of an Idea of Reason, the name of a subject to be emancipated? In the second case we give up the pretension of presenting something in experience which corresponds to this term.[25]

In some details of phrasing – for example, its talk of a 'subject to be emancipated' – this passage might seem true to its Kantian lights and even to that critical 're-reading' of Marx that Lyotard here recommends. But the postmodern scepticism shows up clearly in other, more decisive and symptomatic ways. Thus his nominalist language ('the term "proletariat"', 'the *name* of a subject') betokens Lyotard's refusal to acknowledge that such words could possess any reference outside the discourse of speculative reason.

So it is that the sublime does duty, yet again, as an analogue for those strictly unrepresentable 'Ideas of Reason' whose significance lies beyond the furthest bounds of conceptual or experiential knowledge. For the only alternative, as Lyotard would have it, is a Hegelian reading of Marx on history according to which Ideas become incarnate in the form of a universal class (the Proletariat) whose advent marks the definitive transcendence of all such ontological distinctions.

This shows, to say the least, a somewhat limited grasp of debates within the Marxist theoretical tradition since Lukács's *History and Class Consciousness*. And as a reading of Kant it is even more skewed and tendentious, chiefly on account of Lyotard's desire to aestheticize ethics and politics by deploying the sublime as a figure of ultimate heterogeneity, a wedge (so to speak) or a deconstructive lever that can always be driven between the cognitive and evaluative phrase-regimes. Such ideas thus serve to immaterialize the language of any class-based social analysis or any account of knowledge and human interests that would assign a more than notional (speculative) content to terms like 'society' and 'class'. This whole line of argument bears a striking resemblance to other variations on the end-of-ideology theme, among them Margaret Thatcher's celebrated claim that 'society' doesn't exist, that 'individual' interests, motives, or talents are the only ones that count, and that talk of 'class' is just a tedious irrelevance in present-day social and economic terms. For whatever their express political allegiance – no matter how remote from the numbing banalities of Thatcherite rhetoric – these theorists must be seen as effectively endorsing the same ultra-nominalist position.

It is here that postmodernism feeds back into the 'New Times' thinking of an otherwise shrewd and perceptive commentator like Stuart Hall. Such, after all, is the message implicit in his article on the 1992 election campaign and the reasons for Labour's defeat at the polls. If there is any way forward for socialism in the wake of this defeat then it clearly does not lie through the old left country of class politics, collective social values, or appeals to enlightened interest on the part of an informed and responsible electorate. Rather it must take full account of those factors – upward mobility, the 'classless society', free enterprise, individual 'empowerment' and so forth – whose appeal may be largely or wholly bogus when set against all the evidence to hand, but which have none the less managed to set the agenda for now and the foreseeable future. Such phrases have a ready-made suasive power – an ability to chime with the 'new sociology of aspirations' – which leaves no room for the old left analysis, based as it was on obsolete notions like truth, reality, ideology, critique, and genuine (as opposed to false or distorted) consensus values. If words and styles of talk are indeed all we have, and if those old language-games are now hopelessly outdated, then socialists had better move with the times and adapt their rhetoric accordingly.

Hall is not much given to philosophical excursions in the manner of Lyotard and kindred spirits on the postmodern cultural scene. But his view of current domestic political 'realities' has a good deal in common with that strain of nominalist thinking which claims a starting point and justification in Kant's idea of the sublime. Thus the language of class, of real human interests or the 'subject to be emancipated' may still (for Lyotard or Hall) possess a certain ethical resonance, a power to evoke 'Ideas of Reason' whose meaning cannot be wholly exhausted by setbacks on the socialist road. But we shall be wrong, both agree, if we think that there is 'something experiential' that could ever 'correspond' to such ideas, or if we cling to the cognitivist illusion of 'presenting something in experience' that might actually bear them out. Now of course there is some truth in these arguments, both as a matter of soical observation and (albeit more debatably) in so far as Lyotard would claim to derive them from a reading of the Kantian sublime. Thus it can hardly be denied that class predicates or socio-economic terms of analysis become more difficult to apply, at least in any straightforward representationalist mode, at a time of rapid and complex demographic change when so many of the old class indicators no longer seem to have much purchase. To this extent Hall is fully justified in arguing that any workable socialist politics will need to take account of these factors when considering its future electoral strategy. And there is also a sense in which Lyotard is right to invoke Kant by way of controverting any simple correspondence-theory of history, politics and class-interests. Thus he can cite various passages in the third *Critique* which do indeed proffer the sublime as a token of the gulf between cognitive and evaluative phrase-regimes, the existence of a 'suprasensible' realm beyond the bounds of phenomenal self-evidence, or the confusions that arise when 'Ideas of Reason' are wrongly referred to the cognitive tribunal whose competence extends only to matters of theoretical understanding, namely those cases where sensuous intuitions may be 'brought under' adequate concepts. In short, there are good reasons for maintaining that the interests of justice, or the hopes of social and ethico-political progress, are not best served by a direct appeal to those interests as embodied in the actual experience of some existing class or group. Of course one might well have arrived at this conclusion without benefit of Lyotard's repeated and circuitous detours via Kant on the sublime. For Stuart Hall it is largely a matter of inductive observation, of remarking those current social trends and demographic shifts that pose a problem for more traditional, class-based modes of analysis and critique. But for other theorists on the post-Marxist left there is a plausible (though by its very nature somewhat fugitive) connection to be drawn between the Kantian sublime and issues of a present-day political or socio-cultural import.[26]

Where this connection breaks down, as I have argued, is with the further move that presses such scepticism well beyond the point of a argued appeal to the evidence of demographic change. For it then becomes a pretext for the kind of wholesale nominalist approach that denies what should surely be apparent to any commentator, that is to say, the continuing *facts* of unemployment, social deprivation, unequal opportunities, two-tier health care, educational under-privilege and the rest. No doubt these data have then to be interpreted with a due regard to all the complicating factors – upward mobility, imaginary investment, Hall's 'new sociology of aspirations' – which will strike any reasonably sensitive observer of the current electoral scene. But there is little purpose in pursuing such analyses if they end up, like Lyotard's obsessive ruminations on the Kantian sublime, by denying both the relevance of class predicates and, beyond that, any version of the argument that would link those predicates – however nuanced or qualified – to the lived *experience* of class divisions in an unjust social order. It is for this reason, I would suggest, that the sublime has come to play such a prominent role in the thinking of postmodern culture-critics who are otherwise largely unconcerned with issues of a specialized philosophical nature. What it serves to promote, whether overtly or implicitly, is a sceptical ethos which simply takes for granted the collapse of all realist or representationalist paradigms, the advent of a post-modern 'hyperreality' devoid of ontological grounding or experiential content, and the need henceforth to abandon any thought of criticizing social injustice from a standpoint of class solidarity based on communal perceptions and interests. In short, there is a strong elective affinity between this strain of post-Marxist/'New Times' thinking and the current high vogue for invocations of the Kantian sublime.

IV

In his book *Protocols of Reading* Robert Scholes has some pertinent thoughts with regard to this issue of experience, class and representation as treated by various schools of post-structuralist theory.[27] His point, very briefly, is that critics cannot have it both ways, on the one hand proclaiming their 'radical' credentials and their concern with questions of politics, race, and gender while on the other adopting a nominalist (or 'textualist') stance which denies any possible ground of appeal in the realities of oppression as *known and experienced* by members of the relevant class, community, or interest-group. For theory then becomes just a play-off between different (incommensurable) language-games, an affair of multiple competing 'discourses' or 'subject-positions' devoid of any real-world consequence. Feminism, conversely, 'is based upon the notion of a gendered reader, and is driven by a perception of injustice in the relations between men and women in specific social, economic, and political terms'.[28] Scholes's main target here is the claim advanced by some, mostly male, critics: that since gender is after all a discursive product, a position constructed within language, or according to the roles 'arbitrarily' assigned by this or that set of cultural codes, *therefore* it must be possible for good-willed male feminists to 'read as women', or adopt the kinds of viewpoint typically accorded to the female 'implied reader'. Such arguments understandably possess great appeal for theorists who would otherwise feel themselves *de facto* excluded from having anything relevant to say. But they are nonetheless mistaken, Scholes contends, since they ignore the manifold differences – the real and material (not just 'discursive') differences of interest – that characterize women's experience as subjects and readers.

This is not to say that males have nothing to learn from the encounter with feminist criticism or with work by women writers that foregrounds the issue of gender role representation. Where the fallacy appears – as Elaine Showalter argues in her well-known essay on critical 'cross-dressing' – is with the idea that male critics can somehow divest themselves of masculine attributes and espouse the other viewpoint through an act of well-meaning readerly choice.[29] For this ignores the stubborn *facticity* of sexual difference, its inscription in a collective and individual history which cannot be so blithely transcended in pursuit of some utopian gender-role freeplay. As Scholes puts it:

> Both texts and readers are already written when they meet, but both may emerge from the encounter altered in some crucial respect. Feminist critics have made this semiotic process concrete and intelligible for us all, for gender – if not destiny – is one of those rough spots by which necessity, in the form of culture, grasps us and shapes our ends. Because women in this culture have been an underprivileged class, they have learned lessons in class consciosuness that many men have not. Because it cuts across social class, gender brings the lessons of class consciousness into places normally so insulated by privilege as to be unconscious of the structure that supports and insulates them. Feminism, then, has drawn its strength from the ethical – political domain, by showing that women, as a class, have been regularly discriminated against by a cultural system that positions them as subordinate to men.[30]

This clear-headed passage is important to my argument for two connected reasons. First, it brings out the point that *difference* can only be a fashionable buzzword – like Lyotard's rhetoric of sublime 'heterogeneity' – so long as it is conceived in ideal abstraction from the contexts of real-world experience or the lived actualities of class and gender oppression. Second, it shows how such predicates of class-membership (for instance, 'women as a class') still play a vital descriptive and explanatory role, even – or especially – at times like the present when gender issues must be seen to 'cut across' other, more traditional modes of class analysis.

Scholes's argument here is partly a matter of empirical observation and partly – though he doesn't deploy such terms – the result of what amounts to a Kantian deduction on transcendental or *a priori* grounds. Thus practical experience is enough to confirm that any effective critique of social injustice, oppression, unequal opportunities and so forth will need to identify the particular group whose lives, prospects or conditions of existence have been consequently damaged or curtailed. Such criticism may indeed come from non-members of the group, from male feminists who strive (so far as possible) to 'read as a woman', or from left intellectuals and cultural theorists who adopt a standpoint markedly at odds with their own class-interests narrowly conceived. Even so, they will be working on the prior assumption, *contra* the postmodern sceptics and nominalists, that such a group exists, that its name corresponds (in however complex or overdetermined a way) to certain facts of shared or communicable human experience, and furthermore that criticism can best represent the interests of justice and truth by attempting to identify (and identify with) the experiences thus conveyed. At this point the empirical arguments join with the question as viewed under a Kantian (or 'conditions of possibility') aspect. For just as understanding in its cognitive or theoretical mode requires always that the manifold of sensuous intuitions be 'brought under' adequate concepts, so here it is the case that one cannot begin to grasp the lived realities of class or gender oppression without using terms (like 'gender' and 'class') which render that experience intelligible. And this holds – to repeat – despite all the problems, of an empirical *and* a theoretical nature, that are nowadays confronted by anyone seeking to apply such terms in a non-reductive or sufficiently 'flexible' manner.

One can therefore see why Scholes thinks it important to 'clarify the notion of *class*' as deployed in his argument, and to explain that the term is 'not restricted to socio-economic class, even though that remains as a central type or model for the concept'.[31] His point is not (or not only) that we need such enabling categories in order to wrest form from chaos, or to represent what would otherwise be lost to the flux of inchoate experience. More specifically, he is arguing *on ethico-political as well as on cognitive grounds* that we cannot do justice to these truths of experience, to the record of human suffering and waste brought about by various discriminative practices, unless we acknowledge the applicability of class predicates in this wider sense. The problem about post-structuralism is that it denies the pertinence of all such categorial descriptions, and thus contrives to block the appeal to any kind of real-world knowledge or experience. For if everything is ultimately constructed in discourse – truth, reality, subject-positions, class allegiances and so forth – then *ex hypothese* we could only be deluded in thinking that any particular discourse (for instance, that of feminism) had a better claim to justice or truth than the others currently on offer. And there is also a sense – a quite explicit and programmatic sense – in which post-structuralism works to undermine the very bases of critical or oppositional thought. That is to say, it takes the nominalist view that 'opposition' is itself just a product of discursive differentials, a term whose meaning inevitably fluctuates with the passage from one discourse to the next, and which therefore cannot be assigned any content, any real-world experiential truth, aside from its role in this or that (wholly conventional) signifying practice. And this applies not only to those aspects of inter-cultural linguistic difference (for instance, the various colour-term vocabularies or other such discrepant semantic fields) which post-structuralists often adduce in support of their claims for ontological relativity. Instances of this sort, though striking enough, need pose little problem for a theory of translation that views them as localized exceptions to be set against the broader regularities of human understanding within and across cultures.[32] But post-structuralism goes much further in its drive to relativize meaning and truth to the structures of linguistic representation or the force-field of contending discourses. For it operates on an abstract (quasi-systemic) model of 'opposition' and 'difference' whereby those terms are deprived of all specific historical or experiential content, and treated, in effect, as linguistic artefacts or products of discursive definition.

Such is of course Saussure's account of language as a system of structural contrasts and differences 'without positive terms', a system that requires (among other preconditions for achieving theoretical consistency) the positing of an 'arbitrary' link betwen signifier and signified.[33] This explains his well-known lack of interest in the referential aspect of language, justified as a matter of working convenience or methodological priority. But there is no warrant whatsoever in Saussure for extending this strictly heuristic principle to the point where any mention of the referent – any appeal beyond the self-enclosed domain of signification – is regarded as a lapse into naive ('positivist' or 'metaphysical') ways of thought, to be dismissed briefly with a sigh.[34] What such ideas amount to is a form of specular misrecognition, a confinement to the structural-linguistic imaginary which mistakes its own theoretical preconceptions for the limits of language, thought, and experience in general. (Lacan is perhaps the most egregious example of the way that ontological distinctions – the imaginary, the symbolic, the real – can be so redefined as precisely to invert the order of relationship between them.)[35] Hence post-structuralism's dogged attachment to a nominalist thesis which treats the Saussurian 'arbitrary' sign, or the bar between signifier and signified, as a pretext for rejecting any notion that language might give access to the realm of cognitive or experiential knowledge.

It is at this point that some theorists have perceived a kinship with current readings of the Kantian sublime, a sense in which post-structuralism might be seen as engaged with the same problematic of radically disjunct or 'heterogeneous' discourses.[36] But in both cases such scepticism follows from a failure (or refusal) to grasp Kant's argument in the first *Critique* regarding the conceptually mediated character of all empirical truth-claims, or the requirement of 'bringing intuitions under concepts' in order to establish their cognitive validity. By ignoring this requirement, and switching their sights to the more seductive prospects of the Kantian sublime, these theorists end up with an aestheticized reading of Kant that reduces all forms of knowledge (and knowledge-constitutive interests) to the level of so many subject-positions constructed in and through language. It is worth quoting Scholes at length here since he offers some particularly telling examples of the confusion engendered by a textualist approach to issues of class and gender politics.

> Readers who read as members of a class can be distinguished from those who are members of what Stanley Fish has called an 'interpretive community' . . . in that membership in a class implies both necessity and interest. A member of the class *Jew* in Hitler's Germany or of the class *Black* in South Africa at present is a member of those classes by necessity and has an interest in the situation of the class as a whole. . . . A class, in this sense, is a cultural creation, part of a system of categories imposed upon all those who attain subjectivity in a given culture. . . . One may choose to be a feminist or not, but one is assigned one's gender and may change it only by extraordinary effort. The relationship between being female and being a feminist is neither simple nor to be taken for granted, but there is no comparable relationship between being a deconstructionist and belonging to a class – which is of course not to say that deconstruction is free of interest or beyond ideology. . . . A feminist literary critic writes for other critics, to be sure, but she also writes on behalf of other women and, as a critic, she is strengthened by the consciousness of this responsibility. A male critic, on the other hand, may work within the feminist paradigm but never be a fully-fledged member of the class of feminists.[37]

My one minor quarrel has to do with Scholes's idea that deconstruction is chiefly to blame for dissolving those various categories – among them (as he argues) the interlinked concepts of class-membership and cognitive representation – which alone make it possible to render such experience intelligible. In fact one could say more accurately, at least with reference to Derrida's work, that deconstruction continues to operate with those concepts and respect their rigorous necessity, while at the same time resisting any premature appeal to the binary structures (or logics of exclusion) on which they customarily depend.[38] This is not to deny that there are some texts of Derrida that do give credence to Scholes's charge. Among them are those essays where he touches on the topic of sexual difference and the imagined possibility of 'reading as a woman', or exploring all manner of polymorphous gender-roles, as a strategy for contesting received ('phallogocentric') discourses of meaning and truth.[39] But elsewhere, that is to say, in the bulk of his more considered and analytical work, Derrida is at pains to disavow any notion that difference, as a concept and a fact of experience, can be somehow transformed through the utopian 'freeplay' of a writing that blithely rejects such irksome constraints. Scholes's criticism applies more justly to that facile strain of postmodern and post-structuralist thought which takes it as read – with no philosophical qualms – that truth *just is* what we are given to make of it according to various textual strategies, gender-role constructs, signifying practices or whatever. In which case it would follow (logically though absurdly) that 'there is no significant difference between reading about an experience and having an experience, because experience never simply occurs'.[40]

The essays in this book were written with a view to sorting out some of the muddles and misreadings – especially misreadings of Kant – that currently exert such widespread appeal. For these issues have a relevance, as I have argued here, outside and beyond the specialized enclaves of cultural and critical theory. In fact they are within reach of the single most urgent question now confronting left thinkers in Britain and the United States: namely, what remains of the socialist project at a time when distorted consensus values have gone so far toward setting the agenda for 'informed' or 'realistic' political debate. It might seem just a piece of academic wishful thinking to make such claims for the importance of getting Kant right on the relation between epistemology, ethics and aesthetics; for pursuing the question 'What Is Enlightenment?' as raised in Foucault's late writings on the politics of knowledge; or again, for William Empson's spirited attempt to reassert the values of reason and truth against the orthodox literary-critical fashions of his time. But for better or worse it has been largely in the context of 'theory' – that capacious though ill-defined genre – that these issues have received their most intensive scrutiny over the past two decades. Empson took a fairly sanguine view when he wound up his case for analytical close-reading in *Seven Types of Ambiguity* with the hope that such methods would make us more intelligent, more willing to examine our own preconceptions and routine habits of response. 'It seems', he remarked, 'sufficient justification for so many niggling pages'.[41] Whether or not this applies in the present instance I must leave the reader to decide.

2

'What Is Enlightenment?': Foucault on Kant

Many commentators have noted a marked change of emphasis in Foucault's later thinking about issues of truth, ethics, and social responsibility. For some, this change was characterized chiefly by a certain relaxation of the sceptical rigour – the attitude of extreme Nietzschean suspicion with regard to truth-claims or ethical values of whatever kind – that had hitherto played such a prominent role in his work. Thus according to Roy Boyne the shift can be located with a fair degree of precision, occurring as it does between volume one of *The History of Sexuality* (where Foucault's genealogies of power/knowledge seem to exclude all notions of truth, enlightenment, self-understanding or effective political agency) and the later, posthumously published volumes where this doctrine gives way to a sense of renewed ethical and social engagement.[1] In this work, as Boyne reads it,

> there is . . . the suggestion of a certain Utopian residue. It pertains to the exercise of discipline, but this time it is not so much a question of an alienating imposition, rather one of normatively reinforced self-regulation. . . . The stake in this contest is freedom. A self ruled by the desires is unfree. Therefore moderation equals freedom. Thus the exercise of self-mastery is closely connected to the state of freedom.[2]

This is not to deny that there remain great problems, especially from the standpoint of present-day cultural and gender politics, with Foucault's appeal to those techniques of self-fashioning which he finds best embodied in the ethos of ancient Greek and Roman sexual conduct. Although it offers an escape-route of kinds from his earlier outlook of cognitive and ethical scepticism, still it leaves certain crucial questions unanswered. And most important of these, as Boyne points out, is the question that has preoccupied thinkers from Plato to Kant and beyond: namely, the relation between those various faculties of knowledge, practical reason and aesthetic taste whose claims philosophy has sought to adjudicate.

What is at issue here, especially since Kant, is the status of the subject (the knowing, willing and judging subject) as possessor of a certain strenuously argued autonomy, a freedom of reflective or self-willed choice that finds no place in the phenomenal realm of determinate causes and effects. In his early work Foucault simply rejects such notions, regarding them as a form of transcendental illusion, a product of that subject-centered discourse which typifies Kant's three *Critiques*, and which gave rise to 'man' – the subject-object of the modern 'human sciences' – as a specular image of its own disciplinary concerns. Such, briefly stated, is the argument put forward in texts like *The Order of Things* and *The Archaeology of Knowledge*, works that bear witness (despite all his well-known denials) to the influence of structuralist thinking and its deep-seated strain of theoretical anti-humanism.[3] Moreover, it is an attitude which still finds expression in the writings of Foucault's next 'period', with the shift – often treated as a watershed in his thought – from 'archaeology' to 'genealogy', or from a structuralist attempt to analyse the various discursive formations that make up the history of the human sciences to a Nietzschean project whose avowed aim is to challenge and subvert all the operative notions (truth, reason, history, origins, objectivity) which have so far managed to impose their rule on the conduct of those same disciplines.[4] For here also the subject is conceived as nothing more than a transient side-effect of discourse – in the fashionable parlance a 'subject-position' – which lacks any kind of autonomous identity or selfhood, and whose locus can only be defined in relation to a force-field of contending power/knowledge interests.

To the three cardinal questions that were posed by Kant – What can I know? What should I will? And what can I reasonably hope for? – Foucault thus responds with a Nietzschean denial that these questions make any kind of sense as construed in the normative 'Enlightenment' mode. For it was only when viewed from the illusory standpoint of a transcendental subject-presumed-to-know that such claims could be thought to possess any ultimate truth, any grounding rationale or competence to judge in matters of epistemological or ethical concern. With the demise of that subject – brought about, Foucault argues, by the passage to a new discursive regime, one in which language (or representation) henceforth defines the very limits of thought – we are forced to do without such delusive guarantees and acknowledge that 'truth' is just a nominal predicate, a token of the prestige currently enjoyed by this or that privileged discourse. For if there is nothing beyond this prison-house of language, no perspective from which we could possibly criticize or question the discourses currently on offer, then clearly we had much better leave off thinking in those old-fashioned Kantian-enlightenment terms. And if one result of such a change is to topple the subject from its erstwhile role as 'transcendental' arbiter of virtue and truth, then again (Foucault urges) we should take a lesson from Nietzsche and not strive vainly to resuscitate values whose epoch, or horizon of intelligibility, has receded beyond any hope of recall.

In short, he sees only the history of an error in the various attempts, from Kant on down, to secure the sphere of practical reason (ethics) against the threat of a thoroughgoing determinst creed, on the one hand, or an equally pernicious value-relativism on the other. Whether in its 'archaeological' or 'genealogical' phase, Foucault's thinking manifests a constant desire to strip the subject of its unearned powers and prerogatives, to treat it as merely an epiphenomenon of language, and thus to put the truth-claims of Enlightenment reason very firmly in their place. This it will achieve – as in *The Order of Things* – by revealing their radically *contingent* character, their provenance in a certain period-specific discourse, a localized ensemble of knowledge-constitutive interests that once produced 'man' as the transcendental locus of meaning, morality, and truth. Thus Foucault reads Kant as having failed to make good his promise of breaking with a merely anthropological perspective, that is to say, his arguments for a critical philosophy where the 'faculties' in question (cognitive understanding, pure reason, practical reason, aesthetic judgment) would justify their claims *a priori* through a process of rigorous transcendental critique, and would thereby forego any reliance on mere psychological or naturalistic data. On the contrary, Foucault remarks: 'man in the [Kantian] analytic of finitude is a strange empirico-transcendental doublet, since he is a being such that knowledge will be attained in him of what renders all knowledge possible'.[5] And again:

> If man is indeed . . . that paradoxical figure in which the empirical contents of knowledge necessarily release, of themselves, the conditions that have made them possible, then man cannot posit himself in the immediate and sovereign transparency of a *cogito*. . . . Because he is an empirico-transcendental doublet, man is also the locus of a misunderstanding that constantly exposes his thought to the risk of being swamped by his own being, and also enables him to recover his integrity on the basis of what eludes him.[6]

In his later texts, after the 'turn' toward Nietzschean genealogy, Foucault will not abandon but extend and radicalize this attack on the truth-claims and values of Enlightenment critique. And he will do so chiefly by exposing the subject in its various guises (whether the 'transcendental' subject of Kantian philosophy, the writing subject as discussed in his essay 'What Is An Author?', or the autonomous self of humanist ethical discourse) to a full-scale process of rhetorical deconstruction whereby its existence is supposedly revealed as the merest of contingent historical episodes or superinduced ideological effects.[7] Hence no doubt the great appeal of those middle-period essays to a readership of mainly post-structuralist adepts for whom the 'death of the author', the

obsolescence of Enlightenment values, and the linguistic (or discursive) construction of reality were so many items of received wisdom scarcely in need of
argumentative support. That Foucault himself made considerable efforts to
distance his thinking from any such wholesale orthodoxy was a point that
seldom registered in this heady climate of debate.

Nevertheless the signs were there for anyone willing to read, and they
became more evident, as Boyne rightly notes, with Foucault's shift of stance in
the later volumes of *A History of Sexuality*. What this change amounted to was
a growing sense of the moral and political bankruptcy entailed by any project
that effectively renounced the principles of human agency and choice. Such it
seems was Foucault's main reason for now backing away from the three central
tenets of his Nietzschean–genealogical phase: 1) that all truth-claims are
inextricably bound up with relations of power/knowledge; 2) that the subject is
nothing more than a figment of discourse, a transient 'fold' in the fabric of this
or that system of representations; and 3) that these insights are sufficient
to refute any argument premised on 'enlightened' notions of reason, self-
knowledge, emancipatory interests, *Ideologiekritik*, etc. In the writings of his
last decade Foucault gives voice to some striking reservations with regard to
this entire genealogical approach. Most crucially, he sees it as lacking the
conceptual resources to explain how subjects engage in that process of willed
self-fashioning, that jointly cognitive and ethical endeavour which allows them
to achieve something other (and more) than a passive acquiescence in the codes,
conventions or sexual mores of their time. Thus in the case of the ancient
Greeks, as Foucault writes,

> [o]ne could not practise moderation without a certain form of knowledge that
> was at least one of its essential conditions. One could not form oneself as an
> ethical subject in the use of pleasures without forming oneself at the same time
> as a subject of knowledge. . . . Moderation implied that the *logos* be placed in a
> position of supremacy in the human being and that it be to subdue the desires
> and regulate behaviour.[8]

Boyne cites this passage as evidence of the shift in Foucault's later thinking,
his readiness to credit the subject with at least some measure of thoughtful
and active involvement in the shaping of its own self-constitutive desires.
Nevertheless he finds the problem not so much resolved as conveniently
shelved when Foucault switches from his erstwhile talk of 'power/knowledge'
or 'resistance' to an idiom whose operative terms are those of self-discipline,
moderation or suchlike 'technologies of the self'. For here also it is hard to
comprehend how the subject could achieve any degree of genuine autonomy,
given the extent to which, on Foucault's own submission, this freedom is
necessarily shaped or constrained by existing structures of regulative conduct.

In short, his new conception runs into the same difficulty when it comes to envisaging a realm of ethical values — of choice, responsibility and self-determination — that would somehow escape the strictures imposed by his previous uncompromising rejection of all such values.

Boyne makes this point in connection with what Foucault has to say about the Greek ideal of cultivated sexual discipline, an ethos (more precisely: an *aesthetics*) of attitude and conduct whose virtue was to recognize 'that self-mastery, not the total absence of desire, was the prime condition for leading a life of moderation and reason'.[9] But there still seems little room within this spartan regime for any notion of the 'subject' beyond what is produced by a clash of opposing value-systems or an arena of endlessly contending discourses devoid of effective moral agency and choice. Thus 'all that Foucault identifies here is a mechanism without a principle, a force without direction'. And again, more emphatically:

> The problem of such an absence is that self-domination could lead one to do 'what has to be done'. Perhaps it does take self-discipline to sacrifice a generation or to cut off the village children's arms after the injections given by 'enemy' Red Cross workers. Without a normative regime, we cannot determine the essential parameters of self-discipline, and . . . Foucault has tended throughout to ignore that aspect of desire that seeks the death of the other. . . . The resources of the *logos* are needed to give shape and direction to this power which has its foundation in self-mastery.[10]

Of course there is a sense in which all ethical theories, and especially those in the modern (post-Kantian) tradition, have had to cope with this problem of reconciling two apparently contradictory sets of claims. Thus it is assumed that the highest moral values are those that involve a subjection to the dictates of law, principle or conscience, these latter conceived either as a form of internalized social regulation or — as with Kant — in universalist terms, through the appeal to a 'categorical imperative' supposedly transcending all mere considerations of circumstance or private interest. Such philosophies have this much in common with Foucault's thinking: that they envisage morality as a matter of *resistance*, of desires held in check by the discipline of practical reason, or by the moral law as a salutary curb upon the promptings of instinctual, self-gratifying will.[11] But in his case (as many commentators have noted) the 'subject' becomes little more than a place-filler, a recipient of moral directives which issue from some other, heteronomous source of authority, and which cannot be conceived as in any way belonging to a project of autonomous self-creation. Nor can this dilemma be resolved by arguing that such conflicts of interest and principle are in some sense *internal* to the subject, taking rise from a range of disciplinary techniques — or internalized strategies of surveillance and control – whose aim is to fashion a self in accordance with the highest, most reputable ideals. For then one has to ask the same question over again, namely, what remains of the ethical 'subject' as a thinking, willing and responsible agent of choice if its options are effectively exhausted in advance *either* by the force of self-seeking, unregenerate desire *or* by those disciplines to which it submits as a matter of ethical compulsion? Such is at any rate the aporia soon arrived at if one assumes, like Foucault, that ethical discourse is entirely a product of power/knowledge differentials, and hence that any advance toward greater autonomy (or 'self-determination') will involve a kind of inward policing by the subject of its own thoughts and desires.[12]

As I say, these difficulties are by no means peculiar to Foucault's project or the wider post-structuralist enterprise. In fact they are at the heart of much current debate about the limits of moral philosophy as traditionally conceived, the antinomies of Kantian ('formalist') ethics, and the need for an approach that would take more account of the contingent, historical or situated character of real-world ethical issues.[13] But they are pushed to an extreme by Foucault's insistence, still present in his later writings, that subjectivity is constructed through and through by the various discourses, conventions or regulative codes that alone provide a means of 'aesthetic' self-fashioning in the absence of any other normative standard. For on this account the subject is indeed nothing more than a localized point of intersection, a product of the various contending forces that define its very conditions of possibility. In the early Foucault – the self-styled 'archaeologist' of discourses, knowledges, and signifying systems – there is no real attempt to avoid this bleakly determinist conclusion. What analysis uncovers as it digs down and back into the stratified history of the present is a sequence of rifts in the order of discursive relations, a sequence that reveals the diversity of truth-claims from one epoch to the next, the utter lack of grounds or validity-conditions for judging between these incommensurable paradigms, and the fact that 'man' (or the transcendental subject of humanist discourse) has arrived very late on the cultural scene and is even now heading for oblivion.[14] In his middle-period texts this structuralist approach gives way to a Nietzschean-Deleuzean rhetoric of forces, affects and power/knowledge differentials that would seem, on the face of it, more amenable to notions of practical agency and will.[15] But this appearance is deceptive since he still operates with a minimalist (indeed purely nominal) concept of the 'subject' which gives no hold for the treatment of substantive ethical or socio-political questions. And the problem persists, as I have argued, even in those writings of his final decade where Foucault has a great deal to say concerning the self and its various formative mechanisms. What emerges is not so much a radical re-thinking of these issues as a shift in rhetorical strategy, one that allows him to place more emphasis on the active, self-shaping, volitional aspects of human conduct and thought, but which signally fails to explain how such impulses could ever take rise, given the self's inescapable subjection to a range of pre-existing disciplinary codes and imperatives that between them determine the very shape and limits of its 'freedom'. In this respect at least, with regard to its ethical bearings, Foucault's work continues to generate the same kinds of deep-laid philosophical perplexity.

Thomas Flynn makes the point in a generally admiring essay on Foucault's last course of lectures delivered at the Collège de France in 1984.[16] The lectures were addressed to precisely this theme of ethics (or the claims of moral self-knowledge) in Greek and Roman antiquity, as viewed in relation to the various modes of truth-telling discourse. Flynn finds evidence of a new direction in his thinking, a concern with values of authentic selfhood – as opposed to their sophistical or strategic simulation – which scarcely figured in his earlier work. All the same, Flynn registers a sense that the problems have not been entirely laid to rest; that despite this 'turn' toward an ethics of stoical self-fashioning, and away from the negative rigours of Nietzschean genealogy, Foucault is still unable to articulate clearly what such an attitude would amount to in real-life moral or political terms. Thus: '[t]he issue centers on the *activity* of the subject in this process of self-constitution. . . . Is he/she the mere reflection of structural changes, the simple nodal point of a multiplicity of impersonal relationships?'[17] Posed like this, it is a question that could also be put to the entire structuralist and post-structuralist enterprise, or indeed to any such movement of thought premised on the argument that subjectivity is an effect of those various signifying systems, or orders of discursive representation, which happen to prevail from one epoch to the next. But the doubt extends to Foucault's later writings, even (or especially) those texts where he adopts a language more explicitly concerned with issues of ethical self-knowledge. For 'it is clear,' Flynn writes, 'that Foucault continued to respect those "structuralist" concepts as he insisted that we "rethink the question of the subject"'.[18] And this despite Foucault's numerous denials – going back at least to the late 1960s – that his thinking had ever been much influenced by 'structuralist' theories or methods. For what Flynn is referring to here is not so much a particular (post-Saussurean) approach to questions of meaning, knowledge, and representation, but a wider tendency within the human sciences, pressed to an extreme by the structuralist paradigm, which generates strictly insoluble antinomies in the realm of ethical thought. And most crucial of these is the old familiar issue of free-will *versus* determinism, an issue confronted in various forms by philosophers down through the ages, but posed with maximum force by a thinking, like Foucault's, which conceives subjectivity entirely in terms of discursive formations, effects of power/knowledge, or the kind of self-mastery that comes of a stoical subjection to some given disciplinary regime. It is in this sense that Foucault both inherits and intensifies the paradoxes which structuralism itself carried over from the legacy of Western philosophical thought.

Hence, according to Flynn, the 'uneasiness' that remains if one follows the path marked out by Foucault's late texts, implying as they do that 'such passivity suffices to account for the *self*-constitution of the moral subject'.

> No doubt a form of 'historical *a priori*' makes certain practices possible and excludes others. Courage . . . in face of possible violence, for example, may well be encouraged and even taken for granted in a specific society at a particular time. But as Sartre reminded the Marxist 'economists', Flaubert may be a *petit-bourgeois*, but not every *petit-bourgeois* is Flaubert. It is the question of individual responsibility (a concept Foucault would historicize as well) that assumes particular urgency in the context of moral constitution. The excuse, 'That's just the way I am!' carries little weight in moral exchanges. [19]

Of course Foucault was alert to such criticisms and addressed them repeatedly in the essays and interviews of his last few years. One response was his distinction between 'morality' and 'ethics', the latter conceived as an activity of disciplined self-knowledge in accordance with certain shared or communal norms, the former as a discourse of rule-bound abstract generalities with no real claim upon the self and its modes of jointly private and social fulfilment. Thus 'care for the self is ethical in itself, but it implies complex relations with others, in the measure that this *ethos* of freedom is also a way of caring for others'. [20] And again: '*Ethos* implies a relation with others to the extent that care for self renders one competent to occupy a place in the city, in the community . . . whether it be to exercise a magistracy or to have friendly relationships.' [21] For it is the greatest virtue of such ethical (as opposed to moralizing) thought that it places questions of value and human obligation back where they belong, in the context of a flourishing communal way of life, and thus helps to dissolve those sterile antinomies that have for so long plagued the axiology of Western post-classical reason.

There is a parallel here with the argument of philosophers like Bernard Williams who also put the case for a different way of thinking about ethical issues, one that would break with Kantian or other such 'formalist' approaches, and would take more account of those contextual factors – the variety of culture-specific values, motives and interests – by which we make sense of our day-to-day lives as moral agents. [22] And this is part of a wider movement of thought among liberals of various colour who reject what they see as the overweening claims, the prescriptivist appeal to universal values or abstract principles, bound up with the philosophic discourse of Enlightenment. In its place they suggest a return to that alternative tradition which stresses the essentially communal nature of our ethical commitments and priorities, the fact that such values can only be realized through a project of shared endeavour. Some, like Alasdair MacIntyre, conceive this project in Aristotelian terms, as a doctrine of the practical virtues that would find its highest good in a life devoted to the exercise of jointly civic, domestic and private self-perfection.[23] For others (among them thinkers of a liberal-pluralist persuasion like Michael Walzer) it is a matter of respecting the variety of values, moral viewpoints or cultural 'forms of life' that will always coexist in any genuine participant democracy.[24] And in support of such claims – so far as they are taken to require philosophical support – most often there is some reference to Wittgenstein or other such proponents of an anti-foundationalist view, to the effect (roughly speaking) that those 'forms of life' go all the way down, so that there is no way to justify one's beliefs, values or ethical priorities beyond simply remarking that they make good sense for members of a given cultural community.

When this line of argument is pushed right through, as by current neo-pragmatists like Richard Rorty, then the upshot is to render 'philosophy' pretty much redunddant, along with any version of 'enlightened' thinking or critique of in-place consensus values which claims to distinguish reason or truth from what is presently and contingently 'good in the way of belief'.[25] For on their view there is simply no point in appealing to grounds, principles, validity-conditions, precepts of 'practical reason' or whatever since the only thing that counts is the performative power to carry conviction with this or that 'interpretive community'.[26] And in the end such conviction will always be relative to the values and beliefs held in common by at least some significant proportion of the community concerned. That is to say, one can only be misguided in thinking to criticize 'false' or 'ideological' consensus beliefs if those beliefs make up the very background of tacit presupposition – the cultural 'horizon of intelligibility' – against which such arguments have to be assessed. And in this case (as Rorty cheerfully concludes) we might as well give up the whole vain enterprize and acknowledge that, for all practical purposes, there is *simply no difference* – no difference that makes any difference – between truth and what presently counts as such by our own, albeit contingent and self-interested, cultural lights.

Now of course I am not suggesting that Foucault ever came around to this position of willing acquiescence in the currency of accepted belief. Such an argument would clearly be absurd, given his well-known oppositional stance on issues of sexual politics, psychiatric medicine and penal and legislative practice. Nor can one doubt the close relationship that obtained between Foucault's practical involvement with these issues – his record of active inter-vention at the 'micropolitical' or day-to-day level – and those writings where he sought to engage such questions from a more 'theoretical' standpoint. This connection is plain enough in early works like *The Birth of the Clinic* and *Madness and Civilization*, books which make a programmatic aim of challenging the various normative regimes (or systems of instituted power/knowledge) whose effect had been increasingly to reinforce the line that separated reason from unreason, the mad from the sane, the normal from the deviant and so forth.[27] And the other main products of this early phase – from *The Order of Things* to *The Archaeology of Knowledge* – can likewise be seen as extended meditations on the way that various truth-claims, various orders of knowledge and representation had exercised a kindred disciplinary function by delimiting what should count, from one period to the next, as a legitimate mode of discourse. With his middle-period essays where Nietzsche is the predominant influence, especially those collected in *Language, Counter-Memory, Practice*, Foucault became yet more insistent on the point. Thus one could not write history except as a 'history of the present', a form of Nietzschean *wirkliche Geschichte* which abandoned the false (because impossible) ideal of scholarly objectivity, and which actively contested such 'monumental' projects with a view to liberating hitherto repressed or marginalized voices.[28] Archival research was worse than useless, he argued, if all it did was enable one to pile up a mass of documentary evidence with no such motivating interest in view. Hence the shift from 'archaeology' to 'genealogy' as a favoured metaphor to describe what he was doing: an activity now conceived more expressly in terms of its power to intervene and *make a real difference* at the level of historical discourses or forms of knowledge-production.

Nothing could be further (or so it might seem) from those fashionable doctrines (postmodernist, neo-pragmatist, Wittgensteinian or whatever) which appeal to 'language-games' or cultural 'forms of life' as a bottom-line justification, a means of excluding all arguments save those that happen to fit with what is currently and contingently 'good in the way of belief'. The least knowledge of Foucault's work, early or late, should be sufficient to convince the reader that his was indeed an oppositional voice raised consistently against the complacent self-images of the age. And yet there is a sense in which he laid himself open to just such a reading, one that would emphasise, as Rorty does, the extent to which Foucault's professed ethos of 'aesthetic' self-fashioning goes along with a liberal-ironist acceptance of things as they are, or (more to the point) as they are held to be according to the current consensus wisdom.[29] After all, this is exactly what Rorty most admires about the culture of the 'North Atlantic postmodern bourgeois' democracies: their capacitiy to accommodate the widest possible range of private satisfactions, opinions, life-styles or modes of personal fulfilment, just so long as the individuals concerned do not profess to have theories, principles or grounds with which to back up their preferences.[30] Thus the liberal ironist, on Rorty's view, is one who very wisely foregoes the typical 'Enlightenment' prerogatives – such as criticizing consensus-values or telling other people what to think – and instead seeks to cultivate the 'private' virtues while acknowledging that these can exert no claim to universal significance or truth. On the whole it is the novelists and poets who offer most help in this direction, since they, unlike the system-building theorists and philosophers, are less often tempted to raise their imaginative insights into a wholesale doctrine, a blueprint for social progress, or a form of self-exempting *Ideologiekritik*.[31] Apart from some few choice spirits (among whom Rorty would count 'rogue' thinkers like Nietzsche, Heidegger and Derrida) the philosophers have generally spoiled their case by presuming to lay down the law on such matters and thus failing to recognize the contingent, temporal, or culture-specific character of their own pet notions. And so it has been left to the others – the rogue element – to point out how often those earnest, truth-seeking types have mistaken metaphors for concepts, erected whole systems of legislative theory on the basis of this or that preferred 'final vocabulary', and set themselves up as privileged dispensers of wisdom and truth. Much better, Rorty thinks, to abandon this whole delusory enterprise and see that philosophy is just one more voice in the 'cultural conversation of mankind', a voice with no authority save that acquired – as with the poets and novelists – by addressing the shared values and concerns of a given interpretive community.

My point about Foucault can be put most simply by remarking that Rorty can recruit him with relative ease as yet another thinker who has been travelling this road toward something like a postmodern pragmatist endpoint. Thus Rorty sees no great problem in playing down Foucault's more 'radical' claims – his Nietzschean rhetoric, his activist injunctions, his heady talk of 'power/knowledge' – and playing up that theme of aesthetic self-invention which supposedly aligns him with the liberal ironists and debunkers of enlightenment wisdom. On this view, Foucault worked his way around to a position that was largely disabused of those old-fashioned ideas about truth, knowledge, emancipatory critique, or the 'political responsibility of the intellectuals'. Insofar as he cut these pretensions down to size – as by advocating the role of 'specific intellectuals', in contrast to the 'universal' types of an earlier (superannuated) epoch – Foucault wins Rorty's full approval. Where he lapses on occasion is in tending to suggest that the resultant 'micropolitics' of localized struggle can effectively generate a dissident ethos that would run strongly counter to the currency of received (meaning 'postmodern bourgeois liberal') values and beliefs. To this extent Foucault has failed to take his own best lessons to heart; chief among them the fact that there is no secure vantage-point, no 'sky-hook' (as Rorty engagingly puts it) on which to hang one's arguments, judgments and criticisms, apart from the various kinds of suasive appeal that happen to work in some given cultural context. But of course Foucault knows this perfectly well, having always maintained an attitude of healthy scepticism with regard to the truth-claims of enlightenment critique and their lack of any possible justification, least of all any 'transcendental' grounding, except within the discourse (or the 'final vocabulary') of an outworn philosophic culture. In other words Rorty can read Foucault, along with Heidegger, Habermas, Derrida, Rawls and a good many more, as basically a kind of half-way pragmatist, one who might as well complete the journey by dumping all that pointless 'philosophical' baggage and easing himself back into the communal fold. For it is Rorty's belief that all these thinkers have been heading toward a pragmatist conclusion, despite their various unfortunate hold-ups along the way. And in Foucault's case (so Rorty suggests) the problem can be got around easily enough by discounting his more grandiose or dramatic claims – which would tend to disrupt the ongoing 'cultural conversation' – and valuing his work for what it yields in the way of new vocabularies, metaphors, or styles of inventive self-description.

One highly desirable consequence of this, in Rorty's view, is that we will cease to take Foucault very seriously as a *theorist*, a thinker with definite claims upon the shape and limits of human understanding, ethical self-knowledge or whatever. But any loss of prestige in this department will be more than compensated by the benefits that accrue from reading him as a 'private' moralist, an adept of creative self-fashioning whose work offers a range of role-models or elective self-images for those other (likewise private) individuals who happen to admire his style. And conversely, if there is a *wrong* way of reading Foucault, then it involves the typical 'Enlightenment' idea that there must be some way to bridge the gap between private and public moralities, some means of deriving generalized precepts – or ethical standards that would hold good for everyone – from the quest for autonomy and self-perfection that impels the creative individual. All of which suggests that the best way to view Foucault is as a poet, a 'Romantic intellectual', a maker of fresh-minted metaphors (rather than a purveyor of valid arguments), and hence as belonging to that visionary company whose chief representatives are poets like Blake and Shelley, or 'strong revisionist' interpreters like Harold Bloom.

Of course it may be said that this is dangerous talk since it verges on the kind of Nietzschean extravagance, the strain of wholesale 'aesthetic ideology', that would set up the artist (or his surrogate, the 'inspired' political leader) as a figure beyond good and evil, a shaper of destiny sublimely unaccountable to commonplace standards of human conduct. But Rorty has an answer to this objection, urging that we treat it as just another pseudo-problem, another of those unfortunate confusions brought about by our over-readiness to extrapolate from the private to the public sphere. Thus:

> It is only when a Romantic intellectual begins to want his private self to serve as a model for other human beings that his politics tend to become anti-liberal.

When he begins to think that other human beings have a moral duty to achieve the same inner autonomy as he himself has achieved, then he begins to think about political and social changes which will help them do so. Then he may begin to think that he has a moral duty to bring about these changes, whether his fellow citizens want them or not.[32]

So one can get Foucault off this particular hook by stressing, among other things, his suspicion of Enlightenment concepts such as reason, truth, ideology and critique; his refusal to play the role of 'universal intellectual', whether in a Kantian, a Marxist or other such grandiose ethico-political guise; and above all his concern with the 'private' virtues of autonomy, self-perfection, and creative endeavour. He will then take his rightful place, as Rorty sees it, among the poets, novelists and 'edifying' thinkers who offer us a choice of more or less attractive life-styles or metaphors to live by, rather than telling us what to think like philosophers in the old prescriptivist mode. And if there remain odd passages in Foucault that cannot be reconciled to this pragmatist reading, then we had best treat them with indulgence as merely the result of his over-zealous desire to shake up the complacencies of bourgeois-liberal discourse.

Again, I am not suggesting for a moment that Rorty is right about Foucault, or that pragmatism is indeed where his arguments were always heading, give or take a few lapses into Nietzschean genealogy and suchlike frivolous pursuits. Just how wrong this is may be judged by comparing some of Rorty's remarks with those passages in Foucault's own writing where he addresses the question of ethical responsibility and the relation between private and public spheres. According to Rorty,

> Foucault was trying to serve human liberty, but he was also, in the interest of his personal autonomy, trying to be a faceless, rootless, homeless stranger to humanity and to history. As a citizen, he was trying to achieve the same political consequences which a good humanitarian bourgeois liberal would wish to produce. As a philosopher trying to invent himself, he was, to quote [Charles] Taylor, 'tossing aside the whole tradition of Augustinian inwardness'. . . . Foucault, as I understand him, wanted to do good to his fellow humans while at the same time having an identity which had nothing to do with them. He wanted to help people without taking their vocabulary as the one in which he spoke himself. He wanted to help them while inventing a self which had nothing much (indeed, as little as possible) to do with theirs.[33]

Here, as so often, what we are getting from Rorty is not so much a commentary on the texts in hand but a 'strong misreading' of the type he so admires in Harold Bloom. That is to say, it is a Rortian revisionist account which, *mirabile dictu*, has Foucault coming out in near-perfect agreement with everything that Rorty thinks best about the pragmatist way of handling these

issues. To call Foucault a 'good humanitarian liberal' is not, after all, the kind
of praise that most readily springs to mind when reading works like *The History
of Sexuality* or the essays and interviews of his last decade. Nor is it really much
of a compliment, in Foucauldian terms, to be apostrophized as one who
'wanted to do good to his fellow humans', but whose aestheticist desire for
private self-perfection left him at a loss for any language, any 'vocabulary', that
would link his concerns with theirs. The passage reads somewhat like a
lukewarm obituary or a shrewdly double-edged epitaph, casting around for
nice things to say ('he wanted to help them') while entering certain reservations
for honesty's sake ('a self which had nothing much [indeed, as little as possible]
in common with theirs'). Thus Foucault turns out to be a 'liberal ironist' very
much after Rorty's persuasion, on the one hand indulging his private desire for
autonomy and aesthetic self-perfection, while on the other acknowledging, like
a good pragmatist, that such values can exert no claim whatsoever in the
public or socio-political sphere.

One response to Rorty's essay would be a downright denial that Foucault
could ever have been brought to accept this double-aspect reading of his work.
And indeed, one could instance numerous passages – early and late – where
Foucault affirms just the opposite: that his researches into the history of penal
institutions, of psychiatric practices or gender-role construction should all be
viewed primarily as active attempts to re-shape the collective self-image and
memory of Western culture, and thus to bring about desirable changes in the
way we live now.[43] Certainly he showed small patience with interviewers who
naively raised questions about the 'relevance' of theory to practice, or who
assumed that this 'relevance' should somehow consist in a proven correspondence between the themes of his writing and the activist concerns of his
life as a public intellectual. From the Nietzschean standpoint such questions
appeared strictly unintelligible, assuming as they did that theory or scholarship
could exist in some realm of pure, disinterested knowledge, immune to the
effects of institutional power or the motivating will to subvert or contest
such power. On the contrary, he argued: these discourses were *performative*
through and through, their truth-claims bound up with forms of disciplinary
surveillance and control, or structures of instituted power/knowledge, that
could only be challenged by a counter-discourse with its own performative
efficacy, its own rhetorical power to re-define what counted as a 'relevant'
contribution to debate. All of which suggests that Rorty is absurdly wide of
the mark in his effort to talk Foucault down to the level of an easygoing
pragmatist exchange of views between like-minded partners in the cultural
conversation.

But the picture starts to look more complicated if one asks what implicit
concession Foucault makes to the pragmatist case, thus enabling Rorty to
present this account as anything like an accurate or convincing rendition. For

of course it may be argued that Rorty is just applying the same kind of Nietzschean licence when he reads Foucault, however much against the grain, as a 'good humanitarian bourgeois liberal' intent upon fashioning a private morality and perfectly prepared to renounce all claims on any conscience apart from his own. Thus one has to ask, for instance, why the following character-ization does not seem *entirely* wrongheaded or wide of the mark, despite what amounts to a wholesale severing of the links between Foucault's work as a genealogist of morals and his various commitments in the practical-political sphere.

> I think Foucault should have answered the questions 'Where do you stand? What are your values?', in this way: 'I stand with you as a fellow-citizen, but as a philosopher, I stand by myself, pursuing projects of self-invention which are none of your concern. I am not about to offer philosophical grounds for being on your side in public affairs, for my philosophical project is a private one which provides neither motive nor justification for my political actions'.[44]

This is a flat misreading of Foucault insofar as it ignores his reiterated claim that politics (or 'public' morality) cannot be divorced from those various techniques of ethical self-fashioning that comprise the history of Western practical reason, from the Stoics to the Christian confessional and Freudian psychoanalysis. Moreover, it blithely negates his thesis that the only effective resistance to forms of instituted power/knowledge is one that involves both 'care for the self' – the central topic of Foucault's late writings – and a kindred (indeed an inseparable) concern with questions of social and political conduct that short-circuit any version of the private/public dichotomy. Thus 'on the critical side', as Foucault puts it,

> philosophy is precisely the challenging of all phenomena of domination at whatever level or under whatever form they present themselves – political, economic, sexual, institutional, and so on. This critical function of philosophy, up to a certain point, emerges right from the Socratic imperative: 'Be concerned with yourself, i.e., ground yourself in liberty, through the mastery of self'.[45]

All of which suggests that Foucault would not have taken kindly to Rorty's description of him as an aesthete whose finest, most inventive energies went into the shaping of a private ego-ideal, and whose public gestures involved little more than a sentiment of good-willed citizenly virtue. In effect Rorty has simply made Foucault over into the image of his own liberal-pragmatist beliefs. Any hint of 'radicalism' can now be seen for what it is, a strictly private or self-occupied affair, while in political terms the whole project amounts to an attitude of *noli me tangere*, a plea that the aesthete be left to his or her own devices in exchange for an agreement to play by the rules and uphold the currency of existing consensus values. So much for the 'critical function of philosophy' as Foucault describes it in (presumably) a moment of untypical Enlightenment hubris.

On the other hand, as I have said, there is a sense in which Foucault lays himself open to just such a reading through his avowal of a Nietzschean-relativist stance in matters of interpretive validity or truth. Thus Rorty could argue that he has, after all, respected the spirit if not the letter of Foucault's texts; that it is the interpreter's prerogative, here as always, to practise a form of strong-revisionist reading responsive to present-day cultural needs; and that Foucault was in any case a thoroughgoing sceptic as regards the claims of authorial intention or scholarly objectivity. More than that, he could answer – again with some show of Foucauldian warrant – that we miss the whole point of these texts if we think that they are in any way concerned to offer arguments, reasons or justifying principles for the stance they adopt on various questions of an ethical or socio-political nature. For in Rorty's view this is just another relic of the old foundationalist paradigm, the assumption that anyone with a case to argue – or a new scheme of values to promote – will need to offer more by way of 'philosophical' back-up than a mere appeal to consensus ideas of what is 'good in the way of belief'. But since Foucault is not a 'philosopher' – since he labours under no such delusory burden – we should therefore read him as he asks to be read, that is to say, as a Nietzschean strong self-inventor and source of new-found rhetorical strategies whose meaning is whatever we choose to make of it in pursuit of our own projects. 'Such a reply would sound less shocking', Rorty remarks,

> if one substituted 'poet' for 'philosopher'. For as opposed to poets, philoso-phers are traditionally supposed to offer a 'basis' for our moral obligations to others. . . . Unlike poets, they are supposed to be 'rational', and rationality is supposed to consist in being able to exhibit the 'universal validity' of one's position. Foucault, like Nietzsche, was a philosopher who claimed a poet's privileges. One of these privileges is to rejoin 'What has universal validity to do with *me*?' I think that philosophers are as entitled to this privilege as poets, so I think this rejoinder sufficient. [46]

Such, according to Rorty, is the pragmatist outcome of that 'ancient quarrel' between poetry and philosophy which Plato was the first to articulate, and whose latterday offshoot is the long-running feud between 'continental' and 'analytic' schools. The issue has been resolved pretty much by default – he thinks – since we can now recognise (after Nietzsche, Heidegger, Derrida et al) that philosophy was always just another 'kind of writing', a discourse peculiarly prone to denying its own poetic or literary character, but nonetheless rhetorical for that. In which case it is the merit of Foucault's later work to have taken this message to heart and come up with a strong revisionist line – a poetics of endless metaphorical self-fashioning – which simply collapses the notional difference between philosophy and its old antagonist.

So we can best read Foucault as a 'knight of autonomy' (in Rorty's quasi-Kierkegaardian phrase), a thinker whose quest for ethical well-being went along with a principled refusal to generalize on the basis of his own private needs and desires, or to offer anything that remotely resembled a normative moral creed. For otherwise, as Rorty well knows, there is always a danger that the ethos of aesthetic self-invention will get out of hand and begin to look more like a wholesale 'transvaluation of values', an attempted 'overcoming' of Western metaphysics in the Nietzschean-Heideggerian mode. In short, 'we should not try to find a societal counterpart to the desire for autonomy. . . . Trying to do so leads to Hitlerlike and Maolike fantasies about "creating a new kind of human being"'.[47] But we shall not be led in this direction – any more than Foucault at his liberal-democratic best – if we acknowledge the private/public dichotomy and the fact that such projects have absolutely no claim upon the wider communal interest. Thus 'the point of a liberal society', as Rorty understands it,

> is not to invent or create anything, but simply to make it as easy as possible for people to achieve their wildly different private ends without hurting each other. To work out the details of the continually shifting compromises which make up the political discourse of such a society requires a banal moral vocabulary – a vocabulary which is no more relevant to one individual's private self-image than to another's. In a liberal society, our public dealings with our fellow citizens are not *supposed* to be Romantic or inventive; they are supposed to have the routine intelligibility of the marketplace or the courtroom.[48]

In other words, we can cope with strong revisionists or self-fashioning aesthetes like Foucault just so long as we don't take them seriously – or at any rate read them with a pinch of liberal-ironic salt – when they start pronouncing on matters of public or political concern. That Foucault once in a while indulged this bad habit is evidence, for Rorty, that he hadn't travelled *quite* far enough toward that stance of 'postmodern bourgeois-liberal pragmatist' wisdom which enabled him to view such lapses in others as a symptom of their lingering 'Enlightenment' habits of thought. But we can always operate on a principle of charity, discount for those momentary blind-spots, and read him as a thinker well advanced along the path to private autonomy on the one hand, and on the other an outlook of easygoing tolerance for the public self-images of the age. Thus: '[w]hether he wanted to be or not, Foucault was, among other things, a useful citizen of a democratic country – one who did his best to make that country's institutions fairer and more decent'.[49] And if this reading seems at odds with much of what Foucault had to say – with his Nietzschean (or decidedly jaundiced) view of liberal-democratic values, his treatment of such values as one more regime of oppressive institutionalized power/knowledge, and his relentless drive to subvert the very bases of received morality and truth – then Rorty can only deplore these excesses and voice the fond wish 'that he [Foucault] had been more comfortable with this self-description than he was'. Such problems aside, we had much better give him the benefit of the doubt. For otherwise he will emerge as a truly dangerous thinker, an adept of aesthetic self-fashioning who failed to draw the line between private and public domains, and who thus mistook his own project of 'poetic' invention for something in the nature of a political philosophy or a moralizing tract for the times.

II

I have taken this lengthy detour via Rorty's essay because it shows both the extent to which Foucault can be misread by a well-disposed liberal commentator, and also the way that such a reading can latch onto philosophical, ethical and political problems in his work which tend to be ignored by other, more devoted or *echt*-Foucauldian types. For in one respect Rorty is undoubtedly right. That is to say: if you follow Foucault's sceptical genealogies to a point where the knowing, willing and judging subject becomes nothing more than a transient illusion, a 'face drawn in sand at the edge of the sea', soon to be erased by the incoming tide, then this does give rise to some stark alternatives in the ethico-political realm. More specifically, it opens the way to Rorty's private-aestheticist reading of Foucault by reducing the subject to a nominal entity – a vanishing-point or *tabula rasa* – with no scope for moral agency and choice unless through an act of pure, poetic self-invention.

What this amounts to is a dead-end version of those paradoxes that Kant pointed out in the cautionary section of his first *Critique* devoted to the antinomies of pure reason.[50] That is to say, it combines a form of hard-line determinist creed – in this case, the argument that subjectivity is constituted through and through by the ubiquitous effects of power/knowledge – with the desire to secure some space for autonomy or freedom, for a mode of self-fashioning which would somehow escape that otherwise implacably determinist regime. But of course the only way to envisage such a freedom (given these awkward constraints) is by conceiving it in terms of an existential leap, an *acte gratuite* that delivers the subject from its bondage to this or that conventional discourse, language-game or cultural form of life, and which thus involves the choice of some alternative 'final vocabulary' (Rorty's phrase) by which to achieve at least some measure of 'private' autonomy and self-fulfilment. Not that this offers any genuine solution, any means of transcending the freewill/ determinism problem or treating it, like Kant, as an error brought about by the failure to pose the right sorts of question at various, specifically demarcated levels of philosophical enquiry. For on Foucault's view this was a closed episode in the history of thought, a discourse premised on obsolescent notions such as 'man', 'reason' and the 'transcendental subject'. All that remained now was to analyse the discursive conditions of possibility that had once given rise to these chimerical ideas. But in thus proclaiming an end to the philosophic discourse of modernity Foucault ran into precisely those problems – those deep-laid antinomies – that Kant set out to adjudicate from a standpoint of enlightened critical reason. Most crucially, he left himself no room for manoeuvre when it came to explaining how subjects could exercise a degree of ethical autonomy or choice, a margin of freedom that would not be foreclosed by the pervasive workings of power/knowledge. And his only escape-route, Rorty contends, was one that involved a language of radical 'self-invention', a freedom so absolute or unconditioned that it needs to be confined to the private sphere – to the space of individual imagining – in order to keep the world safe for liberal democracy. For if the 'knight of autonomy' sets up to legislate in the ethico-political realm, then the way is clearly open to those forms of autocratic abuse – those manifestations of the private will-to-power writ large – whose history is a matter of public record.

So Rorty is right about Foucault in the sense of revealing certain problems and liabilities in his thought that tend to be overlooked by other, more orthodox commentators. What makes his reading such an odd piece of argument – though perfectly in line with his own postmodern-pragmatist beliefs – is the fact that Rorty admires Foucault *precisely on account* of his having pushed these problems to the point where they entail a radical disjunction between the private and public domains. The result strikes me as something very like an immanent critique of Foucault's entire project, offered though it is in the guise of a commentary that sets out to praise him for having been a good liberal-pragmatist at heart, despite those occasional lapses into a different (more radical and self-deceiving) rhetoric. Of course it may be said that Rorty is impaling Foucault on the horns of a false dilemma; that all this talk about the private/public dichotomy is just a way of off-loading Rorty's peculiar problems, or an instance of liberal discourse run aground on its own disabling contradictions. But I think this misses the more valuable diagnostic point: that Foucault's work invites such a reading insofar as it swings between the opposite poles of a thoroughgoing determinist creed (the idea that subjectivity is entirely constructed in and through discourse) and an ethics – or aesthetics – of autonomous self-creation which somehow escapes that limiting condition.

What is at this stage absent from Foucauldian ethics – very largely (I would

argue) as a consequence of his turn against Kant and the values of Enlightenment critique – is any sense of the complex relations that exist between those
various modalities of knowledge, will and judgement which all exert a claim
upon the subject's powers of self-knowledge and reflective moral agency. For in
the end Foucault's scepticism leads him to a point where there is just no way of
addressing such issues except genealogically, that is to say, as a form of
transcendental illusion whose emergence – and whose symptomatic blind-spots
– can be seen in Kant's strenuous but ultimately failed attempt to establish a
domain of critical philosophy purged of all anthropocentric residues. As Ian
Hacking usefully reminds us, *The Order of Things* was a project that grew out of
Foucault's work on the foreword to a French translation of Kant's *Anthropology*.[51]
And it is clear that the course of his subsequent thinking, whether in the
'archaeological' or the 'genealogical' mode, was very largely set by this
encounter with Kant and by the effort to articulate a post-humanist or non-
subject-centred history of the social and human sciences. But this raises the
question as to how far it is possible to envisage an *ethics* – in any meaningful
sense of that term – which would treat the subject as indeed nothing more
than an imaginary locus, a side-effect of language, or a product of those
transient discursive formations that constitute the history of Western thought.
It seems to me that this question haunts Foucault's writings up to the end, and
that he never managed to address or resolve it to his own satisfaction.

 Rorty of course sees nothing to fret about here, believing as he does that we
can happily get along with a minimalist notion of the 'subject' which dispenses
with any principle of integrity, selfhood or continuous identity over time, and
which rejoices in the range of optional subject-positions thrown up by this or
that 'final vocabulary'. In fact it is Foucault's great virtue, as Rorty reads him,
to have dumped all those old 'essentialist' concepts of the self, and thus
pointed the way toward a postmodern sense of open-ended creative possibility.
Of course there is a problem – remarked upon by several commentators – in
construing just what Rorty can mean with his talk of 'self-fashioning', 'self-
creation', 'self-invention', etc., given his professed disbelief in the self as
anything more than a floating ensemble of language-games or transient role-
models. But Rorty makes light of such objections, viewing them as merely a
symptom of the old-fashioned craving for some 'deep' further fact about human
selfhood that would answer to Kantian ideas of justice, enlightenment and
truth. What he likes in Foucault is best summed up by a passage from
his essay 'Freud and Moral Reflection', where Rorty puts the case for this
minimalist conception as the last, best hope for private autonomy and, by the
same token, for liberal democracy as its natural counterpart in the public-
political sphere. 'I want to focus,' he writes,

 on the way in which Freud, by helping us to see ourselves as centerless, as
 random assemblages of contingent and idiosyncratic needs rather than as more or

less adequate exemplifications of a common human essence, opened up new possibilities for the aesthetic life. He helped us become increasingly ironic, playful, free, and inventive in our choice of self-descriptions. . . . Freud made the paradigm of self-knowledge the discovery of the fortuitous materials out of which we must construct ourselves rather than the discovery of the principles to which we must conform. He thus made the desire for purification seem more self-deceptive, and the quest for self-enlargement more promising.[53]

And likewise with Foucault, as Rorty reads him: a thinker whose best, most creative energies were devoted to undoing the old (that is, Kantian) paradigm of ethical self-knowledge, and constructing an alternative where the 'self' would figure only as a nominal point of reference, a catachrestic term adopted for want of any handy substitute. Nor can Rorty see any reason to worry about the ethical consequences of this argument, not to mention the logical problems involved in conceiving how 'self-enlargement' could occur in the absence of a self to enlarge. For such problems will only seem urgent to a reader still hooked on 'philosophical' ideas of what constitutes a valid, adequate or good-faith argument. But if one takes it, like Rorty, that 'truth' *just is* whatever counts as such according to the current conversational rules of the game, then one might as well follow such strong exemplars as Freud and Foucault in renouncing that old, subject-centred discourse and embarking on a project of creative self-invention with the best vocabulary to hand.

As I have said, there are difficulties for anyone who contests this reading on grounds of its failure to take due account of Foucault's 'radical' politics, his commitment to a Nietzschean 'transvaluation of values', or his lifelong opposition to forms of instituted power/knowledge. For these objections to carry much weight one would also need to demonstrate, *contra* Rorty, that his writings manifest an argued and principled resistance to the neo-pragmatist account of them, that is to say, the idea that they can best be read as recommending on the one hand a private ethos of autonomy, self-fashioning, liberal irony, etc., and on the other an attitude of public 'solidarity' or consensus-based citizenly virtue. Of course this will strike most readers as a travesty of Foucault's ethico-political beliefs, his activist stance on various issues of social and moral conscience, and his well-known view of the 'specific intellectual' as one who – unlike her enlightened, 'universal' counterpart – engages such issues at the level of localized resistance and direct intervention. On these counts it may be said that Rorty misreads Foucault, or reads him consistently against the grain with a view to promoting his own postmodern-neopragmatist-liberal agenda. But he can still come back with two lines of argument by way of countering this charge. One is the point – as I have suggested already – that if Foucault is understood to be urging a more direct 'non-dichotomous' relation between 'private' and 'public' moralities, then his position leans over into a strain of wholesale aesthetic ideology with disquieting echoes of the Nietzschean will-to-power and similar (decidedly illiberal) notions. In this respect Rorty could claim to be offering a better, more socially desirable reading which saves him, so to speak, from his own worst devices. And the second line of argument open to Rorty is simply to remark that there is nothing in Foucault – no standard of right reading, no ethical criterion, no critical court of appeal – that could possibly count against any 'strong revisionist' or slanted understanding of his work. After all, few writers have done more to undermine the claims of authorial intent, to dislodge the knowing and willing subject from its erstwhile privileged status, and to promulgate an 'ethics' of reading indifferent to issues of interpretative truth and falsehood. In short, Foucault has yielded every last critical ground on which one might otherwise have rested the case against Rorty's shrewdly angled misreading. And he has done so, moreover, as a consequence of abandoning those same values and principles – the legacy of Kantian-Enlightenment thought – which Rorty is likewise bent upon consigning to the scrapheap of obsolete ideas.

Michael Walzer argues to similar effect in his essay 'The Politics of Michel Foucault', a dissident account – as might be expected, given Walzer's mainstream-liberal views – but still one of the best, most cogently argued commentaries to date.[54] Walzer's main objection to Foucault is that he offers no normative standard, no basis of moral or political judgement by which one might distinguish different orders of civil and state authority. For on Foucault's account it would appear that *any* such order – from the totalitarian to the liberal-democratic – must finally be viewed as the product or expression of an omnipresent will-to-power whose mechanisms extend to every last aspect of our private and public lives. Least of all should we suppose (the typical Enlightenment error) that history shows signs of a progress, however halting or uneven, from regimes founded on the exercise of power in its overt, spectacular form to social institutions that temper such excesses through the civilizing influence of reason, democracy, and humanitarian concern. For of course it is Foucault's belief that these developments, along with their academic offshoots in the human and social sciences, are simply a more sophisticated instrument of surveillance and control, a means by which the workings of power/knowledge take hold upon the subject's innermost thoughts and desires. So there can be no question of resisting those effects through the kind of reasoned, principled critique that 'progressive' intellectuals from Kant to Habermas have seen fit to provide. For with each new addition (or expert refinement) to the range of available discourses, knowledges, or modes of 'enlightened' understanding there accrues yet further power to intervene in that process of disciplinary subject-formation whose history Foucault lays open to view. In which case the only option – as he thinks – is to renounce this whole bad legacy of *soi-disant* 'liberating' thought and acknowledge that effective resistance can only come about through the kind of localized, contingent intervention that lays no claim to anything more in the way of justifying principles.

Walzer sees clearly how Foucault is thus led to adopt an extreme voluntarist stance – an 'ethics' of radical self-creation – as the last refuge of freedom and autonomy when confronted with this otherwise implacably determinist regime. 'When Foucault is an anarchist,' Walzer writes,

> he is a moral as well as a political anarchist. For him morality and politics go together. Guilt and innocence are the products of law just as normality and abnormality are the products of discipline. To abolish power systems is to abolish both moral and scientific categories: away with them all! But what will be left? Foucault does not believe, as earlier anarchists did, that the free human subject is a subject of a certain sort, naturally good, warmly sociable, kind and loving. Rather, there is for him no such thing as a free human subject, no natural man or woman. Men and women are always social creations, the products of codes and disciplines. And so Foucault's radical abolitionism, if it is serious, is not anarchist so much as nihilist. For on his own arguments, either there will be nothing left at all, nothing visibly human; or new codes and disciplines will be produced, and Foucault gives us no reason to expect that these will be any better than the ones we now live with. Nor, for that matter, does he give us any way of knowing what 'better' might mean.[55]

It seems to me that this passage goes a long way toward explaining what is wrong with the treatment of these topics in much of Foucault's work. That is to say, it pinpoints all the problems that arise in the course of his protracted attempt to formulate an ethics and a politics which *on the one hand* conserve a credible role for the subject as locus of autonomous, self-acting resistance, while *on the other* they steadfastly reject any appeal to the subject conceived in Kantian terms, i.e., as a knowing and willing agent whose commitments are a matter of reasoned argument, reflective self-knowledge, and principled choice. In the end Foucault is caught – as I suggested above – on the horns of that same dilemma that Kant expounded among the Antinomies of Pure Reason in order to point a way through and beyond it. His thinking oscillates between the twin poles of a determinism pushed to the utmost extreme – where the 'subject' is nothing more than a transient construction out of various discursive registers – and a doctrine of autonomy (or private self-invention) that leans right over into an anarchist ethics and politics.

All of which lends a certain poignancy to Ian Hacking's comments, in his essay 'Self-Improvement', that 'Foucault was a remarkably able Kantian', and that '[t]hose who criticize Foucault for not giving us a place to stand might start their critique with Kant'.[56] For what emerges from Foucault's series of engagements with the legacy of Kantian thought is not so much an over-coming of the old antinomies as a re-run of issues that have not been laid to rest despite all his proclamations of an end to the discourse of Enlightenment critique. And this applies to every aspect of his thought, from the mainly epistemological concerns of a work like *The Order of Things* to the ethico-political questions that preoccupy the writings of his final decade. Take for instance the following curious passage from a 1983 interview where Foucault apparently abandons any notion of the subject as a mere epiphenomenon of discourse, or of knowledge and truth as values that can only be construed in terms of some particular language-game, paradigm, or mode of discursive representation. Such, after all, had been the main working premise that linked Foucault's early archaeological researches to his subsequent, Nietzsche-inspired genealogies of truth and morals. But he now seems anxious to assert just the opposite: that the subject has resources – of will, self-knowledge, or reflective understanding – that *cannot* be accounted for exclusively in terms of its linguistic or discursive constitution. 'What distinguishes thought,' Foucault maintains,

> is that it is something quite different from the set of representations that underlies a certain behavior; it is also something quite different from the domain of attitudes that can determine this behavior. Thought is not what inhabits a certain conduct and gives it its meaning; rather, it is what allows one to step back from this way of acting or reacting, to present it to oneself as an object of thought and question it as to its meaning, its conditions, and its goals. Thought is freedom in relation to what one does, the motion by which one detaches oneself from it, establishes it as an object, and reflects on it as a problem.[57]

Nothing could be further from the governing precept of Foucault's earlier work, the idea that structures of representation, or discourses of power/knowledge, are all that remain once the subject has been dislodged from its position of illusory eminence, revealed as just a side-effect of language or a figment of the humanist imaginary. To his later way of thinking, on the contrary, '[t]he work of philosophical and historical reflection is put back into the field of the work of thought only on condition that one clearly grasps problematization not as an arrangement of representations but as a work of thought'.[58] What has now become clear to Foucault is that there is simply no basis for an ethics – no room for any adequate or workable account of human responsibility, agency and choice – if one accepts this drastically reductive and determinist creed.

In other words he continued to wrestle with issues left open in the settling of accounts with Kant that appeared to be concluded (to his own satisfaction) in a work like *The Order of Things*. And these issues were as much epistemo-logical as ethical or political in nature. For it is among the main principles of Kantian philosophy – one rejected *tout court* by the early Foucault – that practical reason, while crucially distinct from the truth-claims of cognitive enquiry, nonetheless involves judgements of circumstantial truth or falsehood which cannot be upheld without taking due account of the way things stand in reality.[59] Of course Kant denies, as he must, that ethical questions could ever be reduced to a matter of straightforward empirical warrant, or a direct appeal to the facts of the case by way of ultimate justification. After all, he is committed to maintaining the (as he sees it) imperative distinction between judgements in the realm of cognitive understanding whose truth is a matter of determinate necessity (of bringing intuitions under adequate concepts), and ethical judgements whose appeal is always to a realm of 'suprasensible' ideas or maxims, a tribunal where the rule is given through an act of freely-willed compliance or assent.[60] To confuse these realms – as by seeking to ground moral judgements in observations of fact, or claiming to derive an 'ought' straightforwardly from an 'is' – is in Kant's view the kind of category-mistake that produces all the aporias of determinist thinking as applied to issues of human agency and will. But clearly there is no reasoning on ethical principles except by bringing them down to earth, so to speak, in the form of specific case-studies or instances that illustrate the relevant point.[61] Hence the need for a double-aspect theory which on the one hand acknowledges the range of causal and circumstantial factors that must be recognized as bearing upon our thoughts, motives and actions, while on the other maintaining a sense of the autonomous character – the government by rules of its own free choosing – that properly belongs to ethical judgement.[62]

For some recent critics of a liberal-communitarian persuasion – Walzer prominent among them – this Kantian metaphysics of morals is altogether too prescriptive or 'formalist' in nature.[63] Which is to say, it is only capable of offering the most abstract kinds of guidance (like Kant's 'categorical imperative'), and has little to impart by way of guidance or advice when it comes to the sorts of commonplace dilemma – the perplexities of interest and motive – that characterize our day-to-day experience as social creatures. Such issues can only be addressed to any purpose, these critics argue, by abandoning the high ground of Kantian ethics and adopting a perspective more fully conversant with the values, conventions, and habits of belief which prevail within this or that specific cultural context. And for us (for citizens of the present-day Western liberal democracies) this context is defined very largely in terms of those reciprocal rights and obligations, along with the occasional conflicts of priority between them, that enable our active, participant role in the ongoing cultural conversation. Thus Kant goes wrong (and gives rise to a history of misconceived 'liberal' thought) by laying such stress on the autonomy of ethical judgement, or the voice of dissident conscience as opposed to the claims of communal wellbeing or social solidarity. And he does so, in Walzer's view, as a consequence of those same foundationalist precepts that typify the discourse of Enlightenment reason in its other (epistemological) aspect. But this project will appear simply pointless and misguided if one has perceived the benefits of liberal culture in its latter-day, post-Kantian or un-self-deluding form. For it will then become clear to any good-faith member of the relevant interpretive community that there is no court of appeal, no source of justifying grounds or principles, beyond that provided by existing civil and social institutions. Nor are such principles in any way requisite, given the capacity of this liberal culture to sustain the kind of dialogue that allows a fair hearing to all interested parties. In short, one can happily dispense with those Enlightenment notions – truth, reason, critique, ideology and so forth – just so long as the conversation keeps going and everyone abides by the present set of rules.

To put it like this is to emphasize the degree of convergence that exists between Walzer's communitarian viewpoint and Rorty's thoroughgoing pragmatist persuasion that truth is what currently counts as 'good in the way of belief'. It is odd, to say the least, that Walzer should have offered such a shrewd diagnosis of the problems that beset Foucault's ethical and socio-political thought, while himself – elsewhere – adopting a position that effectively sidesteps these issues.[64] For if indeed it is the case that consensus values go 'all the way down', then there is simply no conceiving how resistance comes about, or how anyone could effectively challenge those values from a standpoint of argued and principled dissent. It seems to me that Foucault found himself in the awkward position of one who sought to maintain a strongly oppositional or counter-hegemonic stance, yet whose outlook of extreme epistemological and ethical scepticism left him at the last with no ground on which to stand in advancing these dissident claims. And this is nowhere more apparent than in the record of Foucault's repeated encounters with Kant, from *The Order of Things* (where Kant's philosophy figures as the merest of transient discursive paradigms) to the later writings where Foucault is engaged in what amounts to a full-scale revisionist reading of Kantian ethical themes. To pursue the often complex and circuitous course of these encounters is I think the best way to grasp what is at stake in the current postmodernist turn against the discourse of Enlightenment values and beliefs.

III

The most crucial text here is Foucault's essay 'What Is Enlightenment?', taking its cue from a piece of the same title that Kant published in November 1784 in response to a call for disquisitions on this topic by the liberal *Berliner Monatschrift*.[65] Up to a point Foucault offers what could well be taken as a summary account, a 'faithful' exposition of the various claims that Kant advances on behalf of Enlightenment and its ethico-political bearings. Thus: 'Kant indicates right away that the "way out" that characterizes Enlightenment is a process that releases us from the status of "immaturity"'. By "immaturity" Kant means "a certain state of our will that makes us accept someone else's authority to lead us in areas where the use of reason is called for"' (WIE, p. 34). So Enlightenment is defined, in Foucault's scrupulously Kantian terms, as a certain 'modification of the preexisting relation linking will, authority and the use of reason' (p. 35). Its motto is *Sapere aude*, 'Dare to know!', and it must therefore be construed 'both as a process in which men participate collectively and as an act of courage to be accomplished personally' (p. 35). But while presenting these claims in the mode of paraphrase or shorthand synopsis Foucault finds room for misgivings as regards their 'ambiguous' status, in particular their failure, as he sees it, to resolve certain issues in the realm of practical agency and will. And these doubts become steadily more prominent to the point where commentary shades into overt dissent or a form of immanent critique.

Thus Enlightenment is characterized by Kant on the one hand 'as a phenomenon, an ongoing process' and on the other 'as a task and an obligation'. In which case clearly there is an issue – one confronted by numerous latterday schools of thought, among them Althusserian Marxism and the structuralist 'sciences of man' – as to how these two perspectives could ever be reconciled. 'Are we to understand,' Foucault asks,

> that the entire human race is caught up in the process of Enlightenment? Then we must imagine Enlightenment as a historical change that affects the political and social existence of all people on the face of the earth. Or are we to understand that it involves a change affecting what constitutes the humanity of human beings? But the question then arises of knowing what this change is. Here again, Kant's answer is not without a certain ambiguity. In any case, beneath its appearance of simplicity, it is really rather complex. (WIE, p. 35)

And from this point his essay goes on to remark some of the further problems – the *antinomies*, as Foucault all-but names them – that emerge in the course of Kant's reflections on Enlightenment as 'process' and 'phenomenon'. His treatment preserves an attitude of qualified respect, at least when compared with those pages of arch-sceptical commentary in *The Order of Things* where the Kantian project appears as nothing more than a species of transcendental illusion, a mirage created – and soon to be erased – by the imperious order of 'discourse'. Thus Foucault now acknowledges that 'this little text is located in a sense at the crossroads of critical reflection and reflection on history' (p. 38). Moreover it marks the first occasion on which 'a philosopher has connected in this way, closely and from the inside, the significance of his work with respect to knowledge, a reflection on history and a particular analysis of the specific moment at which he is writing and because of which he is writing' (p. 38).[66]

But these tributes have a double-edged character that emerges more clearly as Foucault expounds what he takes to be the crucial and unresolved tension within Kant's philosophical project. This results from his commitment to a notion of critique which on the one hand takes rise in response to certain highly specific historical conditions, while on the other hand claiming to transcend those conditions through an exercise of the human faculties – of understanding, reason and judgement – deduced *a priori* as a matter of timeless, self-evident truth. On Foucault's reading, this latter must be seen as a form of residual anthropomorphism, a humanist or subject-centred philosophy which fails to take the point of its own best insights as regards the radically contingent or historically situated character of all such truth-claims.

Thus Kant still figures, here as in *The Order of Things*, as one of those thinkers whose will to contest and problematize existing relations of power/ knowledge was itself the product of a finally un-self-questioning drive to establish its own 'enlightened' credentials. And this despite the fact, which Foucault readily concedes, that any competent, good-faith discussion of these issues will have to go by way of a critical encounter whose terms will always very largely have been set in advance by that same legacy of thought. In short, '[w]e must try to proceed with the analysis of ourselves as beings who are historically determined, to a certain extent, by the Enlightenment' (WIE, p. 43). But to this extent precisely we shall have to acknowledge – unlike Kant – that the Enlightenment project is (and always was) just one of those manifold discursive paradigms, those shifting orders of language or representation that make up the structural genealogy of Western reason. So the process of enquiring-back into this history of thought will not, in Foucault's words, 'be oriented retrospectively toward "the essential kernel of rationality" that can be found in the Enlightenment and that would have to be preserved in any event' (p. 43). On the contrary, such thinking 'will be oriented toward "the contemporary limits of the necessary", that is, toward what is not or is no longer indispensable for the constitution of ourselves as autonomous subjects' (p. 43). Clearly this amounts to something more than a mildly revisionist reading of Kant, a modest proposal – in the 'history of ideas' vein – that we take some account of social or circumstantial factors as well as substantive philosophical arguments. For Foucault's contention goes far beyond this amicable parcelling-out of disciplinary domains. What it requires, in effect, is that we read Kant's philosophy as marked *through and through* by this error of mistaking culture-specific for *a priori* valid truth-claims, or 'contemporary limits of the necessary' for limits intrinsic to our very constitution as thinking and willing subjects.

Thus it might well seem on the evidence of 'What Is Enlightenment?' that Foucault has scarcely altered his sceptical stance with regard to the agenda and entire axiology of Kantian critique. But this appearance is deceptive, as soon becomes clear as one reads further into the essay. For it is now Foucault's central concern to articulate an ethics premised on the values of autonomy, freedom, and self-determination attained through an exercise of practical will. And when he comes to describe this project in more detail it turns out remarkably akin to Kant's own, as expressed in the famous threefold question (What can I know? What should I will? and What may I reasonably hope for?). The crucial difference in Foucault's way of posing these questions is that he treats them – in genealogical fashion – as belonging to a certain, historically delimited configuration of knowledge, discourse or the will-to-truth. That is to say, he rejects any version of the strong universalist premise that would hold such values to be more than contingent, more than just a product of our own (now waning) cultural attachment to the philosophic discourse of modernity. What remains of that delusory Enlightenment project is not so much 'a theory, a doctrine, or . . . a permanent body of knowledge that is accumulating', but rather, in Foucault's carefully chosen words, 'an ethos, a philosophical life in which the critique of what we are is at one and the same time the historical analysis of the limits that are imposed on us and an experiment with the possibility of going beyond them' (WIE, p. 50). And again, taking aim at the heart of Kant's distinction between reason in its 'public' (critical) and 'private' (doxastic or opinionative) modes:

> criticism is no longer going to be practised in the search for formal structures with universal value, but rather as an historical investigation into the events that have led us to constitute ourselves and to recognize ourselves as subjects of what we are doing, thinking, saying. In that sense, this criticism is not transcendental. . . . it is genealogical in its design and archaeological in its method. (pp. 45–6)

In fact Foucault precisely inverts Kant's order of priorities. On the one hand he demotes the claims of 'transcendental' reason (or critique) to the status of a merely localized episode in the recent history of thought. On the other he identifies truth – for all practical purposes – with that level of contingent events or shifts in the order of power/knowledge relations which can best be revealed through a jointly 'archaeological' and 'genealogical' approach. Insofar as the Enlightenment project survives, it does so in a sharply delimited or relativized form, as an impetus to the kind of investigative thinking – the enquiring-back into its own genesis and historical conditions of emergence – which can offer no hold for the truth-telling claims of old-style 'universal' reason. To adapt Karl Krauss's famous remark about Freudian psychoanalysis: Enlightenment now shows up as a symptom of the very condition for which it once professed to be the cure.

And yet, as Foucault very pointedly remarks, there is no question of simply having done with that entire heritage of thought, no way of jumping outside it (so to speak) onto some alternative — maybe 'postmodern' — terrain of disabused sceptical hindsight. Such, after all, had been the attitude evinced in those pages on Kant in *The Order of Things* where Foucault proclaimed the imminent demise of 'man' as the specular figment of a discourse premised on obsolete (Enlightenment) truth-claims and values. If he is now less inclined to adopt this style of heady post-structuralist talk it is because he perceives the risk it entails, namely that of 'letting ourselves be determined by more general structures of which we may not be conscious, and over which we may have no control' (WIE, p. 47). In short, Foucault's wager is that we can in some sense 'keep faith' with the project of enlightened critique, while acknowledging that in another sense — on the strong universalist or 'transcendental' reading — that project has long since run its course and relinquished all claims to validity or truth. Thus 'the thread that may connect us with the Enlightenment', he writes, 'is not faithfulness to doctrinal elements, but rather the permanent reactivation of an attitude — that is, of a philosophical ethos that could be described as a permanent critique of our historical era' (p. 42).

What this amounts to is an argument for decoupling ethics from any version of the old 'foundationalist' paradigm, the idea on the one hand that self-knowledge comes about through an exercise of autonomous practical reason, and on the other that this involves a critical reflection on the powers and capacities — as well as the constitutive limits — of human knowledge in general. Of course Kant's philosophy goes a long and sometimes tortuous way around to establish the relation between knowing and willing, or the complex 'architectonic' of the faculties within which the various orders of truth-claim find their legitimate place.[67] Moreover, he lays great stress on the need to respect these distinctions — especially that between phenomenal cognition and judgements in the ethico-political realm — since otherwise such judgements would ultimately fall under the laws of causal necessity, and would thus be deprived of their autonomous character, their standing as freely-willed acts of assent to the requirements of morality and justice. In this sense it might be argued that Foucault — along with postmodernist sceptics like Lyotard — is merely following out the logic of Kant's own position when he seeks to drive a wedge between the truth-claims of Enlightenment reason and the project of ethical self-fashioning that survives the eclipse or demise of those claims.[68] Thus: 'rather than seeking to distinguish the "modern era" from the "premodern" or "postmodern", I think it would be more useful to try to find out how the attitude of modernity, ever since its formation, has found itself struggling with attitudes of "countermodernity"' (WIE, p. 39). In which case Foucault's revisionist reading would in fact be no more than a faithful rendition, an attempt to conserve this liberating impulse, or 'to bring some measure of clarity to the consciousness that we have of ourselves and our past' (p. 45).

So the Kantian questions still have a pertinence, a capacity to provoke critical reflection on the ways and means of 'enlightened' self-knowledge that exist for us now as subjects inscribed within a certain culture-specific discourse. But on Foucault's account they need to be framed rather differently, re-cast in such a form as to exclude any notion of truth or critique as values transcending this localized context of utterance. Thus: 'How are we constituted as subjects of our own knowledge? How are we constituted as subjects who exercise or submit to power relations? How are we constituted as subjects of our own actions?' (p. 49). These are still recognizably the same kinds of question that have occupied thinkers in the modern or critical-enlightenment tradition, from Kant to Habermas.[69] But they differ in respect of the one crucial point: that for Foucault self-knowledge can only come about through the exercise of a freedom — a space of individual autonomy — created in the margins or interstices of an otherwise ubiquitous will-to-power whose watchwords are 'reason', 'enlightenment', and 'truth'. Hence the single most important question for Foucault: 'how can the growth of capabilities be disconnected from the intensification of power relations?' (p. 48). And his answer — to this extent in common with Lyotard and other postmodernizing critics of Kant — is to shift the main burden of enquiry from the relationship between knowledge and ethics (as developed chiefly in the first two *Critiques*) to the relationship between ethics and aesthetics (as taken up in the *Critique of Judgement* with reference to the beautiful and the sublime).[70] For it then becomes possible to re-write the history of the present in terms of an elective genealogy which downplays the critical-enlightenment aspects of the modern, and which instead stresses the aesthetic dimension — the very different 'modernity' of a poet like Baudelaire — by way of contesting that other line of descent.

What is at issue here is an ambivalence that inhabits the key-word 'modern' — almost, one could say, an elaborate pun on the meanings of that term — whereby it comes to signal the passage from philosophy to poetry, or from Kantian critique to the symbolist project of autonomous self-creation through aesthetic means. 'For the attitude of modernity,' Foucault writes,

> the high value of the present is indissociable from a desperate eagerness to imagine it, to imagine it otherwise than it is. . . . Baudelairean modernity is an exercise in which extreme attention to what is real is confronted with the practice of a liberty that simultaneously respects this reality and violates it. (WIE, p. 41)

Hence the great difference between Kant's and Foucault's ways of answering the question: 'What Is Enlightenment?' For Kant, it is a matter of attaining intellectual and moral maturity through the exercise of criticism in its various modes, whether applied to issues of cognitive understanding (where intuitions must be 'brought under' adequate concepts), to questions of an ethical or political order (where practical reason supplies the rule), or again, to issues in the sphere of aesthetic judgement where the relevant tribunal can only be that of an intersubjective community of taste appealing to shared principles or criteria of value. For Foucault, on the contrary, this doctrine of the faculties is the merest of 'transcendental' illusions, an elective self-image whose hold upon the discourse of Enlightenment was soon to be eclipsed by the advent of a 'counter-modernism', a primarily artistic and literary ethos possessed of no such grandiose philosophical ideas. So it is that the aesthetic moves to centre stage as the focal point for everything that challenges, eludes or subverts the truth-claims of enlightenment critique.

Thus: 'modern man, for Baudelaire, is not the man who goes off to discover himself, his secrets and his hidden truth; he is the man who tries to invent himself' (WIE, p. 42). And again, in a passage that anticipates Rorty and his private-aestheticist reading of Foucault:

> this ironic heroization of the present, this transfiguring play of freedom with reality, this ascetic elaboration of the self – Baudelaire does not imagine that these have any place in society itself, or in the body politic. They can only be produced in another, a different place, which Baudelaire calls art. (p. 42)

It is here, midway through his essay, that Foucault abruptly switches over from discussing 'modernity' as a project of enlightened or truth-seeking thought to a sequence of reflections on Baudelaire, aestheticism, and the ethos of poetic self-fashioning conceived as the hallmark of the authentically modern. His main text is Baudelaire's well-known essay on the painter Constantin Guys, an artist of the everyday, of fleeting impressions, of humdrum realities that are somehow 'transfigured' into something more profound and revealing.[71] Thus Guys, 'in appearance a spectator, a collector of curiosities,' should rather be seen (in Baudelaire's words) as 'the last to linger wherever there can be a glow of light, an echo of poetry, a quiver of life or a chord of music; wherever a passion can *pose* before him, wherever natural man and conventional man display themselves in a strange beauty, wherever the sun lights up the swift joys of the *depraved animal*' (WIE, p. 41). What Foucault seeks to emphasize by citing these and similar observations from Baudelaire's essay is the passage, as he sees it, from a discourse of modernity premised on outmoded (enlightenment) ideas of knowledge, reason and truth, to a modernism that not only accepts its condition as a localized, ephemeral state of awareness, but which turns this predicament into a source of new-found imaginative strength by ironically 'heroizing' the present moment and the scope it offers for aesthetic self-creation. In short, 'this deliberate, difficult attitude consists in recapturing something eternal that is not beyond the present instant, nor behind it, but within it' (p. 39).

For Baudelaire, as indeed for Kant, modernity is characterized as a 'break with tradition', a sense of the 'discontinuity of time' and the loss of those certitudes, those items of received commonsense knowledge, that had once seemed to offer enough in the way of ontological or ethical assurance.[72] But where Kant conceived this break as a coming-to-maturity through the exercise of autonomous critical reason, Baudelaire imagines it — in high Romantic style — as the discovery of ever more inventive variations on the theme of aesthetic self-invention. And Foucault follows Baudelaire, rather than Kant, in equating modernity with that spirit of perpetual transformation, that 'feeling of novelty, of vertigo in the face of the passing moment' which alone enables us to grasp what is authentic in our experience of contemporary art-forms and life-styles alike. For it is precisely in 'the ephemeral, the fleeting, the contingent' that consciousness discovers its true vocation as a register of novel modes and intensities of feeling, such as cannot be perceived — much less theorized — by a philosophy still wedded to Enlightenment notions of reason, truth, and critique. What this amounts to, on Foucault's interpretation, is a decisive break with those 'humanist' motifs which attached themselves to the discourse of Kantian critical philosophy, and which prevented it from moving beyond its subject-centred or anthropological orgins. 'Humanism serves to colour and to justify the conception of man to which it is, after all, obliged to take recourse' (WIE, p. 44). But with Baudelaire and the ethos of aesthetic self-fashioning there enters an alternative notion of modernity, one that renounces any such appeal to 'man' as transcendental subject or constitutive source of knowledge and truth. Humanism can thus be opposed, as Foucault now thinks, 'by the principle of a permanent critique and a permanent creation of ourselves in our autonomy: that is, a principle that is at the heart of the historical consciousness that the Enlightenment has of itself' (p. 44).

The word 'critique' has here acquired a meaning very different from that assigned to it by Kant, or indeed by any of those thinkers — Marxists among them — who took it to imply some determinate relation to matters of epistemological warrant, or to issues of truth and falsehood conceived as something more than what is 'good in the way of belief'. It has undergone much the same kind of semantic shift as emerges in Foucault's revisionist usage of the terms 'modernity' and 'enlightenment'. That is to say, these words are no longer construed as signalling a decisive difference in the way that criticism bears upon the currency of commonsense knowledge. Now it is a matter of perpetual self-transformation, a process carried on in the absence of truth-claims or validating grounds, and aimed — very much as Rorty conceives it — toward an ethos of 'private' (aesthetic) fulfilment that would render such notions altogether otiose. This is why Foucault reads Kant with Baudelaire: in order to facilitate the otherwise dubious (not to say sophistical) move which redefines 'modernity', 'enlightenment' and 'critique' on his own preferential terms. All of which lends a certain *prima facie* plausibility to Rorty's claim that Foucault was a good neo-pragmatist at heart, despite his occasional lapses into other, more 'radical' (and hence self-deceptive) styles of talk. For the upshot of Foucault's revisionist reading of Kant is to *aestheticize* issues of politics, morality and social justice to the point where they become, in his own words, a 'transfiguring play of freedom with reality', an 'ascetic elaboration of the self' worked out by the Nietzschean strong individual in pursuit of his or her own desires, or in accordance with that mode of private self-fashioning, that 'ironic heroization of the present . . . which Baudelaire calls art'.

To this extent, Foucault stands squarely in line with those proponents of 'aesthetic education' whose company includes some very diverse figures (from Schiller, Baudelaire and Nietzsche to Heidegger, Marcuse and Rorty), but whose cardinal premise – the ultimate justification of existence as an aesthetic phenomenon – he sees no reason to reject.[73] Hence, as I have argued, his strategy of intertextual reading in 'What Is Enlightenment?', a species of elaborated multiple wordplay which elides the most crucial (historically and philosophically pertinent) distinctions of meaning in terms like 'modernity', 'reason', 'critique', and 'enlightenment' itself. At the end of this process one reaches a point where those terms have lost any genuinely critical edge, any argued claim to link issues of conscience with issues of socio-political concern, and have taken on the kind of private-individualist ethos that would render such claims at best misguided, and at worst – as Foucault frequently asserts – an example of incipient totalitarian thought-control. Only by rejecting this entire tradition of thought, along with its grandiose philosophical claims, can ethics be recalled to what it once was, notably for the ancient Greeks: a cultivation of life-styles, disciplinary techniques, or modes of ascetic/aesthetic self-fashioning which allow the individual a measure of autonomy, a margin of hard-earned private freedom. Least of all can one require, like Kant, that practical reason extend its prerogative so as to legislate not only in the private (autonomous) domain but also on behalf of that wider, indeed universal community of interests where truth and justice would at last coincide in the ethical 'kingdom of ends'. On Foucault's account such ideas can all too readily provide a rationale for what he calls the 'blackmail of enlightenment', the self-promoting ruse by which reason sets up as an ultimate arbiter of truth, justice and right. After all, 'we know from experience' – or at least ought to know in light of events over the past two centuries – that 'the claim to escape from the system of contemporary reality so as to produce the overall programs of another society, of another way of thinking, another culture, another vision of the world, has led only to the return of the most dangerous traditions' (WIE, p. 46). It is with these dire precedents in mind that Foucault, along with Lyotard and other postmodernizing readers of Kant, proposes to shift the main focus of attention from the link between ethics (practical reason) and issues of truth and knowledge to the link between ethics and aesthetic judgement, as theorized by Kant in the third *Critique*. And what especially engages his interest – again like Lyotard – is the role of the sublime as a problematic topos inducing the maximum disturbance of epistemic concepts and categories, the maximum degree of 'heterogeneity' (Lyotard's term) between various orders of phrase-regime.[74] Hence Foucault's desire to transform the very discourse on and around 'modernity' by substituting art for philosophy, or – more pointedly – Baudelaire for Kant. Such is the modernist sensibility as evoked by Baudelaire in his essay on Constantin Guys:

> Away he goes, hurrying, searching. . . . Be very sure that this man – this solitary, gifted with an active imagination, ceaselessly journeying across the great human desert – has an aim loftier than that of a mere *flâneur*, an aim more general, something other than the fugitive pleasure of circumstance. He is looking for that quality which you must allow me to call 'modernity'. . . . He makes it his business to extract from fashion whatever element it may contain of poetry within history. (cited by Foucault, WIE, pp. 40–1)

So we are not to think of the aesthetic attitude, as Kierkegaard and other such high-toned moralists conceived it, as a tactical diversion, a trivial pursuit, or a dwelling on surface appearances in order to avoid real issues of ethical choice. The 'man of modernity' is no mere *flâneur*, no spellbound gazer at the frivolous distractions of life, but a figure embarked upon the quest for truth as that quest inescapably presents itself now, namely, under the aspect of a ceaseless transformation in the styles and modalities of 'authentic' self-knowledge. All the same one is put in mind of postmodern adepts like Baudrillard – purveyors of the shallowest, most enervating brands of present-day cultural junk-theory – when Foucault approvingly cites Baudelaire on Guys, the artist who 'makes it his business to extract from fashion whatever element it may contain of poetry within history'. For it is just this desire to make reality over into an aesthetic phenomenon – to collapse the whole range of ontological distinctions between life and art, fact and fiction, history and poetry, truth and appearance – which typifies the current postmodernist drive against Enlightenment and all its works.[75] And this is nowhere more apparent than in Foucault's assertion (again following Baudelaire) that 'this ironic heroization of the present, this trans-figuring play of freedom and reality, this ascetic elaboration of the self . . . [can] have no place in society itself, or in the body politic' (p. 42). For indeed there is evidence enough, some of it historically near to hand, of what can happen when this desire to aestheticize morality and politics is made over into a wholesale doctrine of society as a *Gesamtkunstwerk*, a spectacle arranged for the benefit of those with the taste or the courage to enjoy such concrete manifestations of the Nietzschean will-to-power.[76]

However it is only fair to remark that Foucault is alert to these dangers and thus, like Rorty, makes a point of denying that this aesthetic *modus vivendi* – this self-willed transvaluation of values – could ever achieve realization on the stage of world-historical events. Such ideas are just a hung-over symptom of the old Enlightenment ethos, the belief that reason is competent to judge in issues of moral, social or political conscience, and moreover – confusion worse confounded – that intellectuals possess this competence in a high degree by virtue of their critical or disinterested, truth-seeking role.[77] On the contrary, Foucault asserts: 'enlightenment' must now give way to 'genealogy' (or the thinking-back into its historical conditions of emergence and possibility) as the sole valid exercise of critical thought in an epoch when values such as 'truth' and 'critique' are irrevocably under suspicion. 'This philosophical attitude has to be translated into the labor of diverse enquiries' (WIE, p. 49). And again: even if 'Kant's reflection . . . is a way of philosophizing that has not been without its importance or effectiveness during the last two centuries', nevertheless that project and its associated values can nowadays only be conceived 'as an attitude, an ethos, a philosophical life . . . and an experiment with the possibilities of going beyond them' (p. 50). Moreover, it follows from this profound shift of critical orientation that the truly 'experimental' attitude – the self-fashioning ethos in its highest, most authentic form – will concern the individual *not* as a matter of his or her wider (civic or socio-political) responsibilities, but as a choice among various life-styles, modes of aesthetic comportment, 'ironic heroizations of the present', etc.. Thus the idea of ethics as an 'art of living' is one that Foucault carries to a point where the relevant comparisons are not only with Baudelaire – his favoured exemplar – but with Pater, Wilde and the discourse of late nineteenth-century aestheticist thought.

These 'decadent' echoes are plainly to be heard when Foucault evokes Baudelaire's passages on 'vulgar, earthy, vile nature', on 'man's indispensable revolt against himself', on 'the doctrine of elegance' which imposes on its subjects 'a discipline more despotic than the most terrible religions', and – most strikingly – on 'the asceticism of the dandy who makes of his body, his behavior, his feelings and passions, his very existence, a work of art' (pp. 41–2). Ethics thus becomes an exercise in rigorous (but nonetheless pleasurable) modes of self-discipline, an activity wherein, as Foucault conceives it, *askesis* and *aisthesis* are by no means opposed but contribute jointly to the shaping of a subject whose desires are both constrained and intensified by those same disciplinary techniques.[78] And it is the *individual* subject that is in question here, the 'modern man' of Foucault's (or Baudelaire's) imagining, one whose 'deliberate attitude of modernity' is 'tied to an indispensable asceticism', and who takes himself 'as object of a complex and difficult elaboration: what

Baudelaire, in the vocabulary of his day, calls *dandyisme*' (p. 41). Such an attitude squarely repudiates the claims of modernity in its Kantian or critical-enlightenment form. That is to say, the subject now engages inventively with his or her desires in an effort of autonomous self-creation, an aesthetics of existence, which exerts no claim to validity or truth beyond the benefits that thereby accrue to the strong-willed 'ethical' individual. 'This modernity does not "liberate man in his own being"; it compels him to face the task of producing himself' (p. 42). And this process can be actively pursued, so Foucault believes, only on condition that we think our way through and beyond the truth-claims of Enlightenment reason, to the point where 'autonomy' is re-defined as a project of aesthetic (or radically individualist) self-creation.

In which case there could be no question of distinguishing, as Kant so steadfastly maintained, between issues that concern reason in the 'public' (ethico-political) sphere, and issues that must finally resolve into a matter of private opinion, individual taste, or mere social convention. For Kant, paradoxically, it was the exercise of 'public' reason that required the subject to think and act with a maximum regard for the dictates of autonomous, self-critical judgement. In 'private' matters, on the other hand, one was always to some degree constrained by the interests of social-institutional morality, of beliefs and obligations accepted in accordance with prevailing consensus norms.[79] What Foucault seeks to do, in effect, is reverse or transvalue Kant's order of priorities, so that ethics equates with the private realm of aesthetic self-fashioning, while reason – or 'enlightenment' in its critical aspect – shows up as little more than a lingering attachment to those old, superannuated habits of thought. For 'we do not break free of this blackmail by introducing "dialectical" nuances while seeking to determine what good and bad elements there may have been in the Enlightenment' (WIE, p. 43). On the contrary: we do so (from Foucault's genealogical perspective) only through a self-willed transvaluation of values, a project of Nietzschean overcoming that admits of no truths save those which conduce to a heightened sense of aesthetic possibility. This is in effect what 'enlightenment' becomes when translated – as Foucault would have it – into an 'attitude', a 'voluntary choice made by certain people', a 'way of thinking and feeling . . . a bit, no doubt, like what the Greeks called an *ethos*' (p. 39). For the upshot of this exercise in persuasive re-definition is to empty 'enlightenment' (the word, the idea, the episode in cultural history) of any sense that might yet be construed as retaining its erstwhile critical and emancipatory thrust.

All this despite the fact, as Foucault duly notes, that 'critique is . . . the handbook of reason that has grown up in the Enlightenment', and moreover that 'the Enlightenment is the age of critique' (p. 38). From his point of view these facts have no more than a localized historical significance, an import that may indeed be crucial for us, as inheritors (for better or worse) of those same values and imperatives, but whose claims no longer possess the least semblance of general validity or truth. To imagine otherwise is to fall straight back into the same old Kantian trap, that is to say, the idea that there *must* exist a difference, a qualitative leap of thought, between mere anthropology (or sociology of knowledge) on the one hand, and critical philosophy (or 'transcendental' reasoning) on the other. Such is the illusion of those thinkers, like Habermas, who would defend and continue the 'unfinished project of modernity'.[80] It is most quickly dispelled, Foucault would claim, by reflecting on the aftermath of Enlightenment as manifest in historical events to date, and also by reading Kant in conjunction with those other modernists (Baudelaire among them) who have drawn out its alternative, more 'radical' implications. We shall then become aware that even Kant's essay – his resounding declaration of philosophic faith – can assume a different aspect when viewed in light of its role within a Foucauldian 'history of the present', a genealogical account of modernity and its discontents.

> It is in the reflection on 'today' as difference in history and as motive for a particular philosophical task that the novelty of this text ['What Is Enlightenment'] appears to me to lie. . . . And by looking at it in this way, it seems to me we may recognize a point of departure: the outline of what one might call the attitude of modernity. (WIE, p. 38)

What this 'attitude' amounts to, we have seen, is a readiness to give up all the truth-telling prerogatives of Enlightenment in exchange for a new-found sense of creative possibility, a 'certain manner of philosophizing' which 'seeks to give new impetus, as far and wide as possible, to the undefined work of freedom' (p. 46). In which case the relevant mode of enquiry is one that leads back to Kant's third *Critique* and to the various unresolved (perhaps unresolvable) issues that arise in connection with aesthetic judgement and its status *vis-à-vis* the discourse of philosophic reason. For it is here, according to postmodernist commentators like Lyotard, that enlightenment comes up against a salutary check to its presumptive, self-authorizing notions of truth. More specifically: what licences the otherwise improbable conjunction of Kant and Baudelaire is the way that the Kantian sublime gives rise to a series of strictly *unthinkable* antinomies, a point at which conceptual understanding is played off the field by the workings of a faculty (or modality of judgement) which somehow manages to 'present the unrepresentable', or to judge in the absence of any adequate concepts or criteria.[81] For Lyotard, this points toward 'heterogeneity' (or the maximization of discursive differentials) as a precondition for the exercise of justice in a postmodern epoch where the old 'grand narratives' no longer command any credence. For Foucault, it suggests that we read Kant henceforth in the intertextual company of poets and aesthetes, those who conserved the authentic impulse of modernity by renouncing its truth-claims and treating it as a wholly *aesthetic* phenomenon, a means whereby the resourceful individual could elaborate endless new strategies of self-invention. Such is 'the asceticism of the dandy who makes of his body, his behavior, his feelings and passions, his very existence, a work of art' (p. 41).

Thus the 'novelty' of Kant's undertaking has nothing to do with his so-called 'Copernican revolution' in philosophy, his claim to have provided a new, a more secure and critically accountable basis for the arbitration of issues concerning epistemology, ethics, or aesthetic judgement. Still less is it a matter of his having established, by means of transcendental critique, a series of *a priori* valid procedures for distinguishing between questions amenable to such philosophic treatment, and questions that fall within the realm of mere opinion, personal taste, or traditional belief. If this was Kant's estimate of his own achievement (and the view of it espoused by mainstream or orthodox commentators) we are none the less free – even in some sense obliged, as Foucault argues – to resist such a reading and seek out the signs of a different, counter-enlightenment image of 'modernity'. And the discourse that serves most effectively to promote this strong revisionist line is the language of autonomous self-invention adopted by aesthetes like Baudelaire, those for whom 'modernity is not simply a form of relationship to the present; it is also a mode of relationship that has to be established with oneself' (WIE, p. 41). Moreover, this attitude is 'tied to an indispensable asceticism' insofar as it radicalizes Kant's idea of the ethical injunction as a kind of self-thwarting, self-denying impulse, a law that seemingly bears from outside upon the subject and its first-order 'natural' instincts and desires, but which in fact, like the Freudian superego, issues from a voice of internal conscience and thereby effectively constitutes the subject as a locus of conflict, division, and ethical choice. Kant would thus figure as indeed the first thinker of modernity, but one whose insights were only followed through to their ultimate, authentically 'modern' conclusion by that radical 'decentering' of the subject accomplished on the one hand by the Symbolist *poètes maudits*, and on the other by Freudian psychoanalysis.

All the same we should be wrong to press too far with this three-sided analogy between Kant, Freud and Foucault. For despite all their differences – not least with regard to philosophy's claims as a privileged discourse of truth – Kant and Freud both maintain (unlike Foucault) an attitude of principled respect for the truth-telling virtues of enlightened thought, its capacity to bring forth redemptive self-knowledge from the chaos of instinctual drives. Nor can it be argued that this Kantian reading of Freud is one that merely suits the purposes of those, like Habermas, who would proclaim the 'enlightenment' lineage of psychoanalysis, and who are thus driven to ignore that whole dimension of the Freudian text where language becomes coextensive with the structures or symptoms of unconscious desire, and where reason is thereby revealed as nothing other than a delusive gesture of mastery, a plaything subject to forces beyond its knowledge or powers of interpretive control.[82] For it was Lacan – most insistent reader of Freud in this latter, post-structuralist vein – who also more than once remarked on Freud's kinship with Kant and the need to comprehend the Freudian text as an *ethical* discourse marked through and through by the symptoms of this conflict between reason and desire, the dictates of internalized (social or moral) conscience and the promptings of instinctual gratification.[83] What separates Foucault from both Kant and Freud (not to mention Lacan) is his aestheticized version of the ascetic imperative, that is to say, his understanding of ethical discourse as premised on a constant exploration of new possibilities, new modes of being whose aim is solely to enhance or intensify the pleasures of 'autonomous' selfhood.

It is in these terms precisely that Baudelaire celebrates the work of Constantin Guys, archetypal 'painter of modern life', for whom ' "natural" things become "more than natural", "beautiful" things become "more than beautiful", and individual objects appear "endowed with an impulsive life like the soul of their creator" ' (WIE, p. 41). For Foucault, this attitude exemplifies not only the discourse of aesthetic (or literary) modernism but also the outlook of 'modernity' in general, including Kant's project in 'What Is Enlightenment?' once shorn of its delusive philosophical props and outworks. Reading Kant along with Baudelaire thus becomes a lesson in the transience of cultural paradigms, in the way that questions of truth and right reason are converted into issues of taste, aesthetic preference, or idiosyncratic life-style. But there can then be no question of conflicts arising – as they do (in different ways) for Kant and Freud – between the realm of instinctual pleasures or desires and the order of properly ethical principles and values. More precisely: what is absent from Foucault's account is any sense that such conflicts could involve something more than a means of intensified self-cultivation, an opportunity for further aesthetic inventions on the same individualist theme. For modernity, we recall, 'is not simply a form of relationship to the present; it is also a mode of relationship that has to be established with oneself' (p. 41). And along with this redefinition of 'modernity' and its cognate Enlightenment terms goes a shift in the meaning of 'autonomous' judgement or reflection, a shift that devalues practical reason in its Kantian (public or critically account-able) sense, and which promotes a view of ethics as entirely bound up with the project of aesthetic self-fashioning. Nor does it count decisively against this reading that Foucault, after all, has much to say about asceticism and the fact that pleasures and desires take shape only in response, or by way of willed resistance, to the counter-pressure of various 'disciplinary' techniques. For these techniques are still deployed, as Foucault describes them, in the service of a 'truth' whose ultimate aim is a knowledge of the self and its potentially manifold styles or modalities of being.

It is largely by means of this semantic slide, this elision of the difference between *askesis* and *aisthesis*, that Foucault so adroitly negotiates the passage from Kant to Baudelaire. That is to say, it enables him to move across, with at least some show of textual and historical warrant, from an ethics grounded in the maxims and postulates of enlightened practical reason to an ethics premised on the Nietzschean will to treat existence as 'justified' solely to the extent that we can view it 'as an aesthetic phenomenon'. And it is for this reason also, as I have argued above, that Foucault's late texts can so easily be appropriated by a postmodern-pragmatist thinker such as Rorty. For those texts undoubtedly lend credence to Rorty's view that 'Foucault, like Nietzsche, was a philosopher who claimed a poet's privileges', and that 'one of these privileges is to rejoin "What has universal validity to do with *me*?"'.[84] And from this point – having set up the Kantian 'universal' moralist as a target for the usual range of knock-down arguments – Rorty then proceeds to enlist Foucault as an ally in what he takes to be the only viable alternative, a project of 'aesthetic' self-fashioning that renounces any claim to normative validity beyond the individual or private domain. In short, there is no reason why a strong revisionist or poet-philosopher like Foucault should feel himself obliged to answer such questions as 'Where do you stand?' or 'What are your values?'. And if he does so answer, then the best response is: 'I stand with you as fellow-citizens, but as a philosopher, I stand off by myself, pursuing projects of self-invention which are none of your concern'.[85] All of which follows, as can hardly be denied, from the aestheticizing impulse – the strain of high romantic or counter-enlightenment thought – that motivates Foucault to read Kant *avec* Baudelaire, thereby constructing his own (decidedly inventive) 'history of the present'.

IV

No doubt it will be said, with some justice, that when Rorty welcomes Foucault as a convert to this way of thinking he is obliged to discount that whole dimension of Foucault's work which bore very directly on issues of a wider socio-political import. And indeed there is no denying his record of involvement with pressure-groups and activist campaigns concerned with (for instance) racial discrimation, abuses of psychiatric medicine, the persecution of 'deviant' minorities, sexual transgressors, victims of the French penal system, and so forth. Moreover, these concerns also found expression in a series of powerfully argued works (from *Madness and Civilization* and *The Birth of the Clinic* to *Discipline and Punish*, *Pierre Rivière* and the multi-volume *History of*

Sexuality) which leave no doubt as to Foucault's belief that scholarship and 'theory' cannot be divorced from real-world issues of moral and political conscience. In this respect he clearly belongs to that company of left-dissident intellectuals – Noam Chomsky and Edward Said among them – who, whatever their differences, stand worlds apart from the self-engrossed frivolities of current postmodernist fashion.[86] All this I would willingly concede, along with the fact that Foucault's writings have undoubtedly done more than most to sustain the existence of a genuine oppositional culture – a 'counter-public-sphere', in Habermasian parlance – during these past two decades of concerted right-wing ideological offensives. My point is not at all to detract from this achievement, which in any case speaks for itself through the range and vitality of debates sparked off by Foucault's various interventions. What interests me more is the odd disjunction between Foucault's highly effective practice as a critical intellectual and the way that he persistently (not to say perversely) deploys every means, in his more speculative writings, to render such a practice untenable. For those writings could be seen to undermine the very ground – the very conditions of possibility for critical discourse – on which he nonetheless and *necessarily* claimed to stand when pursuing his other (historically and politically oriented) lines of research.

In short: there is a near-schizophrenic splitting of roles between (1) Foucault the 'public' intellectual, thinking and writing on behalf of those subjects oppressed by the discourses of instituted power/knowledge, and (2) Foucault the avowed aesthete, avatar of Nietzsche and Baudelaire, who espouses an ethos of private self-fashioning and an attitude of sovereign disdain toward the principles and values of enlightened critique. That he managed to negotiate the tensions of this dual identity – though not without visible signs of strain – is I think one of the more remarkable aspects of Foucault's life and work. For Rorty, of course, this is simply not a problem, or not one that a strong revisionist like Foucault ever needed to confront, having thought his way through and beyond all those tedious old debates about truth, enlightenment, ethical responsibility, the 'political role of the intellectuals' and so forth. Thus we ought to be content, Rorty urges, with a reading of Foucault that honours him, like Freud, for 'helping us to see ourselves as centerless, as random assemblages of contingent and idiosyncratic needs', and for thereby opening up 'new possibilities for the aesthetic life'.[87] But the signs of tension are there, as I have argued, in Foucault's protracted series of engagements with Kant, in the talk of 'truth' – however elusively defined – that figures so often in his late essays and interviews, and above all in his growing resistance to that strain of facile ultra-relativist talk that forms such a prominent (and depressing) feature of the *avant-garde* cultural scene. All of which suggests that he cannot be so easily recruited to a postmodern-pragmatist or counter-enlightenment ethos whose watchwords are the 'end of philosophy', the demise of Enlightenment critique, and the eclipse of the subject – the Kantian knowing, willing, and judging subject – as a phantom entity whose lineaments have now dissolved into a 'random assemblage' of 'contingent and idiosyncratic needs'. For this is simply to say, whether wittingly or not, that we should look back to Hume, rather than Kant, as an elective precursor for the 'new possibilities' that arise with the postmodern passage to a discourse relieved of those old, subject-centred concepts and values. But in Foucault's later writings this idea meets up with a good deal of principled resistance, whatever his attraction (as detailed above) to that wholesale aestheticizing impulse which would otherwise bring him out squarely in accord with the Hume-Nietzsche-Rorty line of argument.

What is at issue in these texts is the notion that truth can be relativized to the point where it becomes nothing more than a reflex product of the epistemic will-to-power, a symptom – as thinkers like Lyotard would have it – of the old 'meta-narrative' drive to transcendence bound up with the philosophic discourse of modernity.[88] Such had no doubt been Foucault's position in his early 'archaeologies' of knowledge, including those remarkable (if also highly questionable) pages on Kant in *The Order of Things*. And it emerges more emphatically in his middle-period essays (such as 'Nietzsche, Genealogy, History') where truth-claims are exposed to all the sceptical rigours of a thoroughgoing relativist creed, a Nietzschean 'transvaluation of values' pushed to the very limits (and beyond) of rational intelligibility. But what Foucault came to recognize as his work went on – notably his detailed researches into ethics, sexuality and the modes of self-knowledge entailed by these emergent disciplines of conduct and thought – was that they only made sense from a critical viewpoint informed by certain distinctively 'enlightenment' values and presuppositions. Hence his remark, in a striking late passage that I have cited once already, that 'thought is not what inhabits a certain conduct and gives it its meaning', but is rather 'what allows one to step back from this way of acting or reacting, to present it to oneself as an object of thought and question it as to its meaning, its conditions, and its goals'.[89] This passage is 'Kantian' not only in the minimal sense that it raises certain questions – of agency, autonomy, ethical conduct, reflective self-knowledge – which were also some of Kant's most important concerns throughout the three *Critiques*. My point is rather that it views them as standing in a complex *but accountable* order of relationship, an order whose specific modalities (like the relations between 'acting' and 'reacting', 'conduct' and 'thought', the 'meaning' of action and its 'conditions' or 'goals') are described in terms that very closely resemble their role in Kant's project of thought.

Not that one could plausibly interpret Foucault as engaged in a covert campaign to resuscitate the Kantian 'doctrine of faculties' in anything like its original form. But what can be said, on the evidence of this and similar passages, is that Foucault came around to a viewpoint strikingly at odds with his earlier (sceptical-genealogical) approach, and that one major consequence was a radical re-thinking of the subject's role in relation to issues of truth, critique, self-knowledge, and practical reason. The following reflections from a 1984 interview are so clearly indicative in this regard that they merit lengthy citation.

> To say that the study of thought is the analysis of a freedom does not mean one is dealing with a formal system that has reference to itself. Actually, for a domain of action, a behavior, to enter the field of thought, it is necessary for a certain number of factors to have made it uncertain, to have made it lose its familiarity, or to have provoked a certain number of difficulties around it. These elements result from social, economic, or political processes. But here their only role is that of instigation. They can exist and perform their action for a very long time, before there is effective problematization by thought. And when thought intervenes, it doesn't assume a unique form that is the direct result or the necessary expression of those difficulties; it is an original or specific response – often taking many forms, sometimes even contradictory in its different aspects – to these difficulties, which are defined for it by a situation or a context and which hold true as a possible question.[90]

Again, this passage goes beyond the mere rehearsal of vaguely 'Kantian' themes and issues. What it raises most crucially is the question – much debated by present-day exegetes, for and against – as to how far Kant's dictates of 'practical reason' must be seen as just a set of empty abstractions, a universalist morality devoid of ethical substance, or (in Foucault's words) as 'a formal system that has reference [only] to itself'. Such had I think been Foucault's view when he composed those pages in *The Order of Things* where 'man', or the Kantian 'transcendental subject', figures in precisely that negative role, as delusory figment of a discourse premised on its own, purely circular or self-confirming 'system' of quasi-universal concepts and categories. And in his subsequent work – notably *The History of Sexuality* – he remained committed to a genealogical approach that stressed the specificities of context, the social and historical conditions of emergence for various ethical codes, rather than anything remotely akin to Kant's universalist maxims. Yet it is also the case, as the above passage makes clear, that Foucault came to think of these conditions as intelligible only from the critical standpoint of an ethics that 'problematized' past or present modes of conduct and belief, and which thus allowed thought to intervene with the effect of 'provoking difficulties' around them. And it is by virtue of this thinking intervention, he argues, that discourse transcends its confinement to the currency of in-place consensus values – those that belong to a given 'situation' or 'context' – and attains a more properly ethical perspective.

Of course these issues are prefigured in the history of rejoinders to Kant, beginning with Hegel's protest in the name of *Sittlichkeit*, of a worldly, a context-sensitive or culturally 'situated' ethics, and echoed in the work of those present-day liberal-communitarian thinkers (Williams and Walzer among them) who likewise reject Kant's supposed appeal to a rule-based morality of abstract precepts and principles.[91] In his later writings Foucault gives full weight to these specific considerations of historical place and time, to the kind of 'thick description' – in Clifford Geertz's suggestive phrase – that takes due account of the various social and political contexts within which different ethical systems have evolved in the passage from antiquity to the present.[92] But he also sees that there is more to ethics than 'elements result[ing] from social, economic, or political processes', or more than can adequately be explained by reference to a 'situation or a context' that happens to promote certain culture-specific values and norms. What is required in order for ethical issues to arise is a certain 'problematization by thought', a sense of conflict or resistance that typically results when established beliefs are thrown into question by an 'original and specific response', a 'difficulty' which cannot be smoothed away by appeal to some prevalent set of consensus values. It is at this point precisely that 'a domain of action, a behavior' becomes subject to ethical scrutiny, or, in Foucault's phrase, finds itself compelled to 'enter the field of thought'. And for this to happen it is prerequisite that certain factors should have 'made it uncertain', 'made it lose its familiarity', or 'provoked a certain number of difficulties around it'. In short, no ethics without resistance, which is also to say – in more Kantian terms – no ethics in the absence of a critical reflection that may always go against both the motives of instinctual self-gratification and the dictates of currently prevailing commonsense belief. For only to the extent that such conflicts are possible can thinking lay claim to any measure of autonomy, any scope for the exercise of responsible judgement in matters of ethico-political concern.

This is not to deny that Foucault comes out in favour of a heterodox reading of Kant, one that treats ethics as primarily a matter of fashioning the self in accordance with techniques, or inventive variations on the strong individualist *rapport-à-soi*, analogous to those of the symbolist poet. As he puts it in a 1983 interview:

> What strikes me is the fact that in our society, art has become something which is related only to objects and not to individuals, or to life. That art is something which is specialized or is done by experts who are artists. But couldn't everyone's life become a work of art? Why should the lamp or the house be an art object, but not our lives?[93]

What such attitudes promote, as I have argued elsewhere, is a wholesale aestheticization of ethics and politics which typically seizes upon certain passages in Kant – most often passages that work by way of analogy or figural comparison – and treats them as a pretext for maximizing the gulf between issues of knowledge or truth, on the one hand, and issues of ethical accountability on the other.[94] Of course this reading finds warrant, up to a point, in Kant's appeal to the tribunal of taste (in particular, to our judgements of the beautiful) as a means of suggesting how ethical judgements can claim intersubjective warrant without the recourse to determinate concepts which would render such judgements superfluous. And it is further borne out (as postmodernist commentators often remark) by those passages from the third *Critique* where Kant invokes the sublime as an analogue for that which absolutely exceeds our powers of cognitive or phenomenal grasp, and which thus – through an inward or reflective movement of thought – gives access to the realm of 'suprasensible' ideas. Such passages undoubtedly justify the claim that, for Kant, there exists a certain affinity between issues of aesthetic judgement and questions in the realm of ethics (or practical reason). But it is equally clear to any attentive reader that Kant never seeks to conflate these realms in the current postmodernist fashion. Nor does he argue, like Lyotard, for a drastically antinomian version of the Kantian sublime, one that would enforce the radical 'heterogeneity' of cognitive and evaluative phrase-regimes, and thus (in effect) create an insuperable gulf between matters of factual understanding and questions of ethical judgement.[95] To be sure, Kant goes a long way around – and deploys a variety of oblique or analogical arguments – in his address to this most problematical of boundary-disputes in the three *Critiques*. But he nowhere endorses the kind of postmodern aestheticist reading that would treat ethical issues as wholly divorced from questions of circumstantial warrant.

Such readings can be seen as the most extreme variant of that objection to the supposed 'formalism' of Kantian ethics which Hegel was the first to articulate, and which is nowadays taken up by critics of a liberal-communitarian persuasion. From this point of view it is a matter of choice between on the one hand an abstract, rule-based morality of generalized precepts or maxims, and on the other an ethics that would sensibly renounce such presumptive universalist claims and take account of the contingencies – the range of social, cultural, political and other such irreducibly context-specific factors – which people have to cope with in their everyday lives as situated moral agents. And from here it is no great distance to Rorty's postmodern-neopragmatist outlook, his suggestion that we give up the misguided quest for reasons, principles, ideas of justice, validating grounds or whatever, and view ourselves rather as creatures whose identity consists in nothing more than a 'random assemblage' of 'contingent and idiosyncratic needs'. For in this way, he thinks, we can best learn to live without those old (henceforth obsolete) ideas, while also enjoying a new-found sense of open-ended creative possibility, a freedom to devise all manner of novel 'vocabularies' in the quest for better, more adventurous modes of self-description.

Such is the private-aestheticist ethos that Rorty proposes as an antidote to Kant, an escape-route from the 'formalist' rigours which he – like the liberal-communitarians – finds so objectionable in Kantian ethics. And for Foucault likewise it appears to offer an alternative to the whole tradition of Enlightenment ethical discourse, a means of conceiving the 'autonomous' self and its actions, thoughts and desires in such a way that it would no longer be subject to the vexing antinomies of Kantian practical reason. It would rather be a question of promoting, in Foucault's words,

> the reflective and voluntary practices by which men not only fix the rules of their conduct, but seek to transform themselves, to modify themselves in their singular being, and to make of their life a work which bears certain aesthetic values and obeys certain stylistic rules.[96]

These 'values' and 'rules' must therefore be thought of as somehow intrinsic to the self, as belonging to that range of 'voluntary practices' (or self-willed disciplinary techniques) by which subjects are 'modified in their singular being', and thereby achieve – like Baudelaire's 'man of modernity' – the greatest measure of autonomy in conduct and thought. Indeed, one is mistaking the import of Foucault's argument if one uses (as I did just now) the two distinct terms, 'subject' and 'self', as if they were more or less synonymous or simply interchangeable. For it is precisely his point that the *subject* as conceived within an ethical discourse like Kant's is always a product of that imaginary, specular mode of self-relation which generates the various endemic conflicts and antinomies of humanist thought. What is required is therefore a non-subject-centred discourse, one that views the self 'in [its] singular being' as the locus of those various 'practices' and 'rules' by which the process of self-transformation somehow comes about. Only thus – so it seems – can thinking regain that long-lost ethical vocation which had not yet suffered the fatal swerve toward forms of internalized conflict or imaginary misrecognition.

Hence Foucault's main purpose in the later volumes of *The History of Sexuality*: to show how it was that the classical ethos of disciplined, aesthetic self-fashioning gave way to a range of ethical standpoints – whether Stoic, Christian, Kantian, Freudian or whatever – which envisaged the subject as a site of conflict between opposed principles or value-systems. But one can see very clearly from the above-cited passage, as indeed from my tortuous commentary upon it, that he fails to articulate this cardinal distinction with anything like the consistency or rigour that his argument requires. Thus what are we to make of those 'reflective and voluntary practices' which seemingly take rise within a 'singular being' whose selfhood is integral and as yet untouched by the alienating ethos, the unhappy conciousness of modernity? What exactly can it mean for this unitary being to enter upon a process of voluntary 'self-transformation' whereby its constitutive 'practices' or 'rules of conduct' are viewed (so to speak) as the raw material for its own aesthetic elaboration? Far from providing an answer to these questions, the passage breaks down into two contradictory lines of argument, the one premised on a notional appeal to the self as a unified, autonomous locus of agency and will, the other enmeshed in a subject-centred language of 'reflection', non-self-identity, or reflexive autocritique. The antinomies persist despite all Foucault's strenuous efforts to think his way through and beyond them. Nor are these problems effectively resolved by invoking the aesthetic as an alternative terrain, a realm wherein the self might achieve true autonomy by shaping its life in accordance with those 'values' and 'rules' that characterize the discipline of artistic creation. For one still has to ask what relationship exists between the 'reflective and voluntary practices' that go toward this project of aesthetic self-fashioning, and the 'singular being' whose life is thus subject to a process of willed transformation. In short, Foucault's argument is deeply confused, not least when he claims to have annulled or overcome the antinomies of Kantian ethical discourse.

My point in all this is not merely to belabour certain local aberrations or laxities of phrasing in Foucault's texts. What they reveal, as I have argued, is a reiterated pattern of hostile yet compulsive engagements with Kant, a pattern whose peculiar dialectic of 'blindness' and 'insight' (to adopt Paul de Man's deconstructive terminology) indicates the presence of fundamental tensions in Foucault's ethical thought.[97] These tensions arise very largely from the fact that Foucault (in common with other present-day commentators) exaggerates the gulf between Kantian practical reason – the 'categorical imperative', as well as the generalized 'maxims' of conduct – and the range of context-specific values, beliefs and motivating interests that apply in particular cases of ethical judgment. That is to say, he goes along with the mistaken view that Kant is a thoroughgoing 'formalist' in ethics, a thinker whose strong universalist claims led him to ignore such merely contingent or localized factors. Jürgen Habermas decisively refutes this view in a passage that also makes short work of Lyotard's line on the absolute 'heterogeneity' of cognitive and ethical phrase-regimes.

> Neither Kantian ethics nor discourse ethics [i.e., Habermas's verion of this project] lays itself open to the charge that, since it defines the moral principle in formal or procedural terms, it can only make tautological statements about morality. . . . The issue is whether we can *all* will that a contested norm gain binding force under given conditions. The content that is tested by a moral principle is generated not by the philosopher but by real life. The conflicts of

action that come to be morally judged and consensually resolved grow out of everyday life. Reason as a tester of maxims (Kant) or actors as participants in argumentation (discourse ethics) *find* these conflicts. They do not create them.[98]

This goes clean against the reading of Kant that Foucault proposes in *The Order of Things* and which finds numerous echoes in Lyotard and other postmodernist commentators. On that view, practical reason becomes just one more illusory attribute of that strange Kantian hybrid, the 'transcendental-empirical doublet', whose advent and demise are coterminous with 'man', himself nothing more than a short-lived figment of the liberal-humanist imaginary. Thus ethics and empirical validity-claims alike – in Habermas's terms, 'maxims' and the 'testing of maxims' – are dissolved into a play of multiple, decentred discourses which allow of no possible adjudication in point of their factual, their rational-discursive, or their ethico-political warrant. What remains, as with Lyotard, is a range of strictly incommensurable 'phrase-regimes', such that any attempted judgement between them will either be obliged to operate 'without criteria', or otherwise – by ignoring their specific 'differend' – risk committing a grave injustice against one or both. Such would be the outcome of Foucault's postmodern-aestheticist 'ethics' if pursued with the degree of perverse rigour that Lyotard brings to his reading of Kant. And indeed it is a consequence that Foucault on occasion seemed willing to entertain, as for instance in his efforts – like the essay 'What Is Enlightenment?' – to assimilate Kant to a version of 'modernity' defined very largely with reference to the aesthetic sublime.

But there was also, as I have said, a counter-impulse at work in Foucault's thinking, an impulse that led him not only to engage in a series of agonistic encounters with Kant, but also to describe his own project in terms that acknowledged (so to speak, *malgré lui*) the ineluctable claims and priorities of Kantian thought. Nor is this in any way an argument that seeks to subvert or invalidate his ethical credentials. For in so far as Foucault remained a critical intellectual (which he manifestly did, whatever his well-known reluctance to assume that role) it was always by virtue of adopting a stance of principled resistance – or reflective detachment – that questioned the prevailing self-images of the age, the modes of currently acceptable conduct and thought. This is why, in the end, Foucault's work cannot be annexed to that otherwise kindred postmodern-pragmatist line which equates truth *tout court* with what is 'good in the way of belief', and which regards ethical values as wholly a product of existing consensus norms. Geoffrey Harpham puts the case against this way of thinking, along with its various conservative-liberal or communitarian analogues, when he asks bluntly: 'could ethics be disarmed and still be ethical?' In other words, is it possible to conceive of an ethics that would merit the name while admitting no appeal to values, principles or truth-claims beyond the sphere of consensually warranted belief?

> The example of MacIntyre's and Williams's hero, Aristotle, suggests that
> the answer is no. Aristotle's silent and complacent acceptance of slavery and
> numerous other forms of privilege and exploitation, his conviction that humanity
> was divided into 'natural types', betrays the secret of an ethics of social con-
> fidence — that it defines values primarily in terms of culturally sanctioned
> attitudes and opinions and promotes the undistanced local social order to the
> status of a universal order of the worthy. Unless it contains a 'moral' image of
> the law as a resistant other to society, history, or to the uncritical beliefs and
> prejudices of the individual, ethics can only be an apology for interest even more
> ignoble than interest itself.[99]

This criticism would apply not only to neopragmatists like Rorty but also (as
Harpham notes) to those theorists — among them MacIntyre and Williams —
who would break with the legacy of Kantian ethical thought by advocating a
'return' to Aristotle, or a conception of the private and public good that defines
itself in terms of a life well lived by the communal standards of the day.[100] It
is not just the fact of Aristotle's having espoused some (to us) unacceptable or
repugnant ideas that renders this position morally suspect. Rather, it is the
way that such ideas tie in with a conformist or consensus-based morality which
would offer no conceivable justification for the *criticism* of these or other
offensive items of belief. For, as Harpham says, 'when cultural values are
unworthy, uncertain, or disputed, only an appeal to some imperative that
convincingly transcends culture and privatized conceptions of interest can
legitimate action'.[101] But this is not to argue — as is often made out by critics
of Kant's supposed 'formalism' — that morality must then be conceived as
exerting its prerogatives in a realm quite apart from the conduct of everyday,
'situated' human existence. On the contrary, Harpham writes: 'the effect of
morality is not transcendental, but worldly; it achieves its worldly force,
however, through its claim to universality and transcendence'.

It is this constitutive tension in the nature of his own project that Foucault
on the one hand seeks to deny through his appeals to an ethos of aesthetic
self-fashioning, while on the other implicitly acknowledging its presence in
passages, like those cited above, whose express purport and logical form are so
markedly at odds. One could multiply such instances from the later essays
and interviews, all of them conveying this uneasy sense that the Kantian
antinomies cannot be so deftly set aside, and that ethical thinking may have no
choice but to formulate its values, interests and commitments in a language
that constantly reduplicates their terms. What this amounts to is the same
dilemma that Rorty faces, although in his case the problem is not so much
confronted as conveniently shelved in the hope that we will soon come around
to some different style of 'post-philosophical' talk. Put simply, it is the
question how such talk could ever make sense, given 1) the presumed dis-

solution of the subject into so many contingent language-games, discourses, 'final vocabularies' or whatever, and 2) the idea of ethics as a project of willed self-fashioning aimed, as both Foucault and Rorty suggest, toward the creation of a truly autonomous 'self' beyond all the deep-laid conflicts and dichotomies of Kantian practical reason. For there is (to say the least) some difficulty in reconciling claims (1) and (2), or in conceiving how the subject – the multiple, decentred, dispersed 'subject' of these postmodern times – can also be thought of as actively engaged in such a process of ethical or aesthetic self-invention. As Rorty sees it we can always just switch vocabularies, or choose to stop raising those pointless philosophical questions by adopting some alternative mode of self-description, some preferable line of talk. And for Foucault, what really matters in ethical terms is 'the kind of relationship you ought to have with yourself, *rapport à soi* . . . which determines how the individual is supposed to constitute himself as a moral subject of his own actions'.[102] In both cases the emphasis falls on those options for the conduct of one's private life – one's aesthetic preferences, modes of self-relation, choices of exemplary life-style, role-model, 'final vocabulary' etc. – which then set the pattern for whatever may result in the wider (social or intersubjective) realm. For it is here, in the process of establishing a distinctive *rapport à soi*, that the self carves out a working space for its projects of ethical self-fashioning. And if this way of putting it involves a fairly obvious paradox – with the self figuring both as subject and object of its own elaborations – then the problem is one that can hardly be avoided, given the peculiar (aestheticized) doctrine of autonomy with which these thinkers operate.

To be sure, there is a marked difference between Foucault's essentially stoic attitude, his view of ethics as always involving a hard-won, strenuous effort of applied self-discipline, and Rorty's style of easygoing pragmatist adjustment to consensus values and beliefs. Moreover, as I have argued, it is a difference that carries across into their sharply divergent ideas of the intellectual's role *vis-à-vis* the social and political discourses of instituted power/knowledge. To describe Rorty as a 'radical' thinker, in this regard at least, would be about as wrong-headed as the converse error of withholding that title from Foucault. And yet there ia a sense in which Foucault invites such a reading through his failure to recognize the consequences of this postmodern shift toward a private-aesthetic conception of ethical issues. What is playing itself out in these debates, as so often, is a re-run of previous episodes in the history of thought, in particular the chapter that begins with Hume and receives its most articulate (and critical) treatment in Kant's doctrine of the faculties. For Hume, famously, reflection on the self led him to a point where identity dissolved into a flux of transient impressions, memories, desires, anticipations and suchlike evanescent mind-states, a stream of consciousness whose unity – or the comforting illusion thereof – could only be explained in terms of associative linkage.[103] For in the end these phenomena involved nothing more than contiguity in space and time, allied to mere force of habit and the influence of ingrained social convention. Thus there was, he concluded, no 'deep further fact' about the nature of human selfhood, no integrating principle that would constitute the subject as a locus of autonomous thought, agency and will. But these issues were bothersome only so long as one considered them philosophically, that is to say, as abstract or armchair problems dreamed up in isolation from the business of everyday social life. From this point of view, Hume thought, they were beyond all hope of argumentative solution or settlement on reasoned grounds. So one simply had to set them aside once in a while and revert to other, more socially responsive activities or companionable forms of life. In which case the problems would simply disappear or show up as just a species of bother-headed 'philosophic' talk, hopelessly remote from the real-world interests and concerns that occupied even the most sceptical philosopher for most of his or her waking hours.

It is not hard to see how Hume's arguments have been revived, albeit in a variety of updated idioms, by thinkers of a postmodern or neopragmatist persuasion. Rorty, like Hume, sees no alternative but to view the self as a 'centreless, . . . random assemblage of contingent and idiosyncratic needs', an assemblage held together by nothing more permanent or dignified than its choice among the currently existing range of life-styles, vocabularies, and modes of self-description. And he also follows Hume – though with fewer 'philosophical' misgivings – in his advice that we should henceforth answer the sceptic *not* by continuing the vain old quest for some ultimate truth about ourselves or the world, but simply by acknowledging (in sensible pragmatist fashion) that 'truth' is nothing more than what counts as such at the present conversational stage of the game. Furthermore, both thinkers exemplify the turn toward aesthetics as an analogue – a substitute even – for the misguided labours of epistemological or ethico-political critique. With Hume this takes the form of an appeal to the polite, civilized or consensual 'standard of taste', while for Rorty it requires the adoption of alternative, more 'literary' notions of the self, notions that can open up 'new possibilities for the aesthetic life' by 'help[ing] us think of moral reflection and sophistication as a matter of self-creation rather than self-knowledge'.[104] Of course there is a shift of emphasis that occurs in the passage from Hume to Rorty, a shift (roughly speaking) from the *beautiful* as a touchstone of harmonized communal taste to the postmodernist or (quasi-)Kantian *sublime* as a watchword for the ethos of private 'self-creation' that Rorty now recommends. But in fact these two ideas cannot get into conflict since the 'private' is conceived as a realm safely apart, a realm wherein people are free to pursue all manner of diverse projects, activities or life-styles just so long as they do so (as Rorty puts it) 'on their own time', and without setting up as critical intellectuals or self-appointed guardians of the public good.

What this amounts to, in short, is a happy conjunction of both those aesthetic modalities of judgement – the beautiful and the sublime – where one provides an image of the ideal, consensus-based order of social existence, while the other holds out a welcome escape-route for strong individualists, self-fashioning aesthetes, romantic ironists, etc. Such a modest proposal has the obvious virtue of respecting cultural differences and allowing everyone to work out his or her 'private' destiny with minimal interference either from the state or from others likewise engaged. All that is needed in order to maintain this civilized *modus vivendi* is a willingness to accept the contingent character of even our most 'basic' values and truth-claims, along with a healthily sceptical attitude – or a measure of liberal irony – as regards any project that oversteps the mark and encroaches on the public domain. So in fact there is less difference than at first might appear between Rorty's high-romantic talk of autonomous self-invention and Hume's broadly conservative appeal to the 'standard of taste' as a commonsense tribunal for issues in the aesthetic or the ethico-political sphere. For the message is the same in each case: that philosophy (or theory) offers no guidance in such matters; that consensus-belief is the court of last appeal, at any rate so far as the public or citizenly virtues are concerned; and that otherwise we are pretty much free to adopt whatever creed or value-system happens to suit our individual tastes and preferences. All of which may seem attractive enough – indeed highly desirable – in so far as it promotes a pluralist ethos and an outlook of easygoing, tolerant regard for the variety of human satisfactions. But it should also be remarked that this leaves no room for any argued or principled critique of consensus values, any notion that there might exist false, partial or distorted modes of consensus belief, and moreover that the private/public dichotomy – as theorized by conservative thinkers like Hume or present-day liberals like Rorty – might count among the most effective means of holding such beliefs in place. For this has always been the role of aesthetic ideology: to sustain the *illusion* of consensus values by projecting a substitute public sphere, a realm of intersubjective agreement – with allowance for the vagaries of private self-invention – where real-world disputes and conflicts of interest could then be resolved in imaginary form. And it has managed to do so only on condition that philosophy give up its critical or truth-telling claims, and henceforth consent to take its bearings from 'taste' (or aesthetic judgement) as the sole arbiter of values.

On the face of it Foucault was as far as possible from endorsing any such consensus morality or pragmatist appeal to what is presently 'good in the way of belief'. In his later writings, it is the strong-individualist ethos – the doctrine of autonomous self-creation – which provides Foucault with both an aim to be striven for and a way back into his various source texts, especially those of classical antiquity. But there is, as I have argued, a deeper sense in which these two apparently antithetical doctrines not only coexist without conflict but work to reinforce each other through what amounts to a convenient *entente cordiale*, a tactical alliance of interests in preserving the public/private dichotomy. And nothing is more surely indicative in this regard than Foucault's long history of visions and revisions as a reader of Kant, a history that leads from the attitude of downright scepticism expressed in *The Order of Things* to the project of strenuous revisionist engagement – the aestheticized reading of Kantian ethics – undertaken most explicitly in the essay 'What Is Enlightenment?' For if Hume is the strong (though unacknowledged) precursor for much of what passes as the current postmodernist wisdom, then it is in Kant, or the criticisms which Kant brings against Hume, that this wisdom encounters the greatest challenge to its powers of creative misprision. In particular, it has to reject Kant's argument that there is indeed a 'deep further fact' concerning the nature of human identity or selfhood, a 'condition of possibility' in the strong (*a priori*) sense without which it would simply make no sense to ascribe thoughts, feelings, or motives to this or that individual subject. Such is Kant's reason for asserting, *contra* Hume, that there exists a 'transcendental unity of apperception', a focal point of conscious experience or reflective self-knowledge that cannot be reduced to the mere succession of transient phenomenal mind-states. And this is not (as Foucault would have it) just a product of certain, period-specific norms and assumptions, a symptom of the typecast 'Enlightenment' drive to constitute 'man' as author and agent of his own autonomous nature. On the contrary, it is nothing less than *prerequisite* for anyone who would address these crucial issues as to the powers and limits of human understanding, the modalities of ethical will, or the relationship between 'private' and 'public' realms as a matter that concerns the 'autonomous' subject in Kant's very different (ethico-political) sense of that term. In short, Foucault's revisionist reading of Kant is still very much caught up with those unresolved puzzles and perplexities that Hume was the first to articulate, and which have now been reinvented – as if from scratch – by the arbiters of postmodern intellectual fashion.

It seems to me that Foucault arrived at this position as a result of his confusing two quite different conceptions of ethical autonomy. One was the existentialist doctrine of good and bad faith, according to which, as Foucault puts it, 'Sartre avoids the idea of the self as something which is given to us, but through the moral notion of authenticity, he turns back to the idea that we have to be ourselves – to be truly our true self'.[105] Like other critics of Sartre (Merleau-Ponty among them) Foucault saw this as a philosophy dangerously prone to elevate the will of the 'authentic' individual to a position of absolute authority in matters of ethical and political judgement.[106] His response is to turn the whole argument around in such a way that *on the one hand* it severs all links between issues of 'authentic' selfhood and questions of social justice, political good faith, and collective responsibility, while *on the other* it redefines 'authenticity' in terms that relate solely to the realm of 'self-invention' or private-aestheticist values. Thus:

> I think that the only acceptable practical consequence of what Sartre says is to link his theoretical insight to the practice of creativity. . . . From the idea that the self is not given to us, I think that there is only one practical consequence: we have to create ourselves as a work of art. In his analyses of Baudelaire, Flaubert, etc., it is interesting that Sartre refers the work of creation to a certain relation to oneself − the author to himself − which has the form of authenticity or of inauthenticity. I would like to say exactly the contrary: we should not have to refer the creative activity of somebody to the kind of relation he has to himself, but should relate the kind of relation one has to oneself to a creative activity.[107]

But this completely fails to grasp the real objection to Sartre's ethics and politics, as argued by Merleau-Ponty. For that objection has to do with Sartre's brand of extreme existentialist voluntarism, his idea of the truly 'authentic' self − or the subject who acts in good faith − as rejecting all claims of conscience, morality or political purpose save those that issue from the peremptory will to pursue his or her own project of autonomous self-invention. So far from resolving this problem, Foucault merely repeats it in a sharper, more insistent or seemingly intractable form. For on his view the Sartrean ethic falls short not by reason of its false (and politically disastrous) polarization of the private and public realms, but because − on the contrary − it doesn't go far enough in acknowledging this same radical disjunction. For if ethics is properly or essentially a matter of the 'relation one has to oneself', and if the most authentic way of conceiving that relation is in terms of how we might (like Baudelaire or Flaubert) 'create ourselves as a work of art', then Merleau-Ponty's criticism is wholly wide of the mark. One might as well radicalize Sartre's position to the point where individuals are conceived as absolute legislators in a self-sufficient world of their own inventing; a world, moreover, whose private (even solipsistic) nature allows of no appeal to the validating standards of public or intersubjective debate. And in this case there can be no effective rejoinder to postmodern ironists such as Rorty, thinkers who take it for a prime virtue of 'liberal' cultures like our own that they offer maximum scope for the enterprise of private self-creation, while keeping such projects safely apart from the maintenance of existing consensus norms.

From Foucault's point of view there would appear little difference between the kind of radical autonomy involved in Sartre's existentialist ethic and the

Kantian appeal to the knowing, willing and judging subject as a locus of responsible action and choice. In each case, he thinks, we are confronted with a species of 'transcendental' illusion, a product of the humanist imaginary which constitutes 'man' as the self-knowing, self-acting subject of his own most intimate thoughts, motives and desires. Much of Foucault's difficulty with Kant, in his long series of refractory encounters, may perhaps have resulted from this failure to distinguish two quite different conceptions of 'autonomy' as related to issues of knowledge and ethical conduct. For clearly it was Sartre whom Foucault, like others of his generation, most often had in mind when attacking the pretensions of the so-called 'universal' intellectual, the figure who exploited his presumed expertise in some specialized discipline (like philosophy) in order to set up as a privileged purveyor of moral and political truths. The passage quoted above is evidence enough that this potentially authoritarian strain in the ethos of 'authentic', truth-telling discourse was one of the factors that influenced Foucault in his choice of an alternative (aestheticized) account of the self and its modalities of being. But by assimilating Kant to the general run of 'subject-centred' discourses Foucault fell into a confusion which created real problems for his own thinking about ethical issues. He failed to register the crucial distinction between Sartre's conception of the self as engaged in a constant, agonistic struggle to preserve its 'good faith' (or moral authenticity) in face of competing projects, and Kant's understanding of the public sphere as a realm wherein subjects could achieve autonomy through the exercise of reasoned judgement in accord with enlightened (critical or truth-seeking) standards of debate. For it is only by rejecting this latter view that freedom is made to seem the upshot of a strong-individualist quest, a goal unattainable except through the kind of 'autonomous' self-creation whose model is to be found in the aestheticist programme of writers like Baudelaire and Flaubert.

V

In his later writings there are many indications that Foucault had come to recognize this troubling liability in his own work to date. They include, as I have suggested, those passages where he broaches a markedly different relationship to Kant and the heritage of Enlightenment critique. This relation is now characterized by Foucault's much greater readiness to concede that the interests of autonomy and freedom may well be advanced, rather than uniformly stifled or repressed, by a discourse that acknowledges certain criteria of truth and reasoned critical enquiry. Thus: 'thought is freedom in relation to what one does, the motion by which one detaches oneself from it, establishes it as an object, and reflects on it as a problem'.[108] Such passages bring Foucault remarkably close to a Kantian conception of practical reason as a thinking whose autonomy consists in its reflective distance from matters of phenomenal self-evidence or straightforward empirical truth, but which nonetheless cannot be conceived (*pace* postmodernists like Rorty or Lyotard) as existing in a separate realm, a 'heterogeneous' phrase-regime wholly indifferent to the claims of real-world, veridical knowledge. Nor is this merely an 'academic' issue that concerns few readers beyond those involved in the specialized study of Kant. For a great deal hangs on those questions of priority – or those modes of complex interrelation and dependence – which Kant brings out by way of adjudicating the 'conflict of the faculties' and their various boundary-disputes. Most importantly, it is a matter of determining on the one hand how ethics relates to issues of knowledge or truth, and on the other just how far ethical values may be treated (in the current postmodernist style) as belonging to the same modality of thought as obtains for the realm of 'taste' or aesthetic judgement. In the range of conflicting responses to these questions – past and present – one can trace out not only a contested area in the reception-history of Kant's ideas, but also some crucial differences of view among moral philosophers and political theorists.

Patrick Hogan puts the case as follows in his book *The Politics of Interpretation*, a work that addresses various problems in the field of literary theory, but mainly with a view to bringing them down to earth in the context of everyday social involvements, teaching and professional ethics. 'Moral concerns,' Hogan writes, 'are posterior to concerns of truth or falsity, not prior thereto.' And this because, most often,

> moral propositions imply and thus presuppose assertions of fact. For example, if we say that the United States is behaving shamefully with regard to Nicaragua, or if we say that we should work to put an end to U.S. Nicaraguan policy, we quite clearly assume there to be a certain fact of the matter. It is precisely the *factual* state of affairs which we assume ourselves to be criticizing. Similarly, when we claim that women should be allowed access to high-level governmental positions, we assume that there is a fact of the matter, specifically, their being denied such access at present. One cannot, so to speak, be more moral than the facts. . . . We can and should work to end U.S. support for Samocista terrorists who burn crops and gun down civilians precisely and only because there is such support for a group of terrorists, former supporters of Anastasio Somoza, who burn crops and gun down civilians. Lacking empirical and logical criteria, as Bertrand Russell so nicely put it, 'truth can be [and, we might add, *will* be] determined by the police', or whoever has power in the relevant area.[109]

One could make the same point in more explicitly Kantian terms by asserting, as in the passage from Habermas that I cited on page 77, that practical reason can never be wholly divorced from the interests of cognitive enquiry, factual understanding, or veridical warrant. For this position is by no means incompatible with Kant's qualifying stress on the autonomous character of ethical judgement, its belonging to a realm of 'suprasensible' ideas or precepts, a court of appeal where the rule is not given *directly or exclusively* by straightforward reference to some factual state of affairs. Of course it may be argued – with plentiful support from the text – that Kant's main object in the second *Critique* is to establish just such a clear-cut separation of spheres, thus ensuring that practical reason retains its essential attributes of autonomy and freedom, since it cannot be reduced (as would otherwise be the case) to the order of determinate concepts or empirical truth-claims. But this is not to say, along with Lyotard and other postmodernizing Kantian revisionists, that the 'language-games' of cognitive and ethical judgement are so utterly 'heterogeneous' that we shall fall into error (or commit some manifest injustice) if we bring factual considerations to bear when adjudicating moral issues. For we should then, as Hogan says, be so completely bankrupt of 'logical and empirical criteria' that nothing could ever count as a valid argument, or a good-faith appeal to the relevant facts, in any given case.

What this amounts to is a form of out-and-out cognitive scepticism, one that takes rise from the 'linguistic turn' – or the adoption of textualist models and metaphors – across a wide range of the present-day humanistic disciplines. Moreover, it is an outlook with disabling consequences elsewhere, not least through its promotion of a dogmatic value-relativism that insists on judging (in Lyotard's words) 'without criteria', and which thus rules out any possibility of reasoned argumentative exchange. No doubt it is a point worth making – and one much emphasized by recent commentators, J. Hillis Miller among them – that Kant pursues some elaborate, even tortuous modes of analogical argument in establishing the relation between his maxims of practical reason and the business of everyday, situated moral judgement. But it is equally clear that he intends those maxims to possess the kind of real-world relevance or applicable force that would save them from floating off into a realm of purely abstract precept and principle. Thus Miller reads Kant very much in accordance with his own textualist imperative when he comments, *à propos* some passages in the *Groundwork of the Metaphysics of Morals*, that 'it is never possible to be sure that duty is not a fiction in the bad sense of an ungrounded act of self-sustaining language, that is, precisely a vain delusion and chimerical concept, a kind of ghost generated by a sad linguistic necessity'.[110] For this reading is plausible only to the extent that one accepts Miller's deconstructionist articles of faith, i.e. that reality is a discursive (or rhetorical) construct, that there is nothing – or nothing knowable – 'outside the text', that reference is the merest of comforting illusions (even if generated, like our sense of moral obligation,

by a 'sad linguistic necessity'), and therefore – as Miller concludes with a
kind of mock-rueful triumphalist flourish – that 'the failure to read or the
impossibility of reading is a universal predicament, one moment of which is
that potentially aberrant form of language called ethical judgement or prescription'.[111] As I say, Miller's conclusions follow on 'logically' enough from
his textualist premises. But otherwise – insofar as one rejects those premises –
the above claims will appear just a litany of postmodern *idées reçues*, and
Miller's 'reading' of Kant just the product of his failure to acknowledge those
numerous instances (in the *Groundwork* and the second *Critique*) where the
maxims of practical reason are applied to a range of specific situations or
working examples.[112]

Nor is Miller's case much strengthened by his noting the frequency with
which Kant has recourse to fictive, allegorical, or imaginary episodes in order
to negotiate this passage. For such episodes work precisely by virtue of their
exemplary or real-world analogical force, their capacity to render a vivid
presentation of dilemmas which might always be encountered in the conduct of
everyday moral decision-making. To treat them, like Miller, as belonging to a
realm of wholly imaginary (or 'textual') contrivance is to ignore the various
kinds of conceptual fit – or orders of verisimilitude – that obtain between
language (fictional language included) and reality. Postmodernism typically
inverts this procedure by declaring 'reality' to be a world well lost now that we
have all lived on into an epoch of texts without referents, signifiers without
signifieds, or language as a giddying *mise-en-abîme* that opens up endless
prospects of rhetorical deconstruction. But it is important to recall – as I have
argued elsewhere – that this whole line of talk has grown up in isolation from
other, more cogent and productive ways of thinking about the relation between
sense, reference and truth.[113] In particular, post-structuralism and its latterday
offshoots – among them, most variants of 'literary' deconstruction – have taken
it as gospel (following Saussure) that 'the sign' is the minimal distinctive unit
of language, rather than the sentence (or the proposition) conceived as a bearer
of articulate meanings and truth-claims which can then be analysed in terms of
their logico-semantic and referential status. By ignoring this alternative – as
developed by philosophers in the broadly Fregean line of descent – post-
structuralist theory has condemned itself, cheerfully enough, to an outlook of
last-ditch cognitive scepticism, along with a species of thoroughgoing value-
relativism whose sole guiding principle is Lyotard's strictly incoherent notion
of 'judging without criteria'. For such ideas can gain credence only on condition that we give up all claims to validity or truth, most especially those that
would commit an injustice, an infraction of the speech-act rules, by seeking to
adjudicate ethical issues on factual, evidential or documentary grounds.

Hence the widespread appeal, at least among literary theorists, of an argument like Hillis Miller's, one that raises the perplexities of 'textualist' doctrine to a high point of method and principle. For again there are alternative (and preferable) ways of addressing the difficulty that Miller so relishes, namely, the fact that Kant often has resort to fictions – or 'parables' – as a means of giving detailed, exemplary content to the otherwise inscrutable dictates of moral law. One might instance the work of those modal logicians – and, more recently, literary critics – who have explored the variety of so-called 'possible worlds', imaginary realms that differ from our own in certain crucial (specified) respects, but which also share with it a greater or lesser number of factual *données*, time-space coordinates, validity-conditions, ontological commitments and so forth.[114] Such approaches have the great advantage, when compared with Miller's pan-textualist line, that they are able to explain with some precision how fictional works can incorporate elements ranging all the way from 'pure' fantasy to items of historical or documented fact. Moreover, these distinctions can be shown to hold not only as between different types of work – for instance, novels in the high tradition of nineteenth-century European realism and recent forms of postmodern, anti-illusionist or experimental narrative – but also from moment to moment in the reading of texts that answer to such accurately hybrid descriptions as 'historiographical metafiction'. Thus it seems, to say the least, a highly dubious argumentative move that would level the difference between 'fiction' (conceived *grosso modo*) and the ethical writings of a philosopher like Kant, one who took elaborate precautions in this matter of establishing the scope and limits of reason in its various legitimate spheres. Above all, it ignores that entire dimension of his argument in the first *Critique* which has to do with the forms of illusion that arise when speculative reason takes wing in the realm of pure 'metaphysical' enquiry, while nonetheless claiming access to a knowledge that can only be had by way of cognitive understanding, that is, through the process of bringing intuitions under adequate concepts. For it is here that Kant lays the groundwork for his subsequent reflections on the various orders of truth-claim, along with all their issues of priority and complex modes of reciprocal dependence, that make up the 'architectonic' of the faculties. And it is with reference to those same issues, albeit couched in a very different idiom, that present-day thinkers – modal logicians among them – seek to clarify the various orders of relation between fictional and real-world truth.

Thus philosophers are not without resources when it comes to handling the kinds of problem that Miller would treat as strictly insoluble, or as leading always to an end-point of textual 'aporia', a disarticulation of sense and reference which blocks any naive or self-assured passage from word to world.[115] For such arguments can only have force against a straw-man position, a positivist doctrine of language, meaning and truth to which few philosophers would nowadays subscribe. In fact there is more naivety – despite all the show of geared-up rhetorical sophistication – in the kind of reflex post-structuralist response that treats any appeal to reality or truth as just another symptom of old-style 'logocentric' thinking. And the same applies to those kindred varieties of set-piece deconstructive argument, like the notion that philosophy is just another 'kind of writing', that textuality goes 'all the way down', or (following Nietzsche) that every concept will in the end turn out to be a species of forgotten or sublimated metaphor. What is ignored in each case – though not, one should add, in Derrida's more nuanced and cogent account – is the fact that we should lack all the needful distinctions, all the terms and criteria for advancing such claims, had they not been provided through exactly the kind of rigorous philosophical critique that the current deconstructors so blithely dismiss.[116] Thus the point about metaphors, like that concerning fictive or possible worlds, is that we are able to make sense of them by perceiving certain points of resemblance to the conditions that obtain for literal (or veridical) discourse, while at the same time noting those other significant respects in which they call for a different, less straightforward mode of application. Only to thinkers who adopt an all-out sceptical or 'textualist' line will this process seem either flatly impossible or a mystery beyond rational comprehension. And it is the same mystifying drive that construes Kant as a postmodern sceptic *avant la lettre*, a philosopher whose professed concern to make sense of real-world ethical issues is everywhere thrown into doubt by his resort to purely 'fictive' allegories of reading.

Foucault never went quite so far as these current revisionists in exploiting Kant as a pretext or alibi for his own interpretive ends. Even at the time of *The Order of Things* – his period of greatest resistance – there is an undertow of grudging acknowledgment that the Kantian project in some sense defines the very conditions of possibility for present-day critical thought, and thus cannot (despite all his programmatic claims to the contrary) be treated as just another episode in the history of bygone discursive formations. This acknowledgment becomes more explicit in his later work, to the point where, with essays like 'What Is Enlightenment?', Foucault seems embarked upon a reading of Kant that is also a kind of belated self-reckoning, a renegotiation of problems bequeathed by his own project to date. What marks this protracted encounter, as I have argued, is a complex pattern of ambivalent (sometimes contradictory) responses, a pattern that repeats itself with singular insistence in the writings and interviews of his final decade. It is a tension that results on the one hand from Foucault's espousal of a Nietzschean or private-aestheticist creed, and on the other from his growing recognition that the truth-values of enlightened thought – of reason in its jointly epistemo-critical and ethico-political modes – cannot be abandoned without at the same time renouncing any claim to promote or articulate the interests of justice, autonomy and human emancipation. Foucault is thus faced with a genuine dilemma, but not the kind of self-delighting paradox or wished-for aporia that figures so predictably as the upshot of readings in the postmodern textualist mode.

Often this conflict is inscribed within the compass of a single sentence, as when Foucault declares (*contra* Kant) that criticism will henceforth 'not deduce from the form of what we are what it is impossible for us to know and to do', but should rather seek to 'separate out, from the contingency that has made us what we are, the possibility of no longer being, doing, or thinking what we are, do, or think' (WIE, p. 46). On the face of it such comments are directed squarely against the residual 'humanist' or 'anthropological' elements that Foucault still detects in Kantian thought. They would then have to be construed as supporting his claim that an ethics (or aesthetics) of radical self-invention is the only kind of project that merits our allegiance in an epoch of postmodern, post-enlightenment thought. Yet it is equally clear that the above sentence corresponds *at every point* to Kant's own claims in the original text 'What Is Enlightenment?'. Once again it is a question – quite as much so for Foucault as for Kant – of thinking our way through and beyond those limits, those various forms of self-imposed tutelage or servitude, which will show up as merely 'contingent' (as socially conditioned or historically produced) only insofar as we exercise our powers of autonomous critical reason. And 'autonomy' in this context can hardly be understood as involving nothing more than the private dedication to a mode of being, a *rapport à soi*, which affords the greatest possible scope for the project of aesthetic self-fashioning. Thus it may well be the case, according to Foucault, that we must henceforth conceive this indispensable 'work of thought' not so much as attempting (in Kantian fashion) 'to make possible a metaphysics that has finally become a science', but rather as seeking 'to give new impetus, as far and wide as possible, to the undefined work of freedom' (WIE, p. 46). But we then have to ask what such claims could amount to in the absence of a public or critical sphere – a tribunal of 'autonomous' judgement, in the Kantian sense – that would serve to evaluate their various orders of truth-telling warrant or ethical accountability. For freedom is not merely 'undefined' but strictly *inconceivable* if located, as Foucault often seems to locate it, in a private realm quite apart from the interests of emancipatory critique. What beckons from the end of this particular road is a postmodern variant of the Kantian sublime which nonsensically counsels us to 'judge without criteria', and whose appeal – as with Lyotard – lies in its evasion of other, more pressing issues of ethical and political conscience.

So Foucault had good reason for shifting ground with regard to post-structuralism and kindred forms of modish ultra-relativist doctrine. The nearest he came to rejecting these ideas outright was in the interview with Paul Rabinow, conducted in May 1984 just a few weeks before his death.[117] Most significant here is the way that Foucault moves on directly from questions of ethics and politics to issues of truth, language and representation, in each case adopting a clearly-marked critical distance from the attitudes and assumptions that had characterized his earlier work. Thus to Rabinow's question 'What is a history of problematics?', Foucault responds by defining those respects in which the 'work of thought' differs from the kinds of analysis – among them, presumably, post-structuralist approaches – which take it for granted that language (or discourse) is the ultimate horizon of intelligibility. Such a work is now conceived as 'something quite different from the set of representations that underlies a certain behavior'; also as 'something quite different from the domain of attitudes that can determine this behavior'. On the contrary, the work of thought becomes possible only insofar as it enables the thinker 'to step back from [a certain] way of acting or reacting, to present it to oneself as an object of thought and question it as to its meaning, its conditions, and its goals'.[118] For it is precisely at the point where 'a given' is translated into 'a question', or some present mode of conduct into an issue concerning that conduct and its ethical implications, that thinking can begin to problematize the grounds of its own more habitual or taken-for-granted beliefs. And if this means abandoning the main tenet of post-structuralist doctrine – i.e., the claim that thought is constituted through and through by the codes, conventions, language-games or discourses that make up a given cultural order – then Foucault seems ready to do just that. Thus: 'the work of philosophical and historical reflection is put back into the field of the work of thought only on condition that one clearly grasps problematization not as an arrangement of representations but as a work of thought.'[119] As it happens this is the closing sentence of the last text collected in Rabinow's *Foucault Reader*. One could hardly wish for a firmer declaration of the distance that he had travelled from the reading of Kant which affords such a brilliant (if negative) climax to *The Order of Things*.

When I cited these passages previously it was in order to suggest the unresolved conflicts or tensions that resulted from Foucault's ongoing quarrel with the truth-claims of enlightenment critique. We can now see how much was at stake in this contest of interpretations, this attempt (at the outset) to represent Kantian philosophy as one passing episode in the history of an error, and then – as the issues posed themselves more sharply – to define his own project in uneasy relation to that same much-disputed heritage. No doubt this change of mind came about for various reasons, among them Foucault's growing opposition to 'structuralism' and its various offshoots, not least on account of their failure to afford any adequate grasp of the complex relations between truth, knowledge, and the ethical 'work of thought'. But there was, I think, another more urgent motive in the problems that Foucault encountered, especially during the late 1960s and early 70s, when called upon to offer some principled justification of his own current stance on moral and ethico-political questions. For it is clear from some of his essays and interviews at the time (notably those translated in the volume *Power/Knowledge*) that Foucault very often came close to endorsing an attitude which resembled Lyotard's post-modernist notion of 'judging without criteria'. That is to say, he briefly went along with what amounted to a private-decisionist creed, one that in principle rejected any form of reasoned, enlightened or 'abstract' morality, and which staked all its claims to ethical good faith on a direct appeal to individual conscience as the sole arbiter of action and choice in this or that particular context. After all, this was the heady period before and after *les événements* of 1968 when French dissident or leftist intellectuals were required to take their stand on numerous issues, and to choose between a range of competing positions – Marxist, Trotskyist, Marxist-Leninist, Marxist-Leninist-Maoist, anarchist, incipient 'post-Marxist', and so on – which could hardly be treated as a matter of straightforward deduction from first principles. At the time it must have seemed that there were as many groupings (or short-lived activist 'groupuscules') as there were local issues and day-to-day turns in the course of political events. In this situation one can fully understand why Foucault should have registered the appeal of a 'micropolitics' that seemed most responsive to these momentary shifts of tactical alliance, these unpredictable 'conjunctures' brought about by the absence of any large-scale unifying movement.

What the times thus required was a flexible attitude – a readiness to abandon high-sounding talk of 'truth', 'principles', 'justice', 'emancipatory interests' or whatever – and a corresponding will to bend all one's energies to various short-term, 'specific' projects of localized resistance and critique. Insofar as such projects stood in need of justification, it could only be a matter of pointing out their strategic usefulness in pursuit of some goal whose desirability was simply self-evident to those pursuing it, but whose ultimate good could never be determined with reference to higher ('universal' or 'trans-cendent') grounds of ethical judgement. For to fall back on such Kantian precepts was a hopelessly obsolete gesture, an evasion of issues that nowadays presented themselves entirely in specific, conjunctural, or local-interventionist terms. Thus for example, when asked by the members of a Maoist collective to offer some thoughts on 'revolutionary justice', Foucault in effect took the line of least resistance by denying that such questions could possibly be answered, or answered with the kind of principled, self-validating argument that his interlocutors apparently required.[120] At this point, as I say, there was little to distinguish Foucault's situationist attitude to issues of ethics, politics and justice from Lyotard's postmodernist treatment of such issues as belonging to a realm of 'sublimely' incommensurable truth-claims, and hence as allowing no appeal to shared standards or criteria of judgement. For this appeal could only carry some degree of argumentative conviction to the extent that there existed a communal sense of what should count as valid, legitimate reasoning in any given case. And therefore, since agreement was so evidently lacking, one had no choice (as Foucault then saw it) but to give up the quest for justifying grounds and respond to each new situation as need or opportunity arose.

In his book *Just Gaming*, a series of dialogues with Jean-Loup Thébaud, Lyotard shows himself quite ready to go all the way with this principled rejection of principles, this notion that 'commitment' can only be a matter of decisions arrived at through an act of unreasoning, spur-of-the-moment choice.[121] Thébaud is less than convinced by Lyotard's case, and at one stage presses him for a clearer statement on the issue of political justice. How could one justify *any* commitment – any choice between conflicting principles – if there were no criteria by which to assess the issues and priorities involved? Lyotard then offers the example of a West German terrorist group who kidnapped and murdered the industrialist Hans-Martin Schleyer. Was their action in any sense 'justified' as a response to Schleyer's involvement (as they claimed) with US war-plans and the military-industrial complex? More specifically: 'is it just that there be an American computer in Heidelberg that, among other things, is used to plan the bombing of Hanoi? In the final analysis, someone like Schleyer thinks so. In the final analysis, the "Baader-Meinhof" group thinks not. It is up to everyone to decide!'[122] But decide *on what basis*, Thébaud reasonably asks, and according to what criteria, whether circumstantial, moral, or political? Does Lyotard himself think it unjust that the American computer should be put to these uses and housed in the Federal Republic? 'Yes,' he replies, 'absolutely. I can say that such is my opinion. I feel committed in that respect.' But when it comes to justifying this commitment – giving reasons for the way he feels – Lyotard flatly refuses to argue the point any further. 'If you asked me why I am on that side, I think that I would answer that I do not have an answer to the question "why?", and that this is of the order of . . . transcendence.'[123] He is anxious that Thébaud should not misconstrue the meaning of this term 'transcendence', not take it as appealing to some kind of mystical or quasi-religious absolute. But it is hard to see what other significance could attach to the word, given Lyotard's thoroughly mystified reading of Kant, his promotion of sublime 'heterogeneity' to a high point of ethical doctrine, and his blank refusal – in this particular instance – to reason out the moral issues of the case. 'When I say "transcendence", it means: I do not know who is sending me the prescription in question.' One could take this perhaps as a version of the Kantian ethical imperative, the duty always to reason beyond one's private, self-interested motives or desires to some idea of the universal good, one that issues from a voice of conscience – an internal yet seemingly heteronomous voice – which thwarts or overrules those desires. Yet this reading goes clean against Lyotard's outright rejection of all such 'enlightenment' values and truth-claims. As he describes it, the call of conscience sounds more like the 'voices' of Shaw's Saint

Joan than the exercise of practical reason in quest of validating grounds and principles.

Foucault might seem to have argued himself into a similiar corner when confronting the 'heterogeneous' claims and counter-claims of late-sixties French political debate. Above all, what this period impressed upon him was the danger of extrapolating too directly from a thinker's theoretical or philosophical concerns to his/her presumed 'position' on issues of an ethico-political nature. In the interview with Rabinow one finds him looking back on these episodes from his earlier career with a mixture of impatience and wry self-criticism. 'There were Marxists', he recalls,

> who said I was a danger to Western democracy . . . there was a socialist who wrote that the thinker who resembled me most closely was Adolf Hitler in *Mein Kampf*. I have been considered by liberals as a technocrat, an agent of the Gaullist government; I have been considered by people on the right, Gaullists or otherwise, as a dangerous left-wing anarchist; there was an American professor who asked why a crypto-Marxist like me, manifestly a KGB agent, was invited to American universities, and so on.[124]

From which Foucault would appear to draw a lesson very much in line with both Lyotard's doctrine of plural, incommensurable 'phrase-regimes' and Rorty's advice that we give up on the quest for any ethics or politics that would bridge the gulf between our 'private' and 'public' spheres of existence. Thus: 'the key to the personal poetic attitude of a philosopher is not to be sought in his ideas, as if it could be deduced from them, but rather in his philosophy-as-life, in his philosophical life, his ethos.'[125] And this ethos presents itself mainly in aesthetic terms, that is to say, as a project of 'poetic' self-invention which has more to do with 'personal' attitudes, beliefs and predilections than with anything in the nature of arguments, principles, or philosophical 'ideas'.

Yet once again there are signs – in the same interview – of Foucault's not wishing to go all the way with this postmodern-pragmatist-aestheticist line, and indeed of his adopting a stance more akin to the opposed ('enlightenment') view. For it is, as he remarks, 'not at all a matter of making a particular issue of my own situation; but, if you like, I think that by asking this sort of ethico-epistemologico-political question, one is not taking up a position on a chessboard'.[126] In other words, there are issues that can (and should) be raised beyond the private-aestheticist sphere, and which cannot be reduced – as he sometimes suggests – to an argument for the merely contingent relation between matters of 'personal' ethos or life-style and questions of a wider (socio-political) concern. Insofar as one takes a stand on such issues one is *not* just adopting some set-piece 'position on a chessboard' ('socialist', 'liberal', 'Gaullist', 'left-wing anarchist', 'crypto-Marxist' or whatever), but arguing a case whose validity-conditions will always involve both factual truth-claims and the appeal to certain standards – certain stated criteria – of right and wrong. Hence the resistance that Foucault puts up to any account, like Rorty's, that would treat him as travelling a long way around to basically postmodern-pragmatist conclusions. For such thinking comes down to a form of inert consensus-ideology, an apologia for existing values and beliefs that would place them beyond reach of counter-argument or effective oppositional critique.

One last example – again from the interview with Rabinow – may help to define more exactly where the difference lies between Foucault and the proponents of a postmodern ethics that exploits the sublime (or its own strong-revisionist reading thereof) as an analogue for the radical 'heterogeneity' which supposedly inhabits (or inhibits) all forms of determinate ethical judgement. Its significance can best be grasped through the contrast with Lyotard's shuffling and evasive response on the question of terrorist 'morality' *vis-à-vis* the claims of legal obligation or citizenly virtue. The example is that of Poland, one that Foucault – speaking in 1984 – regards as indisputably 'touching us all', and therefore as presenting a decisive test-case for anyone who seeks to address these issues in a real-world, practical context. 'If we raise the question of Poland in strictly political terms,' he remarks,

> it is clear that we quickly reach the point of saying that there is nothing we can do. We can't dispatch a team of paratroopers, and we can't send armoured cars to liberate Warsaw. I think that, politically, we have to recognize this, but I think we have to agree that, for ethical reasons, we have to raise the problem of Poland in the form of a non-acceptance of what is happening there, and a non-acceptance of the passivity of our own governments. I think this attitude is an ethical one, but it is also political; it does not consist in saying merely, 'I protest', but in making of that attitude a political phenomenon that is as substantial as possible, and one which those who govern, here or there, will sooner or later be obliged to take into account.[127]

My point is that Foucault – unlike Lyotard – acknowledges the claims of certain moral imperatives that *necessarily* hold for any conscientious subject in possession of the relevant facts, and whose validity cannot be relativized to this or that 'phrase-regime', 'discourse' or cultural 'form of life'. Nor can this be merely a matter of one's private 'attitude', a position arrived at on no firmer basis than Lyotard's opt-out gesture, his voluntarist or decisionist notion of ethics as a leap of faith beyond any standard of reasoned accountability. For as Foucault describes it the posture of 'non-acceptance' is one that follows from a critical review of the best available evidence, a commitment made 'as substantial as possible' by giving due weight to all those factors – historical, political and socio-economic – which enable one to reach an informed judgement. So it is not so much a question of 'judging without criteria' (in Lyotard's oxymoronic phrase) as of asking which criteria properly apply in some particular set of circumstances, and then deciding what should count as a consequent, good-faith, or ethically warranted response.

Thus 'politics' is secondary to 'ethics' only in the sense that ethics confronts such issues at the crucial point where an adequate knowledge of the given situation passes over into a *reasoned and justified* commitment on moral-evaluative grounds. Thus, in Foucault's words,

> when thought intervenes, it doesn't assume a unique form that is the direct result or the necessary expression of these difficulties; it is an original or specific response − often taking many forms, sometimes even contradictory in its different aspects − to these difficulties, which are defined for it by a situation or a context, and which hold true as a possible question.[128]

What this passage brings out is Foucault's eminently Kantian concern to explain how ethical judgement is on the one hand a matter of autonomous, freely-willed choice − since always to some extent underdetermined by the circumstantial evidence − and on the other obliged to take account of such evidence in order to justify its actions, commitments, or evaluative priorities. By this time he had advanced a long way toward abandoning the extreme nominalist position − the attitude of cognitive scepticism linked to a relativist philosophy of meaning and value − that had marked his writings from *The Order of Things* to the period of Nietzsche-inspired 'genealogical' thought. For such ideas had been enlisted in the service of a fashionable 'end-of-ideology' creed which rejected all truth-claims as a matter of course, and which cheerfully embraced the postmodern prospect of a 'cultural conversation' of plural, heterogeneous discourses henceforth given over to judging in the absence of factual or ethical criteria. Whatever their erstwhile appeal for Foucault − or his own central role in promoting them − these ideas now struck him (it is reasonable to infer) as philosophically incoherent and as possessing nothing like the 'radical' charge that their adherents standardly claimed for them.

VI

Had Foucault lived longer this resistance might have taken a more overt and polemical form, a challenge to many of the orthodox notions now canvassed in his name. As it is, one can see from the late essays and interviews − especially those that pursue his engagement with Kant − how far he had come in the process of re-thinking his relation to the project of enlightenment critique. Of course there is no question of claiming Foucault as a good Kantian at heart, a prodigal son who once ventured forth among the vanities and snares of post-structuralist fashion, but who finally acknowledged the error of his ways and embraced the paternal creed. Such an argument would ignore those numerous points of tension – 'aporias' in the strict, not the current all-purpose rhetorical sense of that term – which continue to vex Foucault's later dealings with Kant. Yet very often it is precisely at the moment when Foucault is asserting his distance from this legacy of thought that he also bears witness to its present-day significance, its capacity for raising the right kinds of question with regard to matters of ethical, social and political conscience. Thus 'the thread that may connect us to the Enlightenment is not faithfulness to its doctrinal elements, but rather the permanent reactivation of an attitude – that is, of a philosophical ethos that could be described as a permanent critique of our historical era' (WIE, p. 42). We shall misread this and other passages like it if we take them as signalling a postmodern break with all the values of Enlightenment thought. For what could be more in keeping with Kant's critical imperative than this requirement that philosophy take nothing on trust – its own 'doctrinal elements' included – but persist in the kind of self-questioning activity which allows of no privileged exemptions, no truth-claims (epistemic or ethical) that cannot be justified on reasoned or principled grounds? Such, after all, is Foucault's way of linking the 'work of thought' with the maintenance of a distinctive 'philosophical ethos', one which involves the 'permanent critique' of naturalized attitudes and values. If this is no simple 'return' to Kant, still less can it be thought of – following the current doxa – as a flat repudiation of Kantian ideas in the wisdom of postmodern hindsight.

When Foucault denounces what he calls the 'blackmail of Enlightenment', his phrase can best be taken as referring to the mythical and demonized view of that tradition adopted – with little in the way of corroborative evidence – by doctrinaire postmodernists like Lyotard. And yet one also finds him, just a few sentences later, declaring that 'as an enterprise for linking the progress of truth and the history of liberty in a bond of direct relation, it [the Enlightenment] formulated a philosophical question that remains for us to consider' (WIE, p. 43). This affirmative characterization is demonstrably nearer the mark, both as a matter of adequate description (on philosophic and historical grounds), and as regards the motivating interests of Foucault's own engagement with Kant and the discourse of Enlightenment critique. It explains why he continued to treat such questions as a 'privileged domain for analysis', a 'set of political, economic, social, institutional, and cultural events on which we still depend in large part' (p. 42). Where the conflict arose was in Foucault's uncertainty, still present in his last writings, as to whether those 'events' were historically contingent at bottom, and should therefore be treated as just another (albeit *for us* a uniquely 'privileged') episode in the structural genealogy of Western thought, or whether, on the contrary, they marked the passage to a new and henceforth indispensable mode of socio-cultural analysis. The former reading is undoubtedly borne out by his work from *The Order of Things* to the late 1960s. Thereafter one can find evidence for both interpretations, often – as I have argued – within the same text and in response to the same sorts of question. But the fact that this remained an issue for Foucault, and the more so through successive encounters with Kant, is evidence enough that he never espoused that line of least resistance (or retreat into postures of private-aestheticist whimsy) enjoined by the postmodern sceptics.

In this respect Foucault indeed kept faith with what he saw as the enduring value of Enlightenment thought: its capacity to 'separate out, from the contingency that has made us what we are, the possibility of no longer being, doing, or thinking what we are, do, or think'. On Rorty's account this would simply be a matter of exchanging one life-style or 'final vocabulary' for another, a process that occurs for no good reason save that of momentarily relieving our boredom and providing some new, equally 'contingent' set of topics for the ongoing cultural conversation. One could – if very strongly so disposed – read Foucault's sentence as a straightforward endorsement of the postmodern-pragmatist line. Thus it might plausibly be construed as urging that 'enlightenment' is a thing of the past, that truth is just a matter of what is (currently and contingently) 'good in the way of belief', and that value-commitments only make sense insofar as they carry weight, or possess some measure of suasive appeal, for members of an existing interpretive community. But there could then be no accounting for the logic of Foucault's sentence, as opposed to its vaguely rhetorical drift. That is to say, one would be at a loss to understand his assertion that criticism can 'separate out' those contingent factors that have 'made us what we are' from those other 'possibilities' that remain at present unfulfilled, but which yet provide a standard – in Kantian terms, a regulative idea – for the ethical 'work of thought'. These are not just options that offer themselves randomly according to the current conversational state of play, or within the presently-existing range of language-games, discourses, elective self-images etc. Rather, they are conceived as *conditions of possibility* for that attitude of 'permanent critique' which Foucault identifies with the Enlightenment ethos in its authentic, self-questioning form.

It is here that Foucault implicitly takes issue with that facile strain of counter-enlightenment rhetoric which has often laid claim to his own work, early and late, as a principal source of inspiration. Small wonder that he became increasingly disposed to assert his distance from post-structuralism and its various offshoots on the Francophile cultural scene. For there is nothing more alien to Foucault's thought than the kind of ultra-relativist orthodoxy that erects its own lack of critical and ethical resources into a quasi-universal 'postmodern condition', a terminal indifference with regard to issues of truth and falsehood, or – to paraphrase Jonathan Swift – that state of perfected self-assurance which comes of being blissfully well deceived. And conversely, there was no question more central to the evolving project of Foucault's life and work than the one taken up in Kant's inaugural essay on the theme 'What Is Enlightenment?'. Any reading that manages to sidestep this question, or which returns a confidently negative response, is bound to misconstrue Foucault's project at numerous points.

3

For Truth in Criticism: William Empson and the Claims of Theory

When is a theorist not a theorist? Perhaps when, like William Empson, he starts out by a writing an extraordinary first book (*Seven Types of Ambiguity*)[1] which raises all manner of subtle and far-reaching theoretical questions, but then lives on to develop a hearty dislike of the modern 'Eng Lit' industry, its ethos of geared-up professional expertise and – most especially – its tiresome display of spurious 'theoretical' concern. Such was certainly Empson's response to just about every school or movement of literary theory, from the American New Criticism to structuralism and deconstruction. For a while he made a point of keeping up with these developments, reviewing any books that came his way (though rarely with much enthusiasm), and at least hanging on to the basic conviction – so strong in *Seven Types* – that 'theory' was a worthwhile pursuit just so long as it helped us to puzzle out the sense of some otherwise mysterious passage, and didn't fly off at a speculative tangent, or become tied up in philosophical problems of its own ingenious creating. After all, as he wrote in *Seven Types*,

> normal sensibility is a tissue of what has been conscious theory made habitual and returned to the pre-conscious, and, therefore, conscious theory may make an addition to sensibility even though it draws no (or no true) conclusion, formulates no general theory, in the scientific sense, which reconciles and makes quickly available the results which it describes. (p. 254)

At this time Empson was mainly concerned to head off the objections of those posturing aesthetes ('Oxford' types as he tagged them) who would no doubt regard his book as a monstrous piece of clanking theoretical machinery, an approach that threatened to 'kill the plant' – or destroy the very sources of poetic response – by 'pruning down too far towards the emotional roots'. In face of such attitudes Empson felt justified in adopting a stance of sturdy 'Cambridge' rationalism, an outlook informed by his own keen interest in mathematics, theoretical physics, and the scientific disciplines in general. To this extent at least 'theory' was useful: as a means of persuading oneself and others that poetry – even 'obscure' modern poetry – was best approached with the intellect fully engaged, and without giving way to an aestheticist mystique that would leave readers entirely at the mercy of this or that irrational prejudice. In short, 'it is necessary to protect our sensibility against critical dogma, but it is just because of this that the reassurance given by some machinery for analysis has become so necessary in its turn' (*ST*, p. 253). For otherwise one might as well admit that criticism – especially Empson's kind of criticism – performs a great disservice to poetry by analysing that which of its very nature resists the best efforts of analytic commentary.

It is worth looking more closely at Empson's arguments here since they help to explain both his early, positive attitude to 'theory' and the reasons for his subsequent lack of sympathy with what others were attempting under the same broad description. In *Seven Types* he takes the view that, if poetry makes sense, then its sense-making properties are likely to be continuous with those of our everyday 'prosaic' understanding, even if raised to a much higher power of semantic or syntactic condensation. At any rate it is better to work on this assumption – to press as far as possible toward analysing the character and sources of poetic 'emotion' – than to take easy refuge in a wholesale aestheticist creed which elevates the mysterious nature of poetry to a high point of critical doctrine. Thus:

> things temporarily or permanently inexplicable are not, therefore, to be thought of as essentially different from things that can be explained in some terms you happen to have at your disposal; nor can you have reason to think them likely to be different unless there is a great deal about the inexplicable things that you already know. (*ST*, p. 252)

In other words, there is something wrong – philosophically suspect – about the attitude that treats poetry as somehow vouchsafing imaginative truths, insights or orders of 'paradoxical' wisdom that inherently transcend the powers and capacities of rational thought. Critics who take this line are in much the same position as cultural relativists who argue that there exist languages, world-views, scientific paradigms, or 'universes of discourse' that differ so radically from our own (modern Eurocentric) standpoint that there can, in principle, be no question of 'translating' reliably between them, or at any rate of knowing for sure that such translation had in fact occurred.[2] For you could only be in a position to assert this incommensurability-thesis if you had at least understood sufficient of the language or world-view in question to register the problems of achieving any reasonably accurate or truthful grasp. And then of course the thesis would self-deconstruct, since the very fact of claiming to be in that position, i.e. to *know* where the difficulties arose, would constitute a standing reproof to the claims of any wholesale cultural-relativist outlook.

This is not to deny, as Empson readily admits, that there may be 'things temporarily or permanently inexplicable', whether these have to do with some radically alien set of cultural beliefs, practices, or life-forms, or perhaps (his more immediate concern) with some passage of especially opaque poetry that turns out to baffle the best efforts of rational prose commentary. But to take these exceptional cases as the norm is to fall into the same error that anthropologists, philosophers, historians of science and others make when they conclude on the basis of such localized (however well-documented) problems that translation between languages and cultures is a radically impossible enterprise; that different 'language-games' or 'forms of life' are incommensurable one with another; that there is no judging between various scientific 'paradigms' or 'discourses' since they each set their own, strictly immanent or *sui generis* terms for understanding; or that knowledge (including scientific knowledge) is always a product of the dominant conventions, the professional codes of practice or research-programmes that effectively determine what shall count as such at any given time. These arguments are open to the obvious rejoinder, as above: that without at least some measure of shared understanding across and between languages, disciplines and cultures the sceptic's position would be strictly unintelligible, since it would lack any means of making its point with respect to *particular* or well-attested cases of misunderstanding.[3] In short, this attitude of out-and-out cultural relativism is self-refuting insofar as it trades on a generalized refusal to acknowledge the terms on which *all* understanding necessarily proceeds, at least to the extent that it hopes to make sense in the forum of accountable public debate.

Such – in broad outline – is the case advanced by the philosopher Donald Davidson in his well-known essay 'On the Very Idea of a Conceptual Scheme'.[4] His main targets here are the various forms of currently fashionable cognitive scepticism, among them Whorfian ethno-linguistics (where 'truth' and 'reality' are held to be constructed entirely in and through language),[5] Quine's ultra-empiricist attack on the analytic/synthetic distinction (along with his consequent denial of the possibility of 'radical translation'),[6] Feyerabend's anarchist philosophy of science (which throws out all validity-conditions save those adopted more or less at whim on the part of this or that localized short-term collective),[7] and other such versions of the basic idea that all knowledge is mediated by 'conceptual schemes' (language-games, 'forms of life' etc.) which differ so fundamentally in respect of their sense-making criteria that nothing could justify our claiming to compare them, or to understand, interpret or criticize one in terms of another.[8] To this catalogue Davidson might well have added post-structuralism, postmodernism, Foucauldian 'genealogy' (or discourse-theory), and at least one variety of deconstruction as practised by (mainly American) literary critics.[9] For with these thinkers also it is a high point of doctrine that 'truth' is nothing more than what counts as such according to the codes, cultural conventions, power/knowledge interests, 'intertextual' relationships and so forth which make up the conditions of intelligibility within this or that field of 'signifying practice'. And he (Davidson) would surely have much the same point to make against this latest efflorescence of epistemic scepticism in a textualist or literary-rhetorical mode. For they all raise the question – wholly unanswerable on their own terms – of just what constitutes a valid (or even a meaningful) interpretation when all 'discourses' come down to a play of strictly incommensurable language-games with no rational grounds for adjudicating the issue between them.

It seems to me that Empson is within sight of this question when he devotes the last chapter of *Seven Types* to a defence of 'analytic', as opposed to subjective or 'appreciative' criticism. For the main purpose of verbal exegesis, as he sees it, is to offer a 'machinery' of rational understanding which may not satisfy the aesthete (on grounds of tact, sensibility or mere good taste), but which can at least give heart to the critic in search of more solid grounds for debate. And this machinery is necessary, he writes,

> partly so as to look as if you knew what you were talking about, partly as a matter of 'style', and partly from the basic assumption of prose that all the parts of speech must have some meaning. (These three give the same idea with increasing generality.) Otherwise, one would be constantly stating relations between unknown or indefinite objects, or only stating something *about* such relations, themselves unknown and indefinite, in a way which probably reflects accurately the nature of your statement, but to which only the pure mathematician is accustomed. So that many of my explanations may be demonstrably wrong, and yet efficient for their purpose, and *vice versa*. (*ST*, p. 253)

The situation with criticism is therefore much like that in the sciences, where intuition may go a long way – may indeed be indispensable when it comes to assessing the truth-claims of rival, equally plausible theories – but where one still needs the 'machinery' of rational argument by way of making good some particular claim.

Hence the alternating process, as Empson describes it, between commentary of a broadly 'appreciative' kind and commentary that ignores the rules of good taste and presses as far as it can toward a limit-point of lucid, rational understanding.

> When you have made a quotation, you must first show the reader how you feel about it, by metaphor, implication, devices of sound, or anything else that will work; on the other hand, when you want to make a critical remark, to explain *why* your quotation takes effect as it does, you must state your result as plainly (in as transferable, intellectually handy terms) as you can. (p. 250)

What this amounts to (as perhaps one might have expected, given Empson's early and continued interest in mathematics and the natural sciences) is a theory of criticism that minimizes — even bids fair to collapse — the difference between problems of literary interpretation and problems in the nature of scientific reasoning. His poems of this period show Empson puzzling in much the same way about just how far the more advanced (i.e., speculative) models and metaphors of modern science find expression through modes of 'poetic' reasoning that tend to jump over the logical relations required of a straightforward demonstrative sequence of argument.[10] But it is equally important to recognize that Empson is very far from regarding this as a one-way relation of dependence, a version of the argument (much touted by recent 'radical' philosophers of science) that scientific discovery is ultimately reliant on imaginative 'leaps' that somehow elude all the standard protocols of method and verification.[11] For he is just as keen to make the point that criticism will amount to nothing more than a species of aestheticist self-indulgence if it doesn't give sound analytical *reasons* for coming up with this or that ingenious piece of closely-wrought verbal exegesis. The one idea that he will not entertain is that poetry somehow expresses a wisdom — an order of 'higher', paradoxical or purely intuitive thought — beyond reach of rational analysis. And this was a conviction that stayed with Empson right through to the books and essays of his last period.

In *Seven Types* it produces the strong rationalist conviction that poetry ought to make sense according to the best, most rigorous (if 'prosaic') standards of hard-pressed analytic commentary. Thus 'explanations of literary matters . . . , involving as they do much apparently random invention, are more like Pure than Analytical Geometry, and, if you cannot think of a construction, that may show that you would be wise to use a different set of methods, but cannot show the problem is of a new kind' (pp. 252–3). What I think this means — and the meaning is far from self-evident — is that theory works best if allowed to settle down into a generalized sense that adequate explanations ought to be available, even in cases of 'obscure' modern verse where the meaning (in Wallace Stevens's pregnant phrase) 'resists the intelligence almost successfully'. In other words, criticism has to operate on the principle that any poem worth the effort of detailed exegesis will *most likely* make sense in rationally accountable terms, and that where such efforts fail — or find themselves at last resorting to talk of 'deep' symbolism, obscure private motives, or paradoxical truths — then one can always go back and try another analytical 'construction'. Thus

> [any] advance in the machinery of description makes a reader feel stronger about his appreciations, more reliably able to distinguish the private or accidental from the critically important or repeatable, more confident of the reality (that is, the

transferability) of his experiences; adds, in short, in the mind of the reader to the
things there to be described, whether or not it makes those particular things
more describable. (p. 254)

For it is Empson's firm belief that the only way to read intelligently is to
keep the reasoning faculties fully in gear and not go along with emotivist,
symbolist, Jungian or other such doctrines that would sever all links between
poetic language and the language of plain-prose reason. This is not to say that
there may not be passages, and among them passages of genuinely powerful,
haunting or profound poetry, which in the end turn out to elude all the critic's
dogged sense-making efforts. Such was Empson's experience with the lines
from Wordsworth's 'Tintern Abbey' which he puzzled over at length in *Seven
Types* and took up again – hoping to explain the puzzlement – in a chapter of
his later book *The Structure of Complex Words*.[12] But instances like this, though
not at all uncommon, were best regarded as exceptions that in some sense
confirmed the rule, or cases that could only be dealt with adequately by
keeping one's rational defences up and not (so to speak) admitting defeat at the
first hurdle.

Such was at any rate the lesson that Empson drew from the scientific
disciplines – especially the advances in theoretical physics – that dominated the
Cambridge intellectual scene during his undergraduate years. It was an outlook
as remote as possible from the kinds of extreme cognitive scepticism or the
varieties of relativist doctrine which nowadays pass (at least among literary
theorists) as the last word in *au courant* philosophy of science. Small wonder, as
I have said, that Empson found himself increasingly at odds with an enterprize
(that of professional 'Eng Lit') whose drift he perceived as getting further and
further out of touch with the interests of science and – more urgently – the
needs of enlightened rational understanding. Not that this involved the kind
of vulgar positivist conception of science and truth that literary theorists are
apt to hold up as a foil to their own more 'sophisticated' views. (Barthes's
Critique et vérité has a good deal to answer for here,[13] along with the anti-
cognitivist bias of American New Criticism and, albeit from a very different
angle, F. R. Leavis in his absurd crusade against science during the 'two
cultures' debate with C. P. Snow.) On the contrary: Empson saw very clearly
that such a model was out of the question, not only for literary criticism
but even (or especially) for the kinds of scientific enquiry that most engaged
his speculative interest. In *Seven Types*, as indeed in his poems of the
period, Empson shows himself fully up-to-date with ideas, like Heisenberg's
Uncertainty Principle, which had already done much to problematize the
relation between knower and known, or scientific observation and the order of
'objective' reality. All of which tended to complicate his view that verbal
analysis was the right way for criticism to go, or at any rate a method that

would serve critics better than the lame retreat into various kinds of emotivist, irrationalist or aestheticist doctrine. One had to concede, he argued, that 'the act of knowing is itself an act of sympathizing; unless you are enjoying the poetry you cannot create it, as poetry, in your mind' (*ST*, p. 248).

On the one hand this meant that any claims for 'analytical' as opposed to 'appreciative' criticism had better take account of these deep-laid problems and not pin their faith to an old-fashioned positivist paradigm which no longer possessed much credibility even among scientists. Such would be the view that 'the mind, otherwise passive, collects propositions about the outside world' (p. 248); a view whose application to poetry would at least have the negative virtue of showing up its inbuilt limitations, or 'reduc[ing] that idea of truth (much more intimately than elsewhere) to a self-contradiction' (p. 249). On the other hand, this is no reason — so Empson maintains — to go along with the prevalent idea of poetry as somehow enjoying a special dispensation from the standards of rational accountability or plain good sense. Least of all could it justify what Empson regards as the desperate recourse to emotivist doctrines that entirely sever the link between poetry and other (scientific, philosophical or everyday) uses of language. This last had been the view of I. A. Richards, argued in a series of influential books, notably his *Principles of Literary Criticism* (1927).[14] On Richards's view it was simply a muddle — a species of category-mistake — to worry about the status of poetical truth-claims as if they aspired to the condition of constative (i.e., factual or assertoric) truth. Poems were valuable chiefly for their power of evoking a complex *emotional* response in the reader's mind, a state in which the chaos of our humdrum, day-to-day experience could achieve a momentary 'equipoise' or balance of diverse (normally conflicting) psychological impulses. The greatest poetry, according to Richards, is the product of 'exceptional experiences' in the lives of 'exceptional individuals'. Its power to communicate such privileged moments comes from the poet's peculiar gift for condensing a range of otherwise confused or contradictory emotions into a verbal form that achieves the maximum degree of lucidity and poise. But it can do so only on condition that readers approach it in the proper frame of mind, that is to say, by suspending the standards appropriate to other (truth-functional) kinds of discourse, and effecting that 'complete severance of poetry from belief' which Richards considered the *sine qua non* of its survival in a scientific age.

What this amounts to is a modern restatement of Matthew Arnold's case in 'The Study of Poetry', retaining the stress on literature's vital role as a force for cultural renewal, but adopting the language of behaviourist psychology to back up its claims. The march of science had left small room for those forms of collective belief or imaginary projection that had once made it possible to feel at home in an otherwise hostile or indifferent universe. Poetry can 'save' us, Richards believes, but only if we learn to read it aright, and give up thinking of poetic truth as in any way subject to the governing criteria of factual or veridical discourse. This means accepting that poets deal only in varieties of 'pseudo-statement', sentences which share the grammatical *form* but not, he insists, the assertoric *force* of genuine truthful propositions. Otherwise poetry must forfeit all claim to be taken seriously in an age when science has pressed so far toward defining the terms of rational debate in every other realm of enquiry. Richards would seem to have arrived at this conclusion by endorsing the logical-positivist argument in its strongest (and least tenable) form, i.e., that the only propositions which really made sense were those that squared with the world-view of modern scientific reason, or which lent themselves to verification in accordance with principles derived from that programme. Thus truth-values would apply to just two classes of utterance: empirical truths-of-observation on the one hand and purely analytic (hence empty or tautologous) statements of logical necessity on the other. Hence Richards's unfortunate retreat — as Empson saw it — into a form of dead-end 'emotivist' doctrine that attempted to save appearances by cutting poetry off from any semblance of rational sense.

The American New Critics, Wimsatt and Brooks chief among them, did nothing to challenge this anti-cognitivist bias despite their taking issue with Richards's 'affective' or psychologistic premises.[15] What they managed, in effect, was a wholesale transfer of priorities from the realm of subjective reader-response to that of the poem as 'verbal icon', an inwrought structure of paradox, irony, or multiple meaning under whatever favoured designation. It would then become possible, they hoped, to place criticism on a properly disciplined or methodical footing by avoiding the appeal to reader-response with all its impressionistic vagaries, and attending instead to the 'words on the page', or those various privileged figures and tropes that characterized poetic language. But they retained from Richards the same root conviction that poetry was not in the business of offering arguments, advancing truth-claims, or in any way providing fit material for the purposes of logico-semantic analysis. Indeed their whole approach was premised, like his, on a principle of non-continuity between poetry and other kinds of discourse, a *de jure* principle which required, among other things, that critics should respect the (supposedly) autonomous character of poetic language and form, and thus guard against the manifold 'heresies' of paraphrase, biography, historical source-hunting, sociological background-studies and so forth. What these approaches had in common was a tendency to substitute content-analysis (or an unseemly rush from words to world) for the work of detailed rhetorical exegesis which alone provided an adequate grasp of the poem's meaning and structure. And this applied above all to the 'heresy of paraphrase', the idea that one could so far separate 'form' and 'content' as to offer a plain-prose summary which cashed out the poem's meaning in conveniently simplified terms. In which case

– according to the New Critics – one might as well give up reading poetry altogether, since any difference between it and the various discourses that attempted to analyse, describe or explain it could only be a matter of degree, not a qualitative difference, and would therefore tend to reduce or disappear as soon as one applied the requisite analytic skills. Only by respecting the uniqueness of poetry – its resistance to paraphrase and other such reductive ploys – could criticism make out a convincing case for the continued value of literary studies in an age of rampant scientism or technocratic reason.

Thus the New Critics followed Richards in this respect at least: that they drew a firm line between the rational prose virtues that (supposedly) governed their own interpretive procedure and the realm of poetic meaning where issues of truth and falsehood – or of argumentative warrant – no longer had any significant role to play. For Empson, on the contrary, there seemed little point in pursuing an 'emotive' (or non-cognitivist) theory of poetic language whose effect, as he saw it, was to isolate literature in a self-enclosed realm of feelings or affects which bore no relation to wider practical or socio-political concerns. In *Seven Types* the main thrust of this argument is aganst the kind of woolly-minded 'appreciative' criticism which shies away from verbal analysis for fear of harming our delicate intuitive responses. Empson puts this case most forcefully in a 1930 article responding to John Sparrow's polemical attack on Richards, Cambridge and the newly emergent 'school' of tough-minded analytic criticism.[16] Where Sparrow goes wrong – in company, one might add, with many early reviewers of *Seven Types* – is in trying to separate enjoyment from analysis, or judgements of value (supposedly arrived at on the basis of 'pure' intuition) from the process of patiently figuring out what this or that passage actually means. But he ignores all the evidence, as Empson argues, that 'those who judge in literary matters by "intuition" always assume a legacy of analysis, and complain when it is carried further'. Thus Sparrow treats 'beauty' as a simple noun, a non-natural attribute (like 'goodness' in G. E. Moore's ethical theory) which somhow typifies our best, most responsive and rewarding moments of experience, but which cannot be in any way explained or analysed beyond making the right appreciative noises. To Empson, this seemed nothing more than an easy escape-route, a retreat not only from problems in the realm of aesthetics or literary theory, but also from those very real difficulties which arose at every point in the effort to understand other people's motives and intentions. In short, it is an outlook which 'stultifies the intelligence, abolishes criticism, makes most of the facts about beautiful things unintelligible, and leaves us with a sense that the whole thing is a necromancy to which any charlatan may have the password'.[17] Thus Sparrow is here cast as a typical 'Oxford' aesthete, a critic who refuses to examine the sources of his own emotive reactions, and who therefore remains entirely at the mercy of whatever irrational prejudice may happen to capture his mind. Whereas it is the great virtue of 'analysis', as Empson sees it, to make us more aware of those prejudicial blind-spots and thus more capable of thinking our way through and beyond them.

All the same Empson is willing to concede that there *is* something deeply problematic about the claims of analytical criticism, especially when these are combined – as in Richards – with a sense that poetry needs to preserve its mysterious, 'inexplicable' power if it is ever to provide the imaginative sustenance required in a post-religious world of drastically naturalized meanings and values. To Sparrow this seems nothing more than a cheat on Richards's part, a means of smuggling myth and magic back in by the back-door while exploiting the appeal of a 'method' that trades on its pseudo-scientific credentials. For Empson, conversely, the issue about 'analysis' must be seen as one of those deep and *inescapable* problems which arise as soon as one reflects on the nature and limits of human understanding. In fact his rejoinder to Sparrow at this point reads like a synopsis of what Kant has to say in that section of the First Critique devoted to the 'Antinomies of Pure Reason'.

> The prime intellectual difficulty of our age is that true beliefs may make it impossible to act rightly; that we cannot think without verbal fictions; that they must not be taken for true beliefs, and yet must be taken seriously; that it is essential to analyse beauty; essential to accept it unanalysed; essential to believe that the universe is deterministic; essential to act as if it was not. None of these abysses, however, opened under Mr Sparrow's feet.[18]

Empson's point is that you will not avoid these problems – whether in ethics, epistemology, aesthetics, or literary criticism – by adopting the kind of blinkered emotivist outlook which counts them irrelevant for the purposes of ordinary, day-to-day human understanding. For the result of such thinking, as shown by Sparrow, is to fall back on vague appeals to 'intuition' that make no allowance for the reasoned appraisal of motives, meanings and intentions. So the puzzle about analytic criticism is often within reach of larger questions as to how we can cope with those various vexing antinomies (freewill *versus* determinism, and so forth) which will not disappear through a simple application of intuitive or commonsense criteria.

On this point Empson is fully in agreement with Richards, whatever his differences elsewhere: that the 'scientific' method which Sparrow so despises is better than the any amount of 'appreciative' waffle since it does at least try to sort these problems into some kind of humanly intelligible sense. Richards is right to take a robust line on the question of reader-response (or affective psychology), and is also quite justified – Empson thinks – in treating poetry as fit material for tests under near-laboratory conditions, tests which take it pretty much granted 1) that there is no ultimate mystery about poems, 2) that their

language is continuous with the language of straightforward prose communication, and therefore 3) that any failures of readerly grasp can best be understood, and hopefully remedied, by examining the various causal factors (social,
cultural, psychological) which may be shown to have brought them about. All
this strikes Empson as far preferable to Sparrow's squeamish protests on behalf
of an obscurantist ethos which amounts to little more than a species of 'Oxford'
high-table snobbery. Where he *will* take issue with Richards – increasingly so
in his articles and reviews of the next two decades – is over the argument that
criticism can only practise these needful therapeutic skills on condition that
it treat poetry as an 'emotive' form of utterance, a language-game devoid
of truth-telling warrant, cognitive interests, or veridical force. Only thus,
Richards thinks, can poetry 'save' us from the encroachments of science in an
age given over to positivist conceptions of meaning and method. That criticism
should emulate those methods – that is to say, turn itself into a branch of
applied behavioral psychology – is a development that Richards can happily
endorse since it promises to place literary studies on a footing with the other,
more prestigious 'sciences of man'. But there would be no point in mounting
such a strong neo-Arnoldian case for the high destinies of poetry if it were
not for this saving difference between poetic and other (referential or truth-
functional) varieties of discourse. For on Richards's view – again carried over
from the logical positivists – it is impossible to conceive how poetry could ever
be taken seriously except by suspending those otherwise normative conditions
for valid utterance and treating it as a language of 'pseudo-statements' devoid
of any genuine propositional force.

In his rejoinder to Sparrow there are signs already that Empson is unwilling
to take this doctrine on board. He concedes that the emotivist argument might
be more 'decently plausible' when applied to painting or the other visual arts
since here 'the modes of satisfaction are little understood, and are far removed
from the verbal system on which the discursive intelligence usually supports
itself'.[19] But it shouldn't be so attractive to literary critics whose main
business, after all, is to explain as best they can how language works, including
the language of poetry, and who therefore cannot rest content with 'explanations' which in fact explain nothing bar their own deep puzzlement. This
was why Empson went on, in *The Structure of Complex Words*, to develop a
theory of multiple meaning that would offer precisely a working account of
that 'verbal system on which the discursive intelligence usually supports itself'.
Seven Types, he came to feel, had rather fudged this issue by ranging its
examples on a vaguely-defined scale of 'increasing logical and psychological
complexity', with a clear implication that the best, most rewarding cases were
those that involved a downright clash of contradictory beliefs or atitudes. Thus
the seventh Type is the kind that occurs 'when the two meanings of the word,
the two values of the ambiguity, are the two opposite meanings defined by the

context, so that the total effect is to show a fundamental division in the writer's mind' (*ST*, p. 192). But there is a problem with this if you believe, like Empson, that criticism is most usefully employed in making rational sense of semantic complications that would otherwise open the way to all manner of mystified quasi-religious doctrine or 'paradoxical' pseudo-wisdom. For it did seem to many readers of the book that Empson was implying an equation – or at any rate a strong elective affinity – between full-blown cases of the seventh type and states of psychological conflict in the poet which most often resulted from some 'deep' clash of unconscious motives or desires. And many of his examples – especially the closing *tour de force* on George Herbert's 'The Sacrifice' – tended to support this impression in so far as they focused on religious poetry where the orthodox, Christian-devotional reading came up against the signs of neurotic self-doubt engendered by adherence to a harshly paradoxical creed.

Hence the final image of Christ in Herbert's poem: 'scapegoat and tragic hero; loved because hated; hated because godlike; freeing from torture because tortured; torturing his torturers because all-merciful; source of all strength to all men because by accepting he exaggerates their weakness; and, because outcast, creating the possibility of society' (*ST*, p. 233). It is clear enough, from this passage and others like it, that Empson not only viewed such paradoxes as a great source of poetic concentration and power, but also came to think of them – no doubt in consequence of reading some of Freud's late essays – as compulsively repeating a primal scene of repressed sacrificial guilt and desire which was played out over and again in the consciousness of latter-day 'civilized' reason.[20] Thus 'Herbert deals in this poem, on the scale and by the methods necessary to it, with the most complicated and deeply-rooted notion of the human mind' (p. 233). This idea is taken up in *Some Versions of Pastoral* (1935), where it becomes a kind of ground-bass or running theme for the various stages of thematic transformation, again laid out on a scale of increasing psychological complexity, that characterize the history of 'pastoral' writing in Empson's massively extended definition of that term.[21] Indeed, one could argue that Empsonian pastoral is not so much a *genre* or literary 'form' as a standing possibility for endless variations on a basic structure of feeling, a technique of self-complicating irony ('putting the complex into the simple') whose instances range from the highly conventional – the Renaissance courtier-as-swain – to a poet like Marvell, suggesting profound philosophical puzzles in a style of relaxed contemplative ease, or again works like 'The Beggars' Opera' or *Alice In Wonderland* where Empson finds a cluster of deeply ambivalent (not to say perverse) motives gathering around the figures of MacHeath, the sacrificial victim-hero and Alice, the child as idealized image of adult fantasy-projection. Such is presumably what Empson means when he talks (*à propos* the Seventh Type) about ambiguities that in the end have to do with 'the most

complicated and deeply-rooted notion of the human mind'. For behind all
these variants – even the 'simplest' – there is more than a hint of the primal
scene evoked in Empson's analysis of Herbert, a scene that many readers will
nowadays associate with René Girard and his dark meditations on 'mimetic
rivalry' and the origins of human social institutions in the act of (real or
imaginary) parricide that first gave rise to the bonding-through-guilt of the
parties to that fabulous event.[22]

II

However there is still some doubt in Empson's mind as to whether such 'deep'
ambiguities should really be thought of as fit material for the literary critic's
purpose. Hence perhaps the feeling of excitement mixed with a certain gathering unease that overtakes Empson's writing as he approaches the 'secret
places of the Muse', a domain where the ground-rules of logic appear to be
suspended, where the law of contradiction no longer holds, and where one
ought to feel 'something of the awe and horror which were felt by Dante finally
arriving at the most centrique part of earth, of Satan, and of hell' (*ST*, p. 196).
For indeed one can view the whole book as building up to those extraordinary
instances of the Seventh Type, cases that offer the maximum resistance to
any reading premised on rationalist ideas of language, truth and logic. No
doubt Neil Hertz is right when he suggests that these pages convey a kind
of threshold or liminal experience, an 'allegory of reading' (in de Man's
terminology) or an 'end-of-the-line' encounter (Hertz) which can only find
voice through such a rhetoric of crisis whose nearest equivalent is the Kantian
or Romantic sublime.[23] At least this would explain something of Empson's
disquiet as he moves into regions of conflict, paradox or advanced logical
disorder where the conscious mind seems increasingly out of its depth. One
could then perhaps read the essay on Marvell in *Some Versions* as a kind of
pastoral self-reassurance on Empson's part, a reminder that poetry can evoke
mental states which are 'neither conscious nor not conscious', which involve all
manner of subliminal ideas or thoughts beyond reach of reflective awareness,
but which nonetheless provide an apt stimulus for the poet's 'conceited'
metaphysical style. 'Here as usual with "profound" remarks the strength of the
thing is to combine unusually intellectual with unusually primitive ideas;
thought about the conditions of knowledge with a magical idea that the adept
controls the external world by thought' (*SVP*, p. 99). Many readers have felt
that the essay, like the poem, has a sense of quiet exhilaration which comes of
its somehow holding these antinomies in a state of rapt, near-mystical repose, a
mood rather seldom to be found in Empson's criticism. After all, 'the chief
point of the poem,' as he reads it, 'is to contrast and reconcile conscious and

unconscious states, intuitive and intellectual modes of apprehension . . . like the seventh Buddhist heaven of enlightenment' (p. 99).

It seems to me that this impression has a lot to do with Empson's strongly-felt need, in the early criticism, to find some way beyond all those problems thrown up by the depth-psychological approach, problems that had scarcely been laid to rest in the reply to Sparrow or the closing chapters of *Seven Types*. At least on this occasion – in the reading of Marvell – Empson seems largely untroubled by such problems and ready to follow out the poem's suggestions for a life of unimpeded harmonious balance between instinct and reason, will and self-knowledge, unconscious impulse and reflective awareness. So there is maybe something a bit too portentous – a slight misjudgement of tone – about Hertz's reading of the Seventh Type as an approach to the 'secret places of the Muse' that brings Empson out in the company of de Man and other such essayers of language at the limit. In fact his more usual way of handling these 'deep' ambiguities is to admit that they may point back to some kind of 'deep' psychological disturbance or 'primitive' (pre-logical) confusion, but then suggest various ways to fit them into a rationally intelligible structure. Thus 'although such words appeal to the fundamental habits of the human mind, and are fruitful of irrationality, they are to be expected from a rather sophisticated state of language and of feeling' (*ST*, p. 195). It is at this point precisely that ambiguities of the Seventh Type may be seen to shade off into a version of pastoral, or a mode of understanding which treats them reflexively as topics for the play of self-conscious speculative thought.

Again, these ideas are often within reach of something very like the Kantian sublime, a topos much invoked by present-day theorists of a deconstructive or postmodern bent.[24] That is to say, they figure at the limit-point where thought comes up against some obstacle, some overwhelming force or check to its powers of cognitive grasp, such that the mind at first fails to discover any adequate (conceptual or linguistic) means of representation, but then turns this failure around, so to speak, by finding *within itself* the autonomous potential – the capacity for creative self-renewal – which transforms such experiences into a source of moral and imaginative strength. Empson's chapter on Marvell offers several striking examples, among them *The Ancient Mariner* (where 'so long as the Mariner is horrified by the creatures of the calm he is their slave; he is set free to act, in the supreme verses of the poem, as soon as he delights in them'), and the story by Poe where 'the sailor in *The Maelstrom* is so horrified as to be frozen, by a trick of neurosis, into idle curiosity, and this becomes a scientific interest in the portent which shows him the way to escape from it' (*SVP*, p. 101). Like 'The Garden', though in more dramatic fashion, these works communicate a powerful sense that the mind somehow contains all of nature, is able to comprehend or 'control' it through thought, so that differences between subject and object (or conscious and unconscious knowledge) are momentarily suspended in a state of achieved reflective equilibrium. All of which would tend to support Hertz's claim that Empson was at this time much engaged with issues in the region of the Kantian sublime.

But it is also worth noting how he gives the whole topic a markedly different philosophical slant by stressing the elements of conscious, rational, 'witty' or reflective self-knowledge that enable these poets to attain something like a perspective atop all the vexing antinomies that would otherwise threaten to 'freeze' thinking in a state of self-induced neurotic deadlock or disabling aporia. For here, as in *Seven Types*, Empson sees little hope for improved understanding in the kind of criticism that seeks out 'deep' conflicts – whether of a psychological or an epistemological order – with a view to pointing up the inherent limitations of rational-discursive thought. This is why he prefers to treat of the sublime (or its pastoral equivalent) as essentially a matter of 'putting the complex into the simple', of discovering some social-communicative basis for experiences that would otherwise occupy the realm of private neurosis or psychopathology. This 'grand theme' may have its 'root in magic' but is still very strong, Empson suggests, 'among the mountain climbers and often the scientists' (*SVP*, p. 100). In other words it is a source of very real practical (at times, life-saving) benefits which probably have to do with our capacity – especially when under pressure or in circumstances of extreme physical danger – to perform highly complex mental operations that are only called 'intuitive for lack of any adequate descriptive or analytical machinery. At any rate there does seem a need to distinguish between Empson's strikingly down-to-earth treatment of the sublime and those other (postmodernist or deconstructive) readings that emphasize its aporetic character, its paradoxical claim to 'present the unpresentable', or its power to discompose all the normative categories of thought and perception.

This difference is well brought out in Empson's gloss on the notion of 'transcendence' as it figures in the famous lines of Marvell describing the state of contemplative repose to which pastoral ideally gives access. ('The Mind, that Ocean where each kind /Does streight its own resemblance find; /Yet it creates, transcending these, /Far other worlds, and other Seas'.) His main point is that the paradoxes here can best be interpreted by trying to sort them into some kind of rational order, even while conceding, as the poem powerfully suggests, that there may be states of mind ('unconscious', 'preconscious' or whatever) that lie beyond reach of knowing exegesis or plain-prose commentary. What seems to be involved at this point, according to Empson, is

a transition from the correspondences of thought with fact to those of thought with thought, to find which is to be creative; there is necessarily here a suggestion of rising from one 'level' of thought to another; and in the next couplet not only does the mind transcend the world it mirrors, but a sea, to which it is parallel, transcends both land and sea too, which implies self-consciousness and all the antinomies of philosophy. Whether or not you give *transcendent* the technical sense 'predicable of all categories' makes no great difference; by including everything in itself the mind includes as a detail itself and all its inclusions. (*SVP*, pp. 104–5)

This passage comes as close as any to capturing the subtle transformation that the sublime undergoes when brought into contact with the Pastoral complex of themes, metaphors, or structural ironies. That is to say, there is a shift of philosophical viewpoint which also entails a certain shift of register or tone, a marked disinclination to dwell on the deeper, darker sources of sublime experience, and a corresponding stress on those aspects that belong to the order of conscious, reflective self-knowledge. In part this has to do with Empson's often-stated principle that the mind has to labour against considerable odds of prejudice, self-ignorance, or irrationality, and that criticism should therefore do its best to cast light on these blind-spots wherever they occur, rather than make matters worse by adopting its own kinds of obfuscatory rhetoric. This, as we have seen, is his attitude when dealing with ambiguities of the Seventh Type, and it is an outlook carried over into Pastoral by way of the various adaptive strategies (or techniques for 'putting the complex into the simple') which characterize that protean genre. But there is also, I think, a much stronger claim involved here, one that amounts to something more than just a matter of temperamental bias (i.e., Empson's characteristic 'tone' of sturdy commonsense rationalism), or a bottom-line pragmatist ground of appeal (his feeling that critics are best employed making 'decently intelligible' sense of any puzzles or obscurities that come their way). What is really at stake in all this is the question whether language *can* provide a basis for the kind of rationalist interpretive 'machinery' that Empson wishes to build on it. And indeed, the whole development of his critical thinking after *Seven Types* and *Some Versions* can be seen as an attempt to answer this question in a way that would hold up philosophically as well as helping with interpretive problems as and when they arise.

Pastoral would figure from this point of view as a cover-term or conveniently loose generic description for the kinds of text that enabled Empson to address matters of depth-psychology (or downright conflicts of motive and meaning) without giving way to an irrationalist persuasion that such cases must exceed all the powers of analytic thought. And he thinks it important to maintain this position since otherwise one is left, in literature as in life, at the mercy of impulses or drives that supposedly resist any form of enlightening explanatory grasp. As he puts it in a characteristic passage toward the close of *Seven Types*:

human life is so much a matter of juggling with contradictory impulses . . . that one is accustomed to thinking people are probably sensible if they follow first one, then the other, of two such courses; any inconsistency that it seems possible to act upon shows that they are in possession of the right number of principles, and have a fair title to humanity. Thus any contradiction is likely to have some sensible interpretation; and if you think of interpretations which are not sensible, it puts the blame on you. (p. 197)

As I have said, this adds up to an attitude fairly remote from the kind of brooding intensity or 'end-of-the-line' meditation that critics like Hertz and Paul de Man have discovered in Empson's early criticism.[25] There are two main points that such readings tend to ignore. The first has to do with his principled assumption that any conflicts uncovered by the depth-hermeneutical approach will most likely turn out to have some 'sensible' (that is, rationally explicable) meaning, as for instance when writers have to cope with the demands of opposed or contradictory value-systems and do so by keeping both in play through devices like ambiguity, pastoral, double-irony, multiple plots and so forth. From which it follows, secondly, that Empson sees little virtue in theories that equate the most valuable or furthest-reaching forms of critical insight with a knowledge that lies somehow beyond reach of rational analysis, or in a realm of 'paradox', 'aporia' or flat contradiction where reason fears to tread.

In his middle-period essays and reviews this aversion was most often expressed with regard to the American New Criticism and its bad habit – as Empson thought – of raising paradox into an absolute measure of poetic worth, a doctrine whose effect was to deny poetry any cognitive, assertoric, or truth-telling force and treat it as a purely rhetorical construction out of the various privileged tropes and figures that comprised the New Critical lexicon.[26] What Empson chiefly objects to here is the whole dogmatic apparatus of checks and prohibitions which theorists like W. K. Wimsatt ran up around the tenets of 'old' New Critical orthodoxy. In particular he rejects the twofold ban on 'intentionalist' readings and those that have resort to *paraphrase*, or any kind of plain-prose rendition, in the attempt to clarify nuances of meaning and style. In both cases, Empson argues, these critics are perversely denying themselves access to a level of everyday interpretive competence which operates in *all* varieties of human social exchange, from casual talk to the most complex forms of literary communication. The only result of setting up these absurd 'heresies' is to trivialize poetry and criticism by sealing them off within a realm of purely aesthetic meanings and values, a domain of 'pseudo-statements' where poets are assumed not to mean what they say in any serious sense, and where questions of argumentative validity (or truth and falsehood) cannot be raised without falling foul of one or another prohibition. 'Consider the Law, which might be expected to reject a popular fallacy; it recognizes amply that one can tell a man's intention, and ought to judge him by it. Only in the criticism of literature, a thing delicately concerned with human intimacy, are we told that we must give up all idea of knowing his intention.'[27] And the effect is even worse, as Empson came to feel, when this self-denying ordinance is joined on to an irrationalist craze for 'paradoxical' meanings (or deep symbolist interpretations) which make a full-scale programme of rejecting the appeal to normative standards of debate. For it then becomes possible for the high priests and mystagogues of Eng. Lit. fashion – mostly 'Neo-Christians' of varying doctrinal adherence – to impute all manner of repellent theological beliefs under cover of a theory (the 'intentional fallacy') that prevents the author from *arguing back* to any real or convincing effect.

That Empson felt obliged to take some of the blame for this bad state of affairs is evident in his 1963 review of an essay on George Herbert by T. S. Eliot, undoubtedly the single most influential figure in the Neo-Christian crusade. After all, he now reflects, *Seven Types* had got itself pretty deep into paradox and kindred forms of irrationalist rhetoric, not least in those climactic pages on Herbert that represent Ambiguity at its furthest (and undoubtedly most intriguing) reach. Empson's later thoughts are worth quoting at length since they bring out his reasons for rejecting this approach on moral, intellectual, and scholarly grounds.

> I put 'The Sacrifice' last of the examples in my book, to stand for the most extreme kind of ambiguity, because it presents Jesus as at the same time forgiving his torturers and condemning them to eternal torture. It now strikes me that my attitude was what I have come to call 'Neo-Christian'; happy to find such an extravagant specimen, I slapped the author on the back and egged him on to be even nastier. . . . [Rosamund] Tuve seemed disposed to treat me as a pagan stumbling towards the light. Clearer now about what the light illuminates, I am keen to stumble away from it.[28]

But in fact, if one then turns back to the offending pages, it soon becomes clear that Empson is not really doing himself justice, or has at any rate misremembered certain crucial details, in issuing this retrospective *mea culpa*. For the reading of Herbert by no means goes along with an irrationalist mystique that would elevate paradox (or the mysteries of Christian atonement) to the status of sublime or transcendent truths beyond reach of rational criticism. Indeed, the predominant tone of these pages is one of quizzical detachment mixed with a certain anthropological interest in the way that such ideas – 'deep-rooted' but nonetheless repellent – can exert a hold upon even the most subtle intelligences. Moreover, the effect is to credit Herbert himself with a degree of civilized, self-distancing irony that operates (like Pastoral) to place these harshly paradoxical notions in a larger context of socialized meanings and values. Thus 'the various sets of conflicts in the Christian doctrine of the Sacrifice are stated with an assured and easy simplicity, a reliable and unassuming grandeur, extraordinary in any material, but unique as achieved by successive fireworks of contradiction, and a mind jumping like a flea' (*ST*, p. 226). Such is indeed, as Empson views it, the chief virtue of the so-called 'metaphysical' style: this capacity to handle deep-seated conflicts of motive and belief by treating them *not* as profoundly paradoxical truths beyond reach of further analysis, but as puzzles best approached in a spirit of open-minded readiness for public debate.

So it is Empson's main objection to Wimsatt and the other guardians of New Critical orthodoxy that their precepts, if acted upon consistently, would leave no room for this kind of dialogical engagement, or indeed for any criticism that treated poetry as more than a pure, self-occupied play with its own tropological conventions. That is to say, one could always invoke the 'intentionalist fallacy' against any critic who presumed to find *arguments* (or propositional content) in poetry, and who then went on, like Empson, to suggest how those arguments might link up with questions of a psycho-biographical or wider socio-cultural import. And the 'heresy of paraphrase' would likewise come in handy for discrediting the notion – such a staple of Empson's approach in *Seven Types* – that one can make at least a decent shot at explaining what poems are about by offering a simplified prose re-statement of the passage in question (or multiple attempts to tease out the sense), and leaving the reader to sort these efforts into some kind of working synthesis. That there is no good reason *in principle* why this method shouldn't succeed – no reason, that is, having to do with poetry's uniquely 'paradoxical' mode of utterance, or its belonging to a realm of autonomous values discontinuous with the interests of plain-prose discourse – is an argument everywhere implicit in Empson's quarrel with the New Criticism. In *Seven Types*, writing in an age of happy innocence before these theoretical distractions cropped up, he just takes it pretty much for granted that critics are in the business of hunting out authorial intentions, and that where those intentions prove hard to establish – as happens with cases of 'advanced logical or psychological disorder' – then one had best cast around for some 'rational' explanation that at least gives the author full credit for not taking refuge in this or that half-baked 'paradoxical' creed. Otherwise criticism is liable to fall into a kind of reverse-Pastoral strategy, 'putting the simple into the complex', or making authors out to be more simple-minded – more completely at the mercy of irrational promptings – than need be supposed on a fairly basic principle of interpretive charity.

Empson made the point again in his 1950 contribution to a *Kenyon Review* symposium on 'verbal analysis' or the style of intensive close-reading which he, more than anyone, had been instrumental in promoting. 'These extra meanings are present,' Empson writes, 'not in any deep unconscious, but at the pre-conscious levels where we handle lexicon and grammar, in our ordinary talk, at the speed we do (surely the various current uses of a word must be in the mind somehow, or how can we pick out the right one so quickly?)'.[29] This passage takes up several arguments that are there implicitly in *Seven Types* but which only emerge to full view when Empson finds himself obliged to defend them in face of Neo-Christian, New Critical and other such emergent irrationalist trends. They include 1) the continuity-principle, that poetic understanding is not *essentially* different from the kinds of 'everyday' linguistic grasp required to make sense of straightforward communicative discourse; 2) the idea that criticism (like linguistics) had best focus on the 'preconscious' level of mental activity, since it is here – rather than by burrowing down to some notional 'unconscious' depths – that we are likeliest to get useful results; and 3) that any insights thus produced will involve not only a *semantics* of multiple meaning but also a *grammar* (or a logico-grammatical component) capable of fitting that semantics into a larger context of interpretive theory. Such was indeed the project that Empson had already undertaken in the work that occupied much of his time during the late 1940s, that is to say, the various essays that were eventually collected in his finest (but as yet little understood) book, *The Structure of Complex Words*. What I want to do now is give some idea of how that work developed out of his earlier interests, and then place it in relation to more current schools of literary theory. For if post-structuralists (among others) have much to learn from Empson – especially on questions of logic, language and truth – it will also mean unlearning some cardinal tenets of the latest theoretical wisdom on such matters.

III

I have suggested that Pastoral was one way forward from those vexing antinomies that Empson discovered when trying to make 'decently intelligible' sense of ambiguities of the Seventh Type. In fact one could read the whole sequence of chapters in *Some Versions* as a progress through stages of increasing psychological complexity, but a progress which at every point plays off 'deep' (often Freudian) conflicts of motive and meaning against a sense of the mind's remarkable capacity for turning such conflicts to creative account by treating them as topics for speculative thought. Thus 'there is too much self-knowledge here [in Lewis Carroll's *Alice* books] to make the game of psycho-analysis seem merely good fun' (*SVP*, p. 218). Empson's point is much akin to the argument of Paul Ricoeur in his book *Freud And Philosophy*: that depth-interpretation (the 'archaeological' approach) can only produce worthwhile results if it is joined to a 'teleological' account of how language opens up new possibilities of meaning through the exercise of imaginative powers vested in the nature of all symbolic understanding. There are, in short, 'two hermeneutics', two interpretations of interpretation, 'one turned toward the revival of archaic meanings, . . . the other toward the emergence of figures that anticipate our spiritual adventures'.[30] To concentrate on the first of these dimensions alone – as in the more reductive applications of psychoanalytic method – is to close one's mind to the signifying potential (or the scope for reflective self-understanding) that enables language to transcend the condition of enslavement to deep-seated irrational meanings and desires. As with Empson's reading of 'The Garden', the aim of such a critical hermeneutics would be to occupy the zone of linguistic creativity where symbols can mediate between the two realms of pre-reflective, instinctual desire and knowledge arrived at through the exercise of reason in its 'complex' or speculative mode. 'This [i.e., Marvell's handling of the theme] combines the idea of the conscious mind, including everything because understanding it, and that of the unconscious animal nature, including everything because in harmony with it' (*SVP*, p. 99). Both dimensions are necessary, as Empson (like Ricoeur) sets out to show, since between them they comprise a dialectics of interpretive thought in the absence of which there could be no accounting for language in its everyday, let alone its more creative aspects.

In this sense, Pastoral on Empson's understanding of the term is not so much a genre – a literary 'form' with clearly-marked stylistic attributes – as a kind of subjective correlative for feelings that would otherwise elude the best efforts of critical commentary. As Empson puts it in his chapter on 'Double Plots': 'the value of the state of mind which finds double irony natural is that it combines breadth of sympathy with energy of judgement; it can keep its balance among all the materials for judging' (*SVP*, p. 57). Or again: 'he [the ironist] gives the same pleasure to his audience, [since] the process brings to mind the whole body of their difficulty with so much sharpness and freshness that it may give the strength to escape from it' (p. 56). What characterizes all Empson's versions of Pastoral – and marks the shift of emphasis from *Seven Types* – is this way of translating private or self-locked conflicts into a register of socialized interests and values which can then find expression through various forms of complex ironic displacement. Thus literature is essentially 'a social process . . . an attempt to reconcile the conflicts of an individual in whom those of society will be mirrored' (p. 22). And this process works pretty well, Empson thinks, in so far as it helps to handle the various communicative problems that are sure to arise in any society where conflicting class-interests (or the specialized division of labour) make it difficult for writers to know just whom they are addressing, or at what precise level of 'conscious' or 'unconscious' reader-response.

This is why *Some Versions* often appeals to a certain idea of the theatre audience, especially in the Elizabethan period, as a useful analogue for what goes on when the reader confronts some problematic passage. 'Once you break into the godlike unity of the appreciator you find a microcosm of which the theatre is the macrocosm; the mind is complex and ill-connected like an audience, and it is as surprising in the one case as the other that a sort of unity can be produced by a play' (p. 60). The main advantage of thinking in these terms is that it takes some of the strain off depth-interpretation – or avoids the more dubious forms of 'psychological' criticism – by opening literature up to all the cross-winds of social and cultural difference. And to this extent it gives the interpreter a handle for understanding nuances or shades of implication that would fail to strike any critic too preoccupied with matters of profound psychological import. Empson makes the point with particular reference to Ernest Jones's essay on *Hamlet*, a reading whose chief fault, as he sees it, is the habit of assuming too readily that 'the only ideas with which an audience can be infected unconsciously are the fundamental Freudian ones' (p. 59). The effect is to narrow one's focus of interest to a point where the only 'explanations' that count are those that invoke some well-worn theme (like the Oedipus Complex) which offers little more than a catch-all interpretive slogan. But really the activity of audience-response is a lot more complex and therefore less subject to irrational drives and compulsions below the (presumed) threshold of conscious awareness. As Empson puts it:

> probably an audience does to some extent let loose the hidden traditional ideas common to its members, which may be a valuable process, but it also forms a small 'public opinion'; the mutual influence of its members' judgements, even though expressed by the most obscure means or only imagined from their presence, is so strong as to produce a sort of sensibility held in common, and from their variety it may be wider, more sensible, than that of any of its members. (*SVP*, p. 59)

And one can generalize this argument beyond the special case of plays that involve a 'pastoral' double-plot structure, or indeed beyond the confines of theatrical performance or stage-drama as such. For it is Empson's idea that the same approach would work for any text – lyric poems and novels included – that possessed a sufficient degree of attitudinal complexity, or a tendency to call out varying responses from different readers, social interest-groups, or (in Stanley Fish's phrase) 'interpretive communities'.[31] But he would also want to argue – as against Fish – that this diversity of actual or potential reader-response was enough to prevent such a theory from appealing to any one set of in-place consensus values conceived as placing limits on what counted as a good-faith or competent judgement at any given time. For it is precisely the virtue of this Pastoral attitude – indeed more an *attitude* than a genre, technique or regular structural device – that it does not force the critic to peer too fixedly into the 'very cauldron of the inner depths', and instead offers a reassuring sense that 'the appeal to a circle of a man's equals is the fundamental escape into the fresh air of the mind' (*SVP*, p. 59).

All the same there is a sense in which Pastoral could offer only a tentative and short-term solution to the problems that Empson encountered in his dealing with ambiguities of the Seventh Type. For the Pastoral ironist is a figure set about by all manner of conflicting pressures and demands, among them the claim of political commitment as against the more 'complex', self-occupied pleasures of a rich imaginative life. This dilemma is presented most explicitly in the book's opening chapter ('Proletarian Literature'), where Empson contrasts the various forms or modalities of Pastoral with the line of communist *Agitprop* thinking espoused by Soviet artist-intellectuals like Maxim Gorki. His main problem with work of this sort – despite Empson's plainly left-wing political sympathies – is that 'when it comes off I find I am taking it as pastoral literature; I read into it, or find that the author has secretly put into it, these more subtle, more far-reaching, and I think more permanent, ideas' (p. 23). That is to say, Pastoral has a breadth of appeal, a capacity for handling complex states of psychological and social (class-based) feeling, which Empson misses in the products of party-line Soviet propaganda. All the same he has to admit that there may be good reason for socialists to reject the whole Pastoral bag of tricks, relying as it does on a root metaphor (that of 'putting the complex into the simple') which can easily be used to insinuate some form of covert 'bourgeois' ideology. For there is often more than a hint of the idea – one that Empson finds pervasively at work in Gray's 'Elegy in a Country Churchyard' – that no amount of social or political reform could ever significantly change the basic facts of human injustice, waste and inequality; that 'gifted' individuals somehow have a natural right to their class-privileges, since after all they are the ones best fitted (whether by talent or breeding) to make good use of them; and therefore that such individuals should reconcile themselves to the existing order – despite all its manifest imperfections – in a spirit of tragic pathos mixed with a certain melancholy irony. In other words, there is no prospect of large-scale social improvement – or of lessening the number of mute, inglorious Miltons – so one had better just accept that this is the case and perhaps turn it to creative account through one or another complex variation on the pastoral theme.

Empson is very far from endorsing this sentiment, and indeed expresses sympathy with those readers who, 'without being communists, have been irritated by the complacence in the massive calm of the poem' (*SVP*, p. 12). For there is, he acknowledges, a 'cheat in the implied politics', a naturalizing gambit that enables the author to carry off this piece of class propaganda by exploiting the pastoral convention in a way that cuts out alternative arguments. Thus the tone of melancholy claims that the poet understands the considerations opposed to aristocracy, though he judges against them; the truism of the reflections in the churchyard, the universality and impersonality this gives to the style, claim as if by comparison that we ought to accept the injustice of society as we do the inevitability of death. (p. 12)

On the strength of such passages one might well suppose that Empson shared the feeling expressed by many left-wing critics of pastoral, Raymond Williams among them: that this is a genre so riddled with attitudes of hypocrisy, class-prejudice and patronage that any good-willed effort to redeem its fortunes is liable to fall into the same posture.[32] But in fact Empson goes on directly to claim that Gray's poem expresses one of the 'permanent truths' of human existence; namely, that 'it is only in degree that any improvement in society could prevent wastage of human powers', since 'the waste even in a fortunate life, the isolation even of a life rich in intimacy, cannot but be felt deeply, and is the central feeling of tragedy' (p. 12). As so often with *Some Versions* it is difficult to know where paraphrase shades off into generalizing comment on Empson's part, or where the attempt to view all sides of a problem – one of the main virtues of Pastoral, as Empson conceives it – leans over into something more like an outlook of generous, all-accepting irony. At any rate one could hazard that sentiments of this sort would find little favour with Gorki, or indeed with Raymond Williams at those points in his work where Pastoral figures as a powerful (if oblique) expression of ruling-class interests.

Nor would these critics be at all mollified by Empson's subsequent efforts in this chapter to work out the basis of a reasonable compromise between the claims of Pastoral sentiment and those of straightforward social justice.

Now all these ideas are very well suited to a socialist society, and have been made to fit in very well with the dogma of the equality of man, but I do not see that they fit in with a rigid proletarian aesthetic. . . . They assume that some people are more delicate and complex than others, and that if these people can be kept from doing harm it is a good thing, though a small thing by comparison with our common humanity. (p. 23)

This theme is one that Empson takes up at greater length in his discussion of Shakespeare's Sonnet 94 ('They that have power to hurt and will do none'). But it is present throughout *Some Versions* as a running subtext, a kind of oblique confessional burden that regularly implicates 'the critic' – or the theorist of Pastoral – on terms that create an uneasy sense of the structural injustice, the exploitative order of social relations whereby such figures can assume their privileged mediating role. I cannot begin to summarize the extraordinary twists and contortions of imputed motive that Empson manages to tease out in his reading of Shakespeare's savagely double-edged 'tribute' to the shadowy patron. Indeed it is one of the great ironies of this book that it breezily flouts the New Critical veto on paraphrasing poems – most often by offering multiple attempts at prose summary – while its own interpretations are so complex (or so hedged about with qualifying ironies) that no paraphrase could possibly do them justice.

But if one thing is clear it is the fact that Shakespeare's sonnet is here taking on a surrogate burden of anxieties and obscure guilt-feelings that have to do mainly with Empson's sense of the strong counter-arguments, ethical and political, that rise up against the whole complex of Pastoral ideas. Thus for instance:

> I must praise to you [i.e., the patron] your very faults, especially your selfish-ness, because you can only now be safe by cultivating them further; yet this is the most dangerous of necessities; people are greedy for your fall as for that of any of the great; indeed no one can rise above common life, as you have done so fully, without in the same degree sinking below it; you have made this advice real to me because I cannot despise it for your sake; I am only sure that you are valuable and in danger. (p. 85)

It is a remarkable passage for various reasons, not least the degree of self-implicating irony – or the hint of a readiness to view his own efforts in a similar, none too flattering light – that comes across in Empson's speculative treatment of the background situation in the Sonnets. At any rate it seems only 'sensible' (as Empson might say) to suppose that such otherwise very curious pieces of commentary will turn out to bear some tangible relation to the ironies that characterize the Pastoral stance in its literary-critical guise. And that relation is best understood, I think, in terms of the conflicting values or priorities that emerge so often when Empson touches on matters of ethical or socio-political concern. For it is here that Pastoral once again comes up against the problem he had addressed in the reply to Sparrow and the closing (mainly theoretical) chapter of *Seven Types*: that is to say, the issue of 'analytical' *versus* 'appreciative' criticism, or the question how best to reconcile these seemingly divergent lines of approach.

At that time, we may recall, Empson had declared himself strongly in favour of a rationalist philosophy of mind and language, an attitude that effectively minimized the difference between poetry and other (prosaic or 'everyday') kinds of discourse. After all, as he remarks, 'analytical is more cheerful than appreciative criticism (both, of course, must be present) precisely because there is less need to agonize over these questions of tone' (*ST*, p. 251). But one doesn't have to read very far into *Some Versions* to see how these 'questions of tone' are still an issue, not only as regards the mode of address best suited to literary criticism, but also in relation to the intellectual's role *vis-à-vis* questions of social and political justice. It is only with *The Structure of Complex Words*, his most ambitious and philosophically far-reaching work, that Empson manages to articulate the interests of critical theory with those of a broad-based humanist ethic which no longer runs the risk — ever-present for the Pastoral critic — of finding itself 'forced into tragic isolation by sheer strength of mind'. What seems to have brought this change about (at much the same time, incidentally, as Empson officially 'gave up' writing poetry) was the shift from a mode of verbal exegesis trained up on the depth-psychological approach to a socialized account of meaning and context that enabled an escape into the 'larger air' of open public debate. Toward the end of *Seven Types* he had rather fretfully noted that 'I am treating the act of communication as something very extraordinary, so that the next step would be to lose faith in it altogether' (p. 243). And the best alternative at that stage seemed to be an attitude of sturdy (if 'prosaic') rationalism which at least had the virtue of making poems more accessible to our ordinary waking habits of thought. Besides, 'it often happens that, for historical reasons or what not, one can no longer appreciate a thing directly by poetical knowledge, and yet can rediscover it in a more controlled form by prosaic knowledge' (p. 243). But again this gives rise to all the troublesome antinomies — intuitive/analytic, creative/critical, poetry/prose and so forth — which Empson was to pursue (though never fully to resolve) through the various generic displacements of Pastoral irony. In *Seven Types* he can offer little more than the general observation that 'a poetical word is a thing conceived in itself and contains all its meanings', whereas 'a prosaic word is flat and useful and might have been used differently' (p. 252). In which case the relation between poetry and criticism would remain a highly puzzling, paradoxical affair, best handled — as Empson pragmatically concludes — by 'trying to understand as many things as possible', and not getting too hung-up on philosophical problems.

In *Some Versions* those problems reemerge in the form of a deepening reflective irony which at times takes on a distinctly Hegelian character. In fact Empson mentions Hegel only in passing (p. 24) but the book has numerous passages that suggest at least some measure of familiarity with his thought. Thus the Pastoral progress through stages of increasing ironic detachment finds a parallel in Hegel's phenomenology of Mind on its journey from the first stirrings of reflective thought to the highest, most developed forms of speculative reason.[33] And this parallel is closest when Empson (like Hegel) stresses the element of 'unhappy consciousness', or the internal conflicts and divisions that Mind encounters in the course of its spiritual odyssey. It may be wise not to push these analogies too hard since Empson did not take kindly to critics who hunted out obscure 'philosophical' ideas in his work. All the same there are

passages in *Some Versions*, and indeed whole aspects of the Pastoral genre as
Empson conceives it, which can best be understood in light of such ideas.
(Besides, he had reviewed a good number of books that reflected the lingering
influence of German idealist philosophy on British thinkers, even after the
famous 'revolution' brought about by Russell, Moore and their contemporaries.)
Anyway it would seem at least plausible to argue that these interests are
somewhere in the background when Empson writes (in his chapter on the *Alice*
books) that Pastoral may well involve reflection on 'the mysteries of self-
knowledge, the self-contradictions of the will, the antinomies of philosophy,
the very Looking Glass itself' (*SVP*, p. 232). Such a passage carries overtones
not only of Hegel but of the whole post-Kantian development of thought
which explored these speculative (mirror-like) abysses encountered by consciousness in its quest for self-knowledge. One could even suggest that Pastoral,
on its widest definition, performs the same role as Romantic Irony in the
thinking of those German critic–philosophers (the Schlegel brothers chief
among them) who raised it into a high point and principle of all modern art.[34]
At any rate there is a clearly-marked kinship – especially so toward the end of
Some Versions – between the Romantic Ironist and the Pastoral 'critic-as-hero',
that figure set about by all the vexing contradictions which philosophy is
finally unable to resolve, and which literature can only express through forms
of increasingly complex ironic displacement. '*Wonderland* is a dream, but the
Looking Glass is self-consciousness'; at which point Pastoral undergoes something like a qualitative change, an extreme dissociation of 'conscious' and
'unconscious' realms, such that there exist no social or generic conventions – no
forms of communal understanding – capable of bridging the distance between
them.

I am not the first reader to suggest a certain unacknowledged kinship
between Empson and the avatars of German nineteenth-century idealist and
speculative thought. There is some interesting commentary to much this effect
in an early essay by Paul de Man ('The Dead End of Formalist Criticism')[35]
where he praises Empson as the one figure in recent Anglo-American debate
who had perceived how 'true poetic ambiguity' takes rise from a 'deep division
of Being', an ontological difference (to adopt the Heideggerian idiom) that
cannot be reconciled by any degree of interpretive or hermeneutic tact. 'What
is the Pastoral convention,' de Man asks,

> if not the eternal separation between the mind that distinguishes, negates,
> legislates, and the originary simplicity of the natural? A separation that may be
> lived, as in Homer's poetry (evoked by Empson as an example of the universality
> of its definition), or may be thought in full consciousness of itself as in Marvell's
> poem. There is no doubt that the pastoral theme is, in fact, the only poetic
> theme, that it is poetry itself. Under the deceitful title of a genre study, Empson

has actually written an ontology of the poetic, but wrapped it, as is his wont, in some extraneous matter that may well conceal the essential. (*BI*, p. 239)

His comments are fully justified as regards that aspect of Empsonian Pastoral irony that becomes more complex and elusive – more susceptible to depth-interpretation – as the genre approaches its limit-point in Carroll's curious variations on the theme. In short, de Man fastens unerringly on those elements in the Pastoral complex of ideas which enable him to make the looked-for connection with German Romanticism, Hegel's 'unhappy consciousness', and Heidegger's late meditations on language, poetry and ontological difference.[36] These affinities are, as I have said, well worth noting, and certainly they offer an 'angle' on Pastoral – a philosophic and historical point of entry – which seems to have escaped most of Empson's Anglo-American commentators.

But de Man is less perceptive (indeed quite uncomprehending) when it comes to that other, social and political dimension which plays an equally important role in the various generic transformations that Empson traces down through the history of Pastoral thought. In fact it is a chief claim of de Man's essay that sociological (especially Marxist) approaches are sure to go wrong at a certain point when they allow such short-term political concerns to substitute for the 'deep division of Being' that characterizes all authentic thinking on the nature of poetic language. Thus 'Marxism is, ultimately, a poetic thought that lacks the patience to pursue its own conclusions to their end'. And again, more explicitly:

> having started out from the premises of the strictest aesthetic formalism, Empson winds up facing the ontological question. It is by virtue of this question that he stands as a warning against certain Marxist illusions. The problem of separation inheres in Being, which means that social forms of separation derive from ontological and meta-social attitudes. For poetry, the divide exists for ever. (*BI*, p. 240)

This all follows directly from de Man's Heideggerian conviction that history and politics belong to a merely 'factical' dimension, a level of thought unconcerned with questions of a deeper (authentic or primordial) import. But if there is, undeniably, an aspect of Pastoral that answers to this depth-hermeneutical approach, there is still a great deal that de Man has to leave out of account in order to make his interpretation stick. For one thing, he ignores the Empsonian stress on those countervailing values of wit, self-critical irony and social 'poise' which most often make possible the Pastoral escape into a wider dimension of meaningful exchange between various classes, interest-groups, or interpretive communities. Where this dimension is lacking – or where the writer retreats, like Lewis Carroll, into a near-private world of obsessional motifs where his sanity is barely saved by the shift to a different, narrower range of reader-response – then Empson sees it as a basically *pathological* variant of the Pastoral theme, and not (like de Man) as conveying a fundamental truth about poetry and language.

This difference comes out most strikingly at those points where Empson's commentary seems within reach of a generalized 'existential' brooding on the facts of human isolation, mortality, and finitude. 'Once at least in each book,' he remarks,

> a cry of loneliness goes up from Alice at the oddity beyond sympathy or communication of the world she has entered – whether that in which the child is shut by weakness, or the adult by the renunciations necessary both for the ideal and the worldly way of life (the strength of the snobbery is to imply that these are the same). (*SVP*, p. 230)

It is an extraordinary passage, to be sure, and one that goes so far beyond a straightforward response to the 'words on the page' that it must suggest some similar burden of anxiety on Empson's part, or at any rate a strongly-marked predisposition to find such meanings at work. But again, there is a crucial difference between the sombre pathos of de Man's Heideggerian rhetoric – according to which this 'division of Being' is inherent in the very nature of 'authentic' language, poetry, and thought – and Empson's idea that it only comes about at moments of extreme psychological stress when the normal machinery of communication has somehow broken down. Hence the tone of sturdy rationalism that comes across even when Empson is commenting on the strangest episodes in the *Alice* books.

> One must be struck by the depth at which the satire is hidden; the queerness of the incident and the characters takes on a Wordsworthian grandeur and aridity, and the landscape defined by the tricks of facetiousness has the remote and staring beauty of the ideas of the insane. (p. 232)

Nothing could be further from de Man's in the end rather placid and self-supporting strain of 'ontological' pathos, his assumption (following Heidegger) that language must *always and everywhere* enact that dehiscence or cleft within the thought of Being whose history is that of 'Western metaphysics' at large. For de Man, once more,

> the ambiguity poetry speaks of is the fundamental one that prevails between the world of the spirit and the world of sentient substance: to ground itself, the spirit must turn itself into sentient substance, but the latter is knowable only in its dissolution into non-being. The spirit cannot coincide with its object and this separation is infinitely sorrowful. (*BI*, p. 237)

Again, I would not wish to deny that this commentary responds to something genuinely 'there' in Empson's criticism, a sense of the alarming depths that may always be revealed when Pastoral irony fails to discover any adequate social or communicative means to externalize these deep-rooted conflicts. But to turn this into a profound truth about literature, criticism and language *in general* is to misread Empson in pursuit of a thesis which he would surely and emphatically reject. For it assumes – against all the evidence of *Some Versions* – that the most typical or representative instances of Pastoral are those which stand, like the *Alice* books, on the verge of self-locked neurotic inhibition or a breakdown in the circuits of communal exhange between 'complex' and 'simple' modes of understanding. And this gets the message of the book completely upside-down. What has changed since Marvell so adroitly conjured his witty variations on this theme is the fact that Carroll must now resort to 'child-cult' – a belated, neurotic, self-isolating variant of Pastoral – in order to articulate feelings that can find no alternative mode of expression, no escape into the 'larger air' of socialized values and conventions. As Empson remarks of this curious development, 'the pathos of its futility is that it is an attempt of reason to do the work of emotion and escape the dangers of the emotional approach to life' (p. 231). In short, we shouldn't take such limiting cases of the Pastoral genre – instances that mark a near-crisis or collapse of all its working values and assumptions – as in any sense conveying some ultimate truth at the end of critical enquiry.

Empson makes this point most explicitly when discussing 'The Garden' and Marvell's deft way with the antinomies of mind and nature, subject and object, or conscious and unconscious modes of knowledge. Later on – with the advent of Romanticism and a mystical–intuitive (Wordsworthian) approach to such themes – it would appear that by far the most valuable moments in poetry were those when the mind transcended such bad antinomies and achieved a kind of hypostatic union, a condition of unmediated inwardness with the forms and appearances of nature. In Marvell, however, the emphasis falls rather differently, and Empson makes no secret of his preference for the earlier Pastoral style.

> The value of these moments made it fitting to pretend they were eternal; and yet the lightness of his expression of their sense of power is more intelligent, and so more convincing, than Wordsworth's solemnity on the same theme, because it does not forget the opposing forces. (*SVP*, p. 108)

De Man is just as sceptical as Empson about the visionary claims of 'high romantic argument', the idea – taken over by mainstream scholars of Romanticism like M. H. Abrams – that poetry can actually attain to this wished-for condition of organic communion with nature or pure, self-present, unmediated access to the processes of natural development and growth. In fact it is a notion that he regards as having produced all manner of mischievous effects, among them that potent 'aesthetic ideology' whose avatars range (improbably enough) from idealist poet-philosophers like Schiller to Nazi propagandists like Goebbels. By far the greater part of de Man's critical work from the mid-1960s on, including his classic essay 'The Rhetoric of Temporality', was devoted to the business of deconstructing this mystified organicist creed.[37] But unlike Empson he always took it for granted that the only kind of criticism adequate to this task was one that engaged texts at a level where conscious meanings or motives played little part, and where language itself could be shown to enact the endless dialectical interplay of 'blindness' and 'insight'. This presumption remains constant in de Man across some otherwise very marked shifts of emphasis, including his abandonment of the Heideggerian jargon of authenticity in favour of a more technical, analytic idiom which eschews such potentially coercive sources of rhetorical pathos and instead examines texts in light of the distinction – revived from the classical *trivium* – between logic, grammar, and rhetoric.[38] Still there is no question, for de Man, of criticism concerning itself with 'witty' tricks of style – or 'preconscious' subleties of thought and technique, as in the Marvell poem – that would enable the escape into what Empson breezily calls the 'fresh air of the mind'.

It is impossible to imagine de Man coming up with those passages of joky paraphrase, offhand commentary and sidelong reflection which characterize Empson's chapter on 'The Garden'. But this is very much the point of his essay: that one may do better not to stand on one's dignity – like Wordsworth (or de Man) when confronted with these 'deep' ontological questions – since there is perhaps more wisdom to be had by following Marvell's good-humoured example and allowing the mind full scope for its exercise of 'conscious' and 'unconscious' powers. 'Only a metaphysical poet with so perfect a sense of form and so complete a control over the tricks of the style, at the end of its development, could actually dramatize these hints as he gave them' (*SVP*, p. 119). Again, nothing could be further from de Man's dark-toned meditations on Pastoral, his talk of 'ontological difference' and other such portentous themes. And this is at least partly a matter of *tone*, of de Man's being deaf to those inflections in Empson's writing that do not, as he puts it, 'forget the opposing forces', or the claims of a witty, self-conscious, speculative reason, as against the claims of a depth-hermeneutic that finds no room for such qualities. For it is, according to Empson, one great virtue of the Pastoral complex of feelings that it points a way beyond these deadlocked antinomies, allowing us to glimpse, momentarily at least, a happier state of mind where they would no longer seem anything like so urgent or compelling.

It is the mood well captured by Empson's gloss on some lines from 'The Garden' which, as he reads them, have to do precisely with this wise passivity or state of reflective equillibrium:

Self-knowledge is possible in such a state so far as the unruly impulses are digested, ordered, made transparent, not by their being known, at the time, as unruly. Consciousness no longer makes an important distinction; the impulses, since they must be balanced already, neither need it to put them right nor are put wrong by the way it forces across their boundaries. They let themselves be known because they are not altered by being known, because their principle of indeterminacy no longer acts. This idea is important for all the versions of pastoral, for the pastoral figure is always ready to be the critic; he not only includes everything but may in some unexpected way know it. (*SVP*, p. 103)

One could plausibly say of this passage, as indeed of many others in *Some Versions*, that it moves within the ambit of romantic irony and of all those self-reflexive puzzles and paradoxes that occupy a critic like de Man. But in that case one would have to go on and specify just why this comparison ultimately misses the mark, or how it is that Empson's treatment of the Pastoral theme opens up such strikingly different possibilities of feeling and thought. For it does seem somewhat off the point, as Empson might say, to compare this sequence of deftly-handled paradoxes with the notions of specular regress or textual *mise-en-abîme* that link deconstruction to its intellectual sources in the German romantic tradition. And here it might be useful to recall his gloss on a single word from 'The Garden' which strikes Empson as somehow condensing this entire range of implications.

Happiness, again, names a conscious state, and yet involves the idea of things falling right, happening so, not being ordered by an anxiety of the conscious reason. (So that as a rule it is a weak word; it is by seeming to look at it hard and bring out its implications that the verse here makes it act as a strong one.)
(*SVP*, p. 104)

From de Man's viewpoint – as presented in that early, admiring essay on Empson – this could only figure as a momentary lapse, a retreat from his otherwise exemplary insistence that Pastoral offers no false promise of reconciliation, no means of overcoming the 'ontological difference' (or the deep 'division of Being') that inhabits all forms of authentic reflection on language, poetry, and criticism. For it is a truth beyond question, at this stage of de Man's thinking, that any hint of 'reconciliation' between mind and nature, subject and object or conscious and unconcious thought-processes will always turn out to involve a certain motivated 'blindness' – or strategy of self-willed evasion – on the critic's part.

In fact the essay tells us much more about de Man and his distinctive (not to say obsessive) concerns than it does about Empsonian Ambiguity and Pastoral. So determined is he to find in Empson a strong precursor for his own kind of criticism that he misreads the chapter on Marvell as an exercise in the 'essentially negative activity of thought', one in which the poem's climactic lines ('Annihilating all that's made /To a green thought in a green shade') are glossed as reflecting on the *destruction* of nature through the mind's relentless powers of self-ironizing inwardness or negation. Thus 'it [the word "green"] is reintroduced at the very moment when this world has been annihilated. It is the freshness, the greenness of budding thought that can evoke itself only through the memory of what it destroys on its way' (*BI*, p. 239). One can see very well why de Man wanted to read both the poem and Empson's essay this way. It is a reading that perfectly endorses his idea of how criticism can work to deconstruct the fallacious organicist or naturalizing drive that subtends all versions of 'aesthetic ideology', all attempts to treat poetry as somehow sharing in the life-world of natural processes and forms. But this does not make it any more convincing as an account of what Empson *actually says* in the course of his essay on 'The Garden'. What de Man has to ignore, or consistently play down in keeping with his whole Heideggerian line of approach, is the extraordinary sense of intellectual uplift, the excitement and feeling of new-found creative possibilities, that Empson finds everywhere implicit in Marvell's handling of the Pastoral theme. Thus:

> the personalized Nature is treated both as external to man and as created by an instinct of the mind, and by tricks of language these are made to seem the same. But if they were simply called the same we would not be so easily satisfied by the tricks. What we feel is that though they are essentially unlike they are practically unlike in different degrees at different times; a supreme condition can therefore be imagined, though not attained, in which they are essentially alike. (To put it like this is no doubt to evade a philosophic issue.) A hint of the supreme condition is thus found in the actual one (this makes the actual one include everything in itself), but this exalted claim is essentially joined to humility; it is effective only through the admission that it is only a hint. (*SVP*, p. 112)

Of course it might be said – and any follower of de Man would most likely be quick to make this point – that the crucial sentence here is the throwaway parenthesis; that Empson has indeed managed to evade the chief 'philosophic issue', namely the insuperable distance that exists between beings and Being, or the sheer *impossibility* that mind should achieve such an easygoing commerce with the realm of physical nature. But this is to assume that 'philosophy' (or real, authentic philosophy) can only be construed in Heideggerian terms as a thinking of the 'ontological difference' which will always be found unavoidably installed at the heart of philosophical reflection. And it is precisely this idea that Empson challenges by stressing the mind's capacity, at least on rare occasions, to think its way creatively *through and beyond* the subject/object or conscious/unconcious antinomies.

His point is not at all to reject 'philosophy' (since *Some Versions* is a deeply 'philosophical' book on almost any definition of the term), but to show what possible alternatives exist for the kind of intelligence that can treat these problems at full imaginative stretch. Moreover, the condition for attaining such insight is that the mind should not become too preoccupied with these and kindred ontological questions, but instead take acount of the social dimension – the multiplicity of human interests and values – that Pastoral brings into play. This is why the 'apparently exalted claim' is 'essentially joined to humility', since it can only work at all insofar as it acknowledges the complex nature of its own satisfactions and the force of opposing arguments. Thus 'something of the tone of pastoral is inherent in the claim; the fault of the Wordsworthian method seems to be that it does not show this' (*SVP*, p. 112). And the same might be said of de Man's account insofar as it makes a programmatic point of ignoring (or suppressing) the social aspects of Pastoral, along with that closely-related dimension where 'deep' anxieties discover an escape-route into the 'larger air' of speculative reason.

IV

To say that all this drops out of the picture on de Man's reading of Empson is to point up the shift of priorities that has occurred in recent literary theory. *Some Versions* offers at least the common ground of an interest in romantic irony – though Empson never uses that term – and a readiness to pursue this topic into regions where criticism (in de Man's words) opens up 'unexpected perspectives on human complexity' (*BI*, p. 238). But that is about as far as the resemblance goes, since Empson, as we have seen, wants to keep these puzzles firmly on the side of reflective self-knowledge, rather than raise 'fundamental' questions beyond hope of rational debate. And in *The Structure of Complex Words* he develops a line of argument that goes clean against the working assumptions of just about every modern school of literary-critical thought, from the 'old' New Criticism to deconstruction. All that I can reasonably hope to do, in the limited space available here, is outline some of the book's major claims and suggest what kind of alternative they offer to these taken-for-granted values and beliefs. This will serve some purpose if at least a few readers are thereby persuaded to investigate the book which Empson considered his most important work, but which commentators have treated with reactions ranging from indifference to bafflement or downright uninformed hostility.

Nor are these responses hard to understand, given the extent of Empson's disagreement with various present-day orthodoxies. For *Complex Words* is a book dedicated to several quite explicit propositions. These include 1) the defence of liberal humanism, or of an ethics of interpretation that builds on liberal-humanist values and assumptions; 2) the indispensability of truth, or of a truth-functional approach to questions of literary meaning which comes out squarely against all forms of cultural-relativist doctrine; 3) the idea that literary texts *make statements* (or possess an assertoric force) unaccounted for by any theory that treats multiple meaning in purely rhetorical terms, whether of 'irony', 'ambiguity', 'paradox', 'intertextuality' or whatever; and 4) the argument that criticism therefore needs some grounding in the kind of semantic theory (or analytical philosophy of language) that might hope to provide at least a working basis for the conduct of interpretive debate. To which might be added the 'commonsense' belief, so strong in Empson's writing at every stage, that poetry (and literary criticism likewise) were continuous with the interests of everyday (social and moral) human wellbeing, and were therefore ill-served by any theory, no matter how sophisticated, which made that continuity more difficult to sustain.

Such was his response to the American New Criticism, a movement that Empson increasingly came to see as given over to a species of irrationalist rhetoric (witness the privilege accorded to figures like paradox), joined to a strongly-marked 'neo-Christian' strain of orthodox religious values. Thus 'any poet who tells his readers what he thinks about the world is getting mixed up with Truth, which [Cleanth] Brooks wants to keep out of poetry'.[39] In fact one can see him getting more and more suspicious of 'theory' as the books come in for review, to the point where almost anything with a tinge of philosophical reflection strikes Empson as most likely just a pretext for some new kind of obfuscating abstract talk. But he is also very aware that the appeal to unexamined commonsense values is one that can easily slide over into mere prejudice or inert conformist thinking: 'the English like to assume that they are sensible, therefore don't require abstruse theory, but there is no guarantee of that'.[40] What Empson really found most objectionable in the works of 'theory' that came his way from the early 1950s on was the specialization of lit-crit method as a means of isolating poetry (or fiction) from language in its everyday constative or truth-telling mode. Indeed, as we have seen, it is an issue that goes right the way back to his quarrel with Richards over the latter's idea that poetry belonged to a realm of 'emotive' pseudo-statement, a domain where values of truth and falsehood simply didn't apply. Later on he was to find the same principle at work – despite the large shift of ontological priorities – in the New Critics' thoroughly 'perverse' refusal to entertain questions of authorial intention or relevant background knowledge. For this was just the end-result, as Empson put it, of 'imitating the Logical Positivist in a different field of study', or allowing a narrowly prescriptive idea of what counted as veridical knowledge to dictate in matters far beyond its legitimate scope. The trouble with such self-denying ordinances – no matter how strongly backed up 'in theory' – was that they cut out so much of the rational sense-making activity which, in the end, was the critic's only claim on the reader's interest or attention.

The same kind of prejudice was still much in evidence – or so Empson thought – in those varieties of structuralist or post-structuralist criticism that began to emerge on the Anglo-American scene in the mid 1970s. Thus, of Frank Kermode's *The Genesis of Secrecy*: 'he looks at a landscape with half-closed eyes through a mist, or in a Claude-glass, or upside down from between his legs; and this is not a good way to read a novel, which is usually better read as if it were a history'.[41] What Empson caught more than a hint of in Kermode's book was the idea, nowadays a staple of postmodernist thought, that ultimately all kinds of discourse (history and theory included) come down to a fictive or tropological dimension, a level where the explanations run out and 'truth' can only be a matter of choice between various competing narratives, discourses, or paradigms.[42] This struck him – predictably – as just another instance of the way that 'sophisticated' textualist theories could produce all manner of perverse misjudgement or dead-end sceptical doctrine. In *Complex Words* he had set out to produce nothing less than a full-scale rejoinder to these and other versions of the widespread irrationalist or counter-enlightenment drift which Empson considered such a harmful influence on present-day literary studies. Small wonder, therefore, that he saw little virtue in those forms of 'advanced' post-structuralist theory that not only ignored his book but seemed bent upon denying any relation between literature, criticism and the interests of truth-seeking rational enquiry.[43]

He strikes the same note in a 1977 review of Raymond Williams's *Keywords*, a book which one might have expected Empson to admire – or at any rate treat sympathetically – since it adopts something very like his own procedure, in *Complex Words*, of analysing the verbal 'equations' (or structures of compacted propositional meaning) contained in certain crucial or ideologically loaded terms.[44] On the contrary: Williams (as Empson reads him) has greatly exaggerated the power of such words to influence our thinking in ways that put language beyond all reach of self-critical or reasoned thought. Thus 'part of the gloom, I think, comes from a theory which makes our minds feebler than they are – than they have to be, if they are to go through their usual performance with language'. And the review ends up with a baleful glance in the direction of other recent movements in criticism:

> The longest entry in the book . . . is for *structural*, and here my sympathy breaks down altogether; the theories he is describing seem to me terrible waffle. What he needs to consider is the structure relating two meanings in any one of his chosen words, so that they imply or insinuate a sentence: 'A is B'. Under what conditions are they able to impose a belief that the speaker would otherwise resist? As he never considers that, he is free to choose any interpretation that suits his own line of propaganda.[45]

Of course this amounts to a summary description of exactly the project that
Empson had undertaken in *The Structure of Complex Words*. And it also suggests
why he took exception to that other kind of 'structuralist' thinking – the kind
represented by Williams's *Keywords* entry – which derived mainly from French
developments in the wake of Saussure. For this theory took it as axiomatic
that language was a network of signifying features 'without positive terms';
that meaning was constituted through the play of differential elements (i.e.,
the contrastive structures of sound and sense), rather than forms of logico-
semantic entailment; and therefore that questions of truth and reference were
strictly off limits for any account of language, or any literary theory, that
sought to describe these characteristics in a properly *structural* mode.[46] One
could argue (as I have elsewhere) that this whole development took rise from a
basic misunderstanding of Saussure, a desire on the part of literary theorists to
extend his various heuristic formulations (such as the 'arbitrary' nature of the
sign) from the specialized field of synchronic language-study to the entire
domain of cultural and textual representation.[47] Hence – among other things –
the reflex post-structuralist aversion to that typecast mythical entity, the
'classic realist text', along with the high valuation attached to its equally
mythical counterpart, the text that multiplies meanings to infinity and slips all
the bonds of naturalized reference or 'bourgeois' realism.[48] In any case it is
clear that, to this way of thinking, criticism achieves its best, most 'radical' or
liberating insights when it ceases to concern itself with truth, valid argument
or other such (supposedly) ideological values.

So one can understand why Empson should have viewed these developments
as a mere continuation of the 'old' New Criticism by different rhetorical
means. In *Complex Words* he sets out the alternative case for a rationalist
semantics, or a truth-functional theory of literature and criticism, which would
point the way beyond these various kinds of last-ditch sceptical doctrine.
Although the book was written some two decades before French structuralism
made its appearance on the Anglo-American scene, it does have an Appendix
on Leonard Bloomfield's *Language* – one of the major works of structural
linguistics in its other, US-domesticated form – which anticipates some of the
same basic issues.[49] What Empson chiefly objects to in Bloomfield's approach
is the behaviorist assumption that one can only have a 'scientific' theory of
language insofar as one brackets out all considerations of how the mind actually
works in producing or interpreting words in context. 'This whole notion of the
scientist viewing language from outside and above is a fallacy; we would have
no hope of dealing with the subject if we had not a rich obscure practical
knowledge from which to extract the theoretical' (*CW*, p. 438). And again:
'till you have decided what a piece of language conveys, like any literary critic,
you cannot look round to see what "formal features" convey it; you will then
find that some features are of great subtlety, and perhaps fail to trace some at

all' (p. 437). The main problem with Bloomfield's approach is that he wants to exclude all 'mentalist' criteria – all reference to the powers of cognitive grasp or interpretive 'competence' possessed by individual language-users – while claiming to provide a full-scale structural analysis of language not only at the level of phonetics (where this approach might work at least up to a point), but also when dealing with metaphor, ambiguity, semantic change and other such features that would remain wholly unintelligible if one applied the rule strictly. In fact – as Empson is relieved to point out – the book is much 'larger than its theory', and Bloomfield often comes up with hypotheses that do take account of utterer's intention, interpretive strategies, motivated choice bewteen variant meanings and so forth. But on the strict, anti-mentalist reading of his book it would appear that Bloomfield could have no time for the sorts of logico-semantic investigation that Empson had been pursuing in *Complex Words*. For 'if you take at their face value these remarks that he lets drop, he is saying that such work would be beyond the pale of the exact sciences, impossible to understand, impossible to criticize' (*CW*, p. 443). And this clearly strikes Empson as yet another instance of the way that theorists in the humanistic disciplines, especially linguistics and literary criticism, are liable to pick up scientistic or positivist notions and apply them far outside their legitimate domain.

This quarrel with Bloomfield might seem pretty remote from Empson's differences with the New Criticism and later post-Saussurian variants of structuralist theory. But there is, as I have suggested, a linking factor in his argument that each of these doctrines goes wrong through its refusal to credit the human mind with sufficient powers of self-understanding or rational grasp. And the best way to counter this unfortunate trend, he thinks, is to show what resources or interpretive 'machinery' we do in fact possess for making sense of language in its more challenging or semantically complex forms. At its highest level of generality – that is to say, as a matter of principled rationalist or liberal-humanist conviction – this amounts to a belief that 'the human mind . . . , the public human mind, as expressed in a language, is not irredeemably lunatic and cannot be made so' (*CW*, p. 83n.). This remark occurs in a footnote reference to Orwell's *Nineteen Eighty-Four*, a book which poses real problems for Empson's theory since it appears to show how language can insinuate all manner of ghastly paradox ('War is Peace', 'Ignorance is Knowledge' etc.), and how little resistance the mind can put up to such forms of perverse or irrational belief. Thus 'what he [Orwell] calls "double-think", a process of intentional but genuine self-deception . . . really does seem a positive capacity of the human mind, so curious and so important in its effects that any theory in this field needs to reckon with it' (p. 83n.). But it is a main point of Empson's argument throughout *Complex Words* that although language can sometimes be made to behave this way – as for instance in the paradoxes of

Christian religion ('God is Love'), or other such varieties of potent irrationalist doctrine – nevertheless one can best get a grip on these problematic items by looking more closely at the structures of semantic entailment that mark them out as clearly deviant cases. And this applies just as much when a poet like Wordsworth manages to communicate his pantheist 'philosophy' of interfused mind and nature through a use of vague but powerful rhetorical devices which effectively short-circuit the normal requirements of sense-making logic or reason. Thus 'it does not seem unfair to say that he induced people to believe he had expounded a consistent philosophy through the firmness and assurance with which he used equations of Type IV; equations whose claim was false, because they did not really erect a third concept as they pretended to' (*CW*, p. 305). And this despite the fact, as Empson goes straight on to say, that 'the result makes very good poetry, and probably suggests important truths'.

The problem with Wordsworth was one that Empson had worried at for several 'niggling' pages in *Seven Types*. There he had fastened on the logical grammar – more specifically, the subtle confusions of grammar and logic – in those lines from 'Tintern Abbey' where Wordsworth achieved what is often regarded as the finest expression of his mystical nature-doctrine. Empson does not deny that the lines have great poetic force; even that they may communicate some genuine wisdom at the level of depth-psychology or emotional need. All the same he insists that this is no reason to suspend one's critical faculties, ignore the logico-grammatical confusions, and simply go along with the poem's mood of mystical-pantheist uplift. Empson's commentary is far too complex and detailed to allow for any adequate summary here. The most important points for our present discussion are 1) his claim that the pantheist doctrine involves not so much a transcendence as a collapse of the normal order of predicative (subject–object) relations, an effect that can only be achieved *by rhetorical means*, and at the cost of some highly dubious grammar; 2) his argument, following from this, that the difficulty of grasping Wordsworth's 'philosophy' is really a problem for the poet, not his exegete, since it reflects deep confusions of language and thought; and 3) Empson's principle, taken up and developed in *Complex Words*, that these confusions had best be treated as such, and not declared exempt from rational critique on grounds of their supposedly higher ('paradoxical') truth. After all, as he remarks, Wordsworth appears to have taken these doctrines very seriously indeed, so that it is only reasonable for us, his readers, to 'try to extract from this passage definite opinions on the relations of God, man, and nature, and on the means by which such relations can be known' (*ST*, p. 152). And if it then turns out on a close reading that those relations are strictly unintelligible – that the grammar and the logic of Wordsworth's poem just do not hang together in the way that his rhetoric requires – then this fact had better count in any critical assessment of the poetry's undoubted persuasive or emotional force.

All the same it is clear from the last few sentences of Empson's commentary that he finds it increasingly hard to reconcile these two divergent lines of response. On the one hand 'I must protest again that I enjoy these lines very much. . . . probably it was necessary for Wordsworth to shuffle, if he was to maintain his peculiar poetical attitude'. On the other: 'the reason why one grudges Wordsworth this source of strength is that he talks as if he owned a creed by which his half-statements might be reconciled, whereas, insofar as his creed was definite, he found these half-statements necessary to keep it at bay' (p. 154). In *Seven Types*, working with the admittedly rather catch-all notion of poetic 'ambiguity', Empson had as yet no adequate means of explaining how emotions – or intuitive responses – could get so completely out of touch with the 'machinery' of a reasoned analytical approach, a criticism that did not rest content with such vague sources of poetic satisfaction. In *Complex Words* this problem becomes a main topic of the book's 'theoretical' chapters and one that Empson frequently reverts to in the reading of particular texts. But it is no longer a question – as it was with Pastoral – of pursuing the various 'inward' complications, the reflective ironies and paradoxes of self-conscious thought, that marked out the stages of a history conceived in broadly Hegelian terms. This was Empson's 'phenomenology of spirit' re-written in the mode of a speculative genre-study with the Pastoral figure – especially the 'critic-as-hero' – occupying the roles of protagonist and commentator at each new vantage-point along the way. But it was also, as we have seen, a problematical book, not least on account of its implied message – more explicit in the later chapters – that Pastoral irony required an increasingly difficult balancing-act between the specialized pleasures of a rich and complex intellectual life and the demands of commonplace human sympathy or straightforward social justice. This becomes most evident in his commentary on the *Alice* books, a chapter where one feels that Empson (like Carroll) is juggling with a range of painful antinomies that might at any moment precipitate the collapse into neurosis or total psychotic isolation. 'It is the ground-bass of this kinship with madness, I think, that makes it so clear that the books are not trifling, and the cool courage with which Alice accepts madmen that gives them their strength' (*SVP*, p. 233). At this point the Pastoral conventions are manifestly falling apart under the strain of an increasingly drastic split between conscious and unconscious, 'complex' and 'simple' (or hyper-intellectual and quasi-primitivist) modes of self-understanding.

V

In short, Empson had travelled about as far as possible along that path of phenomenological reflection – allied to a strain of romantic irony – which opened up these alarming prospects of terminal non-communication. *Complex Words* can then be seen as his consequent attempt to provide an alternative, more hopeful (or theoretically adequate) account of the ways in which language can put up resistance to our normal powers of intellectual grasp. And it does so by shifting the focus of interest from conjectural states of mind in the author or reader to complexities of logico-semantic 'grammar' which are understood precisely as specific *deviations* from a shared basis of rational intelligibility. The 'bits of machinery' that Empson proposes in the book's opening chapters are basically those of two-place predicate logic ('A = B'), eked out with a range of fairly homespun ancillary notations to cover those cases where the structure of semantic entailment cannot be coaxed into a clear-cut pattern of compacted logical grammar. W. V. Quine offers a useful brief statement of why this procedure is so important for logicians and how it serves to clear up various sources of confusion in 'natural' language.

> What follows from what is largely a question of the patterns formed within a text by various grammatical connectives and operators, and of the patterns in which the verbs, nouns, adjectives, and pronouns recur and interweave. Predicate logic abstracts those patterns from the embedding texts by substituting neutral letters for the *predicates* – that is, for the verbs, nouns, and adjectives that bear all the burden of subject matter. Just one of the predicates is retained intact, the two-place predicate '=' of Identity, as a distinctively logical predicate.[50]

For Quine – as indeed for Frege, Russell and other philosophers who have written on the topic – such techniques can only operate at a high level of abstract logical regimentation where semantics gives way to syntax, or where the vagaries of meaning that accrue to individual words in context are bracketed out with the object of revealing some crystalline logical structure. In this way, so it is hoped, language can be purged of its rich though messy 'natural' condition and reconstituted in a form more amenable to the purposes of logical analysis and critique. Thus, as Quine puts it,

> paraphrasing and trimming, we can coax vast reaches of language into this skimpy structure. A celebrated example of paraphrase is that of 'if *p* then *q*' into 'not (*p* and not *q*)', which is faithful enough for most purposes. Our identity predicate '=' comes to the fore in paraphrasing 'else', 'except', and the singular 'the'. A complex segment of discourse may, on the other hand, be swept into the framework of predicate logic as a seamless whole and be treated as atomic when its internal structure offers nothing to the logical argument in hand.[51]

In other words the precondition for attaining this degree of analytical clarity and rigour is that complexity of meaning be treated as a function of the logicosyntactic relationship between terms (or stretches of discourse conceived for this purposes as 'atomic' elements), and that semantic questions be as far as possible ruled out of court. Thus the usefulness of the method varies inversely with the scope it provides for interpreting such natural-language features as ambiguity, metaphor, connotative meaning, rhetorical complexity and so forth. Precision comes only at the price of excluding any semantic functions that cannot be 'coaxed' into this kind of minimalist framework.

Empson's most striking innovation in *Complex Words* is to take this approach and see how it works when applied not so much to the logical grammar (or order of predicative relations) *between* various terms, propositional functions etc., but rather to the structure of implicit semantic 'equations' that operate *within* certain highly-charged or ambivalent words, and which thus make it possible for such words to carry a force of implied argument in and of themselves. As I have said, his basic term of analysis is the identity-relation ('='), although compared with Quine he allows much greater scope for the varieties of logical entailment brought about by differing contexts of usage or structures of semantic implication. The following, highly schematic table of functions (reproduced from *Complex Words*, p. 54) will give some idea of Empson's analytical approach:

The major sense of the word is the	Subject	Predicate
The sense demanded by the most immediate context is the . . . . Subject	II	I
. . . . Predicate	III	V
The order of the two senses is indifferent:	IV	

The roman numerals denote the various classes of semantic equation which, according to Empson, provide the most useful 'machinery' for coping with the otherwise unmanageable range of possible meanings or implicative structures in context. Type IV is the most problematical class since it has to include all those dubious instances where there exists no clear-cut order of logical priority, that is to say, no means of deciding between 'A = B' and 'B = A'. Such cases range from the paradoxes of religion ('God is Love') to political slogans, propaganda techniques, so-called 'primitive' uses of language, and expressions like Keats's 'Beauty is truth, truth beauty' whose sense of profound psychological conviction goes along with a certain ambiguity or vagueness of philosophic import. Nevertheless, Empson argues, it is important to see just how these rhetorical devices take effect and at what point precisely they offer resistance to the efforts of logico-semantic paraphrase. After all, 'if he (Keats) leads up with clear marks of solemnity to saying that Beauty is Truth he doesn't want to be told, any more than anyone else, that "of course" he meant nothing at all except to excite Emotion' (*CW*, p. 7).

This is the main ground for Empson's quarrel with the emotivist theory of poetic meaning proposed by I. A. Richards. It is also his reason for rejecting the idea – as argued by Cleanth Brooks and the American New Critics – that poetry embodies an order of 'paradoxical' wisdom above or beyond the requirements of rational prose sense. For this doctrine can just as easily be used to defend any kind of irrationalist or muddle-headed sentiment, any use of language that evades the protocols of sense-making logic and consistency in order to insinuate some 'profound' pseudo-truth under cover of its own special dispensation. At least critics should not raise paradox into a high point of principle or a kind of self-promoting aesthetic ideology that effectively lumps poetry together with the worst, most actively misleading forms of religious or political dogma. Thus when Empson comes back to the lines from Keats later in his book it is by way of taking issue with Brooks's reading and the idea that this poetry is somehow all the better – more authentically poetic – for its not making sense in logically accountable terms. In fact it now strikes him as a Type IV equation, one in which 'the assertion goes both ways round', so that 'either each entails the other, or both are examples of some third notion in which they are included' (p. 372). This is not to say that since the lines establish their own peculiar 'logic' of meaning – what Empson calls a structure of 'mutual metaphor' – they must therefore be regarded as enouncing a truth beyond reach of commonplace rational grasp. On the contrary: his response, here as with the passage from Wordsworth in *Seven Types*, is to press as far as possible toward analysing their effect and then admit frankly that the lines *don't work* – or that they fail to make good their high Romantic argument – if read with a view to their implicit structures of logico-semantic entailment. The main problem is that Keats seems to exploit his Type IV equation (i.e., the reversible order of priorities between 'A = B' and 'B = A') in order to suggest that Beauty and Truth are so perfectly interchangeable that 'there are no ugly truths', so that 'all truths are to be included in some kind of beauty' (p. 372). And such devices are always suspect, Empson believes, when they fall back on vague intimations of a visionary insight or reconciling power inaccessible to plain prose reason. Thus 'here the identity becomes a full case of Mutual Metaphor, or a full parallel to an equation of Type IV, because the third notion which is supposed to be brought forward has not much likeness to either of the two things identified' (p. 373).

Empson is not alone among critics of Keats in entertaining the suspicion that this sentiment is both morally dubious – since based on a form of aesthetic ideology indifferent to the harsher realities of human experience – and overly (even offensively) 'rhetorical' insofar as it lacks any adequate structure of argument by which to back up its claim. Thus one might come to feel – and here he cites Robert Bridges – that 'the last lines with their brash attempt to end with a smart bit of philosophy have not got enough knowledge behind them' (p. 374). But such a negative judgement would only carry weight if one had tried out various possible ways of fitting the lines into some kind of rational sense-making structure, and not simply read them (on Richards's terms) as appealing to a complex of emotional 'attitudes' in the reader, or again – following Brooks – as belonging to a realm of supra-rational poetic 'paradox' where standards of truth or valid argument simply didn't apply. Empson does his best to give the lines a 'sensible' interpretation, and in fact comes up with some plausible ideas of how the poem's crowning statement might be found to follow with a measure of supporting 'philosophical' conviction. All the same he concedes that 'there is perhaps a puzzle about how far we ought to make this kind of effort, and at what point the size of the effort required simply proves the poem to be bad' (p. 374).

His main point, here and elsewhere, is that we will not do justice to poetry or to ourselves as intelligent readers if we give up this effort at an early stage and resort to some saving emotivist or irrationalist formula which consigns poetry to a realm of 'pseudo-statements' devoid of argumentative or truth-telling warrant. 'Emotions well handled in art are somehow absorbed into the structure; their expression is made also to express where and why they are valid' (p. 372). This sounds like a version of Eliot's 'objective correlative', with the crucial difference, for Empson, that the kind of adequacy involved has to do with matters of truth-functional or logico-semantic grasp, and not (as in Eliot) with an imagist appeal to sensuous intuitions supposedly captured in a language of immediate visual or tactile apprehension. In fact Empson has little time for this idea that poetry's proper business is to 'hand across sensations bodily', a quasi-phenomenalist confusion of language with the realm of natural or organic processes which he, like Paul de Man, finds responsible for manifold errors in the discourse of modern (post-Romantic) literary criticism.[52] What Empson means when he says that emotions well handled are somehow 'absorbed into the structure' is that good poetry stands up better to the kind of analytical commentary – the seeking-out of semantic 'equations' or intelligible structures of compacted argument – which enable the critic to avoid such forms of premature phenomenalist appeal. Nonetheless, 'it often happens that a poet has built his machine, putting all the parts into it and so on very genuinely, and the machine does not go' (*CW*, p. 374). And there is still some doubt in Empson's mind, despite all his valiant sense-making efforts on Keats's behalf, as to whether the poem actually succeeds in giving substance to its visionary claims. Hence what many readers have found vaguely offensive in the last two lines: 'there is a flavour of Christian Science; they fear to wake up in Fairyland, and probably the country of Uplift' (p. 373). Empson goes various ways around to contest this view but in the end – as with Wordsworth's

'Tintern Abbey' – he has to admit that this rhetorical 'uplift' is doing much of the work and continues to resist the best efforts of analysis along logico-semantic lines.

It is important to grasp that there is more at stake here than a technical dispute about 'emotive' *versus* 'cognitive' approaches to the language of poetry, or perhaps just a perverse rearguard attempt, on Empson's part, to translate the programme of logical positivism into a method for literary criticism. Certainly *Complex Words* is very much a part of that Cambridge ethos that produced Bertrand Russell's celebrated 'theory of descriptions' and his analysis of refer-ring expressions in terms of their 'logical grammar' and structures of com-pacted propositional sense.[53] (Whether Empson had also read Frege at this stage, especially his cardinal essay on 'Sense and Reference',[54] can only be matter for conjecture.) But there is also a larger, moral or ethical dimension which joins on directly to these specialized researches and which Empson thinks indispensable for any self-respecting practice of literary-critical judge-ment. He takes A. E. Housman as a test-case here since on the one hand Housman's poems undoubtedly 'work' (i.e., succeed remarkably in putting across their peculiar mixture of fatalist gloom, contempt for all 'merely' human values and activities, and outlook of stoic indifference in face of Nature's destructive forces) while on the other their 'philosophy' is one that most readers would reject outright – and quite properly so, Empson thinks – if asked to accept it as a matter of plain-prose argument or practical belief. Thus 'Housman is about as pure a case as you can get of a poet using untruths to excite "attitudes" ' (p. 13). But this does not mean – far from it – that one had better fall back on the Richards line, discount any truth-claims that the poetry might seem to assert, and allow those 'attitudes' to carry one along for the sake of some odd (if intense) emotional experience. In short, 'even here I think it would be a tedious flippancy to say that the truth or untruth of the assertions is simply irrelevant to the poem' (p. 13).

This is why Empson's arguments in *Complex Words* are aimed just as much against pragmatist accounts of meaning and truth as against I. A. Richards and other proponents of the emotivist doctrine. (See for instance his three appendices on 'Theories of Value', pp. 414–43.) Thus on Richards's view 'the acceptance which a pseudo-statement receives is entirely governed by its effects upon our feelings and attitudes . . . A pseudo-statement is "true" if it suits or serves some attitude or links together attitudes which on other grounds are desirable' (cited in *CW*, p. 13). But of course this leaves wide open the question as to just what 'desirable' means in various contexts of evaluative usage; whether attitudes of a plainly irrational or (in Housman's case) a regressive and well-nigh paranoid character might be 'desirable' for readers in search of some vicarious emotional release; or indeed whether poetry has anything to do with questions of truth, right reason or ethical judgement as applied in areas outside this charmed aesthetic domain. Empson puts the case as forcefully as possible when he remarks on the obvious *undesirability* of Housman's poetic creed when considered not only in terms of rational self-interest, narrowly conceived, but also from the wider (other-regarding) stand-point of a shared human interest in the communal good. This outlook — roughly speaking, a Benthamite ethic of 'the greatest good of the greatest number', tempered by a sense that such values must include some measure of enlightened altruism — is a constant point of reference in Empson's criticism, especially his later attacks on 'neo-Christian' interpreters who raised their contempt for all merely human pleasures and enjoyments into a form of perverse self-denying ordinance or high-priestly mystification. (There is a nice example in *Milton's God* where he takes T. S. Eliot to task for suggesting that Milton's Hell is a lot more convincing than his vaguely visualized scenes in the Garden of Eden. 'So long as you gave Mr Eliot images of someone being tortured his nerves were at peace, but if you gave him an image of two people making each other happy he screamed.')[55]

What needs to be understood here is the close relation that Empson perceives between a rationalist approach to questions of poetic meaning and a theory of value (or enlightened mutual self-interest) that likewise avoids the dangerous appeal to modes of 'satisfaction' beyond reach of commonplace human accountability. His simplest statement of the ethical position occurs in Appendix I of *Complex Words*, where Empson sets it down as a matter of logical inference that

> the creature must think 'It is good, in general, to act so as to produce good effects. Good effects are the same when I am there as when I am not, like the rest of the external world, hence they are good in you as well as in me. Hence, it is good for me to produce good effects in you.' Surely this simply follows from the intellectuality of the creature; it does not depend on exciting emotions of fraternal love or what not, though no doubt they are needed if he is to act on the belief when under strain. It is part of the process of believing that there is a real world outside you, an idea which is built up by generalization and analogy. (p. 427)

Going back to the Housman example we can now perhaps see more clearly why it struck Empson both as an extreme case (of 'emotions' getting out of touch with cognitive interests or veridical truth-claims), and also as the type of case that his theory would need to confront if it wanted to offer anything more than a vague sense of rational reassurance. For if Wordsworth and Keats put prob-lems in the way of Empson's analytical approach — problems having to do with the disjunctive relation between logic, grammar and rhetoric — then Housman is a poet whose undoubted power of lyrical utterance goes along with a massive and perverse indifference to the claims of reason, morality and mere good sense.

In Empson's words, 'there is a sullen conviction that no effort is worth making, a philosophy for the village idiot; and the illogicality which we are told to admire (as being typical of poetical language) is not any "freedom" from logic but the active false logic of persecution mania' (p. 13). On the other hand he is also compelled to admit that Housman's poems have a genuine power and intensity of lyric feeling which cannot be ignored whatever their deficiencies at the level of argument or 'philosophic' import. Hence the great problem for Empson's approach in *Complex Words*: that 'on this theory the poetry is very bad, whereas it seems clear that an adequate theory would be able to admit its merits' (p. 13). That is to say, the 'machinery' of verbal exegesis is always liable to encounter cases where the meaning is resistant to further explication, or where the structures of logico-semantic entailment produce some plainly absurd set of attitudes, meanings, or beliefs. Even so, Empson argues, one is justified in sticking to the machinery despite these problems that rise up against it when applied to such anomalous or recalcitrant material. After all, 'what is done in other fields of study . . . is to give symbols to a few elements that seem essential, avoid refining on the definitions till the examples make it necessary, and try how far the symbols will go' (p. 2). This is pretty much Empson's manner of approach in *Complex Words*, and it is one whose occasional (and readily admitted) failures should not be allowed to obscure the book's extraordinary range of speculative insight.

It is worth saying something more about the Housman case since it brings out the extent to which, in Empson's criticism, questions of method (or interpretive theory) always go along with issues in the realm of moral and socio-political concern. The following is typical of many passages in his later work which readers – especially academic critics – have tended to regard as mere 'anecdotal' detail, no doubt of some interest from a life-and-times view-point but otherwise somewhat beside the point.

> I remember a Japanese class of mine reading Housman in 1931, when they were liable to be conscripted to fight in Manchuria, indeed a man had already been drafted from the class and killed in Shanghai, and they wrote down pretty consistently 'We think Housman is quite right. We will do no good to anyone being killed as soldiers, but we will be admired, and we all want to be admired, and anyway we are better dead.' To do the old gentleman [Housman] justice, I think he would have been rather shocked by these bits of schoolwork. (*CW*, p. 13)

His central point here, as throughout *Complex Words*, is that criticism is simply not doing its job if it fails to make a bridge between 'technical' interests (like the status of poetic truth-claims or modes of semantic implication) and issues of a real-world moral and practical kind. Such is indeed his main argument against the 'emotive' theory of poetic language and its various non-cognitivist offshoots: namely, that these doctrines work out in practice as a pretext for critics to focus their attention exclusively on the 'words on the page', and thus to discount all the problems that arise when literature is read and taught in differing socio-historical contexts. Hence Empson's attitude of sturdy contempt for any theory — like the old New Critical veto on talk about intentions, biography, historical background and so forth — which invents 'bother-headed' philosophical reasons for treating poetry as a special kind of language, a self-enclosed domain of purely rhetorical structures and devices. For the effect of such (in his view) mind-warping preconceptions is to persuade critics firstly that they must suspend all their normal waking habits of judgement when interpreting poetry, and secondly that it is some kind of vulgar mistake — or at any rate a breach of critical etiquette — to ask the plain question whether poems *make sense* in terms of propositional content or valid argument.

This is why Empson says (in a footnote to *Complex Words*) that 'the term Ambiguity, which I used in a book title and as a kind of slogan, implying that the reader is left in doubt between two readings, is more or less superseded by the idea of a double meaning which is intended to be fitted into a definite structure' (p. 103n.). The virtue of this approach is that it gives a hold for discussing truth-claims, beliefs and propositional attitudes, rather than talking more vaguely (as in *Seven Types*) about the various possible senses of a word, line or stanza conceived as so many loosely articulated units or atoms of meaning. And it is Empson's argument — one that he shares with some current analytical philosophers of language, Donald Davidson among them[56] — that one can best take account of the real variety of values, world-views, ethical belief-systems etc. *not* by espousing a wholesale relativist creed but by imputing a large measure of shared rationality to all language-users and then making sense of problematical cases as and when they come up. For Davidson this has to do with the much-discussed problem of 'radical translation', the question whether, in principle, one could ever make a start in understanding or translating some alien language, given the fact of 'ontological relativity' (i.e., the scope for a large-scale mismatch between referring expressions, logical constants, modes of ostensive definition, and so on), and the consequent lack of any firm assurance that one had got the 'native informant' right on even the most basic details.[57] Empson, needless to say, does not have much time for such extravagant varieties of sceptical doubt. But it is clear that *Complex Words* is intended in part as a rejoinder to those various forms of non-cognitivist doctrine which imply a similar breakdown of rational confidence in the power of language to articulate meanings across different contexts of informing value and belief. Moreover, he is at one with Davidson in thinking that relativism, at least in its more sweeping or doctrinaire versions, most often takes rise from a single basic error: that of starting out from a theory of language which relativizes words to their whole background context of meanings, assumptions, language-games, cultural 'forms of life' and so forth, rather than looking to the truth-conditions (or the structures of logico-semantic entailment) which then give a hold for interpreting the word in this or that specific context of utterance. Where Empson differs from Davidson and other like-minded analytical philosophers is in locating those structures *within* single words whose range of co-implicated senses and logical relations can thus provide the basis for a worked-out 'grammar' of the various orders of semantic equation.

This argument takes a reflexive turn when Empson considers the key-word 'grammar' itself, a term that is used in two very different (indeed flatly opposite) senses, and whose semantic structure, or force of 'compacted doctrine', is seen to vary according to which takes priority in any given instance. One idea of 'grammar' (the descriptivist attitude) can best be summarized in Empson's words: 'grammar is merely a codification of usage, and therefore must not attempt anything else' (*CW*, p. 311). The other (prescriptivist) account takes an altogether more elevated view of the grammarian's role since it allows him or her to define good usage, or to lay down standards of linguistic competence, according to precedent, rule, or normative criteria. Empson is not so much interested in this old conundrum (though he does have some relevant things to say on the topic) as in the way that 'grammar', as used by both parties, effectively encodes a whole set of attitudes compacted into a single key-term which carries the entire weight of implied argument.

Here again it is Richards who sets his thinking off in this direction by adopting a broadly contextualist definition of 'grammar' according to which the word, like the discipline, takes its sense (or its methodological bearings) from the whole surrounding context of argument.[58] For Empson, on the contrary, 'grammar' (the word and the practice) involves a lot more in the way of directive intelligence or power to influence language and thought through structures of meaning that cannot be explained on a straightforward con-textualist account. Thus Richards's theory

> makes the prelogical (or usual) thinking a matter of whole sentences or paragraphs . . . it is only in logical thinking, which recognises that the definition of a term is different from statements about an already defined term, that the analyst can usefully attend to the meanings of single words. . . . In [this] fluid state the words 'cannot be said to have any meaning'; no doubt the single words have functions, but such a word is hardly more than an aggregate of potentialities, like what you feel for a syllable used for many words. . . . No doubt this process actually occurs. But in general the language performance is about a topic which can be given in a single word. . . . And, precisely because of the fluidity of words in general, the word recognised as the topic is likely to grow a more inclusive structure in the process. . . . Precisely because they have not got single meanings, they can be made to sum up the process of thought. (*CW*, pp. 312–13)

This passage carries echoes of a long line of philosophico-linguistic speculative thought, running all the way from Plato's *Theaetetus* to Gilbert Ryle's essay 'Letters and Syllables in Plato'.[59] That is to say, it raises the question of precisely what constitutes the minimal distinctive unit of sense or intelligibility in language, given that words only signify by virtue of their role in some larger context of articulated meanings or truth-values. Like Plato, Empson sees a useful analogy with the various levels of constituent analysis applied in morphological studies, i.e., the ascending series of integrative functions that starts out from letters, combines them into syllables, and then arrives at the word-boundaries beyond which lexical units enter into larger (syntactic or discursive) chains of utterance. As developed by Ryle this analogy points to the fact that no single word possesses meaning in and of itself; that it is only through a process of higher-level integration — by grasping the word in its 'syncategorematic' role — that we are able to assign the operative truth-conditions and hence the word's meaning in any given context. All this Empson accepts, though with the further (and highly significant) proviso: that such structures of logico-semantic implication may sometimes operate *within single words* so as to give them a certain propositional force, or a capacity for bearing various kinds of 'compacted' doctrine, that could not be explained on any purely contextualist account.

This is why 'grammar' is such an interesting case: because it divides theorists into two chief camps (the prescriptive and descriptive grammarians), both of whom make it a code-word for their sense of priorities *vis-à-vis* usage and correctness, though only from a qualified prescriptivist standpoint could one offer a generalized theory (like Empson's) designed to take adequate account of this 'machinery' and explain how the mind makes rational sense of the semantic operations involved. For there is a 'grammar' of complex words which raises all the same issues, in particular the question whether words take on meaning by absorption, so to speak, from associated contexts of utterance, or whether they can act as a focus and vehicle for structures of inbuilt semantic implication which in turn redefine the very sense of that operative context. Thus it may be the case, as Empson readily concedes, that 'when a man is talking straight ahead he cannot be supposed to give individual words a great deal of attention, and in arguing that one of them has a particular structure the theorist must be supposing he gives it that structure in his subconscious mind' (*CW*, p. 319). But this is after all not so wildly improbable since 'the subconscious mind is patently doing a good deal of work anyhow; for one thing it is getting the grammar in order'. Or again: 'it [i.e., the putative 'grammar'] would be wrong if it did not correspond to anything in the speaker's mind, but he cannot be supposed to string his sentences together without any mental operation at all' (p. 319). What this amounts to, in brief, is a rationalist philosophy of mind, language and interpretation which assumes that literary critics (like grammarians) can best start out from the relevant facts about our

competence or powers of intuitive grasp as language-users, and then go on to
derive a more elaborately formalized account of the processes involved.

Indeed one could draw an interesting parallel with Chomsky's theory of
generative grammar, especially those later (modified) versions of it that take
more account of semantic factors in constructing their models of grammatical
intelligibility.[60] But my main purpose in conducting this excursion through
the thickets of linguistic philosophy is to place Empson's book in the wider
context of modern ideas about language, logic and truth. For it then becomes
clear that *Complex Words* takes its place in a tradition of thought whose major
representatives are Frege, Russell, Davidson, and other such proponents of a
logico-semantic analytical approach which goes clean against the dominant
drift of recent (post-structuralist) literary theory. Thus Empson's objections to
a radically contextualist account of meaning and interpretation would also
apply to those modish varieties of post-structuralist thinking which take it
pretty much for granted (following Saussure) that language is a network of
signifying relations 'without positive terms'; that all our operative notions of
truth, reference, logical entailment, and so forth are contingent upon the
various codes, conventions or 'discourses' in circulation at any given time; and
therefore – what appears the inevitable upshot – that critics are deluded if they
think to offer any workable *theory* of language, logic and interpretive truth
which does not concede the utter relativity of all such notions. Empson's book
appeared long before the post-structuralist vogue but it does engage with quite
a range of adversary positions, among them (as we have seen) several that
anticipate these current ways of thinking.

Complex Words comes up with the following counter-arguments, some of
them explicit, others requiring a degree of extrapolative licence, or what
philosophers politely call 'rational reconstruction'. 1) There is no reason, aside
from various kinds of deep-grained cultural-relativist prejudice, to suppose that
language exhibits such a range of possible meanings, conventions, or signifying
structures that any generalized theory, any 'grammar' of complex words, must
be beyond hope of attainment. 2) The chief point of convergence between
Empson and Davidson: understanding the sense of a given expression is a
matter of grasping its truth-conditions, rather than the other way around. 3)
Following Russell, whom Empson had clearly read with some care, as well
as Frege, whose argument he is perhaps reinventing: one cannot (like the
post-structuralists) erect Saussure's specialized requirements for the project
of synchronic linguistics into a wholesale anti-realist ontology, allowing all
questions of referential truth to drop clean out of the picture, and treating
language as a strictly two-term relation between signifier and signified. For if
indeed it is the case, as Frege says, that 'sense determines reference' in all
instances save those of straightforward ostensive definition, still one couldn't
even make a start in learning, using, interpreting or translating any utterance

unless one had grasped the relevant conditions for what counted as a veridical speech-act or a paradigm case of referential discourse.[61] 4) There is no accounting for our normal capacity as language-using creatures – let alone our ability to interpret metaphors, deviant 'equations', paradoxical utterances and other such 'extraordinary' forms of expression – without imputing a large measure of shared interpretive competence which goes far beyond anything envisaged on the structuralist or cultural-relativist model. 5) This is also an argument against any premature retreat into 'emotive' theories of poetic or literary language, theories which tend to underestimate the extent to which 'feelings' in words (or matters of emotional 'tone') can be analysed in cognitive or truth-functional terms. Thus: 'much of what appears to us as a "feeling" (as is obvious in the case of a complex metaphor) will in fact be quite an elaborate structure of related meanings' (*CW*, pp. 56–7).

From all of which it follows 6) that literary theory cannot get along without at least some grounding in logic, semantics, and analytical philosophy of language, even if it mostly takes them on board by a kind of 'commonsense' intuitive osmosis, without much need for explicit clarification of the formal principles involved. Of course there is a problem about claiming Empson as an ally for 'theory' in the current, highly-charged polemical climate since he later came to feel such a strong aversion toward the various developments – from New Criticism to deconstruction – bearing that name. But what he found most objectionable in these movements was the mixture of geared-up professional expertise – pseudo-expertise, as he thought it – and extreme remoteness from the practical business of interpreting literary texts. His 'Comment for the Second Edition' of *Complex Words* puts the case with regard to ethical theory, but could also serve as a general statement of Empson's approach to such questions.

Someone said that my Appendix on Theories of Value confuses the necessary distinction between meta-ethics and ethics, because it assumes that theories about the meaning of ethical terms also make ethical recommendations; he felt this enough to sweep aside my amateur [arguments]. But I think that they obviously do. A man can generally see that other people's do, though he tends to feel that his own are universal common sense. The idea that the theorist is not a part of the world he examines is one of the deepest sources of error, and crops up all over the place. (p. 445)

His point – taken up in a variety of ways throughout *Complex Words* – is that 'theories', even those of a technical or specialized character, can still have substantive implications beyond their particular domain of expertise. Thus for instance, any linguist (or literary critic) who adopts something akin to Empson's view of the relation between thought, language and interpretation is likely to match it with a high general estimate of human rationality and purposive intelligence. What is more, such an attitude will tend to go along with certain cognate ethical or socio-political beliefs, as in Chomsky's espousal of a left-libertarian stance which derives, or at any rate claims implicit philosophical support, from his arguments for a rationalist philosophy of mind backed up by the evidence of linguistic universals vested in the nature of human understanding.[62] Thus for Chomsky, as for Empson, there is an obvious link between issues in the realm of linguistic theory (or the semantics of complex words) and questions of moral and political accountability.

VI

In Empson's case this commitment takes the form of a preference for words which convey a certain humour of mutual or self-implicating irony, a 'pastoral' sense of the speaker's being somehow caught up in the same kinds of complex social predicament that he or she typically detects in other people. Hence his comment on the key-word 'dog' in its 'hearty' eighteenth-century usage as a term of half-mocking, half-affectionate abuse: that 'when you call a man a dog with obscure praise, or treat a dog as half-human, you do not much believe in the Fall of Man, you assume a rationalist view of man as the most triumphant of the animals' (*CW*, p. 176). The point about such words is that they seem to involve both a generalized 'grammar' of semantic implication with strong universalist claims, and a normative aspect – or force of ethical recommendation – which inevitably brings value-judgements into play. The same applies to 'sense', one of Empson's main exhibits, and a word whose extraordinary range of meanings – from 'sense-impression' *via* 'commonsense judgement' to Wordsworth's prophetic 'language of the sense' or mystical 'sense of something far more deeply interfused' – allows it to convey the most diverse kinds of compacted philosophical doctrine. All the same, Empson thinks, there is a middle ground set of equations clustered around the basic idea of 'good sense' and tending to imply that this quality involves both a healthy respect for the claims of sensuous experience and a 'sensible' degree of scepticism with regard to other, more mysterious or elevated forms of extra-sensory knowledge. In its simplest version this amounts to a kind of phenomenalist doctrine whereby 'good sense' equates with 'trusting to the senses' or getting along, like the 'dog' of popular repute, on a rock-bottom basis of reliable instinct coupled with the elementary social desires imposed by the need for survival. This usage has a distinctly 'period' feel and goes along with the notion, most pronounced in English writers of the early-modern or Renaissance period, that 'a sensible man will be a bit of a sensualist, well rooted in the earth, and that his judgements will be based on the evidence of the senses supposed to be free from "theory" ' (p. 264). But it can also be extended – as Empson shows from various (mostly eighteenth-century) examples – so as to take in the idea that 'sense' and 'sensibility' are related through a structure of mutual entailment, so that having 'good sense' is a fair indication of possessing good feelings (or sufficiently refined moral sentiments).

Of course the two words can get into conflict, as when Jane Austen constructs a whole plot around the rival claims of 'sense' and 'sensibility', playing them off though a series of structural ironies which the reader – at any rate the fit reader – is expected to pick up on cue. And 'sense' can itself give rise to all manner of deviant (indeed pathological) equations, as in Shakespeare's 'problem play' *Measure For Measure*, where the commonsense or 'middle-range' meanings of the word tend to fade into the background, so that everything turns on a drastic confrontation between hedonist and puritan attitudes, both of which reduce to the stark proposition that 'sense = mere sensuality'. Not that one could find all this 'in' the play without possessing at least some working knowledge of the relevant historical 'background'. In Empson's words:

> there was a strand of loathing for sexuality in any form, partly no doubt as an intellectual agreement with the Puritans, but one that he [Shakespeare] recognised as a diseased frame of mind; and contrasting with this a loathing for the cruelty which this line of feeling produced in Puritans, above all for the claim that to indulge the cruelty satisfies justice. (*CW*, p. 272)

But it is Empson's argument that if one knows this much – a fairly basic provision of readerly competence – then all the play's major themes and conflicts of motive may be seen as carried by the key-word 'sense' and its various structures of semantic implication. What makes *Measure For Measure* such a problematic case is the way it cuts out a whole range of meanings normal to that word and brings in a set of alternative equations – some of them deriving (as Empson suggests) from darker passages in the sonnet sequence – by way of exploring this nexus of ideas around puritanism, sensuality, and repressed sexual drives. Thus

> the subtle confusion of the word is used for a mood of fretted and exhausting casuistry; the corruption of the best makes it the worst; charity is good, but has strange and shameful roots; the idea of a lawsuit about such matters is itself shameful, and indeed more corrupt than the natural evil. (p. 273)

But it is still the case, Empson believes, that the 'normal' interpretive machinery must be working somewhere in the background, since otherwise we should have no comparative yardstick, no handle by which to get a hold on these deviant equations. Thus finally the play 'moves over, as the key-word does, from a consideration of "sensuality", to a consideration of "sanity", and then the action is forced round to a happy ending' (p. 287).

Even so, as Empson's comment suggests, this reversal is achieved against large dramatic odds, and with no very plausible show of motivational psychology. The most powerful and oddly convincing passages are those where 'sense' undergoes such extreme contortions of meaning that the play comes across as 'an examination of sanity itself, which is seen crumbling and dissolving in the soliloquies of Angelo' (p. 270). And at this point clearly it places some strain on Empson's rational-humanist conviction that the best, most rewardingly complex instances of poetic language are those that involve some tacit background of argument, some structure of implied propositional attitudes, by which to make good their normative claim, as opposed to the kinds of irrationalist paradox that critics are often over-willing to praise. This is a real problem with *Complex Words*, and one that Empson confronts most directly in his Note on Orwell's *Nineteen Eighty-Four*. Thus 'what he [Orwell] calls "double-think", a process of intentional but genuine self-deception, really does seem a positive capacity of the human mind, so curious and so important in its effects that any theory in this field needs to reckon with it' (p. 83). All the same, as with *Measure For Measure*, Empson thinks that we can best get a grip on such linguistic perversions by applying the more normal interpretive machinery and sticking to the basic rationalist principle, namely that 'the human mind, that is, the public human mind as expressed in a language, is not irredeemably lunatic and cannot be made so'. But the question remains as to whether this amounts to much more than a pious hope, a preference – as manifest in so much of Empson's criticism – for examples that happen to chime with his own rational-humanist beliefs.

Empson had worked during the war in the Far Eastern section of the BBC's foreign service, a job which he found both depressing and instructive. Such work, he wrote later in *Milton's God*, 'cannot narrow a man's understanding of other people's opinions', though it may in the end 'narrow his own opinions'.[63] Milton had done his own share of anti-royalist propaganda – some of it decidedly devious – and Empson found the experience useful as a way into Milton's tortuously complex psychology. But the real challenge to the rationalist semantics of *Complex Words* comes from Orwellian 'Newspeak', the idea of a language wholly given over to falsehood, paradox, and ideological brainwashing. As a specialist advisor to the Indian and Burmese service Orwell had worked alongside Empson in the wartime BBC. Empson had derived some philosophical comfort from the fact that such work could be carried on without abandoning all respect for rational thought. Orwell drew the opposite conclusion: that language was open to a whole wide range of perverted rhetorical techniques which in the end might reach the point of erasing all distinctions between truth and falsehood, fact and fiction, logic and 'the active false logic of persecution mania'.[64] His novel struck Empson as a 'hideously special case' from which it was wrong to draw any generalized conclusions. Its effectiveness depended largely on its power to 'frighten the reader into believing the possibility of what he does not really think possible'. What this argument comes down to, in face of Orwell's 'nightmare' book, is a belief that there are limits to the powers of unreason or the psychopathology of language when placed in the service of this or that mendacious totalitarian creed. And this despite the fact – as he readily concedes – that the paradoxes of Newspeak are not so very different from the kinds of suasive rhetorical device that characterize the language of certain types of poetry. At any rate the rationalist would need to explain how such devices could carry real conviction if on the one hand their truth-claims were manifestly false, while on the other (*contra* Richards) they couldn't be treated as just a species of 'emotive' language, exempt from all the customary standards of veridical utterance or cognitive accountability.

Complex Words may be read as testing this proposal across across a wide range of literary cases which put up varying degrees of resistance. More than once the method threatens to break down entirely, as in the somewhat baffled chapter on Milton's use of 'all', where the word takes on such a massively encompassing range of senses that it feels to Empson like some kind of deep unconscious 'symbol', beyond reach of analysis on rational or logico-semantic lines. In this case – perhaps the most extreme of its kind – the Richards doctrine may indeed be the only one that works, since 'so far from being able to chart a structure of related meanings in a key word, you get an obviously important word for which an Emotive theory seems about all that you can hold' (*CW*, p. 101). Nevertheless Empson thinks it an untypical case and one that reflects not so much some ultimate truth about the nature of poetic language – i.e., its illogicality, resistance to paraphrase, paradoxical character or whatever – but the sheer psychological strain imposed by Milton's attempt to make decent (humanly intelligible) sense of a thoroughly pernicious and mind-bending creed.

> That his feelings were crying out against his appalling theology in favour of freedom, happiness and the pursuit of truth was I think not obvious to him, and it is this part of the dramatic complex which is thrust upon us by the repeated *all*. . . . One could draw up equations for the effect of *all* in Milton, relating not so much senses of the word as whole contexts in which it has become habitual. But they would no longer be tracing a clear-cut, even if unconscious, mental operation, like those which let us talk straight ahead and get the grammar in order; they would be concerned with something more like a Freudian symbol. (p. 104)

It was this line of argument that Empson took up in *Milton's God* (1961) and the other late essays attacking what he saw as the corrupting influence of 'neo-

Christian' values and assumptions when applied to the reading of renaissance and modern texts. It might be argued that his failure to make much headway with the structural-semantic analysis of Milton's 'all' was one reason for Empson's abandoning the abstruse researches of *Complex Words* and going over to a less 'theoretical' kind of criticism, an approach that on the whole abjured such speculative interests and stuck to matters of historical and psycho-biographical import. But in fact these two aspects of his work were closely related, since the main purpose of *Complex Words* was to provide a kind of broad-based theoretical support – a 'machinery' of interpretive procedures and ground-rules – for the liberal-humanist position adopted in his reading of individual texts. Here again it is Empson's great argument that one *can* in fact derive normative principles (or an ethics of interpretive practice) from a generalized theory of language and literature with strong universalist claims.

In *Milton's God* he found the Christian commentators divided into two main camps of opinion. On the one hand were those (C. S. Lewis among them)[65] who recognized the barbarous character of Milton's 'official' theology but saved their belief by arguing that the poet had got things wrong about Christianity in some crucial respect. On the other were those who rejected this easygoing 'liberal' option, declaring that Milton had got things more or less right and that faith – not reason – was required to make sense of God's mysterious (not to say brutally arbitrary) ways. The one interpretation, as Empson saw it, tried to make something tolerably decent of the Christian religion by treating Milton as a great poet but a mixed-up thinker scarcely in command of his material. The other praised Milton for all the wrong reasons: for lending full credence to a system of belief whose sheer illogicality and latent sadism the poem then cynically endorses. On neither view can Milton be seen as coming off with much credit. Empson suggests that both views are wrong, and that the power of Milton's poetry comes from his attempting to defend a creed against which his reason and his feelings alike were constantly crying out. 'If you regard the poem as inherently nerve-wracking in this peculiar way, you do not feel that any separate justification is needed for its extraordinary style. . . . its style is necessary for the effect.' Hardline neo-Christians underrate Milton's moral intelligence (or plain human decency) by taking the poem at its own official word, as a determined vindication of Christian belief. Well-meaning liberals hang on to their faith by detaching the poem from its context of hard-pressed theological argument and thus rendering it safe for the purposes of vaguely ecumenical uplift. On the contrary, says Empson: the poem is so good because Milton had both the intellectual nerve to take on Christianity at its most repellent, and the decency of feeling (at whatever 'unconscious' level) to resist its powers of irrational persuasion.

This helps to explain why Empson's interests veered away so sharply from the style of analytical close-reading for which he is probably still best known.

He came to feel that such techniques were positively harmful when divorced from the attitude of broad-based tolerant understanding which went along with an enlightened rationalist outlook. Otherwise the emphasis on conflict and paradox was liable to lead – as it had at various points in *Seven Types* – toward regions of depth-psychological motive which could always be mined and exploited by the neo-Christian zealots. Hence perhaps the shift of period-emphasis, in *Complex Words*, from those poets of the early seventeenth century (notably Donne and Herbert) whose work offered such a rich field for this style of quasi-theological exegesis, to the later Restoration and Augustan writers in whom Empson found a more congenial emphasis on the 'rational prose virtues' as manifest in key-words like 'sense' and their structures of implied normative judgement. Perhaps the best example is the chapter on Pope ('Wit in the "Essay on Criticism" ') where Empson follows out the intricate logic of a style finely poised between the rival claims of 'wit' and 'sense'. The rather self-supporting dialectics of 'wit' are shrewdly played off against a note of moderating judgement which insists on the merits of plain 'good sense' or the *sensus communis* of civilized reason. 'To play this trick on such a scale', Empson writes, 'comes at last to suggest more dignified notions; that all a critic can do is to suggest a hierarchy with inadequate language; that to do it so well with so very inadequate language is to offer a kind of diagram of how it must always be done' (*CW*, p. 85). Of course this refers as much to Empson's own 'inadequate' language – his machinery of paraphrase, semantic equations and logical operators – as to Pope's more polished and elegant turns of style. To offer a 'kind of diagram' may be the furthest that a theory like Empson's can go toward explaining the extraordinary subtlety and strength of that style. Yet the 'trick', after all, is much the same in Empson and Pope: to keep the high gyrations of 'wit' in play while constantly suggesting a larger background of tacit values and assumptions. 'Putting the complex into the simple' – Empson's root definition of Pastoral – here becomes a kind of working faith for the theorist–interpreter of complex words.

This is what I mean by suggesting that the book's two dimensions of argument – the theoretical and the ethical-normative – in fact fit together in a way that must appear deeply problematic according to widely-held notions of the difference (the unbridgeable gulf, as some philosophers would have it) between these orders of truth-claim. The following passage will give some idea of how this process works with the key-word 'sense', a crucial example from Empson's point of view since it carries such a range of meanings – or compacted arguments – bound up with the shift from a theocentric to a rational-humanist outlook. 'Our present structure of the word,' he writes,

> was invented around the time of the Restoration; speakers then took to regarding the 'good judgement' use as a simple metaphor, in the course of a general drive

toward simplification. And the two types of equation, 'A is like B' and 'A is typical of B', came into play together; the rise of *sense* for 'good judgement' goes hand in hand with the rise of sensationist or plain-man philosophies. . . . The suasive power of the word seems to come from treating all reactions or good judgements as of one sort, though, in fact, they presumably range from the highest peaks of imaginative insight, or the greatest heart-searchings of 'enthusiasm', to fundamental but humble processes like recognising a patch of colour as a table. *Sense* tells you to concentrate on the middle of the range, the man-size parts where we feel most at home; and it can do this because the simple use of the trope (which is now taken as a pattern) is an appeal to you to show a normal amount of good judgement, 'like everybody else'. (*CW*, p. 262)

Now clearly there is a sense in which any such usage will manifest a certain 'period' character, the result of its having developed (as Empson notes) in response to new forms of collective awareness or modes of 'commonsense' perception. To this extent the above passage must be read as a commentary on one particular phase of post-Renaissance European thought. Roughly speaking, this would be the phase that started out with the questioning of divinely sanctioned or absolutist principles of social order, and which arrived at its highest, most developed stage with the advent of a rational-humanist paradigm grounded in the notion of a 'public sphere' identified with the supposedly self-evident, universal values of 'good sense', reason, and enlightened self-knowledge. This is why, as Empson says, 'the historical approach can profitably be used'; because key-words like 'sense', despite their implicit universalizing claims, in fact bear witness to changing structures of consciousness – whether 'residual', 'dominant', or 'emergent', to adopt Raymond Williams's useful terms of analysis – which cannot be understood apart from their historical context. But Empson then goes on in the very next sentence to assert what appears a contradictory claim: that 'it is not true that *sense* could only get from "sensations" to "good judgement" by a metaphor under specific conditions' (p. 262). That is to say, there is a 'grammar' of complex words – a range of structural-semantic possibilities or modes of communicative grasp – which may indeed emerge to most striking effect in certain kinds of usage and at certain historical junctures, but which nonetheless constitute a permanent feature of the human capacity for using and interpreting such language. And it is Empson's argument that words like 'sense' are best suited to demonstrate this underlying grammar since they involve the kind of reflex, self-implicating logic – the 'humour of mutuality' allied to a sense of broad-based public appeal – which allows language the freedom to develop such complex semantic resources.

In brief, the main point about 'sense' and its various cognates is that they open up a space of 'communicative action' (in Jürgen Habermas's phrase) where it is assumed *firstly* that speakers have a rational interest in achieving the best possible degree of enlightened mutual understanding, and *secondly* that any real advance in this direction will involve criticism of existing ('commonsense') ideas and values where these serve only to promote some partisan, self-authorized, or class-based set of interests.[66] That the word can move across such a range of meanings, and convey such a variety of meaningful relations between them, is what gives it the scope for playing this role in the articulation of a 'public sphere' progressively detached from religious or other sources of imposed doctrinal usage. More specifically, it enables language to break with those types of irrationalist 'equation', from the paradoxes of Christian doctrine to the slogans of Orwellian Newspeak, which exploit the ever-present tendency of thought to get into muddles by accepting some form of illicit analogical transfer or 'primitive' identity-relation. Thus 'in reasonable language the notion of identity can shift to that of a relation between the elements, as in the English sentence, and the covert assertion becomes for instance "A is included in the larger class B", "A entails B", or "A is like B in possessing a character prominent in B"' (*CW*, p. 255). Such logical nuances in the semantic 'grammar' of complex words mark a real stage of intellectual and social advance since they offer at least some measure of defence against those various dogmatic creeds and ideologies which can otherwise so easily capture our minds.

This is why Empson insists very firmly (perhaps with a backward glance to the problems encountered in *Seven Types*) that 'I am trying to write linguistics; something *quite* unconscious and unintentional, even if the hearer catches it like an infection, is not part of an act of communication' (p. 31). Here as in Habermas, the word 'communication' carries a strong normative weighting, a commitment to certain basic working principles – among them the good of improved communicative grasp and the potential for a genuine 'public sphere' of enlightened consensus values wherein such a promise might at last be redeemed – which mesh with Empson's 'theoretical' concerns at every point in the book. This is not to say that he blithely ignores all the problems that philosophers have put in the way of any straightforward passage from statements of fact (or theoretical truth-claims) to judgements of value. Nor, as we have seen, does Empson want to suggest that a key-word like 'sense' could take on its role as a bearer of secularizing impulses and attitudes quite apart from the relevant background context of historically specific values and beliefs. In fact these are two aspects of the same basic problem: namely, how to reconcile the general and the particular in matters of interpretive judgement, or how to make allowance for the sheer variety of cultural codes, conventions, belief-systems, 'commonsense' ideologies and so forth, while nonetheless offering some explanatory *theory* by which to render their differences intelligible. For any such theory will always come up against the question of its own value-laden character, its commitment to principles – like Empson's rational-humanist outlook – which to some extent determine what shall *count* as evidence in favour of the theory concerned.

Thus: 'till you have decided what a piece of language conveys, like any literary critic, you cannot look around to see what "formal features" convey it; you will then find that some features are of great subtlety, and perhaps fail to trace some at all' (*CW*, P. 437). Empson's target here is the behaviorist school of structural linguistics exemplified by Leonard Bloomfield; an approach which, according to Empson, erects a false idea of 'scientific' objectivity and so ignores a basic truth about language, that we could not attain the least idea of its workings 'if we had not a rich obscure practical knowledge from which to extract the theoretical' (p. 438). But this point clearly applies to *any* theory, including Empson's own, which lays claim to an order of validity (in his case, a 'grammar' of logico-semantic entailment) beyond mere adhoc observation or interpretive flair. For there is plainly a sense in which the particular kinds of 'subtlety' that most interest Empson are those which on the one hand answer to his strongly held rational-humanist beliefs, and on the other display exactly the kinds of 'formal feature' that his method is predisposed to seek out. What is more, *Complex Words* might appear to present an extreme – almost vicious – variant of the 'hermeneutic circle' insofar as it discovers an historical home-ground in precisely that period of semantic development when words like 'sense' were undergoing a shift toward their modern (distinctively secular) range of meaning. And yet, as we have seen, it is Empson's claim that these changes do have a larger, representative significance; that the kinds of semantic 'machinery' involved are *not* just the products of a certain ideological or period-specific world-view but indicate capacities of the human mind which amount to a 'grammar' of interpretive competence, a generalized theory of what goes on in the production and reception of language. Such is at any rate the argument implied if one puts together the analysis of 'sense' and its various cognates ('sensation', 'sensibility', 'good sense' etc.) with the treatment of 'grammar' as a word that conveys – 'self-reflexively', so to speak – certain features of its own semantic performance which can then be extended to other such complex words.

This point may be clarified by taking account of some remarks from his appendix on 'Theories of Value', written when the book was almost ready for press – that is to say, when most of the 'practical' chapters had been completed – and based on Empson's reading around in the relevant philosophical litera-ture. His main concern here is to offer some rejoinder to the emotivist theory of ethical value propounded by Charles Morris, C. L. Stevenson and other influential thinkers of the period. Empson considers the doctrine misleading – as one might expect – insofar as it cuts value-judgements off from any process of rational appraisal, any means by which to analyse their various entailments with regard to both the logic of evaluative language and the wider domain of human activities, interests, and practical involvements. 'Value,' he says, 'seems to come into the sphere of fact of its own accord, rather like imaginary numbers into the solution of real equations; but for rigorous logic you then have to go back and alter the definitions of the numbers in the equations – they were always complex numbers but with null imaginary parts' (*CW*, p. 421). In other words, there is a genuine puzzle here – a puzzle duly noted by philosophers at least since Hume – but it is still a basic truth of human experience that we *do* make the passage from 'is' to 'ought' (or reach evaluative judgements on a cognitive basis) every day of our lives. And moreover, as Empson's mathematical analogy suggests, this process must involve much more in the way of complex ratiocinative thought, at whatever 'subconscious' or 'pre-conscious' level, than could ever be allowed for by theorists who adopt the straightforward emotivist doctrine.

So there is a close relation between Empson's treatment of the fact/value antinomy and his thinking on the question of 'theory' as applied to matters of historical-interpretive judgement. In both cases, the argument runs, it is a fallacy to suppose that theoretical truth-claims are somehow undermined by their involvement with various kindred evaluative attitudes, or by the fact that they first took rise (like the complex of ideas around the key-word 'sense') at a certain stage of cultural-linguistic development. Such findings are no doubt of genuine interest from the standpoint of critics, including Empson, who seek to explain how language plays a role in the social evolution of values and beliefs specific to this or that period. Thus 'a word may become a sort of solid entity, able to direct opinion, thought of as like a person . . . [and] to get some general theory about how this happens would clearly be important' (*CW*, p. 39). But one could only claim to possess such a 'general theory' on condition that the underlying principle involved – like the 'grammar' of complex words – held good across a decently extended range of historical examples, and thus offered something more than an insight into the local (period-specific) workings of select lexical items. And it is here that Empson's book stands squarely opposed to the relativist drift that has overtaken various disciplines – chief among them philosophy, sociology, and literary theory – during the past two decades.

To recapitulate then: as against the post-structuralists and followers of Saussure Empson *denies* 1) that language is a network of purely 'arbitrary' codes and conventions; 2) that these conventions are best understood in terms of the likewise 'arbitrary' link between signifier and signified; 3) that any aspirant 'science' of structural linguistics will respect this condition and hence not concern itself with issues of truth, reference, propositional meaning or other such 'extraneous' factors; and 4) that such a 'science' must in any case acknowledge its own inevitably culture-bound character, its textual constitution or transient status as a product of this or that localized 'discourse' lacking any

claim to ultimate validity or truth. On the contrary, he argues: there is a
'grammar' of complex words which corresponds to certain basic logico-semantic
operations, and in the absence of which we would be unable to interpret even
the simplest forms of verbal behaviour. Thus 'much of what appears to us as a
"feeling" (as is obvious in the case of a complex metaphor) will in fact be quite
an elaborate structure of related meanings' (*CW*, pp. 56–7). In which case the
Saussurian paradigm is plainly inadequate since it takes no account of those
signifying structures or relations of logical entailment that operate both at the
level of discourse (i.e., of extended propositions) and at the level of individual words insofar as they carry 'compacted arguments', or implied semantic
'equations'. Here, as we have seen, Empson is much closer to philosophers in
the Anglo-American 'analytical' tradition – thinkers like Frege, Russell and
Quine – than to anything in the French post-structuralist line of descent.

He also provides strong arguments against the kind of ultra-relativist
outlook (associated nowadays with Foucault and the avatars of so-called 'New
Historicism') which reduces all questions of truth, method and validity to so
many stratagems of 'power/knowledge', or products of the epistemic will-to-
power that drives the various forms of knowledge-constitutive interest.[67] What
Complex Words enables us to grasp – and this is perhaps its most important
contribution in the present climate of debate – is the fallacy or patent non-
sequitur involved in all such relativist doctrines: namely, the idea that *just
because* truth-claims take rise from some given, historically contingent set of
socio-cultural values and beliefs, *therefore* they can possess no validity beyond or
outside that original context. To Empson's way of thinking – call it 'rational-
humanist' – this simply ignores all the evidence of real intellectual advances
(and improvements at the level of communicative grasp) achieved, very often,
against sizable odds of entrenched dogma and prejudice. As he put it most
concisely in a book-review of 1930: 'it is unsafe to explain discovery in terms of
a man's intellectual preconceptions, because the act of discovery is precisely
that of stepping outside preconceptions'.[68] Any theory that fails to take
account of this fact – like currently fashionable forms of post-structuralist and
neo-pragmatist thinking[69] – will thereby be forced into a last-ditch relativist
position where it becomes simply *unthinkable* that communication could
ever take place between different language-games, paradigms, discourses, or
cultural life-forms. Such arguments may have a certain heady appeal but they
can hardly begin to explain how we interpret even the simplest, let alone the
most complex and challenging, forms of verbal utterance.

This may help to make sense of Empson's claim that his 'equations' have a
normative as well as an historically specific or period-based character. It is a
claim that he asserts most explicitly in a passage from the chapter 'Sense and
Sensibility', in many ways the philosophic heart of the book since the key-

words in question – along with their structures of semantic entailment – raise quite a number of relevant issues in the realms of epistemology, ethics, psychology, interpretation-theory and so forth. In the case of such words, Empson writes,

> it is because the historical background is so rich and still so much alive . . . that one can fairly do what seems absurdly unhistorical, make a set of equations from first principles. When you have so unmanageable a history behind a stock opposition the words get worked down till they are a kind of bare stage for any future performance. It is no longer the first question about the words to ask when and how, in history, the various elements were introduced, which the full form makes possible. What the user needs, and feels that he has, is an agreed foundation on which to build his own version; a simple basic difference between the words from which the whole opposition can be extracted. One is forced to ask what it can be; I suggest that it is a difference in the order in which the similar elements in the words are equated, and that any subsequent difference is put in by developing the type of equation as required. (*CW*, p. 269)

This is not to deny that a word like 'sense' could only have developed as it did at this time – i.e., acquired a range of distinctively secular and rational-humanist overtones – as a result of changes in the social and ideological sphere which allowed such a shift to occur. In fact it is one of Empson's main arguments throughout *Complex Words*, and another clear sign of his distance from the current post-structuralist orthodoxy, that critical theory is a useless endeavour if it does not take advantage of a splendid resource like the *Oxford English Dictionary* by way of reconstructing those semantic changes through a detailed study of particular case-histories. That is to say, there is no point having a theory of language that operates on strictly 'synchronic' principles, thus excluding any reference to the way that words have actually developed in response to such pressures (or new-found opportunities) in the realm of social exchange. It is in this sense that language – as Empson understands it – both registers and actively works to promote the most far-reaching shifts of 'public opinion' on issues of religion, politics, or ethical concern. There is, he concedes, 'a puzzle for the linguist about how much is "in" a word and how much in the general purpose of those who use it'. But on the other hand it is this 'shrubbery' of half-acknowledged values and beliefs, 'a social and not a very conscious matter, sometimes in conflict with organized opinion, that one would expect to find only able to survive because somehow inherent in their words' (*CW*, p. 158). In which case clearly the critic's main task is that of reconstructing the development of such words 'on historical principles', like the *OED*, and not coming up with some abstract theory in the structural-synchronic mode.

VIII

The obvious comparision here – and one that deserves more extended treatment – is with Mikhail Bakhtin and his lifelong project for a 'sociological poetics' alive to the diversity of meanings and values that jostle for priority in each and every act of communicative utterance.[70] Like Empson, Bakhtin mounts a trenchant critique of those 'idealist' theories of language – Saussure's pre-eminent among them – which think to achieve the condition of a genuine 'science' by defining their object in rigorously abstract terms (*la langue*), and hence disregarding the variety of contexts, of rival ideologies or competing value-systems which are everywhere at work in real-life socialized discourse.[71] There is also common ground between the two critics in their marked preference for words, genres or modalities of usage that challenge the values of official ('monological') discourse by opening it up to all the counter-currents of subversive popular sentiment. For Bakhtin this tradition starts out with the rise of Menippean satire (as opposed to more decorous, 'classical' forms); achieves perhaps its fullest expression with Rabelais and the style of unbuttoned 'carnivalesque' humour directed against every form of authority, religious and secular; and then comes to characterize 'novelistic' discourse insofar as the novel – at least when not subjected to didactic or moralizing purposes – displays a high degree of 'dialogical' exchange between various (overt or implied) narrative voices.[72] For Empson likewise, language attains to its best, most rewardingly complex uses when it manages to break with those (mainly theological) systems of instituted value and belief which had hitherto placed firm limits on the range of permissible thought and sentiment.

This may be an important matter for any society, he thinks, 'because its accepted official beliefs may be things that would be fatal unless in some degree kept at bay' (*CW*, p. 158). And again, in a passage that will surely strike a familiar note with readers of Bakhtin:

> The web of European civilization seems to have been slung between the ideas of Christianity and those of a half-secret rival, centering perhaps (if you made it a system) round honour; one that stresses pride rather than humility, self-realisation rather than self-denial, caste rather than either the communion of the saints or the individual soul. (p. 159)

Moreover, both critics show a similar tendency to conflate theoretical and normative claims, since they both – as I have noted already of Empson – find their central ideas about language most strikingly embodied in certain speech-forms, idioms or genres that invariably carry a strongly-marked ethical or evaluative toning. A good example is Empson's unpacking of the key-word 'honest', giving numeral values to the various head senses, letters to the predicates imposed by context, and plus or minus signs by way of denoting what he calls 'appreciative' and 'depreciative' pregnancy. The development of this word during the seventeenth and eighteenth centuries

> was supported by the philosophical ideas of the Enlightenment, which have not yet been given up, nor should I want to give them up myself; the man who satisfies his own nature ('3+') and is honest to himself ('4') is expected to have generous feelings ('1b+') from his own unobstructed nature, not from the rules of '1−' or the effort of principle in '2'. (*CW*, p. 216)

What is interesting about this passage, aside from the complex apparatus of notation, is the way that it moves across so readily from a generalized defence of 'enlightenment' values to a paraphrase of 'honest' (or its grammar of semantic implication) which clearly offers backing for that same set of values by claiming both descriptive adequacy and ethical-normative force. From this point of view there is simply no separating questions of value from issues in the realm of theoretical and cognitive enquiry.

All the same it would be wrong to press too far with the comparison between Empson and Bakhtin. For one thing, Empson has some pointed reservations about raising 'rogue-sentiment' into a kind of systematically inverted morality, an ethics of purely anarchic, antinomian or subversive character which − as Bakhtin would have it − somehow works to promote the communal good by casting down all the idols of custom and conventional restraint. 'Chat about rogues and other Rabelaisian figures tends to be cosy from a safe distance,' Empson writes; 'they may have been of great value to our society but very nasty' (*CW*, pp. 158−9). And indeed his book provides some striking examples of the way that such words ('rogue', 'dog', 'fool', 'honest', even 'sense') can take on a range of pathological meanings, or twisted cynical implications, sharply at odds with their usual ethos of tolerant mutual understanding. Where he differs from Bakhtin is in offering the means − the normative and logico-semantic resources − by which to interpret such markedly deviant structures of meaning and explain how they managed to get a hold under certain specific social and historical conditions. His chapters on '"Sense" in *Measure for Measure*' and '"Honest" in *Othello*' are predictably the two essays where this approach finds its most challenging material. Thus it is hard not to feel that 'the way everybody [in *Othello*] calls Iago honest amounts to a criticism of the word itself; that is, Shakespeare means "a bluff forthright manner, and amusing talk, which get a man called honest, may go with extreme dishonesty". Or indeed that this is treated as normal, and the satire is on our nature not on language' (*CW*, p. 219). But the main point about Shakespeare's cynical variations on the word is that they only work at all, or can only achieve their singular dramatic effect, by making such a contrast with the structure of meanings more usual at this time, that is to say, the implicit 'humour of mutuality' that allowed 'honest' to develop as a token of secular-humanist values. In short, 'it is the two notions of being ready to blow the gaff on other people and frank to yourself about your own desires that seem to me crucial about Iago; they grow on their own, independent of the hearty feeling that would normally humanize them' (p. 221). And of course this claim takes for granted the idea that there exists a normative 'grammar' of complex words, a capacity for grasping such superinduced ironies – parasitic on the usual structure of meaning – which requires both a highly developed sensitivity to nuances of historical usage and a grasp of those other, more basic forms of semantic entailment whose logic Empson sets out to explain.

One could summarize the divergence of approach between Empson and Bakhtin in terms of the differing emphasis they place on theory (or the claims of analytical reason) *vis-à-vis* the multiplicity of languages, speech-genres, value-systems, socialized codes and conventions etc. Bakhtin's attitude, roughly stated, is one that holds 'the more the merrier', an outlook of undifferentiating pluralist 'freeplay' that celebrates diversity for its own sake and equates such values as reason, truth and method with the workings of a grim paternal law of oppressive 'monological' discourse. For Empson, conversely, this amounts to a species of what might be called 'infantile leftism', a failure to grasp that such anarchic tendencies can just as well lean over into forms of vicious irrationalist sentiment – like those he analyses in Iago's 'honest' – which scarcely justify Bakhtin's claims for the radical or liberating power of language when released from all normative values and constraints. 'To get some general theory about how this happens would clearly be important; if our language is continually thrusting doctrines on us, perhaps very ill-considered ones, the sooner we understand the process the better' (*CW*, p. 39). And this also has clear implications for the issue of priority (if such it is – and Empson would I am sure reject such a claim) between 'historical' and 'theoretical' approaches to literary criticism. For on his view it is evident that both come in at an early stage in the process of interpretation; that you cannot get any sense of how an author is using some particular 'complex word', or range of such words in context, without *first* learning as much as possible about the relevant historico-semantic background, and *second* attempting to fit the various period-senses into a working structure, a 'grammar' of implicit semantic equations by which to understand their argumentative force. But this would involve a good deal more in the way of 'theoretical' exposition than Bakhtin and his followers seem willing to provide.[73]

One area where these questions have an obvious bearing is that of lexicography, or the long-running debate – taken up by Empson in his chapter 'Dictionaries' – on how best to cover the historical ground while also giving users a practical grasp of the semantic resources (as well as the pitfalls) encountered by language-learners and specialists alike. Empson begins by stating plainly 'what I hope is already obvious, that such work on individual words as I have been able to do has been almost entirely dependent on using the majestic object (the *OED*) as it stands' (*CW*, p. 391). But he then goes on to offer a series of proposals for a different, less cumbersome and hence more effective practice of dictionary-making, one that would not simply list the various senses of a word in roughly chronological (or topic-based) order, but apply something more like Empson's own system of extracting the relevant semantic 'equations' and thus conveying a sense of the operative 'grammar' that needs to be grasped by any competent user. 'This amount of symbolism, however indecorous it might appear, really does seem to be needed, because it is important to make the reader notice that the senses can combine and interact' (p. 396). And again, more explicitly: 'what they [native speakers as well as foreign learners] need is an English-to-English dictionary which is guaranteed against circularity, does on the other hand give working rules to distinguish near-synonyms, and also gives warnings of the unexpected tricks that a word might play, especially by an unlooked-for sense poking up' (p. 397).

Empson's chief point with these proposals – worked out in some detail across a range of more-or-less problematic cases – is that even the most dedicated efforts of archival research or philological scholarship won't much help the dictionary user if they do not give some account of the semantic grammar, or the logic of (often unnoticed) propositional attitudes, that defines what passes for a 'competent' use of the word or idiom in question. And this links up in turn with his approach to questions of interpretive method in the literary-critical chapters. That is to say, it combines a lively sense of the historical relativities of language-usage with a firm persuasion – on argued theoretical grounds – that one can only explain these semantic and socio-cultural shifts from a rationalist standpoint sufficiently prepared to analyse the logic of their various (more or less covert) structures of implication. Hence his quarrel with Raymond Williams over the latter's book *Keywords*: a fine piece of dictionary-hunting, Empson thought, offering lots of handy source-material, but apt to give the wrong impression by treating language-users as passive creatures of habit, entirely at the mercy of their pet words and slogans. Thus Williams 'decides that many of our common words regularly tempt us to accept wrong beliefs, usually political ones. . . . He does not say that resistance to them is beyond human power, which would make his book entirely useless, but his introduction offers very little hope from the technique he provides'.[74] Not that Empson was inclined to underestimate the suasive power of such words, or the extent to which people's thinking could be influenced, on a wide range of moral and political questions, by exactly these kinds of subliminal prompting. His own experience of wartime propaganda work was enough to make Empson keenly aware of this fact. But he saw no reason to treat it as a basic truth about language – a grimly Orwellian truth – that such rhetorical effects were so pervasive that no kind of analysis along logico-semantic lines could hope to explain or indeed counteract their influence. Oddly enough Empson cites a whole series of examples from *Keywords* – like the entries on 'interest', 'materialist', 'common', and 'educated' – where Williams *does* in fact offer something very like his own type of argument on rational-reconstructive lines. It is hard not to feel that his response in these cases has more to do with politics – or with Empson's suspicion that Williams has smuggled in a Marxist ideological agenda under cover of his seemingly 'disinterested' method – than with any deep-seated theoretical difference. (Thus 'many of the entries are not political, and they show great breadth of mind, especially in showing that a controversial word contains both sides of the controversy in itself'.)[75] But his argument here, as always, is that you cannot really separate questions of method (or 'theory') from questions of substantive ethico-political 'interest'; that theory does best when it acknowledges the sheer variety of such interests at work in language; and that any method which narrows down the range of intelligible motives and meanings is sure to miss the point in some potentially harmful way.

It is in this sense, as I have argued, that Empson's complex words (or the 'machinery' he offers by way of understanding them) can be seen to controvert any doctrinaire version of the fact/value antinomy. They involve on the one hand a *theory* of interpretation – an account of how we, as competent language-users, habitually 'do things with words' – and on the other an *ethics* of mutual understanding with its own distinct set of humanist and rationalist values squarely opposed to all forms of religious or proto-theological dogma. Of course these are principles hardly likely to commend Empson's book to literary theorists who uncritically endorse the current strain of anti-humanist, non-cognitivist, counter-enlightenment or 'postmodern' thought.

If one had to cast around for a present-day figure who agrees on all the main points at issue then undoubtedly Habermas would be the prime candidate. Like Empson, he sets out a strong defence of 'enlightenment' values and truth-claims, basing that defence on a theory of language (or 'communicative action') which involves both descriptive and normative elements.[76] What Empson has to say about the reciprocal character – the self-implicating logic or 'humour of mutuality' – manifest in key-words like 'sense' finds a parallel in Habermas's regulative notion of an 'ideal speech-situation', a public sphere or optimal context of free and open debate where the various parties would no longer be subject to the distortions, injustices and failures of communicative grasp brought about by currently-prevailing social conditions. Moreover, one could point out a similar shift of emphasis in the course of their respective enquries into language, meaning and interpretive method. Thus where Habermas moves from the 'subject-centered' or epistemological concerns of a work like *Knowledge and Human Interests*[77] to the language-based approach of his later writings (notably *Communication and the Evolution of Society*), Empson follows a similar path (as I argued in more detail above) from the analysis of complex mind-states (*Seven Types*) or modalities of reflective self-knowledge (*Some Versions*) to the study of language in its logico-semantic and more broadly social dimension. Above all, they are both committed to the basic principle – as against the current drift of postmodernist fashion – that thinking cannot simply abandon those 'enlightenment' values of truth, reason and critique that have come to define what Habermas calls the 'unfinished project of modernity'.

All the same there is one major point of disagreement between Habermas and Empson, a point that is so significant as to constitute the most original and striking aspect of *Complex Words*. For it is Habermas's contention that poetry – or literary language in general – belongs to an order of 'world-disclosive', aesthetic or imaginative discourse quite distinct from those other kinds of language (science, philosophy, law, ethics, literary criticism) which have separated out during the past two centuries in the course of evolving their own specific standards of cognitive and evaluative truth. Such is indeed the precondition of maintaining that enlightened 'public sphere' of differential truth-claims which Habermas sets out to defend against its current detractors. Thus he sees nothing but error and confusion in any attempt to erase the 'genre-difference' between literature and philosophy, a charge which Habermas – wrongly, I think – tries to lay at Derrida's door, but which certainly applies to many others in the wider postmodern-neopragmatist camp. This argument is worked out in great detail by Habermas in his book *The Philosophical Discourse of Modernity*.[78] My only point here is that it sets him decidedly at odds with Empson, since the latter's central claim, refined and developed throughout *Complex Words*, is that one cannot (or should not) treat poetic language as somehow existing in a realm quite apart from the logic of truth-conditional discourse, the standards of cognitive accountability, or the interests of rational understanding. Such, after all, is Empson's chief objection to Richards's theory of 'emotive' meaning, as well as to the American New Critics and their talk of 'irony', 'paradox' and other privileged tropes, as a result of which poetry is conceived to exist in a self-enclosed sphere of aesthetic values devoid of truth-telling warrant. Thus to Empson's way of thinking there could be no warrant for Habermas's exclusion of literary language from the 'public realm' of enlightened discourse where truth-claims are properly tried and tested through the process of uncoerced critical debate.

So the comparison with Habermas, though useful and suggestive, breaks down at the point where Empson asserts his most distinctive literary-critical claim: that poetic understanding is *in no way discontinuous* with the kinds of sense-making judgement and analysis brought to bear upon other (whether 'everyday' or specialized) genres of language usage. And this applies even to metaphor, traditionally thought of, at least since Aristotle, as the hallmark and touchstone of language in its creative or 'literary' aspect. Thus, as Empson puts it, 'a metaphor goes outside the ordinary range of a word, [while] an equation "argues from" the ordinary range, treating it as a source of traditional wisdom' (*CW*, p. 332). But even so one can offer a more elaborate scheme of equations, analogical transfers, 'appreciative pregnancies', contextual cues and structures of compacted argument by which to explain how metaphors work without resort to woolly notions of 'emotive' meaning or mysterious modes of 'primitive', 'pre-logical' or irrationalist thought. As Empson writes,

> The mind does not in general use words without attaching to them both a class and its defining property, however vaguely, but owing to the creative looseness of the mind it can sometimes use defining properties which, apart from the aggregate of experience which can be tapped by one word, remain obscure. Cases where a word seems to leave its usual range successfully often occur when the conscious mind has its eye on a few important elements in the situation and the classifying subconscious is called on for a suggestive word. . . . The process may be like a 'construction' in Euclidean geometry; you draw a couple of lines joining points which are already in the diagram, and then the proof seems obvious, though till then the right 'aspect' of the thing was nowhere in sight. (*CW*, p. 335)

Empson's chapter on metaphor can thus be seen as a firm repudiation of theories that assert some basic, irreducible difference between literal and figural modes of language, or those which maintain – like Habermas – that it is simply wrong, a species of category-mistake, to apply the standards of cognitive (truth-seeking) discourse to language in its 'world-disclosive', metaphorical, or literary aspect. If Empson is right – and his ideas about metaphor have been strongly endorsed by (among others) the philosopher Donald Davidson[79] – then there is no good reason to adopt this line. Such arguments would be seen as amounting to just another form of that widespread irrationalist or aestheticizing tendency in present-day thought which Habermas, ironically, sets out to challenge in *The Philosophical Discourse of Modernity*.

But what of those poets – Wordsworth especially – whose language resists such treatment to the point where Empson's rationalist semantics seems very nearly played off the field? In *Seven Types*, as we have seen, he devoted some strenuous but finally rather baffled commentary to the climactic lines from Wordsworth's 'Tintern Abbey', professing to admire the poem whole-heartedly, yet finding its logical grammar 'shuffling and evasive' when it came to the high points of pantheist doctrine. The major advance in *Complex Words* is the fact that it can address these problems without arriving at an ultimate deadlock, or a kind of uneasy stand-off, between the claims of reason and those of Wordsworth's inspirational rhetoric. Thus the chapter in question ('Sense in The Prelude') explores the more benign or less actively misleading kinds of paradox involved in the language of Romantic nature-mysticism. And it is able to do so by virtue of the shift from a somewhat mistrustful depth-psychological approach to one that operates with a better understanding of the logical grammar – the order of unconscious but nonetheless describable truth-claims or 'equations' – that characterizes Wordsworth's high prophetic strain. Thus 'the whole poetical and philosophical effect', Empson writes, 'comes from a violent junction of sense-data to the divine imagination given by love, and the middle term is cut out' (*CW*, p. 296). That 'middle term' is the commonsense ground of moderating rational judgement, as contrasted (say) with the high dialectics of 'wit' in Empson's reading of Pope's 'Essay On Criticism'. By using language in such a way as to jump clean over this stage in the argument Wordsworth moved into regions of paradox pregnant with irrationalist hints and possibilities. In effect, he persuades the reader to accept his pantheist creed through the 'firmness and assurance' of these Type IV equations, structures of implied argument 'whose claim was false, because they did not really erect a third concept as they pretended to' (p. 305). Yet Empson still very readily admits that 'the result makes good poetry, and probably suggests important truths' (ibid.).

His reading thus steers a difficult path between two opposed philosophies of language, truth and meaning. It refuses the straightforward emotivist option of ignoring the truth-claims and taking what Wordsworth has to offer in the way of inspirational uplift or luxuriant sentimental appeal. At the same time it sees that there are powers of suggestion vested in poetic language which might always elude any normative grammar based on too rigid or prescriptive a use of the logico-semantic categories. '[This] ecstasy both destroys normal *sense* and fulfils it, and the world thus shown is both the same as and different from the common one' (*CW*, p. 295). Of course such perplexities could be simply set aside by assuming that poetry just *is* paradoxical, that it exists *sui generis* in a realm quite apart from the entailments of rational prose meaning or commonsense logic. Thus 'what Wordsworth wanted to say', according to Cleanth Brooks, 'demanded his use of paradox . . . , could only be said power-fully through paradox'.[80] But this does no more than translate the emotivist view into a language of high formalist principle that could offer no convincing account of the difference between Wordsworth's exalted 'language of the sense' and the semantic perversions of Orwellian Newspeak. Empson's point is that the reader (or the competent reader) is indeed capable of making such distinc-tions, most often by going through a series of tentative efforts to sort the meaning into some kind of logical structure, and then – if the passage still puts up resistance – allowing for the presence of rhetorical effects that finally elude such treatment.

Thus valuable (as opposed to meretricious or merely propagandist) examples of the kind will tend to evoke a much greater range of possible meanings and structures, even if none of them turns out to satisfy the strictest requirements of logical sense.

> 'Sensation is Imagination' is a possible slogan, but both this and its inverse seem very open to misunderstanding without making the real point. 'Sensation and Imagination are included in a larger class' is merely dull; besides, the important thing may well be that they overlap to form a narrower class. 'Sensation and Imagination interlock' seems the best way to put it. But I think it is fair to say that Wordsworth had not got any translation ready; he was much better at adumbrating his doctrine through rhetorical devices than at writing it out in full. (*CW*, p. 299–300)

Empson's involvement with Basic English, a cause he took up at Richards's behest during the years of preparatory work on *Complex Words*, is very evident in this passage.[81] Along with the experience of teaching in China and Japan, it led him to conclude that complexity in language need not (indeed should not) become an excuse for adopting the kind of high-toned obscurantist attitude that placed poetry beyond reach of plain-prose rational explication. 'Writing it out in full' is not at all the same thing as pedantically murdering to dissect, or refusing the wisdom and enjoyment that poetry has to offer for the sake of some hard-bitten intellectualist creed. On the contrary: it is the best way to understand a poet like Wordsworth, one who expressly believed that 'poetry had better be made out of the "simple language of men", though he made good poetry out of hard words as well'.[82]

This sentence comes from a 1940 broadcast talk on 'Wordsworth and Basic English', one of several pieces that Empson wrote by way of trying out the Basic programme as a technique of practical criticism. Such an exercise is useful, he thinks, not because it gets the full meaning across through an adequate prose paraphrase, but because it sets one off in the right direction, or the right frame of mind, for finding out where the problems lie and then going on to make another, better attempt. 'In looking for the reason why your first answer was wrong, you are sent on to the important questions about poetry. So this process makes the structure of the poetry much clearer.'[83] And again:

> We do not commonly get the ideas opened up, and see the reasons for the feelings. So all this argument about the effect of the lines has come straight out of our attempt at putting the sense into Basic. Without that start we would probably not see what was important, in the structure of the thought.[84]

In retrospect it is clear that this was already the attitude behind Empson's passages of multiple paraphrase in *Seven Types* – such an affront to orthodox

New Critical doctrine – as well as bearing a distinct kinship to the root notion of Empsonian pastoral, that of 'putting the complex into the simple'. But it was only with the writing of *Complex Words* that he managed to bring these interests together in a generalized theory of language and interpretation that could encompass both the normative logic of everyday discourse and the kinds of paradoxical truth-claim implied by a poet like Wordsworth.

IX

When he reviewed A. J. Ayer's *The Foundations of Empirical Knowledge* in 1941 Empson was already convinced that 'the whole development of rationalism since the sixteenth century has been playing round "sense" '.[85] As might be expected it is a broadly sympathetic review, approving Ayer's attitude of sturdy commonsense reason and also – up to a point – his attack on 'metaphysics' in the name of a logical-positivist programme grounded in the methods, procedures or evidential protocols of modern science. All the same Empson points to certain difficulties with Ayer's phenomenalist talk of 'sense-data' and his suggestion that 'we can only build up our knowledge out of what the senses give us'. Such is of course the doctrine (or the structure of implied equations) that Empson discovers in one major use of the key-word 'sense', that is to say, an outlook of secular and rationalist confidence in the basic reliability of the senses and the power of human reason ('sense' = 'good judgement') to arrive at a knowledge of the world on this basis. But if one pushes the normative claims too hard – as by equating 'rationality' with a refusal to go beyond the evidence of the senses, or by treating metaphysics *tout court* as a species of mystified word-magic – then one ends up by endorsing a phenomenalist creed where 'sense-data' (or unmediated sensory perceptions) are the only valid items of knowledge, and where nothing could count as evidence against some 'commonsense' delusion presently imposed by the limits of our physical powers of observation. Thus:

> the plain man may remark that the universe has been sturdily indifferent for eons to the observers to whom its reality is reduced; Mr Ayer will reply that we only *can* be referring to logically possible observations. But he seems very anthropomorphic about observers. Bees see ultra-violet light; perhaps birds feel the points of the compass; some people say atoms have dim sensations – is it logically possible for me to be an atom? The objection to assertions about matter is that we can't conceivably observe it. How are we better off by reducing it to sense-data which we can't conceive ourselves as having? Here again, we know less about the sense-data than we do about the things.[86]

This amounts to a defence of commonsense reason against the kinds of philosophical perplexity that arise when that same set of values – as carried by a key-word like 'sense' – is allowed to harden into abstract dogma. But Empson also makes the point that even scientists could not get along with anything like so a rigid a conception of what counts as genuine (veridical) knowledge. Thus 'one impulse "active in the phenomenalist" is a desire to push out of sight the immense queerness necessary in the universe before we can get any knowledge of it at all'.[87] This argument is partly a Kantian response to Ayer's strain of Humean radical empiricism: a response which holds that we had better start out from 'the fact that the universe is one which can be observed by the creatures it contains', creatures – that is to say – whose knowledge-constitutive interests and capacities are highly evolved and likely to reflect a fair measure of truth about that universe and its physical laws. There may indeed be 'innumerable other universes', but ours is after all 'the only one that could produce a book describing itself'.

However, Empson's main objection to the hardline logical-positivist programme – or to Ayer's narrowly phenomenalist construal of the sense of 'sense' – is that it cuts out so many of those meanings and beliefs that have developed alongside the discourse of scientific rationalism, thus providing a context, a 'public sphere' of differential truth-claims, values and so forth, by which to adjudicate in matters of wider (non-scientific) concern. This is why, as Empson says, 'to a literary man his [Ayer's] idea of the purposes that govern a choice of words seems naive; there are generally several purposes at once, and even the chooser may not be clear about them till later'.[88] So a rationalist semantics – even a strong version of the thesis like Empson's – must also find room for varieties of language that do not make sense on the narrow (positivistic) account, but which may nonetheless both suggest important truths and supply some 'machinery', some grammar of equations, by which to interpret them. It was this line of argument that he later took up in the chapter on Wordsworth in *Complex Words*, a chapter which tests his theory to the limit by focusing mainly on those passages where 'sense' carries the whole weight of high romantic argument. Thus 'the word, I maintain, means both the process of sensing and the supreme act of imagination, and unites them by a jump; the same kind of jump as that in the sentence about crossing the Alps, which identifies the horror caused by the immediate sensations with the exaltation that developed from them' (*CW*, p. 304).

What Empson is describing here is of course that revelatory moment of transition from the order of sensuous (phenomenal) experience to the order of 'suprasensible' ideas which critics and philosophers since Kant have treated as the mark of sublime imagining. Clearly he approaches such claims with a measure of scepticism, or at any rate an attitude of principled doubt with regard to their epistemological and ethical correlates. To this extent (and despite all the differences I have noted) Empson anticipates the thinking of a critic like Paul de Man, especially those essays – among them 'The Rhetoric of

Temporality' – where de Man challenges the privileged terms of mainstream romantic scholarship, terms such as metaphor and symbol which purport to establish a relation of direct, unmediated union between mind and nature, subject and object, language and the realm of organic processes and forms.[89] Here also the critique proceeds by way of a meticulous attention to details of language – most often discrepant or anomalous details – which in turn signal the presence of elements irreducible to any such mystified organicist doctrine. Thus the valorization of symbol and metaphor (the master-tropes of romantic discourse in the German and English traditions) gives way, on this account, to the more prosaic figures of metonymy and allegory, figures that are linked, as de Man argues, 'in their common demystification of an organic world postulated in a symbolic mode of analogical correspondences or in a mimetic mode of representation in which fiction and reality could coincide' (*BI*, p. 222). Hence his objection to the orthodox reading of romantic poetry proposed by theorists such as M. H. Abrams and Earl Wasserman: that they adopt what amounts to a fideist position, accepting the truth-claims of metaphor and symbol at face value, and failing to notice those complicating factors, those moments of aporia or non-coincidence between meaning and intent, which effectively undermine such a reading.[90] Thus Abrams typically 'makes it seem . . . as if the romantic theory of imagination did away with analogy altogether and that Coleridge in particular replaced it by a genuine and working monism' (p. 195).

In the essays of his last period de Man traced this tendency back to its origins in the widespread misreading of Kant – especially of Kant's passages on the sublime in his third *Critique* – which first gave rise to this 'aesthetic ideology' by ignoring the various problematical tensions that characterized the discourse of romanticism.[91] And he did so primarily in order to resist that powerful strain of post-Kantian idealist thought – starting out with Schiller's *Letters on Aesthetic Education* – which raised the idea of the 'organic' artwork, or its subjective correlative, the balanced and harmonious consort of human faculties, into a model for the conduct of human affairs under their ethical, social, and political aspects. 'The "state" that is here being advocated,' he writes, 'is not just a state of mind or of soul, but a principle of political value and authority that has its own claims on the shape and the limits of our freedom.'[92] For it is partly by way of this aestheticizing drift – this extension of organicist themes and motifs from nature, through art, to the realm of morality and politics – that subsequent ideologues were able to envisage the nation-state as an ideal expression of the unified collective will, an expression manifest at every level of language, culture, and history. At very least there is a strong elective affinity between doctrines of a late-romantic transcendentalist cast – especially the idea of symbolic language as achieving a consummate union of time and eternity, the particular and the universal, contingency and necessity – and those potent forms of nationalist mystique that exploited a similar rhetoric in pursuit of more sinister political ends.

It is worth noting in this connection that Empson's talk on 'Wordsworth and Basic English' was broadcast at the outset of World War Two, and that it makes some of its points through a comparison of the late-published (1850), more conservative and doctrinaire version of *The Prelude* with the original 1805 text. What Empson brings out by means of this parallel reading is a general falling-off in the poet's powers of detailed local observation, along with a marked increase in the number of first-person pronouns (putting Wordsworth, rather than nature, at the centre of his own imaginative world), and also – most importantly – a coarsening of the verbal textures whereby words like 'sense' came to lose a great deal of their previous suggestiveness and semantic range. The effect, Empson says, is like 'turning the guns around from firing at the Germans and pointing them against the French',[93] a simile whose application at the time must have carried somewhat more than a casual force. The implication. I think, is that a lot more hangs on the usage of such words – whether in poetry, politics, or everyday parlance – than could ever be explained on any version of the emotivist or non-cognitivist approach. And this idea is reinforced by the implicit analogy that Empson draws between the older Wordsworth's revisionist stance, his disenchantment with French political events and desire to cover the traces of his own revolutionary past, and the troubled situation of 1940 when Europe was once again entering a period of extreme ideological turmoil. It hardly needs saying after recent revelations about de Man's wartime journalism that in his case also the experience must have left a keen sense of the wider political issues bound up with these seemingly specialized concerns in the realm of linguistic and interpretive theory.[94]

This is not the place for a detailed exposition of de Man's writings on aesthetic ideology. Suffice it to say that he, like Empson, holds out against any too willing acquiescence in paradox or other such (supposedly) characteristic marks of 'literary' language; that they both find this attitude potentially complicit with forms of ideological mystification; that de Man's deconstructive strategies of reading are aimed, like Empson's, at uncovering the sources of precisely this suasive or rhetorical power vested in the discourse of romantic poetry and criticism; and finally, that Empson and de Man both insist on maintaining some version of the working distinction between logic, grammar and rhetoric, in de Man's case more explicitly by suggesting a return to the forensic model of the classical *trivium*,[95] and with Empson – by the time of *Complex Words* – through a detailed attention to the structures of logico-semantic 'grammar' that can always be short-circuited (as by poets like Wordsworth) to produce a whole range of paradoxical truth-claims or 'Type IV' equations inherently resistant to the powers of rational understanding. De Man makes this point most often by locating the moments of 'aporia' (or interpretive undecidability) which result from the conflict between literal and figural, logical and rhetorical, or constative and performative dimensions of language. What he will not accept, unlike the 'old' New Critics, is any notion that logical criteria (or standards of truth and falsehood) have to be suspended in the reading of literary texts, since these embody an order of 'paradoxical' wisdom above and beyond the requirements of plain-prose reason. And for Empson likewise it is a suspect move – a strategy of evasion or line of least resistance – for the critic to adopt such a blandly accommodating view of the relation between logic, grammar, and rhetoric. One must, he says, 'distinguish a "fallacy", which depends on your not noticing the logical contradiction, from a "paradox", in which it is recognized and viewed as "profound". It is only the paradox which is apprehended as a contradiction, and could become a candidate for listing as "X = −X"' (*CW*, 53n.). But it is clear from what Empson has to say elsewhere in *Complex Words*, especially the chapters on Wordsworth and Milton, that very often these cases cannot easily be distinguished, so that the fittest state of mind in which to appreciate poetry is one that casts around for some rational machinery by which to reformulate the paradox, and only then (when the available options run out) falls back on the 'profound' interpretation. Otherwise, as he felt, the way was wide open to the kinds of really harmful irrationalist mystique that could always crop up when rhetoric got the upper hand over logic, or when Type IV equations were taken on faith as 'deep' paradoxical truths, beyond reach of rational judgement.

So some kind of 'theory' was evidently needed in order to resist this recurrent strain of literary-critical fashion. On the other hand Empson disliked the way that 'Eng. Lit.' was becoming a geared-up affair of competing systems and theories. Often they struck him as rationalizations of a new technique for drilling the students into an attitude of religious or political orthodoxy. Most offensive were those 'Symbolist' readings (of Shakespeare especially) which equated profundity with a total lack of interest in commonplace worldly motives and values.[96] During the 1960s Empson reviewed quite a number of books, mostly by American academics, in which he detected this perverse 'neo-Christian' ideology at work. Of Maynard Mack's *King Lear in our Time* he remarked that the professors only seemed to feel safe with a Lear who had renounced all claim to sanity and entered a state of near-lunatic transcendental 'wisdom'. 'It is a very Eng. Lit. theory; developed I think because an impressive obscurantism, teaching the kids to revere things that are very odd or plainly evil, is imagined to be the only way to prevent them going red.'[97] In the face of such readings Empson insisted over and again on the importance of 'attending to the story' and not giving in to the prevalent cant of other-worldly meanings and values.

This was probably the chief reason why Empson turned aside from the relatively specialized interests of *Complex Words* and devoted most of his time over the next three decades to the task of resisting this pervasive drift towards pious orthodox creeds. It led him flatly to reject any 'theory' which distracted attention from the urgent business of rescuing Shakespeare, Donne, Milton, Coleridge or Joyce from the hands of their perverse modern exegetes.[98] What these critics were attempting, Empson thought, was a wholesale annexation of literary studies to the High Church monarchist values handed down by Eliot and his numerous acolytes. The canonical 'tradition' of Eliot's devising had already been effective in closing many students' minds to the virtues of any poetry (like Shelley's) that might set them thinking about politics or doubting the truth of Christian revelation. The radical side of Milton had likewise been pushed out of sight by a technique of focusing on (largely irrelevant) 'problems' of style and thus excluding any serious discussion of the poet's life-history, political involvements, and – above all – his embattled theological stance. It remained for the critics to take a poet like Donne – central to Eliot's 'tradition', but uncomfortably prone to heterodox ideas – and make him safe for modern readers by reinterpreting the poems so as to keep those ideas out of view. Empson noticed this technique at work in some of Eliot's own later writing on Donne.[99] The trick was to concede that the ideas were there, but only as a springboard for the poet's neat turns of 'irony', 'paradox' or metaphysical 'wit'. The twenties view of Donne as radical *thinker* – in matters of sexual politics, science and religion alike – could thus be ignored and the poems reclaimed for a latter-day ethos of pious conformist zeal.

Empson became increasingly gloomy about the prospects of turning back this tide of neo-orthodox unreason. In 1967 he was still relatively sanguine, holding out the hope that literary studies might yet be saved from these effects of doctrinal and ideological distortion. Such gross abuses 'are bound to crop up', Empson writes, 'and might destroy it; but with periodic sanitary efforts it can probably be got to continue in a sturdy, placid way, as is needed'.[100] But as time went on the situation worsened, so that Empson felt obliged to devote himself almost full-time to countering the trend in its various forms. In the case of Donne this meant taking on not only the critics (including, most recently, John Carey's hard-boiled debunking approach)[101] but also the editors whose attentions, in Empson's view, were increasingly apt to disfigure the poetry. Brought up on Grierson's pioneering edition of 1921, Empson now found numerous instances where the latest texts either muffled an argument or reduced the poem to a cynical caricature of 'decent' human feelings. The editors (whether wittingly or not) were in league with the critics in using these techniques to distort the plain sense of what they read.[102] Empson's own poems of the Cambridge years had been written partly in excited response to the current 'rediscovery' of Donne, encouraged both by Eliot's early essays and Grierson's classic edition. All the greater was his sense of betrayal when Eliot's

influence turned out to promote a very different and (to Empson) very damaging line of literary-critical fashion. This took the form of ignoring Donne's
arguments and imputing various kinds of subtle irony (or 'deep' symbolic
meaning) to ensure that any ideas left over were deprived of all real argumentative force. The blame for this approach he placed squarely at the door of
Eliot and those who had developed and refined his technique. 'Mallarmé and
Verlaine, it seems fair to remember, did not employ their treasured Symbols to
insinuate scandal, as at a cats' tea-party; this bold application of the method
was invented by our pious Establishment critics.'[103] As with Donne, so with
Milton, Coleridge, Joyce and others: the plain task now (Empson thought) was
to clear away the fog of creeping orthodox revisionism which threatened to
obscure these authors from view.

It is hardly cause for surprise that Empson's later writings have often been
ignored by those who would assign him a handy slot in the history of modern
criticism. *Seven Types* is still seen as his greatest single achievement, with *Some
Versions* a somewhat puzzling sequel (not least on account of its ambivalent
politics), and *Complex Words* a curious mixture of homely commonsense
wisdom and clanking theoretical machinery. Beyond that, *Milton's God* is
sometimes picked upon for polemical reasons, but otherwise treated by 'serious'
Milton scholars to a virtual conspiracy of silence. Empson, after all, reached
the point of rejecting just about every movement of ideas in contemporary
critical debate. Theory itself became suspect insofar as it propped up perverse
and damaging creeds (like the anti-intentionalist doctrine) which then gave rise
to objectionable readings. 'A critical theory is powerful indeed,' as he once
remarked of Bentley and Pearce on Milton, 'if it can blind its holders to so
much beauty' (*SVP*, p. 129). Yet Empson has a certain admiration for those
eighteenth-century rationalist scholars whose methods, he feels, at least had
the merit of not giving in to the forces of unreason or letting the issues go by
default. In *Some Versions* he thinks it a cause for regret that they 'lost so many
points' in the wrangling over Milton, since their defeat in the long run 'had a
bad effect on criticism' (p. 130). And in *Seven Types* he puts the case more
strongly with reference to the earliest editors of Shakespeare and their attempts
to make rational sense of disputed or obscure textual details. As Empson
remarks: 'we no longer have enough faith to attempt such a method, but its
achievement must be regarded with respect, because it has practically invented
some of Shakespeare's most famous passages' (*ST*, p. 82). There is much the
same ambivalence about Empson's theorizing in *Complex Words*. On the one
hand it is needed in order to rebut the more harmful forms of emotivist
doctrine and provide at least the basis, the enabling groundwork, for an
alternative approach to such questions. On the other it threatens to get in the
way of a critic's intuitive responses, an objection that Empson cannot afford to
disregard since his main point about words like 'sense', 'fool' and 'honest' is

that their structures developed out of a rich background of tacit values and assumptions, a background which the reader has to grasp intuitively before he or she can make a start in understanding the logico-semantic 'machinery' involved. Thus 'we must not develop tender feelings towards our little bits of machinery; they need to be kept sharply separate from the delicacy and warmth of the actual cases they are to be used on. . . . there might really be a harmful effect from using this kind of analysis if the two things were liable to get mixed up' (*CW*, p. 19). Hence the often startling fluctuations of tone, between passages of hard-pressed verbal explication and others where the bluff, no-nonsense approach takes over.

This is what makes it impossible to claim Empson for either side in the current, drastically polarized debate about 'theory' and its uses in literary criticism. In *Seven Types* he aligned himself squarely with those who put their faith in 'analysis', rather than mere 'appreciation', as the fittest state of mind in which to understand a poem. Forty years on he reaffirmed that position in response to an American critic who seemed to regard it (symptomatically, Empson thought) as just a species of youthful eccentricity.

> In the year when I. A. Richards was tutoring me some of my friends at Cambridge . . . thought that his 'scientism' was philosophically very absurd, and I could usually, after my weekly hour with Richards, go and tell them some particularly absurd thing he had just said. They, of course, were following T. S. Eliot, early members of the Neo-Christian movement.[104]

'Scientism' here stands in for the attitude of open-minded rational debate which Empson so admired about intellectual life at Cambridge in the 1920s. He never lost faith in this idea, and showed little patience with those (like Leavis) who made a wholesale crusade out of rejecting science, 'technocratic' reason and all their works. Having theories and testing them against the evidence was part of the normal way in which the mind got to grips with experience. And besides, as Empson's poems had shown, there was no firm line to be drawn between the speculative interests of modern science – especially astronomy and nuclear physics – and the needs of a rich emotional life. Yet along with this belief went a feeling that theory could easily harden into dogma and produce all kinds of vicious result. 'The trouble with modern criticism, a wonderfully powerful instrument, is that it is always liable to be applied upside down.'[105] This remark occurred in the course of a letter on the topic (once again) of Orwell's *Nineteen Eighty-Four*. The 'Eng. Lit.' equivalents of Doublethink and Newspeak were, he thought, fairly harmless by comparison, but still required a sturdy effort of mind to resist their corrupting effects.

Empson was disappointed but not altogether surprised that *Complex Words* had met with such a negative response among its early readers and reviewers. He hoped one day to get down to a full-scale revision of the book which would bring the theoretical portions more closely into line with the chapters of 'practical' criticism. In the end this comes back to the old problem of 'analytical' *versus* 'appreciative' criticism, an issue he had addressed in that early response to John Sparrow, and which crops up again at various points in *Complex Words*.

> The thing becomes disagreeable to read, and also likely to excite suspicion, quite rightly I think, because the only way to decide about the examples is by 'taste' (granting that taste needs a good supply of examples and an adequate assurance that contrary ones have not been suppressed), and if you are being badgered by theory at the same time it is hard to keep taste in focus. (p. 202)

Even so, the book as it stands is by far the most original and sustained effort of literary theory to have appeared in this country during the past hundred years. Nor should its importance be lost upon the linguists, analytical philosophers and (above all) the adepts of post-structuralist or deconstructive criticism, since Empson's argument engages at so many points with the issues thrown up by these otherwise disparate schools of contemporary thought. But it is likely that Empson will always resist any attempt to annex his writings to this or that corporate academic enterprise, no matter how avowedly 'interdisciplinary' its interests. In a note to one of his poems Empson remarked (with a sidelong glance at Leavis) that 'this being over-simple . . . is itself a way of escaping the complexity of the critic's problems'.[106] It was Empson, more than anyone, who held out against such simplified solutions and worked to keep the problems steadily in view.

4

Kant Disfigured: Ethics, Deconstruction and the Textual Sublime

In this chapter I shall discuss two recent lines of approach to some issues in the area of Kantian epistemology, ethics and political theory. The authors concerned – Onora O'Neill and J. Hillis Miller – have so little in common as regards their intellectual orientation and sense of what counts as a valid philosophical argument that it might seem perverse to couple them in this way. Miller is a deconstructionist literary critic whose book *The Ethics of Reading* (1987) has a chapter on Kant much influenced by the work of Paul de Man.[1] O'Neill is a philosopher in the broadly 'analytic' tradition who prizes the virtues of clarity, rigour, and adequate conceptual grasp. In *Constructions of Reason* she offers what amounts to a revisionist reading of Kant, but one that still claims to respect Kant's intentions and expound them more convincingly than other, less percipient commentators.[2] That is to say, she assumes first that his arguments make sense; second, that they have somehow given rise to certain forms of prevalent misunderstanding; and third, that the business of constructive criticism is to clear away these sources of confusion by explaining where exactly they have got Kant wrong. To this extent – in common with most analytical philosophers – O'Neill is committed to a fourth basic premise: namely that texts may stand in need of conceptual exegesis (or 'rational reconstruction') in order to clarify their logical structure or to give more emphasis to details of argument that might otherwise pass unnoticed.

From which it follows that philosophy is not, in Richard Rorty's phrase, just another 'kind of writing' whose vaunted truth-claims should henceforth be viewed as a species of rhetorical imposition, an assemblage of metaphors masquerading as concepts, or a language-game that once in a while comes up with some new conversational twist, some welcome change of vocabulary or style, merely to relieve the boredom.[3] Nor can it be assimilated to literature, if by 'literature' we mean a kind of writing where there exist no protocols of truth or valid argument, and where meaning is whatever we make of it in light of currently prevailing interpretive norms.[4] On this view – as maintained by some literary theorists, Hillis Miller among them – philosophical texts are in no way different from novels or poems, and should therefore be read chiefly with an eye to their covert metaphors, fictive strategies and structures of rhetorical implication.[5] To suspend (or deconstruct) the notional difference between philosophy and literature is simply to acknowledge that philosophers, like literary critics, have no means of access to meaning or truth except by way of the 'words on the page', or the activity of textual close-reading. In which case they had better relinquish all ideas of philosophy as a first-order, truth-telling discourse, and show themselves willing to learn a few lessons from the critics and literary theorists.

For O'Neill, on the contrary, philosophy has to do with arguments, truth-claims, validity-conditions and modes of conceptual exegesis which cannot be reduced, in pan-textualist fashion, to this level of an undifferentiated 'writing' devoid of all distinctive generic attributes. Of course there is a trivial sense in which philosophy, like every other discipline, depends upon writing as a means of communication and, beyond that, as a repository of knowledge and ideas which would otherwise be subject to the errors and vagaries of short-term oral transmission. To this extent writing (or 'textuality') may indeed be thought of as a condition of possibility for the entire philosophical enterprise.[6] But there is no justification for pressing this argument to the point at which philosophy is conceived *through and through* as a textual or 'literary' discourse, a product of imaginary misrecognition where metaphors are mistaken for concepts, or where truth-claims (in Nietzsche's famous phrase) turn out to be merely a 'mobile marching army' of sublimated tropes whose figural sense has long been forgotten in the drive for theoretical mastery. To adopt this line is merely to mistake a contingent fact about its mode of transmission for a constitutive feature of all philosophical discourse.[7] It is also, of course, a move with great appeal for literary critics who can thereby seem to turn the tables on philosophy by treating it as just another text with none of the authority traditionally claimed by all those earnest truth-seeking types, from Plato on down, who have relegated literature (or literary criticism) to the realm of mere illusion, mimetic seduction, or false seeming. For if the texts of philosophy are indeed just that – an assortment of rhetorics, favoured vocabularies, subliminal metaphors and covert 'allegories of reading' – then clearly this offers a welcome opportunity for people in departments of English or Comparative Literature to get one up on their overweening colleagues down the corridor. And it also raises the more important question as to whether philosophers can go some way with the 'linguistic turn', that is to say, the currently prevailing view that issues of language, meaning and representation are inseparable from questions of truth, reason and right understanding, while at the same time resisting the 'textualist' drift toward a standpoint of extreme cognitive scepticism or an all-out deconstructive rhetoric of tropes.

This resistance can take various forms, from the Wittgensteinian appeal to 'language-games' (or cultural 'forms of life') as a hedge against sceptical doubt, to Fregean arguments which maintain – *contra* Saussure – that any workable account of language will have to articulate the complex order of relationship between sense, reference, logic, and propositional truth.[8] Then again there is the kind of ethical philosophy exemplified by thinkers like O'Neill, an approach that presupposes the existence of relations – analogical relations, to be sure, but none the less relevant for that – between issues of real-world moral concern and their representation by means of exemplary (narrative and some-times fictive) case-histories. What unites these otherwise diverse schools of thought is the belief that textuality (or rhetoric) does not exhaust the field; that philosophical writings can be read, construed, criticized and engaged in constructive debate at a level beyond the 'words on the page'; and that this is indeed where philosophy differs from other kinds of writing (like literary criticism) where interpretive 'truth' is always *to some degree* a product of persuasive definition or rhetorical strategy. And this remains the case, O'Neill would argue, even when philosophers (Kant among them) make use of various fictive, imaginary or 'literary' examples in order to illustrate some otherwise abstract or generalized point of principle. For those examples take effect – that is to say, give rise to the appropriate forms of enhanced self-knowledge or reflective moral concern – precisely insofar as we perceive their relevance to the sort of situation that might always be encountered in the conduct of our everyday, practical lives. Only to literary theorists dead set on discovering all manner of 'textualist' aporias will it seem that their fictive or allegorical status is such as to endlessly baffle or obstruct the passage from word to world.

What this amounts to, in short, is a system of inverted ontological priorities, a deconstructive reversal of the relationship commonly held to obtain between truth and fiction, reality and representation, or language in its primary (cognitive or referential) mode and language as a play of ungrounded tropes or figural swerves and substitutions. It is in these terms that Miller defines the 'ethics of reading', an ethics whose main obligation is always to read with a maximum regard for the words on the page, and not be seduced into treating those words as somehow giving access to a realm of 'extra-textual' themes, intentions, concepts or referents. Only thus can we be true to that readerly imperative – that 'law of the text', as Miller expounds it – whose demand is nothing less than a freely-willed suspension of all our normative, 'commonsense' habits of response. For we shall otherwise fall prey to the most naive of illusory (undeconstructed) beliefs, namely the idea that language can indeed give us knowledge of the world, as opposed to a knowledge of its own problematical workings as revealed through the close-reading of particular texts.

Nor is this a lesson exclusively vouchsafed by works that bear all the overt markers of fictive, allegorical or poetic status, that is to say, of their belonging to a language-game where truth is not directly or primarily in question, and where meaning is uncoupled from the usual constraints of veridical or referential discourse. For in this regard, contrary to normal assumptions, those texts that we call 'literary' are in fact more aware, more rigorously cognizant of the way that all language (in Paul de Man's phrase) opens up 'vertiginous possibilities of referential aberration'.[9] Thus it is wrong to think of literature as a realm apart, as enjoying an exemption from the normal modes of truth-telling discourse or speech-act entailment, so that tropes like 'ambiguity', 'paradox' or 'aporia' can here be enjoyed in safe isolation from the context of real-world communicative utterance. Such notions, prominent in the 'old' New Criticism and in various schools of formalist doctrine, create what amounts to a false sense of ontological security by thus fencing literature off within a separate aesthetic domain.[10] Quite simply, there is *no* kind of language – scientific, philosophical, factual-documentary or whatever – that would bypass these rhetorical complexities and thereby attain to an ultimate truth (whether empirically grounded or logically derived) beyond reach of deconstructive analysis. For, as Miller reminds us, the very notion of 'ground' is itself just a species of subliminal metaphor, a trope whose conceptual or explanatory force – like other such 'foundationalist' figures – in the end derives solely from its rhetorical character.

This is why we have to recognize, for better or worse, that 'the most resolute attempts to bracket linguistic considerations in the study of literature, to take the language of literature for granted and shift from the study of the relations of word with word to the study of the relations of words with things or with subjectivities, will only lead back in the end to the study of language'.[11] Rhetorical exegesis is therefore 'indispensable' insofar as it blocks the presumptive passage from text to world, or puts up resistance to thematic readings that trade upon 'naive' referential or realist assumptions. 'Any conceivable representation of the relations of words to things, powers, persons, modes of production and exchange, juridical or political systems (or whatever name the presumably non-linguistic may be given) will turn out to be one or another figure of speech.'[12] In which case it is demonstrably wrong to take the line of those Marxists, New Historicists, or sociological critics of various persuasion who denounce deconstruction for its 'formalist' or 'textualist' approach, its lack of concern – as these opponents maintain – with questions of history and material context. For such arguments will always in the end have recourse to some privileged explanatory trope, some figure such as metaphor (involved in all notions of 'mimesis, mirroring, reflection or representation') or metonymy (glossed by Miller as the trope relating 'part to whole, work to surrounding and determining milieu, text to context, container to thing contained').[13] Thus critics can have no strong case, let alone argumentative 'grounds', for attacking deconstruction on account of its supposedly text-

centred, 'ahistorical' or politically disengaged stance. To make this charge stick
one would have to achieve the impossible, that is to say, gain access to a
cognitive standpoint outside or beyond the realm of linguistic representation.
And this – to borrow Thomas Nagel's apt phrase – could only be a 'view from
nowhere', a perspective that in fact was no perspective at all, since it aspired to
transcend all the limiting conditions of attainable human knowledge.[14]

If deconstruction thus presumes to make short work of empirical truth-
claims, it is likewise equipped with a range of textual strategies for dealing
with the supposed priority of logic over language in its 'merely' figural, fictive
or rhetorical modes. Here it is a matter of reversing that priority by showing –
like Paul de Man in a series of by now canonical essays – how rhetoric radically
'suspends' the relationship between language, logic and truth; how it tends
to subvert the classical model of the *trivium* by exposing logic (which traditionally enjoyed pride of place above grammar and rhetoric) to a series of
tropological swerves and displacements whose effect is to complicate this
orderly arrangement.[15] On the received view, as de Man puts it, 'grammar
stands in the service of logic which, in turn, allows for the passage to a
knowledge of the world'.[16] This model depends for what de Man calls its
'smooth functioning' on the confinement of rhetoric to a strictly ancillary role,
an aspect of language whose workings have to do with mere persuasion
or 'performative' efficacy, and which can thus pose no threat to the structural homology between grammar (conceived as an 'isotope' of logic) and
propositional truth. But this relationship remains untroubled only so long as
rhetoric abides by the rules, or so long as rhetoricians – including the majority
of literary theorists – consent to regard it as a separate dimension of language,
devoid of any cognitive or epistemological consequence. Such was (for instance)
I. A. Richards' idea – adopted in response to the reductive rigours of logical-
positivist thinking – that poetry dealt in 'pseudo-truths' or in varieties of
'emotive' statement which could not be held accountable to the standards of
straightforward veridical utterance.[17] And the same attitude prevailed among
the 'old' New Critics, for whom poetry involved a range of rhetorical devices
(ambiguity, paradox, irony etc.) the effect of which was to constitute the
poem as a self-sufficient structure of inwrought meanings, a 'verbal icon'
whose autonomy could only be maintained insofar as it refused all commerce with questions of 'extraneous' validity or truth.[18] Even among critics
more concerned with rhetoric as a systematic field of study – theorists like
Jakobson, Greimas or Genette – the dominant approach was one that tended to
'grammaticize' the workings of figural language by taking it for granted that
they could finally be reduced to some kind of orderly, taxonomic account. But
problems arise with this model, de Man argues, at precisely that point of
resistance where 'it is no longer possible to ignore the epistemological thrust of
the rhetorical dimension of language', or 'to keep it in its place as a mere

adjunct, a mere ornament within the semantic function'.[19] For what then becomes apparent is the extent to which tropes have a wayward 'logic' of their own, a tendency to generate aberrant meanings or chains of figural implication that cannot be reconciled to any such clear-cut methodological approach.

And so it turns out, on de Man's understanding, that 'literariness, the use of language that foregrounds the rhetorical over the grammatical and the logical function, intervenes as a decisive but unsettling element which, in a variety of modes and aspects, disrupts the inner balance of the model and, consequently, its extension to the nonverbal world as well'.[20] Nor can this be taken, as the formalists would have it, for a property peculiar to those deviant or specialized 'uses of language' that typify literary, as opposed (say) to historical, philosophical or other kinds of text. For it is precisely de Man's point that such distinctions collapse, or begin to look much more complicated, as soon as one reads those other texts with an adequate attentiveness to matters of rhetorical detail. Thus the attempt to keep rhetoric separate from logic and grammar – as in the classical *trivium* model – is also what is at stake in present-day quarrels (most notably, those between philosophers and literary theorists) with regard to the integrity of academic disciplines, or the confusions that arise when thoroughgoing 'textualists' like Miller or de Man get to work on material outside their proper, 'literary' field of competence. 'It is therefore not surprising,' de Man remarks, 'that literary theory came into being from outside philosophy and sometimes in conscious rebellion against the weight of its tradition.'[21] After all, that tradition, from Plato on down, has defined itself squarely against the idea that its texts might be read (or its arguments construed) on a level with those of the poets, rhetoricians, or other such purveyors of false wisdom. And this resistance is always most vigorously present where rhetoric threatens to get out of hand, or to stray across the bondary-lines conventionally drawn between language in its logico-grammatical function and language in its so-called 'literary' uses. For it is here – in the province of deconstruction, of literary theory or what de Man terms the 'epistemology of tropes' – that thought comes up against the greatest challenge to its powers of self-assured conceptual grasp. Thus 'no grammatical decoding, however refined, could claim to reach the determining figural dimension of a text'.[22] Moreover, it is this aspect of rhetoric which 'adds a subversive element of unpredictability' and which 'makes it something of a wild card in the serious game of the theoretical disciplines'.[23]

II

What has all this to do with ethics? it might well be asked. And the answer would have to be 'everything' or 'nothing': everything on Miller's and de Man's account, and nothing from the viewpoint of those (like O'Neill) who would doubtless regard it as a frivolous distraction from the proper business of reasoned ethical enquiry. Where these answers diverge is most crucially on the issue of linguistic representation, or the extent to which language can be thought of as providing a reliable means of access to questions of real-world factual, moral or political concern. For Miller there must always come a point in the reading of texts – whether novels, poems or works of ethical philosophy – when those texts turn out to be self-deconstructing, to 'allegorize' the nature of their own rhetorical predicament, or to generate the kinds of linguistic aporia that prevent one from naively extending their import to the realm of 'nonverbal' actions, episodes, or events. Language 'dissociates the cognition from the act' in the sense that it creates insuperable obstacles to any reading premised on the notional correspondence between word and world, the idea that one could pass from the set-piece narrative examples of ethical conduct offered by a philosopher like Kant, to a knowledge (or a maxim of practical reason) which could then be relied upon for useful guidance in real-life situations of moral choice. But this position is untenable, according to Miller and de Man, insofar as it takes as self-evident certain working assumptions about language, logic and truth which are thrown into doubt by a close deconstructive analysis of the way that such passages actually function. For their language can then be seen to oscillate between a rhetoric of 'proof' and a rhetoric of 'persuasion', or – as de Man variously formulates this difference – between 'constative' and 'performative' modes of utterance, the 'grammatization of rhetoric' and the 'rhetorization of grammar', or again, between logic, grammar and rhetoric as theorized (against all the rhetorical odds) by proponents of the classical *trivium* schema.[24] And the result of this chronic instability is to undermine the credit of readings that are based on a tacit continuity-principle, that is to say, on the assumption that 'grammar stands in the service of logic which, in turn, allows for the passage to a knowledge of the world'.[25]

Clearly such an argument has large implications for any theory of knowledge that would presuppose at least the possibility of attaining an adequate correspondence between concepts, propositions and factual states of affairs. Nor can it be simply brushed aside by invoking the current line of anti-foundationalist thought which appears to reject all ideas of truth-as-correspondence, and to require only, in holistic fashion, that one's claims hang together with a sufficient range of sentences currently taken as true.[26] For even on this account there are certain minimal criteria – of coherence, non-contradiction, valid inference, logical compatability – which have to be respected if the holist doctrine is to make any kind of sense. But in de Man's late texts, especially the chapters on Nietzsche in *Allegories of Reading*, the point is made over and again that rhetoric 'unsettles' or 'radically suspends' all such criteria of well-formed argument, with the result that any utterance beyond a certain level of linguistic or discursive complexity will always be subject to conflicting 'logics' of literal and figural sense.[27] And if this creates problems for epistemology then it is equally the case, on de Man's submission, that the 'ethics of reading' is a topic more elusive than anything envisaged by philosophers who operate on 'naive' (referential or thematic) assumptions. For there still remains the question, as he puts it with reference to a passage in Proust, as to 'whether a literary text is *about* that which it describes, represents, or states'.[28]

Of course this goes without saying for the majority of critics, philosophers and exegetes, those for whom a text is self-evidently 'about' whatever it expressly or implicitly takes as its theme. Nor is this belief significantly challenged by Freudian, Marxist or other such variants of the modern 'hermeneutics of suspicion', the idea that reading has to probe beneath the surface of the text in order to uncover its latent dimension of covert, repressed or ideologically motivated meaning. For here also the assumption holds sway that there must be *some* correspondence – however obscure or subterranean – between that which the text overtly expresses as a matter of thematic concern, and that which analysis brings to light through its various expert or depth-hermeneutical techniques. On de Man's view, such readings are no less naive than the orthodox or literalist readings they aim to supplant. What unites these approaches despite all their manifest differences of method and principle is the belief that there must always be an end-point to the process of textual or rhetorical decoding; that finally even the most complex, duplicitous or 'self-referential' of texts will turn out to *mean* something intelligibly related (at whatever 'unconscious' or 'ideological' remove) to its overt professions of thematic intent. To de Man's way of thinking, on the contrary, there is no good reason – force of habit apart – to believe that this must or should be the case. For the result of close-reading in the deconstructive mode is more often to demonstrate the utter lack of grounds for any such doctrine of preestablished harmony as regards the thematic (or 'constative') import of a text and its meaning as revealed through a detailed analysis of its constitutive tropes and figures. Hence – to repeat – the question that de Man finds implicit in the passage from Proust: the question 'whether a literary text is *about* that which it describes, represents, or states'.

As it happens, this passage is 'about' reading in the sense that it overtly celebrates the rewards of an inward, contemplative, imaginative life, a pleasure that is contrasted, for the young Marcel, with those other, more stressful activities that take place in the world outside his self-enclosed realm of creative reverie.[29] But we should be wrong, de Man argues, to take this episode at face value, or to suppose that its meaning can be read straight off as the passage quite expressly asks us to read it. What a closer examination reveals is the way that Proust's language subtly – even 'surreptitiously' – shuttles back and forth between a range of opposed meanings, figural analogies, and associative values which cannot be reduced to any reading in the straightforward thematic-referential mode. Most important of these, in rhetorical terms, is the contrast set up between *metaphor* and *metonymy*, the former equated (traditionally enough) with the values of inwardness, creativity, imaginative insight and visionary transcendence, while the latter – very much the poor relation – would appear confined to those mundane or prosaic orders of experience that depend upon external (sensuous) impressions, and are thus subject to all manner of distracting or merely 'contingent' influence. 'In a passage that abounds in successful and seductive metaphors and which, moreover, explicitly asserts the superior efficacy of metaphor over that of metonymy, persuasion is achieved by a figural play in which contingent figures of chance masquerade as figures of necessity.'[30] As it asks to be read Proust's 'allegory of reading' is one that affirms the qualitative difference between these realms, and which moreover posits metaphor, along with all its cognate values, as the means of creating an imaginative world redeemed from the vicissitudes of time and chance. Such is at any rate the overt or manifest sense that emerges from this typically 'Proustian' moment of interiorized narrative recollection. Thus the passage invests all its powers of persuasion in a rhetoric that would elevate metaphor over metonymy, the inward over the outward, imagination over mere sensory experience, and the 'dark coolness' of Marcel's room – his secluded retreat – over the 'summer warmth' that can only be enjoyed by grace of contingent physical circumstance, and which besides leaves one momentarily exposed to various kinds of natural hazard or irritant. At the level of thematic self-evidence, of what the text is explicitly and knowingly 'about', this reading is one that stakes a fair claim to interpretive validity and truth.

On de Man's view, conversely, it is a mystified, naive or uncritical reading which allows itself the pleasure of being carried along by Proust's seductive rhetoric of transcendence while failing to register those problematic details, or moments of figural aberration, that would otherwise pose a real problem to its powers of idealized recuperative grasp. For what emerges from a detailed tropological account of that same passage in Proust is a series of striking (if well-concealed) instances where 'the figural praxis and the metafigural theory do not coincide', and where 'the assertion of the mastery of metaphor over metonymy owes its persuasive power to the use of metonymic structures'.[31] In part this has to do with Proust's covert deployment of images drawn from the 'outside' world – the realm of contingency, sensuous experience, transient perceptions – in order to characterize modalities of being that supposedly belong to the 'inner' world of self-sufficient imaginative life. It is by means of such duplicitous transfers of sense – analogies whose figural logic belies their suasive or 'performative' import – that the passage manages to pass itself off (at least on a superficial reading) as having actually *achieved* that recollected state of inwardness and mental repose. So it is that, in de Man's words,

> the text asserts the possibility of recuperating, by an act of reading, all that the
> inner contemplation had discarded, the opposites of all the virtues necessary to
> its well-being: the *warmth* of the sun, its *light*, and even the *activity* that the
> restful immobility seemed to have definitively eliminated. Miraculously enriched
> by its antithetical properties, the 'dark coolness' of the room thus acquires the
> light without which no reading would be possible, 'the unmediated, actual, and
> persistent presence' of the summer warmth, and finally even '. . . the shock and
> the animation of a flood of activity'. The narrator is able to assert, without
> seeming to be preposterous, that by staying and reading in his room, Marcel's
> imagination finds access to 'the total spectacle of Summer', including the attrac-
> tions of direct physical action, and that he possesses it much more effectively
> than if he had been actually present in an outside world that he could then only
> have known by bits and pieces.[32]

If the 'figural' and the 'metafigural' readings fail to coincide, it is on account of
this conflict – an unavoidable conflict, as de Man would have it – between
metaphor's claims as a visionary, transcendent or 'totalizing' figure of thought,
and the way that metonymy works to undo (or deconstruct) such claims
through its prosaic reliance on associative links with the realm of contingent
cause-and-effect, of external phenomena or accidents of time and place.
What occurs *in the text*, as distinct from its reading by hoodwinked or
'mystified' interpreters, is a complicated process of figural exchange which on
the one hand openly solicits such a reading, while on the other it provides all
the necessary materials for its own rhetorical deconstruction.

Thus 'precisely when the highest claims are being made for the unifying
power of metaphor, these very images rely in fact on the deceptive use of semi-
automatic grammatical patterns'.[33] Such patterns are 'grammatical' in the sense
that they operate, like metonymy, on the basis of a linkage between discrete
but contiguous terms, or on a quasi-mechanistic principle which associates
meanings, ideas and sensory stimuli without the least claim to that order of
unified 'organic' thought and perception that typifies the language of metaphor
and symbol. As a matter of suasive efficacy, these tropes may perform their
task so well that the reader is unresistingly beguiled into taking the word for
the deed, or the *theme* of achieved metaphorical transcendence for the *actual
attainment* of that same condition in and through the language of Proust's
exemplary narrative. They can thus be seen to constitute 'a more or less hidden
system of relays which allows the properties to enter into substitutions,
exchanges, and crossings that appear to reconcile the incompatabilities of the
inner with the outer world'.[34] But this appearance is deceptive, de Man
maintains, since it relies upon the reader's predictable 'blindness' to exactly
those devices of language, those 'more or less hidden' figural mechanisms,

whose metonymic structure is so easily disguised by the suasive pseudo-logic of metaphor.

At this stage the question arises as to *why* one should read so doggedly against the grain, especially if – as can hardly be denied – one thereby renounces much of the pleasure (of achieved, sympathetic or 'inward' understanding) that comes of what de Man would no doubt call a 'naive' or 'complicitous' involvement. His response can best be gauged from the following passage where the argument moves from a pinpoint diagosis of the Proustian disjunction between logic, grammar and rhetoric to a strain of commentary with markedly ethical (indeed, almost moralistic) overtones. Proust, de Man writes,

> can affect such confidence in the persuasive power of his metaphors that he pushes stylistic defiance to the point of stating the assumed synthesis of light and dark in the incontrovertible language of numerical ratio: 'The dark cool of my warm room was to the full sunlight of the street what the shadow is to the sunray, that is to say equally luminous . . .'. In a logic dominated by truth and error the equation is absurd, since it is the difference of luminosity that distinguishes between shadow and light: 'that is to say' ('c'est-à-dire') in the quotation is precisely what cannot be said. Yet the logic of sensation and of the imagination easily remains convinced of the accuracy of the passage and has not the least difficulty in accepting it as legitimate. One should ask how a blindness comes into being that allows for a statement in which truth and falsehood are completely subverted to be accepted as true without resistance. There seems to be no limit to what tropes can get away with.[35]

One can hardly ignore the ethical tonality – the insistence on arriving at a principled judgement as between 'naive' and 'rhetorically aware' modes of reading – that marks de Man's language here and at numerous other points in his late work. On the one hand there is always the seductive option of allowing the text to have its way with us, of being 'easily' convinced by its suasive rhetoric or its overt statement of thematic intent. Such a reading is content to suspend all questions of determinate 'truth and falsehood' in order to enjoy the maximum yield of imaginary gratification. For there can be no doubt – as de Man often remarks when addressing this topic of 'aesthetic ideology' – that the yield is much greater (or at least more immediate) if one simply goes along with the mystified language of metaphor and symbol, rather than seeking to resist or deconstruct that language through what amounts to a strong-willed renunciation of its 'easy' pleasures.

The choice is spelled out in a sentence from his essay 'Reading and History', where de Man invokes Nietzsche in support of his argument that 'the aesthetic is, by definition, a seductive notion that appeals to the pleasure principle, a eudaimonic judgement that can displace and conceal values of truth and falsehood likely to be more resilient to desire than values of pleasure and pain'.[36] Only thus can one account for the ascetic imperative, the tone of self-denying critical austerity, that typifies so much of de Man's writing in these essays of his last decade. What it counsels in effect is a form of instinctual abnegation, a resistance to the pleasure of readerly involvement or imaginary identification which requires nothing less, on de Man's view, than a rigorous practice of textual close-reading, one that would guard against any such lapse into 'naive' habits of thought.[37] Still it might be asked why on earth one should *want* to make this effort, given firstly that there seems little harm in enjoying Proust's epiphanies at face value, and secondly — as many critics would argue — that de Man's readings are in any case the upshot of a perverse drive to complicate the reading of texts to a point where only deconstructionists will not fear to tread. But here, as so often, he preempts such a charge by finding it implicitly rehearsed or prefigured, and its terms called into question, by the text presently to hand. Thus Proust's passage on the pleasures of reading 'has to attempt the reconciliation between imagination and action and to resolve the ethical conflict that exists between them'.[38] And it does so only to the extent that one is persuaded ('easily convinced') by a rhetorical sleight of hand, a system of covert links and substitutions whose metonymic character is 'more or less hidden' by their constant resort to a range of seductive metaphorical figures. In which case the need to resist such forms of beguiling 'aesthetic ideology' would present itself not only in 'literary' terms — that is to say, as a matter of proving one's competence in the close-reading of texts — but also as an ethical imperative with claims upon the reader's exercise of judgement and will.

For the effect of Proust's passage — when read metaphorically, or in compliance with its own suasive designs — is to offer an imaginary world elsewhere, an escape-route to that realm of aesthetic self-communing or idealized creative reverie where issues of practical, real-world choice can happily be set aside. And this reading has all the more appeal, de Man observes, in so far as it exploits seductive figures (like metaphor and symbol) whose 'totalizing' claims go along with a rhetoric of transcendence, a promise that they can somehow 'reconcile' all those bad antinomies — as between subject and object, imagination and action, the inner and the outer worlds, freedom and necessity, the noumenal and the phenomenal — which plague the discourse of plain-prose reason. But such pleasures can only be had at a certain cost, a cost whose implications have to be reckoned in ethical as well as in purely 'literary' terms. What this *promesse de bonheur* requires in exchange is a willingness, on the reader's part, not to look too closely at the figural mechanisms by which metaphor manages to assert (or to insinuate) its claim. And it also requires that one accept — like Marcel — the inherent superiority of the inward life (of reading, imagination, creative solitude) over anything that pertains to the 'outside' world of contingent actions and events. So long as this value-system is in place – that is, so long as the reader assents to it – there can be no doubt as to metaphor's sovereignty, its imaginative powers of 'transcendence' or 'reconciliation'. Thus:

> a literal and thematic reading that takes the value assertions of the text at their word would have to favor metaphor over metonymy as a means to satisfy a desire all the more tempting since it is paradoxical: the desire for a secluded reading that satisfies the ethical demands of action more effectively than actual deeds.[39]

But such assurance is inevitably 'put into question', de Man goes on, if one suspends this faith in thematic self-evidence and 'takes the rhetorical structure of the text into account'. For what then becomes clear – albeit as the upshot of a highly resistant or counter-intuitive reading – is the fact that Proust's overt (metaphorical) claims are by no means borne out by tropological analysis; that they rely upon occult, even devious structures of metonymic substitution and exchange; and hence that 'the co-presence of intra- and extra-textual movements never reaches a synthesis'.

To arrive at this strenuously negative conclusion, despite and against all the pleasures to be had in reading Proust at his word, is no doubt (as de Man's critics would argue) the kind of killjoy exercise that gets deconstruction a bad name. But such responses miss the point, he contends, since they can only fall back on that same attitude of willing self-delusion which substitutes 'values of pleasure and pain' – in this case, the interests of straightforward reader-satisfaction – for 'values of truth and falsehood'. They can therefore count for nothing if one wishes to achieve a truthful (rhetorically adequate) understanding of the Proustian text, as opposed to an 'aesthetically responsive' reading that is compelled to ignore its tropological complexities. 'The relationship between the literal and the figural senses of a metaphor is always, in this sense, metonymic, though motivated by a constitutive desire to pretend the opposite'.[40] This desire is 'constitutive' insofar as it provides both the motivating impulse to write, read and interpret a text like Proust's, and the means by which language most often succeeds, through the reader's complicitous blindness, in concealing those ulterior (metonymic) structures that subtend the discourse of metaphor or symbol.[41]

III

I have taken this example from de Man as a pointer to the kinds of issue that arise for an 'ethics of reading' premised, like Miller's, on the textualist principle of trusting to nothing but the sacrosanct 'words on the page'. What this amounts to is an attitude of extreme cognitive scepticism, an approach that begins (in familiar post-structuralist fashion) by suspending the relation between word and world, and which ends – as de Man and Miller both assert – by establishing a radical disjunction between the overt (that is, the constative, thematic or referential) aspects of a text and the level at which those meanings are undone by its modes of figural implication. It is in this sense, they argue, that reading becomes a properly 'ethical' activity, one that holds out against our otherwise irresistible tendency to read texts always in accordance with our own preconceived notions of interpretive validity and truth. Only to the extent that we renounce such forms of naive, if pleasurable, response can we hope to maintain a relation to the text that is not both deluded (since blind to its fictive or figural workings) and open to the charge of ethical bad faith (since aimed toward satisfying the reader's idea of what the text should or must be 'about'). In which case we shall also need to reckon with de Man's repeated claim – so offensive to critics of an orthodox liberal-humanist persuasion – that rhetoric 'radically suspends logic and opens up vertiginous possibilities of referential aberration'.[42] For no matter how perverse or counter-intuitive this conclusion may seem, it is nonetheless arrived at (on his own submission) through a labour of 'rigorous' or strictly consequential analysis which cannot be gainsaid simply by protesting in the name of common decency, humane understanding, or straightforward experiential witness.

What such protests ignore is the disjunct relation between logic, grammar and rhetoric, a relation that can only be relied on to maintain its relatively un-problematical character so long as rhetoric is safely confined to a 'performative' or 'ornamental' role. And if this has been the role traditionally assigned to it by a long succession of philosophers and literary theorists, from Aristotle to Greimas and the present-day formalists, then we should ask just why they have felt thus obliged to avoid confronting its more wayward or troublesome (but also more 'rigorous') dimension, that aspect of rhetoric that de Man terms the 'epistemology of tropes'. The reason is to be found in the order of priorities encoded in the classical *trivium* model, and likewise – more generally – in our commonplace beliefs about truth, knowledge, language and experience. It is the assumption (to cite de Man's lapidary sentence once more) that 'grammar stands in the service of logic which, in turn, allows for the passage to a knowledge of the world'. But this continuity-principle can only hold on condition that we take its *de jure* claim as a matter of self-evident, *de facto* truth, that is to say, as a manifest feature of the way that grammar articulates logical (propositional) structures of thought which in turn correspond to real-world states of affairs. On the contrary, says de Man: 'only if the sign engendered meaning in the same way that the object engenders the sign, that is, by representation, would there be no need to distinguish grammar and rhetoric'.[43] Once abandon that doctrine – once admit the possibility that rhetoric may complicate or subvert the structural homology between logic, grammar and referential discourse – and such beliefs will come to seem nothing more than a species of tenacious (but nonetheless questionable) commonsense doxa. And this applies even to those passages of 'self-reflexive' commentary in a novelist like Proust which appear to take the pleasures and superior (imaginative) truth-claims of reading as an overt topic of discussion. On de Man's view 'this procedure in fact begs the question', since 'we cannot *a priori* be certain to gain access to whatever Proust has to say about reading by way of such a reading of a scene of reading'.[44] And again: 'if reading is truly problematic, if a nonconvergence between the stated meaning and its under-standing may be suspected, then the sections in the novel that literally represent reading are not to be privileged'.[45]

All of which follows, de Man suggests, from the 'rigorously' deconstructive mode of textual exegesis that questions any version of the presumed homology between logic, grammar and rhetoric. The episode from Proust is an *allegory* of reading in the sense that allegory, like metonymy but unlike metaphor or symbol, implicitly concedes this truth about language: the fact of its belonging to a realm of 'arbitrary' significations where there is no safe passage, no natural or self-assured means of transition from *what the text says* concerning its exemplary status as a scene of instruction to what it *actually means* (or turns out to signify) when subjected to the deconstructive rigours of a full-scale tropological analysis. And if this argument holds – as it clearly does for Miller and other proponents of a de Manian 'ethics of reading' – then its consequences extend beyond literary (fictive or poetic) texts to *any* kind of writing, philosophy included, which resorts to such exemplary scenes by way of bridging the gulf between issues of ethical theory and matters of real-world moral concern. On the standard assumption – the continuity-principle, as I have called it – there is no great problem here, or nothing that could justify Miller and de Man in adopting their extravagant 'textualist' position. O'Neill speaks firmly on this side of the argument when she discusses the role of illustrative instances ('parables', as Miller would tendentiously describe them) and their relevance to the discourse of moral philosophy. Any difficulties that arise from the use of 'literary' examples have to do with the fact that such cases are judged from a purely detached or 'spectator' viewpoint, without leading on to a moment of decision when that judgement issues in some practical *choice* between various competing principles or courses of conduct. But this is far from saying that we are thereby debarred (on pain of showing up as 'naive' readers) from construing these examples in thematic terms, or with reference to the kinds of real-world dilemma that moral agents might typically or exceptionally confront. After all, as O'Neill remarks, 'examples can only have a point if they illustrate a principle; illustrations must be illustrations of something' (O'Neill, p. 112). The problem is to explain on the one hand how 'examples' (or illustrative cases) link up with 'principles', and on the other how our judgement of such set-piece ('literary') instances can offer real guidance in the conduct of our everyday, practical, decision-making lives.

O'Neill is by no means inclined to underestimate these difficulties, or to treat them as merely 'academic' in relation to the moral concerns of humankind. Indeed, it is a chief virtue of her book that it keeps such problems squarely in view while urging the case for Kantian ethics – against its present-day detractors – as a discourse that avoids the disabling extremes of abstract 'formalism' on the one hand, and on the other a relativist (or communitarian) appeal to what is currently and contingently good in the way of belief. But she yields no ground to the kind of all-purpose textualist argument which would take it as read (like Miller and de Man) that ethical issues can only be raised through the resort to a fictive or figural language that places them beyond all hope of adjudicative treatment. If problems arise with Kant's doctrine of practical reason, then these are problems that can and should be argued out in the public sphere of reasoned moral debate, sometimes – where appropriate – with the aid of 'literary' analogues. For whatever their acknowledged limitations, such examples at least have the merit of allowing us to test moral precepts in the context of an imagined (but nonetheless detailed and specific) set of actions, circumstances and events. That is to say, they provide us with a range of exemplary case-histories which possess some degree of narrative verisimilitude, some points at which their import – or thematic content – can be seen to bear upon issues that might be confronted by real-world (knowing and willing) moral agents in comparable types of situation. To deny the possibility of making such connections – or to treat them, in the deconstructive-textualist mode, as instances of 'naive' reading – is an argument that would count the world well lost in exchange for the delights of paradox, aporia, or 'undecidability'.

Among literary critics this results in nothing more harmful than the current pseudo-radical vogue for a rhetoric of infinitized textual 'freeplay', coupled most often with reflex jibes against its equally mythical counterpart, the 'classic bourgeois-realist text'.[46] Such notions took rise from a reading of Saussure – an 'abusive extrapolation', in Perry Anderson's phrase – which treated the 'arbitrary' nature of the sign as a high point of method and principle, a support for its ultra-nominalist assault on the claims of mimetic realism.[47] For Saussure, on the contrary, this principle had served in a strictly heuristic capacity, that is to say, as a means of constituting the science of structural-synchronic linguistics, as opposed to those other (diachronic or philological) approaches which had hitherto ruled the field.[48] Such was his purpose in proposing the model of language as an autonomous system of immanent differences 'without positive terms', a system where the sign could then be conceived as partaking of a twofold structural economy (signifier and signified), and where its referential aspect could be bracketed – provisionally left out of account – in the interests of greater conceptual precision. Only on a resolutely partial (not to say blinkered and dogmatic) reading could Saussure be construed, in post-structuralist terms, as having simply ruled out all talk of linguistic reference, or shown it to be merely a product of naive (bourgeois-realist) habits of reader response. This position is not only counter-intuitive to the point of manifest absurdity but also maintained in steadfast ignorance of other, more cogent and sophisticated arguments. These have been the subject of much recent commentary, some of it expressly concerned to remedy the shortcomings of post-structuralist thought, so I shall not rehearse them in detail here.[49] Sufficient to remark that there exists a wide range of alternative approaches to the issue of truth, reference and meaning – among them arguments deriving from the work of Frege, Russell, Kripke, Davidson, Quine and others – which differ very markedly one from another, but which nonetheless constitute a standing reproof to this textualist mode of out-and-out cognitive scepticism.[50]

What unites these thinkers at bottom is the simple understanding that a theory of language or representation is unlikely to be of much use if it ends up by totally severing the link between sense and reference, word and world, propositions and facts, or again (in de Man's favoured terminology) between logic, grammar, and rhetoric. Post-structuralism blithely decouples these terms to the point where 'textuality' (or 'unlimited semiosis') takes over from the old oppressive regime of reality, truth and reference. But if this were the case – if those relations were indeed 'arbitrary' through and through, as the sceptics would have us believe – then it is hard to explain how language could communicate even the most basic items of everyday practical knowledge, let alone the kinds of complex articulated truth-claim that make up the discourse of the present-day natural and human sciences. And indeed, for all its talk of self-reflexivity and textual *mise-en-abîme*, post-structuralism is clearly caught on the horns of a familiar relativist dilemma when advancing its own more assertive claims as regards the obsolescence of truth-values, the demise of enlightened ('meta-narrative') discourse, the illusion of referentiality, etc. At very least there is an element of self-disabling paradox – a performative contradiction – involved in these sweeping pronouncements that affect to undermine the veridical status of any such utterance, their own (presumably) included. Of course this line of counter-argument has long been used against sceptics and relativists of various persuasion, from Socrates *versus* Protagoras to the current debate around canny rhetoricians like Richard Rorty and Stanley Fish. And the latter have always bounced back – as now – with some version of the standard knock-down response: that 'truth' is nothing more than what is currently perceived as such according to the language-game, the cultural 'form of life', the interpretive framework or conceptual scheme which happens to prevail at some particular time and place.[51] In this sense one could argue that the new textualism is just an updated version of old relativism, with the difference that it goes more elaborate ways around – or adopts more sophisticated strategies of rhetorical deconstruction – in order to make its otherwise familiar point.

As I say, such ideas are unlikely to do much harm when applied to the reading of literary texts, an activity where truth-claims are commonly regarded as subject to a wider degree of interpretive latitude, and where indeed it is a matter of traditional wisdom – from Philip Sidney to I. A. Richards and the 'old' New Critics – that meaning (not truth) is the relevant concern, that validity-conditions are relaxed (or suspended) in the case of fictive or poetic statements, and that here what counts as a 'truthful' reading cannot be determined on any other grounds than its degree of imaginative insight or interpretive yield. The idea is much the same whether expressed in Sidney's Renaissance idiom of poetic feigning ('Now, for the poet, he nothing affirmeth, and therefore never lieth'; 'things not affirmatively, but allegorically and figuratively written') or in the manner of a text like Barthes's *S/Z*, no doubt its most extreme and virtuoso exposition to date.[52] Where these theorists concur, along with just about every major school of Western post-classical literary criticism, is in arguing that literature in some sense 'nothing affirmeth', since its characteristic forms or modalities of utterance (metaphor, allegory, ambiguity, paradox, irony, fictive statement, *oratio obliqua* and so forth) are such as to preclude any straightforward assessment in veridical or referential terms. And philosophers have mostly accepted some version of this amicable division of realms, preferring not to prosecute the 'ancient quarrel' that Plato perceived between the interests of authentic, truth-seeking wisdom and the falsehoods put about by the poets, rhetoricians and other such sophistical perverters of reason. Thus they have come up with a variety of saving devices, from Aristotle's doctrine of poetic mimesis to the present-day talk among modal logicians of fictive 'possible worlds', or the argument – as advanced by speech-act theorists like John Searle – that literature involves a tacit suspension of the kinds of 'illocutionary force' that characterize our normal modes of communicative utterance.[53] In short, there is general agreement – across some otherwise sharp divergences of view – on the principle that literature somehow enjoys a privileged dispensation, a release from the standards of cognitive, veridical, or factual accountability. As I remarked in chapter three, William Empson is one of the very few literary theorists who have maintained a contrary position.

Thus it might seem unduly alarmist to regard post-structuralism or deconstruction as in any way posing a serious challenge to 'discourses' outside its own highly specialized domain. After all, these arguments have mostly been mounted by literary critics whose main concern is with the rhetoric of fictive or poetic texts, and whose larger ('philosophical') ambitions – as for instance with de Man's deconstructive readings of Kant and Hegel – are still recognizably a product of their training in literary modes of rhetorical exegesis.[54] In which case surely their 'textualist' claims are no more than a series of localized raids and incursions, a takeover-bid for the high disciplinary ground from the literary side of the fence. But this response will appear less convincing if one considers (for instance) what de Man has to say about the 'epistemology of tropes', or the extent to which rhetoric unsettles and subverts all the truth-claims of philosophic reason. If de Man is right — if his readings hold up — then there is simply no recourse to that line of least resistance that would treat literature as a realm safely apart, and deconstruction as a language-game whose 'literary' talk of aporias, undecidability and metaphors masquerading as concepts has no real bearing on the conduct of serious (philosophically accountable) debate. For if there is one thing that marks deconstruction off from previous (e.g., New Critical) approaches to the reading of literary texts, it is the argument that language is just as problematical — just as apt to create such conflicts of sense between logic, grammar and rhetoric — whether the text concerned is a poem, a novel, a piece of historical narrative, a contribution to the philosophy of mind, or a treatise on ethics and politics. To suppose otherwise is merely to seek refuge in a set of *de jure* generic distinctions, or a parcelling-out of disciplinary regimes, which cannot stand up to the undeceiving rigours of a full-scale deconstructive analysis.

So there is a great deal at stake when a theorist like Miller proposes an 'ethics of reading' that would treat *all* texts, whatever their nominal classification, as so many instances of a generalized 'linguistic predicament' that blocks any passage to a knowledge of the world, or which renders such knowledge strictly undecidable as regards its ethical bearings. For on Miller's account it is the merest of delusions to suppose that moral law (or the dictates of Kantian practical reason) could ever achieve articulate form unless with the aid of narratives, fictions, parables, metaphors, allegorical *mises-en-scène*, or other such 'literary' devices. And this despite all Kant's determined efforts to situate that law above and beyond the mere contingencies of circumstantial time and place. After all, as Miller rhetorically asks, 'what does Kant's theory of ethics have to do with narrative, with storytelling, or even with history as the story we tell about the changes of society through centuries?' (Miller, p. 23). To which the answer would again appear to be 'nothing or everything'; nothing insofar as Kant *explicitly rejects* such compromising grounds of appeal, but everything insofar as he *does in fact resort* — most often at crucial points in his argument — to narratives, fictions, or extended similes. Moreover, these are not just handy illustrations brought in to exemplify some otherwise rather abstract (but nonetheless binding and valid) maxim of practical reason. On the contrary, and despite all Kant's protestations, there is simply no way to interpret moral law — to figure out its meaning, its specific implications, or its relevance in real-world terms — except by means of such 'literary' devices adopted in default of any direct relation between these radically disjunct realms.

Thus on the one hand, as Miller paraphrases Kant,

the moral law is above and beyond all that. It remains absolutely the same at all times and places and for all persons. No person can be more than a contingent example of it. No story, it would seem, can do other than falsify it by entangling the law in the meshes of the extrinsic particulars of a time and place, imaginary or real. (Miller, 23)

Such is at any rate what *ought to be the case* if we take Kant at his word, that is to say, if we accept the absolute order of priority which holds it as a truth self-evident to reason first that moral law stands 'above and beyond' all contingent (narrative) exemplifications, and second that any recourse to illustrative stories, parables or anecdotes must at all costs maintain a firm sense of the distinction between 'real' and 'imaginary' story-telling modes. But on the other hand Kant is unable to follow his own prescription, since the 'law of the text' turns out to require both narrative instances and, more alarmingly, instances which allow of no clear-cut judgement as regards their veridical or fictive status. Thus in spite of Kant's explicit formulations, and 'as if to give [them] the lie', his reader can observe what Miller describes as 'a shadowy narrative and the inadvertent demonstration of the necessity of narrative in any account of ethics slowly emerge as Kant develops his concept of respect' (p. 23). More specifically, that concept can only be expounded by way of certain similes or analogues – notably constructions in the 'as if' (*als so*) mode – whose presence would appear just a passing concession to the need for illustrative cases, a concession that Kant is quite willing to make just so long as we recall their strictly figural (and hence inadequate) character. For 'respect' as Kant conceives it is a moral imperative whose dictates transcend all merely 'personal' interests or attachments, and which cannot be reduced to a matter of regard for this or that specific individual in this or that set of contingent motivating circumstances.[55] Yet he is unable to offer any working definition of 'respect' that doesn't have recourse to some such analogy, some more or less 'inadequate' example, in order to interpret those absolute dictates in humanly intelligible terms.

It seems to me that Miller's reading of Kant is a cautionary instance of what goes wrong when a doctrine of extreme (and largely unargued) epistemological scepticism joins up with a hypercultivated interest in textual puzzles and perplexities. Of course there will always be room for disagreement about the relevance of this or that case, or the extent to which it offers justification for the theory or principle concerned. Thus O'Neill cites a number of passages from Kant where he expressly denies that this relation could be codified to the point of achieving a determinate match – a one-to-one rule of correspondence – between the precepts of pure practical reason, the maxims into which those principles translate, and the various kinds of situation (real or imaginary) wherein such maxims might be tried and tested. For Kant, judgement may in some respects be likened to 'mother-wit' (*Mutterwitz*), which is to say that it involves an exercise of intuitive wisdom, insight or sympathy 'whose lack no school can make good'.[56] And yet, as O'Neill goes on to remark, '[Kant] presumably means only that there can be no *algorithms* for judging and no formal instruction, for he allows that "sharpening of the judgment is indeed the one great benefit of examples"' (O'Neill, p. 167). For Miller, conversely, there is no getting around the 'aporia', the moment of radical undecidability, that results from this lack of any self-assured link between precept and practice, moral law and its narrative analogues, or 'respect' as a matter of absolute, unconditional obedience to law and 'respect' as manifest in this or that particular instance.

It is the same dichotomizing habit of thought – the predilection for starkly exclusive 'either/or' choices – that leads post-structuralists to veto all talk of reference, reality, or truth on account of the problems that are seen to arise with any simplified, positivist approach to such issues. Thus: *either* it is the case that language provides a direct, unmediated access to reality, *or*, failing that, we are obliged to acknowledge that 'reality' is a wholly discursive construct, a realm of linguistic ('textual') representations which constitute the real so far as we can possibly know it. If these were indeed the only alternatives – if the case for truth and reference stood or fell on the existence of a one-to-one demonstrable match between word and world – then the sceptical conclusion would follow surely enough, along with all the deconstructive aporias drawn out by textualist adepts like Miller and de Man. That is to say, there could then be no resisting de Man's claim that rhetoric 'radically suspends' the relation between logic and grammar, introducing an element of undecidability (as between the constative and performative aspects of an utterance) which cannot be accounted for in propositional terms. In which case deconstruction would leave no room for the kinds of logico-linguistic analysis propounded by philosophers like Frege and Russell, arguments to the effect – briefly stated – that propositions (not 'signs') are the bearers of determinate truth-values, and that therefore we need to distinguish between properly referring expressions and those other (fictive, counter-factual or hypothetical) types of utterance that possess 'sense' but not 'reference'.[57] Such arguments would rest on nothing more secure than a naive ontological commitment, a foregone assumption *first* that 'reality' and 'fiction' are realms apart; *second*, that factual states of affairs may be captured in propositional form; *third*, that grammar 'stands in the service' of logic to the extent of enabling this passage from language to a reliable 'knowledge of the world'; and *fourth*, that rhetoric is a 'mere adjunct' to logic and grammar, an ornamental function whose effects are confined to the suasive or performative dimension.

Of course, as de Man readily concedes, these premises must appear nothing less than self-evident from a commonsense or mainstream philosophical viewpoint. But once called into question, as occurs most tellingly in the deconstructive reading of literary or philosophical texts, they will always at some point run up against unlooked-for complications which subvert the received order of priorities between logic, grammar, and rhetoric. Nor are these disruptions solely a matter of epistemological consequence, of problems encountered (as at various points in Kant's first *Critique*) in the passage from phenomenal or sensuous intuitions to concepts of understanding. For their effect is most apparent – so Miller would claim – in the case of those texts (like the second *Critique* or the *Foundations of the Metaphysics of Morals*) where Kant's concern is with ethical issues, in particular the question as to how moral law can be acted upon, interpreted or exemplified, given its utter remoteness from the contexts of everyday human experience. At this point, he argues, the aporias of textual close-reading are the nearest we can come to an 'adequate' sense of the gulf that exists between practical reason (the categorical imperative or its derivative maxims) and the need that we should somehow interpret those precepts in humanly intelligible terms. Ethics 'by an intrinsic necessity gives rise to storytelling', and in the telling of stories – *vide* de Man on Rousseau's *Confessions* – we can never be sure that the interests of truth have not been overtaken by other, more complex or ambivalent modes of narrative self-justification.[58]

This latter example should make it clear just how easily the textualist position of cognitive or epistemological scepticism leans over into a strain of downright contempt for the truth-claims of enlightened ethical reason. On de Man's view it is only a 'naive' (referential or thematic) reading of Rousseau that would take the *Confessions* at anything like face value, that is to say, as relating to certain actual episodes in Rousseau's recollected life-history, and moreover as concerned to present those episodes for the reader's judgement without trying to redeem or excuse their more shameful aspects. For this is to ignore the element of rhetorical duplicity that inhabits all such 'confessional' discourse, the fact that it proceeds on the one hand from a desire to lay bare one's various crimes, transgressions, acts of betrayal and guilty secrets, and on the other from an equally imperative desire to *do oneself justice* by constructing a narrative which offers no end of welcome opportunities for this exercise of 'honest' self-reckoning. In short, 'there can never be enough guilt around to match the text-machine's infinite power to excuse'.[59] Furthermore, 'the only thing one has to fear from the excuse is that it will indeed exculpate the confessor, thus making the confession (and the confessional text) redundant as it originates'.[60] This is partly a matter, de Man argues, of the undecidability as between factual and fictive statements, or the way that such writings deny us any recourse to criteria of truth and falsehood beyond what the text would persuade us to believe through its use of various rhetorical devices aimed toward creating just such an ethos of confessional authenticity. Rousseau's very success in this endeavour, his ability to impose his own version of the truth on naive or credulous readers, is all the more reason to regard that truth as a product of *post hoc* narrative contrivance. Thus it is always possible 'to face up to any experience (to excuse any guilt), because the experience always exists simultaneously as fictional discourse and as empirical event'.[61] And since the words on the page are all we have to go by – since de Man allows no legitimate appeal to 'extraneous' or extra-textual sources of evidence – then quite simply 'it is never possible to decide which of these two possibilities is the right one'.

Nor could we ever be justified in supposing that Rousseau's discourse must in some sense be *about* those various guilt-laden memories, like the famous episode of the 'purloined ribbon', which a thematic reading would regard as both central to the narrative and as bearing witness to his (no doubt belated) act of confessional good faith.[62] What the text asks us to believe is that Rousseau himself stole the ribbon; that the servant-girl Marion was dismissed (and her life utterly ruined) as a consequence of his not owning up to the theft; that this conduct on Rousseau's part lacked any kind of intelligible motive, unless – as might be suspected – some prompting of obscure sexual jealousy or desire; that the action has haunted his conscience ever since, not least on account of its seemingly gratuitous character; and that now he intends to come clean on the matter, offering no excuses but making some amends to Marion (whatever became of that unfortunate woman) through his own self-humiliating narrative. But this is not at all how de Man reads the episode, concerned as he is to demonstrate the naivety, the simplistic or rhetorically innocent character, of any interpretation that lends credence to Rousseau's confessional claims. Thus:

> What Rousseau *really* wanted is neither the ribbon nor Marion, but the public scene of exposure which he actually gets. . . . This desire is truly shameful, for it suggests that Marion was destroyed, not for the sake of Rousseau's saving face . . . but merely in order to provide him with a stage on which to parade his disgrace, or, what amounts to the same thing, to furnish him with a good ending for Book II of his *Confessions*.[63]

All of which follows from the lack of any possible decision-procedure, any adequate means or criterion for judging between factual and fictive, truthful and duplicitous, or 'constative' and 'performative' modes of narrative discourse. The latter distinction is especially problematic in the case of self-styled 'confessional' texts since such discourse can always be read *either* as an instance of authentic, truthful self-reckoning *or* as a technique for tacitly excusing the author's guilt by displaying his or her admirable readiness to offer such a warts-and-all autobiographical account. Thus 'the more there is to expose, the more there is to be ashamed of; the more the resistance to exposure, the more satisfying the scene, and, especially, the more satisfying and eloquent the belated revelation, in the later narrative, of the inability to reveal'.[64] And if de Man is right about this – if 'confession' and 'excuse' are speech-act modalities that constantly oscillate in Rousseau's text to the point of rendering their difference strictly undecidable – then it is no great stretch to his (and Miller's) larger claim: that the 'ethics of reading' has nothing to do with themes, intentions, authorial motives, or any such appeal to factors outside the play of ungrounded linguistic or textual representations. 'If we are right in saying that *"qui s'accuse s'excuse"*, then the relation between confession and excuse is rhetorical prior to being intentional.'[65] For then we should have no option but to follow de Man and Miller in viewing ethics as a wholly 'linguistic predicament', as the product of a 'structural interference' between various (for instance, constative and performative) codes, or as issuing always in a moment of deadlocked aporia where the precepts of morality, or practical reason, are placed forever beyond reach of adequate statement or narrative representation.

IV

As I have said, these arguments cannot be dismissed as so much trivial 'literary' talk among critics whose desire is simply to score points off all those earnest philosophical seekers-after-truth. No doubt this motivation plays some part in the present faculty wars, as it has at various times down through the history of what Plato was already calling the 'ancient quarrel' between poets and philosophers. But there are two main respects in which the latest phase of this quarrel differs from previous such episodes. One has to do with the supposed breakdown of traditional disciplinary boundaries, more specifically, the way in which theorists like de Man and Miller extend their techniques of rhetorical close-reading – techniques well established in literary criticism – to works that philosophers would usually regard as no fit material for such treatment. And of course this connects with what deconstruction has to say about those various binary oppositions (concept/metaphor, reason/rhetoric, truth/fiction, philosophy/literature and so forth) which have always, so the argument goes, privileged the one set of terms at the other's expense, and thus maintained philosophy's role as the discipline inherently best equipped to arbitrate their periodic boundary disputes.[66]

The second point concerns the level of argumentative rigour, real or apparent, with which deconstruction claims to have challenged that traditional order of priorities. For it is no longer a question – as once it was for the 'old' New Critics – of acknowledging philosophy's juridical right over issues and texts in its own domain, while protesting that literature involves a different kind of language, a rhetoric of irony, paradox or ambiguity which cannot (or should not) be held accountable to philosophic standards of logical rigour and truth. On the contrary, de Man argues: it is most often in the reading of literary texts that we are brought to recognise those complicating factors – those symptoms of the 'resistance to theory' put up by language in its figural or narrative aspect – which philosophy would much prefer to ignore. Such is the difference between (say) 'paradox' and 'aporia' as bottom-line terms of rhetorical analysis. For the New Critics it was a high point of principle that poetic truth (like the truth-claims of religion) could only be apprehended through a language of paradox, such that contradictions, or what looked like contradictions from the standpoint of plain-prose reason, could be taken as somehow granting access to a realm of deeper, more authentic, or humanly revealing truth.[67] For de Man, conversely, it is the measure of a 'rigorous' (a rhetorically demystified) reading that it offers no refuge in 'literary' or 'aesthetic' values from the aporias that open up between metaphor and metonymy, grammar and rhetoric, or language in its constative and performative modes. It may well be in the interests of philosophy and criticism alike to maintain their uneasy tactical truce, a division of academic labour that effectively replicates the *trivium* model, assigning philosophy a *de jure* competence as regards issues of reason and truth, while conserving a fenced-off rhetorical domain where literature (and criticism) can safely indulge their alternative, less 'rigorous' modes of enquiry. But this is to ignore de Man's 'epistemology of tropes', the dimension of figural language that may always turn out to subvert or undermine the ideal continuity assumed to exist between logic, grammar and our knowledge of the world as given through the forms of phenomenal cognition. 'To empty rhetoric of its epistemological impact,' he writes, 'is possible only because its tropological, figural functions are being bypassed.'[68] And again: such readings ignore the way in which rhetoric induces a 'disturbance of the stable cognitive field', the order of self-assured relations and priorities taken to extend 'from logic to grammar to a general science of man and of the phenomenal world'.[69] In short, philosophers are demonstrably wrong – deceived by their own self-authorizing rhetoric – if they think to treat 'literature' (poetry or fiction) as a realm of special licence where language can be allowed to go on holiday without prejudice to the truth-claims or validity-conditions that properly obtain elsewhere.

Hence de Man's knowingly provocative claim: that philosophical texts are just as much susceptible to a deconstructive reading, a 'literary' reading only in the sense that it elicits those hitherto unnoticed rhetorical structures, those symptoms of 'rigorous unreliability', that inhabit all writing beyond a certain level of discursive elaboration. And if this applies to issues of knowledge, truth and representation – issues that philosophy has seen fit to categorize as ontological or epistemological – then it is equally the case for any discourse on ethics that would offer more than an abstract appeal to some set of universalist precepts or maxims devoid of real-world applicability. Such a charge has often been laid against Kant by a long line of critics from Hegel to the present. They have voiced this objection in various ways: through the appeal to Hegelian *Sittlichkeit*, to Wittgensteinian 'language-games' or 'forms of life', to a revived Aristotelian doctrine of the virtues, or again, as with liberal communitarians like Michael Walzer, to a pluralist ethics of social concern sustained by the diverse practices and values of an ongoing cultural conversation.[70] But Kant always figures in a prominent role as the source of much that is wrong with present-day ethical and political theory. That is to say, he is reproached for his sternly unyielding morality of precept and principle, his attachment to notions (like the categorical imperative or the maxims of practical reason) which leave no room — so it is argued — for the everyday contingencies of situated human existence.

So these critics are oddly in agreement with Miller as regards the problem — or the plain impossibility — of bridging that gulf between 'moral law' and its worldly or context-specific entailments. But they differ decisively in thinking this a reason either to reject Kant's doctrine outright or to bring it down to earth by discounting the 'formalist' (quasi-universalizing) aspects, and treating what remains as more or less amenable to their own communitarian account. For Miller, on the contrary, Kant stands as an exemplary thinker — or his texts as an object-lesson in the 'ethics of reading' — *precisely insofar* as he raises these problems to a high point of 'rigorous' undecidability, a point where we are obliged to encounter the aporias of language, knowledge, representation, reason, justice, and truth. What strikes the objectors, from Hegel to Walzer, as a manifest shortcoming in Kantian ethics strikes Miller as a strong-willed facing up to the ultimately narrative or linguistic predicament that confronts all reflection on the antinomies of pure or practical reason. And those antinomies cannot be avoided (*contra* Kant's present-day revisionist interpreters) by reducing them to the level of an open-ended pluralist exchange between members of this or that interpretive community. For they will always inescapably reemerge as soon as one asks what relation exists between 'morality' as that which should not be compromised by involvement with private, self-seeking motives like fear and desire, and 'ethics' as a matter of practical adjustment to the limiting conditions of real-world agency and choice. To regard such problems as simply unreal, or as merely the unfortunate (and corrigible) upshot of Kant's 'formalist' legacy, is to underwrite the kind of inert, consensus-based ethics that identifies truth (or moral principle) with what is currently 'good in the way of belief'.

The same must apply, Miller argues, to any naively 'thematic' reading of Kant that would take moral law as adequately embodied — or unproblematically represented — by the various tropes, figural displacements, parables, allegories, narrative analogues and so forth which often stand in for what cannot be expressed in more direct, literal terms. The communitarians may think to resolve this perplexity by acknowledging that ethics must indeed have recourse to such homely figures of thought, but treating them as a means to reject Kant's abstract ('formalist') morality and lead ethical discourse back, via the community, home. On this view – a kind of 'naturalized Hegelianism', as Richard Rorty describes it – there is nothing in the least problematic about the idea that all ethical values have an inbuilt narrative component, a tacit dimension where the interests of communal 'solidarity' are promoted through the sense of playing one's role in an ongoing liberal-humanist enterprise.[71] But Miller must of course reject this easygoing option, determined as he is to push the Kantian 'aporias' – especially that between moral law and narrative exemplification – to a point of non-negotiable deadlock such that no appeal to communal values can possibly resolve the issue. Thus on the one hand 'narrative as a fundamental activity of the human mind, the power to make fictions, to tell stories to oneself or to others, serves for Kant as the absolutely necessary bridge without which there would be no connection between the law as such and any particular ethical rule of behavior' (Miller, p. 28). But on the other hand, again according to Kant, moral law is supposed to be 'above and beyond all that', to occupy a realm of pure practical reason 'which remains absolutely the same at all times and places and for all persons' (p. 23). In which case 'no story . . . can do other than falsify it by entangling the law in the meshes of the extrinsic particulars of a time and place, imaginary or real' (p. 23). And this latter distinction itself breaks down – becomes (*qua* Miller) strictly 'undecidable' – at those points where Kant does indeed fall back upon modes of narrative or figural expression, passages that contravene his own strict requirement that law should have no truck with mere contingencies of time and place, or with motives, like those of fear and desire, which would similarly compromise its sovereign claims. Such instances block any straightforward (e.g. communitarian) appeal to narrative understanding as a faculty continuous with our everyday, commonsense, or unproblematical modes of being-in-the-world. For they must also be read as *fictive* – as 'imaginary', not 'real' – insofar as they involve this necessary resort to tropes, parables, or story-telling devices which Kant has to use in default of any means by which law might be adequately represented.

I shall cite just one more extended passage from Miller before moving on to criticize his arguments with reference to O'Neill's very different understanding of these problems in Kantian ethics. It is a passage that dwells with sombre deconstructionist relish on Kant's difficulty in distinguishing 'respect' (*Achtung*) as a law of pure practical reason from 'respect' as a merely contingent response characterized by motives of fear, inclination, or desire. Miller's point is that Kant simply *cannot do without* certain fall-back strategies – metaphors, narrative examples, similes, 'as if' (*als ob*) constructions, etc. – which evoke precisely those all-too-human motives even while he rules explicitly against them as a matter of principled respect for moral law. 'What, then, is the law as such?' Miller asks, in a rhetorical question that clearly expects rather little in the way of enlightening response.

> Well, Kant cannot tell you exactly what the law as such is, in so many words, nor can he tell you exactly where it is, or where it comes from. . . . [But] he can nevertheless tell you to what it is analogous. Into the vacant place where there is no direct access to the law as such, but where we stand respectfully, like the countryman in Kafka's parable 'Before the Law', are displaced by metaphor or some other form of analogy two forms of feeling that *can* be grasped and named directly. Respect for the law is said to be analogous to just those two feelings which it has been said not to be: inclination and fear. The name for this procedure of naming by figures of speech what cannot be named literally because it cannot be faced directly is catachresis or, as Kant calls it, 'hypotyposis'. . . . Kant's linguistic procedure in this footnote is an example of the forced or abusive transfer of terms from an alien realm to name something which has no proper name in itself. . . . What is 'forced' or 'abusive' in this case is clear enough. Kant has said that respect for the law is not based on fear and inclination, but since there is no proper word for what it is based on, he is forced to say it is like just those two feelings, fear and inclination, he has said it is *not* like. (Miller, pp. 20–1)

I have quoted this passage at length because it offers a set-piece example, not only of Miller's working procedures but also of the broader post-structuralist approach to issues of textual understanding. Such criticism operates on the following assumptions: 1) that the real (or our knowledge thereof) is wholly contingent upon our languages, discourses, or modes of representation; 2) that all language is radically figural (or fictive) insofar as it involves the use of 'arbitrary' signs devoid of real-world, referential content; 3) that any illusions we might have to the contrary are merely a product of 'naive' (referential or thematic) modes of reader-response; 4) that there is nothing 'outside the text' – no appeal beyond the play of linguistic or rhetorical figuration – that could possibly put a stop to this vertiginous *mise-en-abîme*; 5) that ethical judgements are likewise ungrounded, since on the one hand they can claim no demonstrative factual or veridical warrant, while on the other their only access to 'law' is through tropes, allegories, or other such oblique devices; and therefore 6) that the 'ethics of reading' must perforce acknowledge this 'linguistic predicament', this 'law of the text' – as Miller describes it – which leaves ethical judgement forever suspended in a state of 'rigorous undecidability', and which regards thematic readings (whether of novels or philosophical exempla) as hopelessly beside the point. 'We read novels,' Miller reassuringly suggests, 'to see in a safe area of fiction or imagination what would happen if we lived our lives according to a certain principle of moral choice' (Miller, p. 30). But such assurance is no sooner offered than withdrawn, turning out as it does to be just another version of philosophy's claim to make literature 'safe' by delimiting its sphere of rhetorical or fictive operations. For what is always revealed by closer analysis is the relation that exists between 'the necessity of narrative in any discourse about ethics' and, more disturbingly, 'the necessity of using analogies or figures of speech in place of an unavailable literal or conceptual language' (p. 33).

V

O'Neill's *Constructions of Reason* has nothing to say about Miller, de Man or other such proponents of this textualist 'ethics of reading'. Despite what might seem a pointedly apposite title, her book makes no attempt to engage with deconstruction but addresses itself squarely to philosophers within the Anglo-American analytic tradition of debate. Nevertheless it mounts a defence of Kantian ethics which the textualists might do well to consider before reiterating some of their more preposterous claims. In using this adjective I take a lead from Miller, one of whose favourite deconstructive ploys is to seize upon some passing figure of speech and literalize its meaning to the point where it becomes the very governing trope (the condition of possibility) for a whole complex structure of argument. Thus: 'preposterous', from the Latin *prae-postero*, is defined as the act of 'putting before what normally comes after', or reversing the commonplace (logical or causal) order of priorities through a trick of linguistic figuration. From which derives the present-day – no doubt 'radically' metaphorical – sense of the word: 'contrary to nature, reason, or common sense; perverse, foolish, utterly absurd'.

Such is for instance Miller's claim with regard to the role of promises in Kant, the fact that the verb *versprechen* (to promise) can also signify 'to misspeak oneself', 'to say the wrong thing', or – on a freer but not too fanciful rendering – 'to betray one's intent through a more-or-less significant slip of the tongue'.[72] For Miller, this is no mere etymological curiosity but an aspect of Kant's 'linguistic predicament' which in turn has real (indeed ominous) implications for his theory of promises and other such forms of morally binding speech-act commitment. Kant's reasoning here is of course based firmly – or precariously, as Miller sees it – on his doctrine of the 'categorical imperative', that is, the principle that one should act always in accordance with maxims (guidelines for conduct) which can be generalized to cover the entirety of human actions and choices, without in the process giving rise to incompatible or contradictory entailments. Thus for instance if lying (or making false promises) were erected into a universal law, then according to Kant 'there would be no promises at all, inasmuch as it would be futile to make a pretence of my intention in regard to future actions to those who would not believe this pretence or – if they overhastily did so – who would pay me back in my own coin. Thus my maxim would necessarily destroy itself as soon as it was made a universal law.'[73] But this argument works, on Miller's submission, only so long as one takes for granted what is here most urgently at issue, namely the priority of practical reason (or moral law) over its modes of linguistic expression. For if once it is allowed – 'preposterous' as this might seem – that language both *precedes and radically suspends* the conditions of good-faith promising, intending, meaning what one says and so forth, then there can be no assurance that any such speech-act is morally binding in the Kantian (categorical) sense.

This is the disturbing possibility that Miller finds shadowed in the verb *versprechen*, a verb whose prefix 'may be either an intensive or, conversely, a privative, a negation' (Miller, p. 36). What it signals to the wary reader is the way that language subverts Kant's meaning – fails to make good his argumentative promise – through the 'latent contradiction' which inhabits that tell-tale prefix. Of course one might respond (as O'Neill doubtless would) that this is just a piece of wilful or opportunist wordplay, an example of the well-known deconstructionist penchant for mistaking the plain sense of things in pursuit of some ingenious rhetorical twist. On the contrary, Miller asserts: this word is symptomatic in the strong sense that it condenses all the problems, all the strictly *inescapable* conflicts or aporias that attach to language in its ethical, performative or promissory aspect. 'Kant says something other than what he means to say. This something betrays a hidden flaw in his argument and makes that argument a non sequitur or an anacolouthon, a failure in following' (p. 36). And the fact of his resorting to such figures of speech is sufficient indication that Kant's project cannot make good on its cardinal claims. What he 'actually shows' (as distinct from what his argument explicitly asserts) is that 'the social order depends on a precarious intralinguistic and interpersonal agreement to go on meaning the same thing by words' (pp. 36–7). In which case the maxims of practical reason – along with their presumed source and guarantee, the categorical imperative – must likewise be acknowledged to rest on nothing more than a deluded (though perhaps indispensable) belief in their language-transcendent authority.

Kant's reader is thus left in the unfortunate predicament of being wholly unable to decide 'whether the morality of promising is grounded in the law as such', or whether – as on Miller's deconstructive reading – it offers 'an example of an ungrounded act which would define morality as a linguistic performative to be judged only by an internal temporal consistency which the example shows, as by a slip of the tongue, can never be achieved' (p. 38). Nor can these uncertainties be kept at bay, or prevented from doing much harm, by an appeal to the various speech-act conventions – the criteria of good-faith utterance – taken to hold within this or that context of shared ethico-linguistic values. For it is precisely Miller's point – driven home with relentless deconstructionist 'rigour' – that any such appeal will end up by subverting its own most basic principle, i.e., the necessity that moral laws (respect for other persons, keeping one's word, promising in good faith) should *not* be just a matter of conventional adherence to the dictates of custom or social propriety. Hence the unsettling (even 'terrifying') message that Miller finds implicit in Kant's failed attempt to demonstrate the categorical impossibility of erecting false promises, or deliberate lies, into a universal maxim of human conduct. What this example in fact shows is that 'in the end it may not be possible to distinguish between a promise made with the intention to keep it and one made with the intention not to keep it. . . . Whether I intend to lie or do not intend to lie I lie in any case, by an intrinsic necessity of language' (p. 38).

O'Neill helps to show what is wrong with this entire line of argument when she, like Miller, takes up the issue of Kant's dependence on narrative examples, figural expressions, and other such 'literary' devices. For there is a problem here, she concedes, if one asks what relationship exists between moral law as a matter of generalized precept and as exemplified in some particular instance of (real or imaginary) human conduct. On this point at least she would be willing to acknowledge some of the reasons for Miller's perplexity, if not the strain of *a priori* scepticism – the refusal to entertain constructive solutions – which leads him to dismiss as 'naive' any account that attempts to answer those problems. Their disagreement comes down to the difference between two philosophical traditions and two opposed views of what properly counts as an adequate critical reading of a text. Where Miller reads always on the lookout for aporias, for instances of rhetorical 'undecidability' which threaten to collapse the whole edifice of Kantian critical thought, O'Neill is more inclined to construe Kant's arguments in the rational-reconstructive mode, that is to say, as capable of justification in terms that respect his philosophical purposes while answering to the best, most accountable standards of current philosophical debate. For Miller there is a kind of negative foreknowledge, an *a priori* certainty always borne out in the reading, that texts will at some point subvert or deconstruct their own most crucial argumentative claims. For O'Neill, conversely, it is likelier than not that any issues arising in connection with particular passages will either be clarified (and perhaps resolved) elsewhere in Kant's work, or at any rate lend themselves to constructive exposition on the part of well-informed commentators.

Not that one is thereby compelled to take Kant entirely at his word, or somehow obliged, on ethical grounds, to treat his work as having always made good on its own argumentative claims. Such are the stark alternatives as Miller conceives them: *either* a reading naively premised on uncritical 'respect' for an author's manifest intentions, *or* the kind of reading that finds those intentions everywhere subverted – rendered 'undecidable' – by the play of aberrant linguistic figuration. But there is no good reason to accept these as the only alternatives on offer, unless (that is) one shares the deconstructionist's need for a straw-man opponent who can always be relied on to adopt the most simplistic of fideist assumptions with regard to the relation between truth, meaning, and authorial intent. What Miller ignores – what he is obliged to ignore if his readings are to carry any credence – is the third possibility that O'Neill keeps steadily in view throughout *Constructions of Reason*. Her point, briefly put, is that localized problems of interpretation do not necessarily leave thought suspended in an ecstasy of 'undecidability'; that there is more to understanding a text than dwelling on some isolated moment of (real or imagined) rhetorical perplexity; and that the main purpose of philosophical commentary, of exegesis and critique in the analytic mode, is to offer conceptual clarification of precisely such interpretive issues. Whatever the obstacles to an adequate grasp put up by this or that passage, one can always look to other passages – or to arguments and instances offered elsewhere – in the hope of discovering some better, more perspicuous or intelligible treatment of the problem.

This is not to deny that such difficulties may be real or that Kant may sometimes fall short of resolving them to the commentator's full satisfaction. What it does reject as perverse is the idea that such issues can *never* be resolved since language (or rhetoric) always and inevitably works to undermine the truth-claims of 'logocentric' reason. For there could then be no question of criticizing Kant, let alone criticizing his work to any constructive purpose. And this because the very idea of constructive criticism rests on the presumption (*contra* Hillis Miller) that philosophy is not just a 'kind of writing', that concepts are not merely so many disguised or sublimated metaphors, and furthermore that there are standards of conceptual or logical validity in argument which do not inevitably self-deconstruct when exposed to a reading in the textualist-rhetorical mode. Which is also to say that when Kant uses metaphors or figural examples one is not thrown back upon the desperate expedient of declaring Kant's text to be *wholly a product* of the tropes or the 'fictive' analogical devices that occasionally figure in his argument. For this would only be the case if those passages functioned aporetically in the strict sense of that term, i.e., if they blocked all possible routes through and beyond the particular instance of referential or conceptual 'undecidability'. Miller has reasons (or motives) of his own for insisting that no such escape-routes are available. But his arguments amount to little more than a litany of textualist *idées reçues*, among them the notion – taken up from de Man in a spirit of unswerving doctrinal adherence – that philosophy possesses no conceptual resources sufficient to withstand the self-styled 'rigours' of rhetorical close-reading.

We can best get a hold on these issues by looking at what O'Neill has to say about metaphor and narrative (or 'literary') examples as they function in the discourse of Kantian ethics. For this is clearly within reach of the larger question as to how moral law can be rendered humanly intelligible, given its austere remoteness from the contexts of everyday practical application. O'Neill takes the point of this criticism but sees no reason to regard it (like Miller) as an absolute and unresolvable aporia which leaves morality suspended in the void between precept and practice, rule and instance, or language in its constative and performative modes. The following passage is I think her most explicit statement of the problems involved.

> When we come to apply the Categorical Imperative (or any derivative principles) to *actual* cases — where we have to act or decide — we face the difficulty that, however detailed the subordinate principles previously worked out, however diverse the examples of action that have been pointed out, these can at most help us to discern the moral status of a maxim of proposed action, but can never determine fully just what sort of act should be performed. Hypothetical examples, being themselves principles of action, must evidently remain indeterminate even when relatively specific, and so cannot fully determine any act. The acts or persons or lives that are pointed to in ostensive examples may, in themselves, be fully determinate. But their relevance to a case in hand must (since there is never total correspondence of features) be guided by some (necessarily indeterminate) understanding of the morally significant aspects of the example. Ostension, as is well known, is always equivocal and requires interpretation. *Judgment* is therefore always needed when principles are applied to particular cases or when ostensive examples are adduced as relevant guides. Neither principles nor examples alone can guide action. (O'Neill, p. 167)

There are several points here that would seem to fall plump into Miller's deconstructionist sights. Thus O'Neill concedes the problematical gap — the lack of any 'fully determinate' match — between principles (or maxims) and the various cases which are taken to illustrate those principles. Such reasoning will always be 'equivocal', she thinks, to the extent that it must always leave room for alternative ideas of what counts as a relevant case, maxim or principle in any given instance. Moreover, there is the difficulty that even if one does come up with some example whose relevance is generally accepted, still it can only function 'hypothetically', that is to say, as a set-piece illustrative case where all the pertinent issues and choices have already been worked out in advance, and where nothing remains of the dilemmas encountered by real-world moral agents whose lives are not constructed on any such providential pattern. These are what O'Neill calls 'literary' examples, whether in the usual sense of that term (taken from novels, plays or poems) or as applied to case-histories, real or invented, which likewise occupy a separate realm of foreclosed existential choice. The trouble, once again, is in seeing how anyone could derive moral guidance from a narrative whose exemplary character consists in its ideal remoteness from the sphere of contingent motives, actions and events. 'We do not have to decide whether to turn Raskolnikov in or whether to find Billy Budd guilty' (O'Neill, p. 175). And this objection applies equally on the one hand to 'hypothetical' instances and on the other to historical or real-life episodes which are nonetheless cited, mentioned or narrated in order to point up some generalized ethical conclusion. For 'just as we cannot challenge the interpretation of a literary example beyond appropriate bounds of literary interpretation, so we do not have to do anything, beyond "deciding what we want to say" about the example and making sense of it' (p. 175).

Such examples are frequent in the work of philosophers – especially those influenced by Wittgenstein – who argue that the only way to make sense of ethical issues is by relating them, via narrative instances, to the various culture-specific 'language-games' or 'forms of life' that alone provide a relevant interpretive context.[74] From this point of view it is the bad legacy of Kantian ('formalist') thinking which produces all those problems and antinomies that plague the discourse of present-day ethical thought. Hence the marked shift toward narrative paradigms – or instances of 'thick description', in Clifford Gertz's usefully resonant phrase – to be found in the work of Peter Winch, Bernard Williams, Michael Walzer and other thinkers of a broadly communitarian persuasion.[75] But O'Neill finds this approach inadequate, mainly on account of its tendency to endorse some existing (consensual) set of values and beliefs, taken as constituting the horizon of intelligibility for moral agents brought up within that particular tradition. For if this were the case – if ethical judgements could only be construed in relation to the interests of a given cultural community – then there could be no question of challenging, opposing or criticizing those interests from a standpoint of reasoned or principled dissent. From which it would follow (a conclusion willingly drawn by neopragmatists like Richard Rorty) that 'reasons' and 'principles' are wholly redundant, or perhaps worth invoking just so far as they provide an added measure of suasive appeal among those – e.g., fellow-citizens of the Western bourgeois liberal democracies – already predisposed to respect such talk.[76]

On this account, as O'Neill puts it, 'moral reasoning presupposes shared moral traditions and practices', so that 'only within such a context can moral discourse about examples take place, and questioning of the shared framework of moral practices is not possible' (O'Neill, p. 172). In the end there is no convincing anyone unless we and they are sufficiently on a wavelength – possessed of enough common values, beliefs or ideas of what counts as a valid, good-faith argument – to make the whole effort worthwhile. Otherwise, lacking such communicative means, we shall have to acknowledge that the differences run so deep as to render meaningful dialogue impossible, since nothing we say could ever make sense, let alone carry moral conviction, from their point of view. And to the extent that others are persuaded to our way of thinking, this cannot be a matter (so Rorty would argue) of offering 'reasoned' or 'principled' grounds for abandoning beliefs which they once found persuasive but which now, thus enlightened, they regard as no longer worthy of acceptance. For in order to arrive at such agreement (and indeed, to have grasped each other's reasons for not so agreeing in the first place) the parties concerned must *already* have shared a whole range of operative values, assumptions and beliefs, in the absence of which their dialogue would never have got started. In short, any localized differences of view will always be resolved, so far as this is possible, by appealing to the kinds of suasive strategy that count with them and with other members of the same interpretive community, however broadly defined. Which is also to say that the differences cannot after all have run so deep, since both disputants shared enough ground (or were open to persuasion on sufficiently similar terms) to make their quarrel a minor thing by comparison. And failing such agreement, Rorty thinks, there is no further recourse – no appeal to 'principles' or 'reasons' – that could possibly settle the issue between them. At this point the argument simply runs out since the parties will be talking at cross-purposes, invoking different (perhaps radically incommensurable) criteria of reason, justice or truth, and hence rendering the whole debate futile. So we might as well accept the pragmatist case that persuasion (or rhetoric) is what counts in the end, and that agreement according to our cultural lights is the best that we or anyone can hope for.[77]

Although O'Neill makes no mention of Rorty she sees very clearly the connection that exists between the narrative or communitarian turn in recent ethical theory and the desire to talk moral issues down to the level of consensus belief. Moreover, she regards the use of 'literary' examples – whether fictive or in the wider (Wittgensteinian) sense of that term – as likewise promoting a relativist outlook which ignores the real conflicts that may always arise between different moral value-systems, or again, between practice and principle within some particular 'interpretive community'. Her point is that such conflicts tend to be smoothed away by any approach that takes language-games, 'forms of life' or narrative exempla as the bottom line of ethical discourse, the stage at which meaningful argument has an end since beyond it there exist no shared criteria for debating the issue one way or the other. 'This position leads readily both to moral conservatism and to moral relativism' (O'Neill, p. 173). For if indeed it is the case (as these thinkers would have it) that ethical arguments cannot do more than appeal to some shared set of values and beliefs, then clearly there could be no principled resistance, no argument on dissident or counter-consensual grounds which carried the least weight with members of the relevant cultural community. And it is here, I would suggest, that the two kinds of 'literary' approach to ethical issues – Hillis Miller's and the narrative-communitarian line – come together in an otherwise improbable alliance. For they both view such issues as strictly unintelligible outside the various discourses, narratives or languages of moral appraisal that happen to exist either within some given socio-cultural context or, as with Miller, in the reading of some particular problematic work or passage. That is to say, they take it pretty much for granted firstly that linguistic (or narrative) understanding is the paradigm case of understanding in general, and secondly that any talk of 'reasons' and 'principles' – any high-toned Kantian talk – can in the end be justified only by virtue of its suasive or story-telling interest.

Of course Miller has different aims in view, seeking as he does to draw out moments of textual 'undecidability' where the two kinds of language (constative and performative, or 'moral law' and its various narrative analogues) can be shown to generate a series of wholly unresolvable linguistic aporias. From a Wittgensteinian standpoint these problems would appear nothing more than a bad case of philosophy's besetting vice, its 'bewitchment by language' or propensity to be over-impressed by sceptical predicaments of its own elaborate devising.[78] But as O'Neill remarks, both approaches are 'literary' in the sense that they exclude all principled judgements other than those than find warrant in this or that localized interpretive case-study. Thus on the one hand 'it is hardly open to a Wittgensteinian to adopt principles of interpretation – whether radically subjectivist or deconstructive – that call in question the possibility of a shared, open reading of a text' (O'Neill, p. 172). But on the other such readings in the 'literary' mode (whether Wittgensteinian or deconstructive) are themselves confined to a treatment of moral or interpretive issues which cannot go beyond the terms laid down by the text or narrative example in hand. What they exclude, more specifically, is any account of the way that shared practices or 'forms of life' – along with their modes of narrative representation – may get into conflict not only with each other but also with principles taken to transcend such communally sanctioned values and beliefs. 'Precisely because of the variety and transience of ethical practices, to which Wittgensteinian writers draw our attention, we cannot easily lead our lives without raising questions that are not just internal to but about local practices' (p. 174). Moreover, 'if examples *are* the pivot of moral thought, this is not only because there is no acceptable theory, but also because they are instances of problems in human lives that stand in need of resolution' (p. 175).

This is why there is less difference than at first might appear between Miller's deconstructive (or all-out sceptical) approach to the 'ethics of reading', and the work of those philosophers who think that such scepticism is best answered by appealing to examples – whether narratives, speech-acts, or other such language-based conventional practices – by way of justifying argument. For O'Neill, on the contrary, these practices themselves stand in need of principled justification, since to assess them 'internally' (i.e., in accordance with their own criteria, their own implied standards of reason, truth and justice) is of course to find that everything is perfectly in order. 'Reflection and even understanding are not enough to bring to human difficulties – unless, of course, these difficulties are merely imagined, as they are in works of literature' (p. 175). Such is the disabling (relativist) consequence of Wittgenstein's famous dictum: that philosophy should properly 'leave everything as it is', rather than seeking to adjudicate problems from a different (critical or principled) standpoint. For such an attitude will always lead to some version of the incommensurability-thesis, the idea that practices can only be judged on terms that would make sense or carry conviction with members of the relevant cultural community, and hence that any criticism which rejects those terms – or which calls those practices into question – must simply have failed to grasp their meaning at some elementary level. On this view 'traditions and practices . . . must be shared if there is to be any moral discourse; and if they are shared we can conduct discussion of particular ethical cases and what "we" might agree to say about them without invoking any principles or theories that are not implicit in those practices' (O'Neill, p. 176). From which it follows that belief-systems set their own terms for valid or meaningful discussion, and that any criticism that rejects those terms – or which treats them as open to principled dissent – is *ipso facto* ruled out of court.

VI

Peter Winch is O'Neill's main exemplar of this conservative-relativist trend. But she might well have cited Jean-François Lyotard as an instance of what results when Wittgensteinian talk of 'language-games', 'forms of life' etc. is joined to an attitude of high postmodernist contempt for all the truth-claims and principles of enlightenment critique.[79] In both cases there is a failure to conceive how moral agents could ever adopt a principled stance that would not amount *either* to a choice among the range of presently-existing codes and conventions, *or* to a species of grandiose self-deception, a claim to occupy the moral high ground outside and above those same communal norms. Merely to multiply the language-games on offer – to talk, like Lyotard, of 'dissensus', rather than 'consensus', as the optimal condition for a postmodern liberal polity – is scarcely to provide any answer to this problem. For it still treats justification as *internal* to each and every language-game, as a matter of strictly 'heterogeneous' criteria which apply only to particular cases, and which cannot be used to judge in other instances without thereby inflicting a wrong on one or other of the parties concerned. Hence Lyotard's pronouncement of an end to those various 'enlightened' meta-narrative theories – Kantian, Hegelian, Marxist or other – which have sought (as he reads them) to suppress such differences in the name of universal reason and truth. Hence also his idea of our current 'postmodern condition' as one in which the sheer multiplicity of language-games (or 'first-order natural pragmatic narratives') can best ensure the interests of equality and justice by denying any single discourse the right to judge others on its own terms. It is this appeal to what Lyotard calls *the differend* – the diversity of 'phrase-regimes' with no last instance of sovereign juridical rule – which provides the sole measure of ethical good faith in a liberal-pluralist culture. For injustice comes about when one phrase-regime (for example, discourse in its factual-documentary, epistemic or truth-telling mode) sets up to give the rule in contexts beyond its legitimate sphere of application. Moreover, he concurs with Hillis Miller and other revisionist ('literary') readers of Kant in regarding the sublime as an index or analogue of this radical heterogeneity, this point at which reflection exceeds all the powers of determinate (conceptual) understanding, so that judgement has somehow to operate 'without criteria' from one such singular instance to the next. What the sublime thus figures, on this postmodern reading, is the gulf that opens up between the cognitive phrase-regime (where intuitions are 'brought under' adequate concepts) and judgements of an ethical, socio-political or kindred evaluative order.[80] To ignore this differend, Lyotard would argue, is not only to commit a category-mistake but also to inflict a grievous wrong upon one or other party to any such dispute. For justice demands that one should treat each case (and every witness, every argument or item of evidence adduced in each case) as a narrative instance whose truth-claims are strictly *sui generis*, and not to be judged by criteria other than its own.

Of course it may be said that Lyotard's thinking is more post-structuralist than Wittgensteinian, and that indeed the whole point of Wittgenstein's appeal to language-games and cultural forms of life is to coax philosophers down from such forms of self-induced sceptical puzzlement. But O'Neill seems to me much nearer the mark when she observes that this widespread linguistic turn is inherently liable to produce just the opposite effect, since it leaves no room for reasons, principles or justifying arguments other than those conventionally sanctioned by this or that cultural discourse. For if the criteria for judging a practice are strictly 'internal' to the practice itself, then on the one hand any validating arguments are trapped in an endlessly circular process of self-justification, while on the other any criticisms or principled objections must be viewed as 'external' to the practice (or language-game) in question, and hence as quite simply beyond the pale for members of the relevant community. It is not just postmodern sceptics like Lyotard, or deconstructionist adepts like Miller, who have seen fit to push their case to a point where the communitarian appeal begins to look somewhat less than reassuring. One may doubt, for instance, whether Kripke's 'solution' to the Wittgensteinian paradox about following a rule is really much more than an elegant re-statement of the same conventionalist doctrine, the idea that rules (whether of conduct, language, logic, or mathematics) cannot be justified beyond pointing out the existence of some relevant communal practice.[81] For this still leaves a path wide open to the sceptical conclusion that what counts as 'following a rule' is wholly contingent upon practices that lack any further (reasoned, argued or principled) means of justification. And from here it is no great distance to other, more extreme versions of the sceptical-relativist doctrine, whether couched in Lyotard's postmodernist idiom of radically 'heterogeneous' phrase-regimes, or (as with Miller) in the deconstructive parlance of textual aporia, undecidability, *mise-en-abîme* and so forth.

Such giddy excesses may seem far removed from the tone of down-to-earth, commonsense wisdom, the appeal to shared meanings and values, that typifies the writing of liberal communitarians or ethical philosophers in the Wittgensteinian line of descent. But the underlying kinship becomes more evident if one asks what defence the latter can mount against the kinds of extravagant 'textualist' position adopted by postmodern thinkers like Lyotard or deconstructors like Miller and de Man. For if indeed it is the case that truth-claims, reasons or principles can only be judged in accordance with criteria internal to this or that language-game, and if close-reading in the deconstructive mode can reveal moments of conflict or divergence between logic, grammar and rhetoric, then there is simply no avoiding the sceptical upshot so eagerly embraced by these thinkers. Nor is it an adequate response to argue, from a Wittgensteinian standpoint, that deconstruction raises problems where no real problems exist, since language-games just *do* make sense in the context of those various practices or 'forms of life' which provide them with all that is needed in the way of criterial justification. For once again this misses the crucial point: that these readings do have their own kind of rigour, one that results – in de Man's case especially – from a combination of sedulous attentiveness to the text or passage in hand and conceptual exegesis of a high (albeit highly heterodox) order. Which is not of course to deny that the results are often so counter-intuitive, so sharply at odds with the mainstream interpretive tradition as to strike many readers (philosophers and literary critics alike) as merely wrong-headed or perverse. Such responses are wholly predictable, de Man maintains, since deconstruction foregrounds the rhetorical dimension of language (the 'epistemology of tropes') to the point where it disrupts all our naturalized ideas of language, logic and truth. Moreover, those ideas have the backing not only of intuitive self-evidence but also of a deep-laid philosophical conviction, one that presupposes 'the interconnection between a science of the phenomenal world and a science of language conceived as definitional logic, the precondition for a correct axiomatic-deductive, synthetic reasoning'.[82] Small wonder that de Man's writings have met with such hostility, bafflement or downright indifference from thinkers in the broadly analytic tradition. But just as significant, I would argue, are the obstacles that they place in the way of any alternative appeal to 'ordinary language' as a possible escape-route from the problems encountered by epistemological (or 'foundationalist') modes of thought. For what de Man's readings also bring out with unsettling regularity is the fact – simply put – that ordinary language is often more 'extraordinary' than it seems, or more apt to generate issues undreamt of on the conventionalist or communitarian account.[83]

My point is that these problems will always arise with any approach that denies itself recourse to truth-claims and principles beyond those embodied in some localized language-game, discourse or cultural 'form of life'. This is why, as O'Neill remarks, '[even] those Wittgensteinian writers who reject relativist readings of Wittgenstein do not offer an account of moral practice and decision that goes beyond the practice-based conception of ethical decision offered by relativist writers' (O'Neill, p. 175). They are unable to do so for the simple reason that if internalist criteria are the only ones available – if justification always comes down to what counts as right or true within some existing cultural community – then anyone who adopts different criteria in order to criticize or challenge its practices will necessarily be working on assumptions at odds with the reasons, motives or life-forms shared by members of that same community. Thus O'Neill cites the argument of Peter Winch that 'a decision can only be made within the context of a meaningful way of life'.[84] Here the word 'meaningful' is taken to encompass all those language-games, practices or tacit presuppositions which make up the communal *Lebenswelt* of situated moral agents, and which therefore (Winch thinks) allow of no valid or relevant appeal to principles outside their shared horizon of understanding. But in this case clearly one is back in the relativist predicament, having no possible grounds on which to criticize even the most (to us) irrational beliefs or repugnant moral, social or political practices. Winch may argue that we can act (as well as interpret) on the basis of contextualized examples, since this process involves both 'making a hypothetical agent's judgement' and 'reflecting on what I would think it right to do in such a situation'. But he also maintains, as against Kant, that 'the universalizability principle is idle' insofar as we are not thereby committed to 'judgements about what others in a like situation should do'.[85] From which it would follow that relativism must have the last word (whatever that could mean), since any 'judgements' thus arrived at would be valid only for agents – ourselves or others – who shared the same criteria for deciding what counted as a good-faith, principled or reasoned response.

All the same, O'Neill remarks, Winch in fact has no choice but to operate on a 'weak' version of the universalizability principle. For otherwise 'there would be no reason for thinking that any literary example or any hypothetical agent's judgement has *any* implication for action' (O'Neill, p. 176). This is a consequence of the procedural difficulty that Miller raises to a high point of textualist aporia: namely, in O'Neill's words, that 'the move from an example and the judgement reached by reflecting on the example in the light of our shared practices to a decision about an actual case, which is unlikely to match the example in all respects, is far from obvious' (p. 176). Her argument here is worth pursuing more closely since it bears on a number of the questions raised by this notion of language-games (or narrative instances) as the furthest one can get in the way of justification. An example-based ('literary') approach to ethics may indeed be 'without costs' in the case of novels or poems, since here we are concerned with interpretive issues only, and are under no further obligation to decide – to settle upon some consequent course of action – in light of any judgement thus arrived at. But the same cannot apply to instances outside this conveniently self-enclosed domain, instances where (contrary to Wittgenstein's teaching) it is simply not enough to reflect on the variety of in-place customs, conventions, language-games, or communal forms of life. For here ethical judgement may find itself in need of other, more principled resources, arguments that enable it to go against the grain of received (consensual) wisdom, and to criticize existing habits of thought from a stand-point of adequately reasoned moral dissent. Thus, according to O'Neill, 'it is difficult to see how the transition from articulated and intelligible literary or hypothetical examples to moral decisions is to be made without the mediation either of principles or of theory that indicates or suggests which *sorts* of correspondence between example and actual case are important and which trivial' (p. 176). Most important here is the implied relation between 'principle' and 'theory', the one having to do with moral judgements that claim a more than localized or context-specific validity, while the other involves a similarly Kantian appeal to truth-claims (or cognitive criteria) that secure the conditions of intelligibility for judgements of real-world relevance and point. For lacking such criteria, she argues, 'the spectator perspective from which Wittgensteinian moral reflection begins dooms it to a "moral connoisseurship" that fails to resolve the problems we actually face' (p. 176).

What O'Neill has to say about narrative or 'literary' examples, and the uncritical perspective often entailed by the use of such examples, would apply even more to Miller's deconstructive 'ethics of reading'. For on this account the destabilizing effects of language in its figural/tropological dimension are such as to subvert – to render 'undecidable' – all the grounds for distinguishing between fact and fiction, reason and rhetoric, or narrative as a means of exemplifying real-life ethical dilemmas and narrative as an 'allegory' of the obstacles encountered by any such naive referential or realist approach. And this is demonstrably the case, Miller argues, with those passages in Kant (especially his *Foundations of the Metaphysics of Morals*) which attempt to flesh out the maxims of practical reason by providing some illustrative instance, some well-chosen anecdote, parable or narrative *exemplum*. If we read them as Kant clearly intended, then these passages should help to counter any charge of ethical 'formalism', any argument which holds that the categorical imperative (along with its derivative maxims) operates at a level of extreme – indeed, near-inhuman – abstraction from the conduct of our lives as situated moral agents. For Miller, on the contrary, this narrative 'turn' is one that not only fails to resolve such problems but sharpens them to the point of an ultimate aporia in the nature of all ethical thinking. Thus, 'the moral law gives rise by an intrinsic necessity to storytelling, even if that storytelling in one way or another puts into question or subverts the moral law' (Miller, p. 25). And again, with regard to Kant's 'parables' in the *Foundations*: 'it is never possible to be sure that duty is not a fiction in the bad sense of an ungrounded act of self-sustaining language, that is, precisely a vain delusion and chimerical concept, a kind of ghost generated by a sad linguistic necessity' (p. 38). In which case it is the merest of 'commonsense' errors, one soon dispelled by the undeceiving rigours of tropological analysis, to suppose that language could ever give access to any truth beyond this melancholy knowledge of its own 'self-sustaining' (but also self-subverting) character.

But one will only be forced to such desperate conclusions if one accepts the premise that Miller shares with Wittgensteinians, postmodernists, and kindred proponents of the current narrative–linguistic–textualist turn. Otherwise it will seem nothing short of self-evident 1) that language *can and does* very often refer to real-world objects, actions and events; 2) that narrative utterances range all the way from the factual-documentary, *via* novels and stories in the classic realist mode, to instances of postmodern, anti-mimetic, 'meta-fictional' or suchlike *avant-garde* literary genres; 3) that these involve a variable balance – and a constant process of readerly adjustment – between knowledge of the relevant truth-conditions and knowledge of how those conditions may some-times be suspended; and 4) that in the case of narrative examples (e.g., those offered in works of ethical philosophy) we are *not* therefore condemned, as Miller would have it, to a state of chronic indecision as regards their veridical or fictive status. It may well be, as I have suggested above, that his arguments follow with a kind of necessity from the stance of extreme cognitive scepticism, and the relativist doctrines of meaning and value, manifest in the turn toward 'literary' analogues across various disciplines of thought. This is why the work of conceptual rhetoricians like Miller and de Man can indeed claim to be 'rigorous' or 'compelling' on its own argumentative terms, that is to say, once allowed the deconstructionist premise that textuality goes all the way down, or that rhetoric radically 'suspends' the relation between language, logic, and truth. Thus 'technically correct rhetorical readings may be boring, monotonous, predictable and unpleasant, but they are irrefutable.' Moreover, as de Man goes on to assert in his typically offhand yet apodictic style,

[such readings] are also totalizing (and potentially totalitarian) for since the
structures and functions they expose do not lead to the knowledge of an entity
(such as language) but are an unreliable process of knowledge production that
prevents all entities, including linguistic entities, from coming into discourse as
such, they are indeed universals, consistently defective models of language's
inability to be a model language. They are, always in theory, the most elastic
theoretical and dialectical model to end all models, and they can rightly claim to
contain within their own defective selves all the other defective models of
reading-avoidance, referential, semiological, grammatical, performative, logical,
or whatever. They are theory and not theory at the same time, the universal
theory of the impossibility of theory.[86]

It is right to find such passages disturbing, even outrageous, in their placid
rejection of every last truth-claim, every principle or standard of valid argument other than the knowledge that nothing can be known beyond the self-
deconstructing play of linguistic figuration. Yet it is wrong to dismiss them
tout court as merely showing what nonsense these super-subtle theorists can
come up with when released from the constraints of competent peer-group
review, or from the plain obligation that their arguments make sense in
humanly intelligible terms. At least this will seem an inadequate response – an
evasion of the issue – to any reader who has endeavoured to engage de Man's
writings at their own level of hard-pressed rhetorical exegesis.[87] What he
remarks about Nietzsche in a similar context – that 'Nietzsche has earned the
right to this inconsistency by the considerable labour of deconstruction that
makes up the bulk of his more analytical writings' – is a comment worth
recalling when confronted with de Man's counter-intuitive claims.[88] In order
to contest them one will need to push the argument much further back, to the
point where deconstruction in effect joins company with other (as it seems less
sceptical or troublesome) variants of the linguistic turn. For it is here, with the
later Wittgenstein especially, that thought starts out on its not-so-long march
towards the various strains of ultra-relativist doctrine (among them the aporias
of deconstruction) which currently exert such a widespread appeal.

VII

We can now turn back to O'Neill's *Constructions of Reason* with a sharper sense
of the issues at stake in her defence of Kant against his present-day critics and
revisionist interpreters. What this case amounts to is a point-for-point critique
of the consensus view which takes it for granted that Kant's project has
been rendered invalid, or at any rate deeply problematic, by the collapse of
'foundationalist' arguments in any shape or form.[89] One response to this

perceived failure is the line adopted by followers of Wittgenstein and liberal-communitarians: that is, the idea that we can readily dispense with such delusive 'transcendental' guarantees, just so long as we maintain a healthy respect for the variety of viewpoints (or narrative perspectives) that characterize an open-ended pluralist 'conversation of mankind'. This position still leaves some room for talk of 'principles' and 'reasons', at least insofar as one interprets such talk in relation to a given socio-political or cultural context of debate. But when subjected to a bit more sceptical pressure, as for instance by neo-pragmatists like Rorty or postmodernists like Lyotard, it very easily transmutes into fashionable variants on the 'end-of-ideology' theme, the strain of anti-enlightenment rhetoric that assimilates truth (along with reason and principle) to what is locally and contingently 'good in the way of belief'.

This is why O'Neill devotes the major part of her book to clarifying the relation between Kant's epistemology, as developed in the first *Critique*, and the account of ethical judgement, or practical reason, which these and other commentators often view as belonging to a separate (in Lyotard's terms an 'incommensurable') order of thought. O'Neill argues that these critics have got Kant wrong, that they have ignored or misconstrued certain crucial passages in his work, and that no such gulf need be taken to exist between the interests of epistemological enquiry and the interests of reason in its ethico-political mode. Moreover, such readings have been largely instrumental in promoting the current relativist orthodoxy which holds that moral judgements can only be assessed – as Wittgenstein, Winch or Lyotard would assert – in terms of the immanent criteria provided by this or that language-game, discourse, interpre-tive community, cultural 'form of life' or whatever. And the same applies to any conception of ethics (like the 'literary' example-based approach) which rules out the appeal to reasons or principles – to values of 'enlightened' critique – beyond those embodied at the level of what Lyotard calls 'first-order natural narrative pragmatics'. For in this case there could simply be no criticizing the beliefs, values and practices that happened to prevail within a certain com-munity at a given point in time. In other words, a lot hangs on the Kantian claim – as O'Neill vigorously expounds it – that practical reason *does* have resources which cannot be reduced without remainder to the currency of in-place consensus belief.

One major source of confusion here is the idea common to many of these thinkers that Kant is a 'foundationalist' in the Cartesian sense of requiring truth-claims to establish their authority quite aside from any process of public debate or communal (intersubjective) validation. On the contrary, O'Neill argues: Kant not only goes out of his way to repudiate any such apodictic starting-point, but makes it a maxim *of cognitive understanding and practical reason alike* that all such claims be referred to the 'tribunal' of enlightened collective judgement. Thus:

the reason why Kant is drawn to explicate the authority of reason in political metaphors is surely that he sees the problems of cognitive and political order as arising in one and the same context. In either case we have a plurality of agents or voices (perhaps potential agents or voices) and no transcendent or preestablished authority. . . . Reason and justice are two aspects to the solution of the problems that arise when an uncoordinated plurality of agents is to share a possible world. Hence political imagery can illuminate the nature of cognitive order and disorientation, just as the vocabulary of reason can be used to characterize social and political order and disorientation. Kant frequently characterizes scepticism as a failure of discursive order, hence as anarchy; just as he characterizes dogmatism (rationalism) as a form of despotism, a triumph of unjust discursive order. (O'Neill, p. 16)

This passage is important for three main reasons, each of them with large implications for the issue between postmodernism and what Habermas calls the 'philosophical discourse of modernity'.[90] First, O'Neill rejects any reading of Kant that would argue, most often for polemical purposes, that his entire critical enterprise stands or falls on the 'foundationalist' paradigm of reason and truth, the Cartesian mirage of a knowledge arrived at through access to an *a priori* privileged realm of clear and distinct ideas.[91] This reading ignores those passages in Kant where he expressly denies that reason can assume such ultimate, self-legislating powers, and where the point is often made – as O'Neill reminds us – through the political analogy with rationalist 'despotism', or the 'triumph of unjust discursive order'. Hence her second main argument: that in order to grasp Kant's reasons for rejecting this 'despotic' (foundationalist) paradigm, we shall need to take account not only of the complex relationships that exist between the various modalities of reason, understanding and judgement as developed in the three *Critiques*, but also of those shorter texts (among them 'What Is Enlightenment?', 'What Is Orientation in Thinking?', 'The Conflict of the Faculties', and 'On the Common Saying "This May Be True in Theory, but It Does Not Apply in Practice"') where Kant more explicitly addresses such issues from an ethico-political viewpoint.[92] For what then becomes clear, on O'Neill's submission, is the fact that these essays 'are a part of Kant's systematic philosophy, and not marginal or occasional pieces'; also that 'the entire critical enterprise has a certain *political* character', in which case 'it is no accident that the guiding metaphors of the *Critique of Pure Reason* are political metaphors' (O'Neill, p.29).

Now of course this might seem to play straight into the hands of those – neopragmatists like Rorty, postmodernists like Lyotard, deconstructors like Miller – who can live quite happily with the notion that all concepts come down to metaphors in the end, or to the kinds of extended (allegorical) metaphor that constitute fictional narrative. But for O'Neill (third point) there is no good reason to suppose that Kant's use of metaphor or narrative necessarily gives his examples a 'literary' turn, or (much less) that it renders them somehow 'undecidable' in point of their real-world ethical import. For it is simply a species of category-mistake – albeit one common to a good many schools of present-day literary theory – which regards all forms of narrative representation (historical narratives included) as inherently fictive insofar as they involve a tropological or story-telling aspect.[93] As I remarked above, this position is credible only on the postmodern-textualist premise that all discourse aspires to the condition of unlimited semiosis, or to the point where 'reality' becomes just a figment of this or that arbitrary sign-system, language-game, or set of narrative conventions. Such ideas have understandably possessed most appeal for literary critics (not to mention a few *avant-garde* sociologists, historiographers, cultural theorists and philosophers of science) keen to catch up with the latest waves of postmodern fictional experiment.[94] What they ignore, however, is the extent to which narrative understanding *always* depends on certain items of knowledge, cognitive frameworks or modes of inference from the world 'outside the text'; also how far this knowledge is prerequisite even to the grasp of fictional works that deliberately put up maximum resistance to any such recuperative reading.[95] For lacking such resources we should be in the position of cryptanalysts confronted with some utterly alien code, some system of (presumably) meaningful notations whose significance would nonetheless defeat our best efforts of applied interpretive theory.

Nor is one at this point obliged to take refuge in an appeal to mere 'commonsense' assumptions, a rhetoric of taken-for-granted belief which post-structuralists (having picked up a trick or two from Barthes) could speedily consign to the 'cultural code' of bourgeois-realist ideology. Such reflex responses display nothing more than a steadfast adherence to their own forms of sceptical *doxa*, coupled with an ignorance of developments elsewhere – like the writings on fiction by modal logicians and 'possible worlds' theorists – which offer a far more nuanced account of the relation between factual and fictive discourse.[96] And the same applies to metaphor, or at least to that 'radical' (Nietzschean) interpretation of metaphor which argues from its assumed omnipresence within language to the sheer impossibility – likewise assumed – of our ever attaining a knowledge of the world except under some wholly 'arbitrary' metaphorical description. Once again, this ignores a large body of work by cognitive psychologists, historians of science, epistemologists, linguistic philosophers and others, seeking to define those various points of transition – or stages of scientific advance – where what *begins* as a metaphor may then come to function as a concept or a regulative framework for the conduct of disciplined truth-seeking thought.[97] In short, new textualism is merely old scepticism in a geared-up rhetorical guise, offering no more in support of its position than a set of dogmatic (if negative) premises, and a flat refusal to entertain arguments that would count strongly against those premises.

O'Neill's reading of Kant is especially pertinent in the context of this widespread drift toward forms of extreme anti-cognitivist and relativist thought. For while acknowledging Kant's frequent reliance on metaphors and narrative analogues, O'Neill also gives good reason to reject any argument, whether liberal-communitarian or postmodern-textualist, which would see nothing more in Kantian ethics than a bottom-line appeal to the stories or language-games that make up some existing cultural form of life. Her point is that these metaphors and narratives do not function simply as illustrative ornaments, nor again – as on Miller's deconstructionist account – in the role of stopgap figural devices that have to stand in for the ineffable dictates of pure moral law. Thus for Miller the most thought-provoking metaphors in Kant are strictly instances of *catachresis*, figures that possess no literal or plain-prose equivalent, and which therefore, like the Kantian sublime, cannot be brought under the cognitive phrase-regime which requires that intuitions be matched with adequate concepts. Such tropes – *hypotyposes* as Kant calls them – are an index of the bafflement that afflicts practical reason when required to offer some account of its workings in humanly intelligible terms. At the narrative level they generate 'allegories' or 'parables' whose effect is likewise to suspend understanding in a state of indecision (or interpretive aporia) which resists all attempts to adjudicate the issue on principled or reasoned grounds. For O'Neill, conversely, there is nothing that could warrant such extremes of textualist scepticism, unless perhaps the (wholly mistaken) idea that metaphor and narrative are 'literary' (fictive) modes of expression that always necessarily block the passage to an enhanced understanding of real-world moral dilemmas.

We can best come to see what is wrong with such ideas by examining O'Neill's extended treatment of three central metaphors in Kant: those which cast reason in the figurative roles of a *debate*, a *tribunal*, or a *community*. In each case, she argues, the metaphor is 'political' in the sense that it invokes the validating context of public dialogue or open argumentative exchange. This is why it is mistaken to regard Kant as a 'foundationalist' thinker, one who supposed, like Descartes, that philosophy could proceed upon self-evident grounds or on the basis of truths known *a priori* through the exercise of pure reason. After all, as Kant remarks in the first sentence of his preface to the first *Critique*, 'human reason has this peculiar fate: that in one species of its knowledge it is burdened by questions which, as prescribed by the very nature of reason itself, it is not able to ignore, but which, as transcending all its powers, it is also not able to answer'.[98] Such questions may indeed be illegitimate from the standpoint of epistemology (or theoretical understanding), where they transgress the primary rule of correspondence between concepts and sensuous intuitions. But they are raised *inescapably*, Kant contends, at the point where reason goes on to enquire into the conditions of possibility for its own critical project, or the kinds of knowledge-constitutive interest which enable thinkers to pursue that project in the sphere of enlightened communal debate.

Nor does this entail – as postmodernists like Lyotard would have it – a radical disjunction or heterogeneity between the 'phrase-regime' of cognitive judgement and those other kinds of discourse (ethics included) where such truth-claims are simply not at issue. Their readings typically shift the focus of attention to those passages in the third *Critique* where aesthetic judgement in its sublime modality – 'presenting the unpresentable', as Kant paradoxically describes it – is taken for a sign of the incommensurability (or the absence of common criteria) that supposedly inhabits Kant's doctrine of the faculties. It is the same idea that Miller promotes with his talk of catachresis (or hypotyposis) as a figure of thought that radically disrupts all the commonplace certitudes of 'naive' reading. But on O'Neill's account these arguments simply miss the point. That is to say, they assume firstly – most often for knock-down polemical purposes – that Kant is a 'foundationalist', rejecting all appeals to standards of discursive or inter-subjective validation; and secondly, following from this, that any metaphors (or narrative detours) in Kant are symptoms of a latent figural dimension which his project vainly strives to repress. For O'Neill, on the other hand, Kant's metaphors can best be understood by beginning where enquiry should properly begin, at the outset of the first *Critique*, and grasping their role as heuristic figures (or regulative ideas) for the conduct of philosophical enquiry. Her point is that these metaphors should not be divorced from the overall plan, the governing project or 'architectonic' of Kantian critical reason. Of course it is always possible to treat them, like Miller and other such 'literary' commentators, as localized tropes which can be taken out of context and then exploited for the maximum yield of paradox, aporia, rhetorical 'undecidability' and so forth. But in this case one is not so much reading Kant as performing a standard deconstructionist routine on materials that might just as well have been encountered in the reading of some quite different text.

O'Neill's argument in *Constructions of Reason* goes precisely the opposite way around. Her purpose is to show 'how and why the account of reason's authority that Kant develops is articulated in political metaphors and how this determines the form of his vindication of reason' (O'Neill, p. 9). Only by proceeding in this way can Kant (or constructive commentary on Kant) avoid the kind of vicious circularity that results if reason sets up to legislate on questions of truth, knowledge or ethical judgement from a foundationalist standpoint that takes its own authority for granted, rather than testing its claims through a process of open participant debate. Such, after all, is the guiding rule that Kant adopts as a first principle of enlightened thought: that 'reason must in all its undertakings subject itself to criticism', since otherwise, 'should it limit freedom of criticism by any prohibitions', then '[reason] must harm itself, drawing upon itself damaging suspicion'. And again:

> Nothing is so important through its usefulness, nothing so sacred, that it may be exempted from this searching examination, which knows no respect for persons. Reason depends on this freedom for its very existence. For reason has no dictatorial authority; its verdict is always simply the agreement of free citizens, of whom each one must be permitted to express, without let or hindrance, his objection or even his veto.[99]

For the sceptics – postmodernists, deconstructionists, counter-enlightenment ideologues of various colour – this passage must be read as reducing to a species of downright performative contradiction. Thus on the one hand it invokes a high-sounding rhetoric of citizenly freedom, participant democracy, unrestricted liberty of conscience, etc., while on the other it issues the sovereign command: 'always think and act in accordance with the dictates of enlightened reason'. But this argument collapses if one takes Kant's point, amplified by O'Neill, that such precepts are arrived at *not* on presumptively self-evident rational grounds, but through a process of self-critical argumentation which rejects any taken-for-granted appeal to the authority of reason and truth. Hence Kant's use of metaphors drawn from the domain of juridical, parliamentary or communal debate; metaphors which cannot be reduced (*contra* Miller) to so many figures of narrative unreadability, or of a moral law forever beyond hope of reasoned or principled justification.

Indeed Kant himself anticipates just such a reading when he characterizes scepticism (in O'Neill's words) as 'a failure of discursive order, hence as anarchy', while dogmatic rationalism figures conversely 'as a form of despotism, a triumph of unjust discursive order' (O'Neill, p. 16). Variations on this theme include a series of interlinked metaphors which treat reason in its various forms (dogmatic, sceptical or critical) by analogy with an architectural project or, again, with the different kinds of building, dwelling-place or mode of habitation that characterize the diverse modes of communal existence. Rationalism failed, according to Kant, because it 'took no account either of the paucity of materials or of the disagreements about the plan among the fellow workers' (p. 12). That is to say, it proceeded on the dogmatic assumption that reason alone could draw up the ground-plan, provide all the necessary (metaphysical) foundations, and follow its project through without regard to any possible disputes along the way. In so doing, moreover, 'it relied on the fiction of a unitary and authoritative architect, whose innate ideas correspond to their real archetypes, to construct the edifice of human knowledge' (p. 12). This may seem a fairly extravagant flight of metaphor, one surely ripe for literary treatment in the deconstructive-textualist mode. But on reflection it possesses a good deal more in the way of explanatory grasp, not only as regards Kant's critique of preceding (rationalist) metaphysics but also – proleptically – in terms of the current debate around 'modern' and 'postmodern' schools of architectural thought. What the analogy suggests (and I do not have room to develop the argument in detail here) is that postmodernism only gains its appearance of a liberating movement when set against that false image of modern ('enlightened') rationality and truth which presupposes the existence of self-authorizing grounds for the conduct of reasoned debate. It is at this point – where such grounds prove simply unattainable – that thought embraces the opposite extreme of an attitude wholly given over to forms of extravagant sceptical doubt.

Here also Kant has resort to a metaphor with striking contemporary overtones: that of *nomadism* as a state of perpetual exile, an existence deprived of any settled habitation and resigned to the necessity of pitching camp on whatever new terrain it chances to discover in the course of its endless wandering. Readers of Deleuze and Guattari will recall how this figure plays a crucial (if scarcely an 'organizing') role in their book *A Thousand Plateaus*, by far the most sustained postmodernist assault on all the concepts and categories of Western intellectual tradition.[100] For them, the nomadic is *par excellence* the trope of a thinking that abandons the security of method and system, that adopts the 'line of flight' (as opposed to the fixed point of origin) as its mode of being in the world, and which thus suggests a way beyond the psychotic ('molar') life-forms that predominate in a closed conceptual order to the schizoid ('molecular') intensities of impulse and desire that would offer, they claim, a route of escape from this authoritarian regime of truth, knowledge and representation. This is not the place to describe in more detail the arguments they deploy, or the tactics they adopt, in pursuing their out-and-out polemical crusade against 'enlightenment' reason in every shape or form. My point, taken up from O'Neill, is that Kant both anticipates their favoured metaphor and treats it as a symptom of the various pathological disorders that result when unworkable ('foundationalist') conceptions of knowledge and truth give way to a wholesale scepticism with regard to *any* kind of rational, principled or truth-seeking argument. Such an attitude must condemn us, in O'Neill's words, to 'a "nomadic" existence that does not meet our deepest needs, including the needs of reason' (p. 12). For it ignores what Kant goes on to demonstrate: that those needs can only be met through a process of enlightened reciprocal exchange which abjures the presumptive (authoritarian) appeal to self-evident grounds, but which maintains the possibility of arriving at adequate criteria or validity-conditions for arguments offered in the public sphere of accountable reasons and principles.

This is why, as O'Neill says, 'the materials assembled in the "Transcendental Doctrine of Elements" are constraints on the building that can be built; but they do not determine what the plan should be' (p. 19). To conceive of such a plan as somehow preexisting the process of its own validation is to fall into the kind of uncritical dogmatism which Kant is at pains to disavow. It is like the idea of reason as a master-architect, a sovereign disposer whose authority entitles him or her to ignore any differences of view that might arise among those assigned to construct or inhabit the edifice. Kant deems such a project strictly unthinkable on three main counts. Firstly, it assumes (like the rationalist metaphysicians) that reason is a self-grounding activity which provides all the knowledge, all the necessary principles on which to build a 'lofty tower' – Kant's phrase – that would then provide a vantage-point of absolute truth, allowing the architect (or philosopher) to survey the whole process of design and construction from start to finish. The manifest absurdity of this metaphor is also the absurdity of all such presumptive truth-claims. For they ignore (secondly) the crucial point: that reason can be justified only insofar as it remains a self-reflexive or critical project, taking nothing on faith but appealing always to those reasons and principles that emerge in the course of open argumentative debate. So it is wrong to regard Kant's 'architectonic' of the faculties – pure reason, theoretical understanding, practical reason, aesthetic judgement - as an 'edifice' built upon (supposedly) firm foundations and unfolding in accordance with a ground-plan whose directives govern that project from the outset.

This leads on to O'Neill's third main argument: that 'the discussion of philosophical method *must* come at the end of a critique of reason' (p. 13), rather than where one might expect to find it, that is to say, in those early passages (like the 'Transcendental Doctrine of Elements') which offer what amounts to a preliminary survey of the field. 'At the beginning', she writes,

> we had no 'material' to discipline; now a hypothesis about how we might embark upon the tasks of reason has supplied some material, but has not shown how this material is to be combined into the edifice of knowledge. It has, however, provided a vantage-point for a reflexive task, which could not be undertaken initially, but only retrospectively, reflectively, toward the end. (p. 14)

This is the heart of O'Neill's case for a strong reading of Kantian ethics – including a defence of the categorical imperative and its various cognate maxims – that would meet the sceptics on their own ground by taking full account of anti-foundationalist arguments. On the currently widespread assumption (shared by postmodernists and liberal-communitarians) such a reading would necessarily involve some appeal to *a priori* grounds or 'formalist' precepts adopted for no better reason than their presumed self-evidence according to the dictates of Kantian moral law. In which case of course they would be open to the charge of providing nothing more than a circular justification for principles that were always already implicit in Kant's working premises, and which therefore invite a sceptical response by virtue of this vicious circularity. 'Are we not then left with the thought that there is no authority for thinking, and that the images of "nomadic" restlessness to which Kant gestures are all that remains when we dispel metaphysical illusion?' (O'Neill, p. 16). Such would be the outcome – the nomadic 'line of flight', in Deleuze/Guattari's idiom – which supposedly results from the failure of enlightenment to make good its own foundationalist claims. But 'before drawing this conclusion', O'Neill advises, 'we must see why Kant's account of the authority of reason uses not only the images of plurality but specifically those of constitutional and political order' (p. 16). For it is by way of these cardinal metaphors – subject as they are to a process of critical enquiry and reflection throughout the course of the three *Critiques* – that Kant both answers the standard line of anti-foundationalist argument and nonetheless asserts reason's capacity to vindicate its claims in the open forum of enlightened participant exchange.

Hence also Kant's appeal to that other main group of metaphors which invoke the idea of communal debate – or the tribunal of the faculties in parliament assembled – as a regulative precept for the interests of truth-seeking thought. This aspect of O'Neill's argument brings her close to the variety of 'transcendental pragmatics' or the notion of an 'ideal speech-situation' which Jürgen Habermas postulates by way of distinguishing between false (partial or distorted) and genuine (enlightened) states of consensus belief.[101] Again, it turns on the crucial difference between truth-claims imposed by arbitrary fiat or through the workings of external coercive restraint, and other such claims whose validity is established in the public sphere of reasoned and principled debate. These metaphors have a more than casual relevance insofar as they achieve regulative status through precisely this process of reflexive application to their own contexts of usage. Thus, according to O'Neill,

> the metaphor of a 'debate' goes beyond that of a 'tribunal' not because it provides 'positive' instruction (it does not), but because it displays the recursive character of the enterprise of critique of reason. Debate cannot survive the adoption of principles of destroying debate. The most fundamental principle for disciplining thought and action among any plurality is to reject principles for thought and action that cannot be shared. Reason's authority is established recursively, rather than resting on secure foundations; this authority is only negative, yet it constrains thought and action. (O'Neill, p. 21)

It is here that Kantian ethics differs from the straightforward consensualist or pragmatist appeal to what is currently 'good in the way of belief' within a given interpretive community. This argument, when pushed to its extreme by adepts like Rorty and Fish, must treat any talk of 'reason' or 'principle' as strictly internal to the culture in question, and hence as nothing more than a species of suasive utterance, adopted for the sake of carrying conviction with those (fellow-members of the same liberal community) who can always be counted on to respect such talk. For Kant, conversely, the *sensus communis* of enlightened public opinion is a regulative idea that reason proposes as the end-point of critical enquiry, and is not to be confused with any existing state of in-place consensus belief. Only by maintaining this crucial distinction, as against the pragmatist or cultural-relativist view, can ethics be redeemed from the kind of disabling circularity which treats issues of truth, justice and right as strictly unintelligible aside from the currency of this or that ongoing discourse, language-game, cultural 'form of life', etc. And at the end of this road – as I have argued above – one encounters those extreme or hypercultivated forms of sceptical doubt which reduce ethics to a play of 'incommensurable' phrase-regimes (Lyotard), or to an allegory of textual 'undecidability' (Miller) which acknowledges no critical tribunal save that of the perplexed and solitary reader, 'face to face with the words on the page'.

VIII

So there is reason to think that O'Neill is not tilting at windmills when she takes issue with recent 'literary' interpretations of Kant. What these accounts presuppose – and always, by their own lights, turn out to reconfirm – is the plain *impossibility* that such issues could ever be argued at a level beyond the pragmatist resort to cultural-linguistic conventions or presently existing values and beliefs. This would also apply to Kant's idea of the *sensus communis* if the pragmatists were right and it offered nothing more than a suasive (rhetorically efficacious) variant of the standard communitarian line. But such a reading ignores the relationship that exists in Kant's thought between practical (ethico-political) reason and those knowledge-constitutive interests that aim beyond the current doxastic view of what should count as a warranted belief. Thus the *sensus communis*, as Kant describes it, is 'a critical faculty which in its reflective act takes account . . . of the mode of representation of everyone else, in order, as it were, to weigh its judgment with the reflective reason of mankind'.[102] Insofar as this judgement is 'reflective' and 'critical' it cannot be equated with the pragmatist appeal to those values and beliefs that currently enjoy widespread (even universal) assent. For it might always transpire that they rested on a partial, a premature or otherwise distorted understanding of the issues involved; or that their presumed universal appeal was in fact just a product of localized interests which failed to acknowledge their own (as it might be) ethnocentric or class-specific character. In such cases there must always be a further court of jurisdiction, one whose authority is vested in the claim that reason *can and should* continue to criticize the currency of established belief, including those items (reasons and principles) that are presently taken to constitute the very nature of enlightened thought. For it is only insofar as it meets this requirement – the test of self-reflexive application – that reason can avoid falling prey to its own kinds of authoritarian coercion.

O'Neill makes the point as follows in a passage of crucial significance for her reading of Kant.

> Whereas 'common sense' is used to refer to understandings that are actually shared, in an *actual* community or more widely, the *sensus communis* consists of [those] principles or maxims that constrain understandings, indeed practices of communication, that can be shared in any *possible* community. . . . They articulate the self-discipline of thinking that will be required if there is to be communication among a plurality whose members are not antecedently coordinated. (p. 25)

It is for this reason that an adequate grasp of Kant's project in the three *Critiques* must also take account of those other, seemingly less central texts (like 'Perpetual Peace' and 'The Idea of a Universal History') where Kant elaborates a theory of communicative action aimed toward defining the conditions of possibility for enlightened ethico-political discourse. Such conditions cannot be specified in advance but can only emerge through critical reflection on the process by which truth-claims, reasons and principles are tested in the forum of public debate. On the standard view, as O'Neill describes it, 'Kant's political writings are at most a corollary of his ethical theory, whose critical grounding is suspect' (p. 4). But this account assumes firstly that the 'grounding' is a matter of self-evident (foundationalist) principles, a reading for which O'Neill finds no adequate warrant in the text, and secondly that Kant's political metaphors – like those of the tribunal, the debate or the *sensus communis* – are incidental tropes whose only contribution is to lend a mere semblance of democratic process to the otherwise fully autonomous dictates of practical reason. Both assumptions are wrong, O'Neill argues, since they ignore on the one hand Kant's explicit rejection of any such foundationalist paradigm, and on the other the extent to which those metaphors are refined, developed and heuristically justified in the course of Kant's critical enquiry. From which it follows not only that 'the entire Kantian enterprise has a certain *political* character', but also that 'practical uses of reason are more fundamental than theoretical uses of reason' (p. 29).

In short, this amounts to a strong defence of the Kantian categorical imperative as a ground-rule (more precisely: a regulative idea) which applies just as much to epistemological as to ethical or political issues. For just as human agents have a shared (knowledge-constitutive) interest in attaining more adequate, accurate or truthful cognitive representations, so likewise they are united, as a 'suprasensible' community, in seeking an enlightened consensus on principles that would raise morality and politics above the mere clash of competing beliefs or rival interpretive communities. Hence the significance of those various metaphors – in the first as well as the second *Critique*, and pervasive in the shorter writings – which offer (so to speak) a testing-ground for Kant's conception of practical reason.

> If the discussion of reason itself is to proceed in terms of *conflicts* whose *battlefields* and *strife* are scenes of *defeat* and *victory* that will give way to a lasting *peace* only when we have established through *legislation* such *courts*, *tribunals* and *judges* as can weigh the issues and give *verdict*, then it is perhaps not surprising that Kant links his discussions of politics very closely to larger issues about the powers and limits of human reason.
>
> (O'Neill, p. 29)

This is not to say – though it is a common misconception among critics of Kant and Habermas alike – that at the end of enquiry we shall at last have achieved the kind of perfect, unimpeded communion of minds (or of rational agents harmoniously united in the public sphere of shared purposes and interests) that would render all conflicts henceforth unthinkable. Kant's thoughts on the topic of 'perpetual peace' should be enough to dispel this illusion, marked as they are by an ironic awareness of the problems, the intractable real-world difficultites, confronted by any such naive utopian faith. In the same way moral agents may find themselves placed in situations where the maxims of practical reason either fail to provide specific guidance or generate conflicts of motive and principle that cannot be resolved by any rational decision-procedure. Furthermore, there is no reason to suppose that self-knowledge (individual or collective) could ever arrive at that stage of reflective transparency where agents could be sure of thinking and acting in accordance with their own most enlightened interests. Thus Kant often remarks 'on the opacity of the human heart and the difficulty of self-knowledge'; also on the fact that 'merely asking an agent what his or her maxim is in [a given] situation may not settle the issue' (O'Neill, p. 85). To suppose otherwise is to fall into the rationalist error, the belief that if we just had enough detailed knowledge (of the relevant circumstances, historical background, cultural context, motivating interests and so forth) then reason could proceed algorithmically to determine what is right or wrong in any specific case.

This is the confusion which Kant so consistently warns against: that of mistaking 'regulative ideas' (which are justified in the 'tribunal' of pure reason) with the truth-claims of theoretical understanding (whose validity is established by bringing intuitions under adequate concepts). Its equivalent in the socio-political sphere would be (for instance) to understand a document like the Charter of the United Nations as possessing no legitimate authority except insofar as its terms were borne out by the record of real-world actions and events. Most often, as recent history has shown, such frustrated high hopes very quickly give way to the opposite (reactive) extreme of cynical disenchantment. All this O'Neill concedes, along with the point that maxims must always be interpreted, and that any interpretation may be open to challenge from some other (on its own terms) equally principled or reasoned account of the issue at stake. Kant is far from claiming that these are 'dispellable difficulties', or that simply by applying an alternative, more perspicuous decision-procedure one could somehow resolve the conflict of viewpoints and arrive at a *method* for settling such disputes without prejudice to any of the parties concerned. On the contrary, O'Neill writes, 'these limits to human self-knowledge constitute the fundamental context of human action' (p. 85). But there is still a crucial difference to be marked between the pragmatist assertion that 'truth' is purely and simply a matter of consensus belief, and the Kantian claim that such beliefs are always subject to criticism, that is to say, always open to a principled challenge which adopts a more informed or enlightened standpoint as regards both the relevant maxims and their bearing on the case in hand. Thus 'the underlying intentions that guide our more specific intentions are not in principle undiscoverable. . . . Even when not consciously formulated they can often be inferred with some assurance, if not certainty, as the principles and policies that our more specific intentions express and implement' (p. 85). What is typically involved in such reasoning is a process of critical review whereby the maxims implicit in some actual or proposed course of action are judged both in terms of their own (cultural or context-specific) criteria and in the light of principles and truth-claims that may always turn out to problematize those first-order (naturalized) habits of belief.

At this point of course the pragmatist will argue that one might as well drop all the self-deluding Kantian talk and accept that any principles or reasons thus offered will themselves carry conviction only to the extent that they persuade fellow-members of the relevant interpretive community.[103] But such an argument is ill-equipped to explain how (for instance) conscientious objectors could be justified in opposing a war or a policy of racial persecution that enjoyed a wide measure of consensus support among those whose opinions defined the currency of taken-for-granted belief. The pragmatist might always respond by pointing out 1) that the objectors would then be appealing to a different, more 'principled' but nonetheless culture-specific set of justifiying motives or reasons, and 2) that in any case their arguments would fail unless there existed at least a minority of like-minded persons with whom the objectors could communicate. But again this fails to account for the possibility that just *one* such voice of conscience might conceivably be raised despite and against the pressures of an otherwise wholesale consensus view. That such a circumstance can rarely (if ever) have obtained is no reason to consider it a case irrelevant for the purposes of ethical theory. For on the one hand it is just the kind of testing limit-case that ethics is obliged to take into account, while on the other – more importantly – it is not so remote from the predicament of moral agents in an unjust (for instance, racist or persecuting) social order who find themselves compelled to think, judge and act without benefit of any such supportive moral community. Here the only available grounds of appeal are to those other-regarding maxims of justice and reason which may be systematically flouted by the culture in question, but whose flouting gives rise to the kinds of aporia – the conditions of impossibility, as it were – that Kant seeks to demonstrate, for example in the case of bad-faith promises or maxims adopted solely with one's own self-interested ends in view. Hence Kant's idea of the *sensus communis* – the discourse of enlightened (yet-to-be-attained) inter-subjective agreement – as opposed to any version of the pragmatist argument that equates truth and justice with some *presently existing* state of consensus belief. For this latter would foreclose on the very possibility that agents should perceive what is wrong with that existing order and should do so, moreover, for reasons of conscience that are capable of argued and principled justification.

One example that comes to mind is that of Huck Finn, defying the conventional mores of his time and place by declaring that he would rather go to hell than turn in his friend the runaway slave. This is not, it is worth noting, a 'literary' example in the sense criticized by O'Neill, that is, one that treats some historical or fictive episode as interpretable only in terms of the language-game or cultural 'form of life' which the episode is taken to illustrate. On the contrary, it points up the limits of any such (e.g., Wittgensteinian or communitarian) approach by posing very squarely the question of how Huck's decision could possibly be justified, given that it issued from a downright rejection of the values and beliefs in which he had been brought up. Nor is it really much help to remark that there must have been some other language-game around, some alternative 'form of life' (Wittgenstein), 'final vocabulary' (Rorty) or 'phrase-regime' (Lyotard) that enabled Huck to arrive at his stance of lonely principled dissent. For what such arguments lead to – most explicitly in Lyotard's case – is an extreme form of ethical decisionism that in effect leaves moral agents suspended between diverse, wholly incommensurable claims upon their sense of justice and right. But the point about Huck's declaration is *not* that it results from some ultimate leap of faith, some commitment arrived at (as Lyotard would have it) by judging 'without criteria', or in the absence of any reasons that might be spelled out by way of argued justification. Rather, it is prepared for through a detailed narrative *mise-en-scène* which enables us both to reconstruct those reasons and to grasp the conflicts of motive and principle that lay behind the final act of choice.

According to the current textualist wisdom such a reading is naive in its ascription of moral agency to 'characters' whose existence can only be a product of fictive contrivance or imaginary projection. But this argument holds only if one takes it as read – or on the say-so of sceptics like Miller – that an 'ethics of reading' begins at the point where we renounce those various illusory comforts ('theme', 'character', 'motive') and accede to the hard-won deconstructive knowledge that nothing exists beyond the play of ungrounded textual representations. Otherwise it will surely seem absurd that theorists should be driven to the point of denying what any good novel-reader quickly learns in the course of his or her successive encounters with the variety of fictive 'possible worlds'. Even Miller is obliged to allow as much when he remarks, *à propos* George Eliot's 'experiments in life', that 'we read novels to see in a safe area of fiction or imagination what would happen if we lived our lives according to a certain principle of moral choice' (Miller, p. 30). Of course he goes on to retract this concession by denying on the one hand that novels give access to a knowable world of shared human experience, and on the other that any ethical issues thus raised could ever provide more than a salutary lesson in the 'rigorous unreliability' of language or the self-subverting character of all such examples. But there seems, to say the least, small merit in a theory which elevates these moments of perplexity or bafflement to a high point of readerly virtue.

O'Neill is clear enough that the use of literary instances can point in a different direction, one that avoids both the relativism entailed by Wittgensteinian or communitarian arguments and (beyond that) the textualist aporias so cherished by theorists like Miller. Among her examples is the case, taken from Sartre's 'Existentialism Is a Humanism', of the young man who has to decide between caring for his sick mother and joining the Free French resistance movement.[104] It will be helpful to quote her commentary at length since it speaks so directly to our present concerns. This episode is purportedly used, O'Neill writes,

> not to illustrate a moral principle but to show that moral principles and codes cannot make our decisions for us. However, the entire force of the example – the reason that it so evidently casts decision back on the agent – depends on the fact that the young man (and Sartre's readers) can see the situation as a conflict of moral principles or ideals. Only those who see relevance both in personal devotion and in a certain conception of public duty can appreciate this dilemma. Sartre works to leave his readers on the cusp. Both loyalties are vividly characterized. Hence this example, while theory-dependent, cannot be set out schematically. Its power depends on making it difficult for us to think that giving precedence to either loyalty would be right. But turning example against theory in *this* way does not require us to see such examples as independent of theory. On the contrary, the principle of construction of the example is entirely

theory-led. The anguish that Sartre sees in moral responsibility reflects a conception of principles as still having a central part in the moral life. We find ourselves confronted with problems and dilemmas whose force derives from certain moral positions and principles that, tragically, lack the resources to resolve the problems they generate. (O'Neill, p. 169)

It should be evident from this that the 'theory' O'Neill has in mind is vulnerable neither to the standard line of knock-down antifoundationalist argument nor to the kind of pragmatist reading that would treat any talk of 'reasons' or 'principles' as intelligible only from within some existing cultural form of life. Moral arguments are 'theory-dependent' insofar as they invoke criteria of good-faith, ethically accountable conduct which go beyond the mere *de facto* appeal to this or that interpretive community. That this can always give rise to genuine conflicts of principle – as distinct from Lyotard's pluralist ethos of strictly 'incommensurable' language-games – gives reason to suppose that such issues transcend any pragmatist attempt to talk them down to the level of communally warranted belief. In the case of Huck Finn the conflict is resolved through his decision to reject a conformist morality or an ethic of Hegelian *Sittlichkeit* (loyalty to family, social custom, the civic mores of his own time and place) in favour not only of a prime obligation to his friend, the runaway slave, but also of a higher, more enlightened set of principles which include those of justice, equality, reciprocal understanding, and respect for the community of human needs aside from all merely contingent differences of race or social class. For Lyotard this decision would presumably figure as an instance of judging 'without criteria', of opting for one or another course of action in a context where choice is 'of the order of transcendence', and where no amount of reasoning or principled argument could settle the issue either way. But this ignores the extent to which the reader of Twain's novel is engaged in a complex but by no means unfathomable process of interpretive inference, a process that enables us to reconstruct the motives and reasons which lead up to Huck's seemingly precipitate moment of choice. What is enacted here, albeit in fictional form, is the kind of moral discovery – the principled critique of existing social and ethical norms – which has marked every stage of human advance beyond an ethos of inert consensus-values.

With the example from Sartre the case is more complicated since it involves two such principles, each with an overriding claim upon the protagonist's conscience, but between them creating a predicament of moral deadlock. However, we shall miss the whole point of this example if we view them as merely alternative conventions or cultural 'forms of life', affording no common criteria of judgement and therefore incapable of generating conflicts beyond the style of easygoing pluralist 'conversation' envisaged by a thinker like Rorty, or the postmodern ethos of maximized 'dissensus' – the play of 'heterogeneous' phrase-regimes – which Lyotard aims to promote. What this approach rules out is the very possibility that agents might have reasons *either* for adopting a principled stance in opposition to consensus values and beliefs, *or* for arriving at the pained (even tragic) awareness that there exist no resources, no ethical grounds for resolving some ultimate conflict of principles. But these latter, as and when they arise, will concern real issues of moral conscience (like the case instanced by Sartre), and not the sorts of notional 'linguistic predicament' which figure in the work of some Wittgensteinians and – more egregiously – in Miller's textualist 'allegories of reading'. Kant's ethical writings are distinctive, O'Neill argues, 'for [their] articulation of the relationships between moral theory or principles, illustrative examples and the judgment that is involved in actual moral decisions, none of which he thinks a dispensable part of the moral life' (p. 168). In this respect they differ from the 'spectator-attitude' or the outlook of 'literary connoisseurship' that contents itself with remarking the variety of moral beliefs, judgements, or value-systems, and which views all talk of 'reasons' and 'principles' as relative to one or another such ethical life-form. Thus 'it is all too easy to agree with [Peter] Winch of such examples that each is *sui generis* and in itself a complete example of moral thinking that can provide no basis for prescribing for others, and so, more generally, that moral theories are redundant, since no task remains to be done once examples have been fully articulated' (p. 171). But, again, this leaves the road wide open to a form of thoroughgoing cognitive and ethical scepticism that would end up by blithely deconstructing the difference between 'literary' (textual) instances of undecidability and real-life issues of moral and political conscience.

IX

'Is it possible,' Miller asks, 'to say that our respect for a text is like our respect for a person, that is, it is respect not for the text in itself but respect for a law which the text exemplifies?' (Miller, p. 18) Yes indeed, O'Neill might reply, and such respect must surely involve at very least an attitude of principled regard for what the text has to say, explicitly or implicitly, concerning its own thematic content, its intended purport, or the kind of reading that most adequately answers to the author's motivating interest. After all, the main precept of Kantian ethics is to treat other people as autonomous agents, as co-equals with ourselves in that universal 'kingdom of ends' which forbids us to exploit them merely as a means toward our own instrumental purposes. Such would be the 'law' – the categorical imperative – that each and every text could be taken to 'exemplify', and whose claims would thus constitute the basic requirement for good-faith reading in general. But this is not at all what

Miller has in mind when he proposes the analogy with Kant. On the contrary, the 'law of the text' as Miller construes it is a law that cannot be expressed, represented, or in any way adequately thematized; a law whose edicts are obscurely figured forth in the guise of parables, fictions or allegories of reading which resist interpretation almost to the point of some ultimate hermetic mystery. And nowhere is this more apparent, Miller thinks, than in Kant's various efforts to bridge the gulf between 'pure practical reason' and the contexts of everyday, situated agency and choice. For at such points Kant is obliged to adopt a whole range of fall-back strategies – whether fictive examples or rhetorical devices like metaphor, catachresis, and simile – by way of oblique communication, or in order to convey what would otherwise elude all the powers of human understanding. The reader is thus placed like Kafka's bewildered supplicant in his parable 'Before the Law': knowing that this law is in some sense intended for him, that its edicts are peremptory, absolute and binding, yet with nobody to explain what those edicts are or how best to apply them.[105]

As I have said, this current line in 'literary' readings of Kant is one that starts out from a predisposed bias toward the third *Critique*, and especially those passages concerning the sublime as a figure for that which surpasses the limits of conceptual grasp or adequate representation. Miller points straight to the source of these readings when he instances Heidegger's influential argument in *Kant and the Problem of Metaphysics*.[106] Thus, according to Heidegger, 'it was Kant's "recoil" from recognizing what his thought was leading him toward, namely toward a concept of the founding power of the imagination, that marked the turning point in that thought' (Miller, pp. 38–9). On this account the single most momentous discovery of the three *Critiques* is the way that Kant's entire project turns out to rest on a series of more-or-less covert appeals to the modality of aesthetic judgement. For this faculty serves both to mediate between sensuous cognition and conceptual understanding (as in the 'Transcendental Aesthetic' of the first *Critique*), and also to point toward that realm of 'suprasensible' ideas wherein moral agents, like the arbiters of aesthetic taste, attain to a mode of reflective judgement which transcends the limiting conditions of cognitive-phenomenal experience. For Miller (as likewise for Lyotard) this amounts to something of a scandal at the heart of Kant's project, an unlooked-for reminder of imagination's role as the *sine qua non* – the condition of (im)possibility – for philosophy's attempt to ground its own truth-claims in the exercise of enlightened critical reason. What they both take for granted – following Heidegger – is firstly the ineluctable need for this dependence on aesthetic metaphors and analogues, and secondly the idea that Kant's use of the term 'aesthetic' *in different contexts of argument* must always signal some ultimate appeal to artistic, poetic, literary or 'imaginative' modes of apprehension. For it is only insofar as one accepts these assumptions (thus ignoring some of Kant's most explicit and elaborate disclaimers) that such literary readings will appear to possess any warrant in the Kantian text.

Miller puts the case as follows in a typically wire-drawn passage of argument from *The Ethics of Reading*.

> Just as the blank place where respect is indefinable, can be given no predicate, is filled by the figurative analogy with fear and inclination, two things respect is not, and just as art or the work of art is defined in the *Critique of Judgment* as the only possible bridge between epistemology, on the one hand, the work of pure reason, and ethics, the work of practical reason, on the other (which would otherwise be separated by the great gulf, *die grosse Kluft* between them), so here within the theory of practical reason itself another chasm open up. This chasm too can only be bridged by a species of artwork, though one not openly defined as such by Kant. Across the gap between the law as such and the immediate work in the real world of practical reason must be cast a little fictional narrative. This narrative . . . must be within the law as such, and it must at the same time give practical advice for the choice of the pure will in a particular case in the real work of history, society, and my immediate obligations to those around me. (Miller, p. 28)

Carried along by Miller's deft analogical footwork it is easy to forget just how remote this all is from what Kant has to say, as distinct from what Miller can construe him as implying, about the relations between epistemology, ethics, and aesthetic judgement. Thus Miller assumes (*contra* Kant, but in line with Heidegger's dubious reading) that any mention of the 'aesthetic' as a mediating category – as between concepts and phenomenal intuitions, or between 'pure' and 'practical' reason – must always involve the appeal to a *fictive* or *literary* realm of imagining, an appeal which leaves judgement forever suspended over the 'gulf' of its own inevitable failure to link up the dictates of 'law as such' with the demands of real-world morality. The source of this confusion is Miller's idea, again wrongly fathered upon Kant, that aesthetic judgement always has to do with *artworks* (primarily, for Miller, fictive or literary texts), rather than characterizing a certain modality of thought whose role in the first *Critique* brings it most closely into relation with epistemological issues, but which also (in a different but related capacity) prefigures the link between such knowledge-constitutive interests and those of practical (ethico-political) reason. The trick is carried off in that telltale sentence which on the one hand asserts that the 'chasm' can only be 'bridged by a species of artwork', while on the other conceding that the 'work' in question is 'not openly defined as such by Kant'. So far is it from being thus defined that Kant goes out of his way to deny any such identification. But having once made the point through a species of aestheticizing wordplay ('work' = 'artwork' and 'immediate work in the real world of practical reason') Miller can proceed to exploit the equation for all that it is worth. Thus the 'artwork' becomes a 'little fictional narrative', an allegory of reading whose message, as always, is that ethics must be viewed as a textual, a linguistic or a 'literary' (fictive) predicament. And this applies not only to the 'law as such' (that figment of Kafkaesque imagining) but also to 'the real work of history, society, and my obligation to those around me'. For in each case – Miller would have us believe – the 'work' in question cannot be other than a fictive example (or catachrestic trope) adopted in default of any firmer bridge between these two utterly disjunct realms.

Such arguments go way beyond anything that O'Neill has in mind when she criticizes the 'literary' turn in recent ethical theory. But there is, as I have suggested, an underlying kinship between such example-based or narrative lines of approach and those forms of extravagant sceptical doubt that issue in Miller's deconstructive allegories of reading. Thus both very often start out from a rejection of Kantian thought as 'foundationalist' in its epistemological aspect and 'formalist' in its ethical bearings. The latter is taken to follow from the former through Kant's typically 'enlightenment' drive to exclude all evidence of social or cultural diversity in pursuit of an abstract categorical appeal to the dictates of universal reason and truth. One great merit of O'Neill's book is to show how such readings are wide of the mark insofar as they ignore the discursive (socially and politically mediated) character that Kant ascribes both to ethical judgements and – as against the foundationalist account – to reasons advanced in the sphere of cognitive or theoretical understanding. But she also makes it clear that this position is not adopted at the cost of espousing a pragmatist view that would collapse the difference between communally warranted belief and truth-claims arrived at through the process of open argumentative debate.

Hence the two main axioms of Kant which O'Neill sets out to defend: first, that 'the practical use of reason is more fundamental than its theoretical or speculative use', and second, that 'the Categorical Imperative is the supreme principle of reason', this latter defined in its classical Kantian form, i.e., as requiring that thought and action be 'based only on maxims through which one can at the same time will that they be universal laws' (p. 3). Not that O'Neill fails to register the force of those arguments that have often been raised against Kant by communitarian critics who urge us to respect the plurality of cultural life-forms and the need for an ethics sufficiently open to the range of socialized beliefs, practices, and modes of moral reasoning. This is why, as we have seen, she makes a point of insisting that such claims cannot rest on the presumptive appeal to self-evident grounds or principles, but must always be subject to reflexive critique and procedures of intersubjective validation. However, these critics are mistaken (she maintains) if they interpret Kant's categorical imperative as a formalist or abstract-universalist precept that excludes all reference to the kinds of disagreement that may always arise when moral agents engage in this process of ongoing collective debate. For what emerges from a reading of the three *Critiques* in conjunction with the various shorter essays is a very different view of Kant's project, one that stresses both the role of practical reason as a source of principled judgements and the primacy of open dialogical exchange as a regulative notion – a condition of possibility – for the conduct of ethical thought.

To suppose that these requirements are somehow incompatible (or that Kant renders them so) is to take no account of those crucial passages where the interests of reason are precisely figured as pertaining to a community, a tribunal or parliament of the faculties whose juridical warrant can only be secured through its continuing exercise of those same self-reflexive and self-critical powers. 'Those who act on such maxims are not guaranteed agreement, at all points; but if they wholly reject it, communication and interaction (even hostile interaction, let alone coordination) will be impossible' (O'Neill, p. 23). For postmodernists like Lyotard this impossibility appears a consummation devoutly to be wished, a means to maximize 'dissensus' (or discursive differentials) among all parties concerned by ruling that each and every language-game disposes of its own immanent criteria, so that no one game can rightfully or intelligibly presume to criticize any other.[107] In company with Miller he . takes this position as warranted by a reading of the third *Critique*, more specifically by reflection on the Kantian sublime as a limit-point where thinking is obliged to renounce all ideas of a rational consensus arrived at through the joint application of epistemic, ethical, socio-political and other such shared human interests. From this point of view there is much less mileage in Kant's notion of the beautiful, premised as it is on the twofold appeal to a harmonious interplay of the faculties (understanding and imagination) and a *sensus communis* of disinterested judgement whereby rational subjects are enabled to agree upon mutually-acceptable standards of taste. Such ideas can carry little weight in the context of current postmodernist theory, a theory that rejects all 'enlightenment' talk of truth at the end of enquiry, and which equates ethics with the realization – brought home most forcibly by the Kantian sublime – that nothing can bridge the absolute gulf between epistemic truth-claims and judgements in the ethical or socio-political sphere. But this reading must appear distinctly partial, not to say skewed, if one considers that Kant's thoughts on the sublime were pretty much common currency at the time, not least among conservative ideologues like Burke who raised the incommensurability-doctrine (or the 'differend' between theory and unreflective customary practice) into a high point of conservative principle. What is thus disavowed, then as now, is any prospect that reason might attain to a critical understanding of the shared human interest in dispelling those sources of error and delusion that mask behind such obfuscatory rhetorics.

Of course this was none of Kant's purpose in his own treatment of the sublime. On the contrary, he viewed it as pointing the way to that realm of 'suprasensible' judgements whose rule was given not by the cognitive requirement that concepts match up with sensuous intuitions, but by the exercise of reason in that higher tribunal where issues of aesthetics could be seen as analogous with issues of ethical conscience. In Kant, however, the sublime figures precisely by way of a suggestive *analogy*, a means of maintaining the essential distinction between determinate judgements of cognitive truth or falsehood and reflective judgements arrived at through the process of freely-willed autonomous choice. Thus Kant nowhere goes so far as to claim – like Lyotard and Miller – that such choices have nothing whatsoever to do with questions of cognitive or factual validity, since they come about solely through an act of ungrounded ethical decision which necessitates our somehow judging 'without criteria', or in the absence of any possible justification by appeal to the facts of the case. This reading will only look plausible insofar as one approaches Kant with a fixed determination to place ethical issues beyond reach of adjudicative treatment in the public sphere of reasoned and principled debate. More specifically, it results from a shift of focus on the part of postmodern commentators who view the sublime as a salutary reminder of the strictly unbridgeable gulf between the 'language-game' of factual-veridical discourse and the 'language-game' of practical or ethico-political reason. This involves on the one hand a turn toward the third *Critique* as a privileged text for such readings, and on the other – within that text – a marked playing-down of Kant's reflections on the beautiful (where ideas of an enlightened community of judgement are still very much to the fore) and a countervailing stress on the sublime as a marker of this radical disjunction of realms. What these thinkers ignore in pursuit of their own postmodernist (or counter-enlightenment) agenda is the close relationship that Kant always perceives between the interests of truth-seeking rational enquiry and the interests of justice as a collective project aimed toward an ideal speech-community delivered from the distorting pressures of this or that falsified consensus or ideological *parti pris*. Only thus – by exploiting the sublime as a figure of radical incommensurability – can Lyotard gain credence for a reading that discounts or rejects so much of what Kant has to say.

O'Neill provides a useful corrective, as so often, when she defends Kant against his various detractors by denying that there need be any conflict of aims between an ethics of principle and an ethics that acknowledges the variety of socialized values, motives, and belief-systems. The critics divide into two main camps: those who read Kant as a formalist (or abstract-universalist) thinker indifferent to the claims of localized or communal tradition, and those who interpret his use of examples as effectively yielding so much ground to the opposing (communitarian) case that any talk of 'principles' or maxims of practical reason becomes more or less redundant. But as O'Neill points out, 'what we need, minimally, if there is to be some possibility of a more than locally comprehensible applied ethics, are some ways of appraising and judging the sorts of cases with which we have to deal' (p. 180). Otherwise ethical reflection will dissolve into the kind of 'moral connoisseurship' that contents itself, in the fashion of some Wittgensteinian thinkers, with just lining up examples and treating them as instances of so many diverse language-games or cultural forms of life, interpretable only by their own *sui generis* criteria, and hence beyond reach of principled judgement or critique. Starting out from an attitude of tolerant respect for the range of communally sanctioned beliefs, this position can easily be pushed to the point where it produces a failure of moral and intellectual nerve, a refusal to conceive that *some* such beliefs (along with their resultant practices) may be downright abhorrent.

Such relativism has gained ground very largely on account of those language- or discourse-based theories that treat all cognitive and evaluative judgements as irreducibly context-specific. It is open to a number of objections, among them the argument put forward by Donald Davidson: that we just couldn't begin to interpret other people's languages, cultures or beliefs except on the assumption (the so-called 'principle of charity') which takes it *firstly* that most of what they say and believe is true, and *secondly* that we and they share enough knowledge – or a wide enough range of ontological and other commitments – to render communication possible.[108] (Otherwise we would not even know when some failure had occurred in the communicative process through this or that localized instance of misunderstanding, cultural difference, aberrant translation or whatever.) A similar point is made, though with stronger moral and political overtones, by Hilary Putnam in his rejoinder to Rorty and other pragmatist thinkers.[109] For if indeed it were the case, as they argue, that truth-claims and value-judgements only make sense from the internalist perspective of those who subscribe to them, then clearly the ultimate wielders of hermeneutic power – those (to put it crudely) with the cultural clout to decide in such matters – would be members of that community most favourably placed to interpret others on its own preferential terms. In fact they could have no choice but to do so since those terms would constitute the limits of intelligibility for anyone (even a good-willed liberal pluralist) brought up on that particular set of interpretive assumptions. And as Putnam remarks, this casts an odd light on the pragmatist claim, when advanced by well-placed US or 'First-World' liberal intellectuals like Rorty, to be speaking from a standpoint that allows full scope to the variety of human interests, values and beliefs.

O'Neill argues to similar effect against those versions of the cultural-relativist approach that start out from Wittgenstein's language-game doctrine, or – in related vein – from the idea that ethical enquiry is best pursued through a case-by-case treatment of narrative examples, each taken to embody some distinctive form of life with its own judgemental criteria. 'Traditional ethnocentrism,' she writes, 'was prepared to override the practices of those beyond its pale; it preached and practised a colonialist ethic, offering to "natives" at most the opportunity for "them" to assimilate to "us"' (p. 174). Wittgensteinian ethnocentrism, by contrast,

> has nothing to say to those who live beyond 'our' local pale; in the face of a world in which adherents of distinct practices meet increasingly it proposes a retreat to the cosiness of 'our' shared world and tradition. Perhaps it is not surprising that such a conception of ethics should flourish mainly in the academies of a former imperial power, and that it should focus predominantly on judging what has been done. Precisely because of the variety and transience of ethical practices, to which Wittgensteinian writers draw our attention, we cannot easily lead our lives without raising questions that are not just internal to but about local practices. (p. 174)

Her point, like Putnam's, is that relativism may turn out to have consequences sharply at odds with its professed ideal of an easygoing tolerance for the range and diversity of viewpoints adopted by denizens of this or that cultural life-world. Rorty is engagingly up-front about this, conceding that pragmatism is very much a homegrown US (or 'North Atlantic postmodern liberal bourgeois') outlook, but urging that we take it on board all the same, whatever its ethnocentric bias, since quite simply it is the best thing going in a world where those values have carried the day.[110] Nor would Rorty be lost for a reply if one remarked on the convergence between his line of argument and those current variations on the 'end-of-ideology' (or 'end-of-history') theme promoted by New World Order ideologues such as Francis Fukuyama.[111] For he would see them as arguing, like everyone else, from a position whose suasive efficacy depends not so much on its appeal to justifying 'reasons' or 'principles, but merely on the fact of its happening to fit with what is nowadays perceived as good in the way of belief. (Which is not of course to deny that this purpose might be served very well by a *rhetoric* of reason and principle if such talk carries weight with a broad enough section of the relevant interpretive community.)

X

This is why O'Neill sees a close kinship between the linguistic (or narrative) turn in recent ethical theory and the drift toward forms of consensus-based ethical theory which reject any appeal to grounds of judgement beyond those internal to the practice in question. For the upshot of such relativist arguments is to promote the surely untenable view that each and every practice is justified by its own moral, social, or communal lights; that (for instance) it was right to own slaves, and wrong to oppose the institution of slavery, in the antebellum American South, or that Nazi ideologues were morally superior to those who resisted the regime so long as National Socialism still held sway. And the same must apply to any comparable instance of beliefs that may once have seemed self-evidently right to most members of a given community, but which strike us now – and perhaps struck some of its members then – as failing to meet the most elementary standards of justice and common decency. All of which tends to support Bernard Williams's forthright rejection of cultural relativism as 'the anthropologist's heresy', and as 'possibly the most absurd view . . . to have been advanced in moral philosophy'.[112] This conclusion is endorsed by Richard Freadman and Seumas Miller in their recent book *Re-Thinking Theory*, a philosophical critique of relativist doctrine as it figures in the discourse of post-structuralism, postmodernism, New Historicism and other such radically 'textualist' modes of thought.[113] What these critics fail to recognize, according to Freadman and Miller, are the disabling ethical consequences that flow from a treatment of 'the real' as a wholly discursive product, a figment of textual representation, and of 'the subject' as likewise constituted through and through by the signifying practices specific to this or that localized cultural context. For on this account one might as well go the full distance with the partisans of moral relativism and declare that all beliefs are equally valid within their own cultural context, since there is nothing – no argument on factual, reasoned or principled grounds – that could possibly provide any justification for criticizing what seem to us false or unacceptable beliefs. In short, new textualism is simply old relativism writ large, with the difference that it goes more elaborate (rhetorical or deconstructive) ways around in order to subvert every notion of truth or ethical accountability.

Freadman and Miller put the case most forcefully when they remark on the fact that 'proponents of doctrines such as Fascism and Apartheid have [very often] embraced moral relativism'. More specifically, 'if Fascists or white racists believe that a particular policy is right – in virtue of that policy being the expression of, say, the *Volk* – then that (ostensibly) makes it right'.[114] Further:

> if a particular culture has as a central social practice and unifying ideology the destruction of other supposedly inferior groups (say Australian aborigines), then according to cultural relativism it is morally right for that culture so to destroy those other groups. For if genocide is their social practice, then genocide is morally right.[115]

This may all seem utterly remote from the concerns of post-structuralist criticism or the straightforward pragmatist recommendation that we let up on talk of 'reasons' and 'principles' and acknowledge that these are just the way we happen to see things from our cultural neck of the woods. But the point is *not* to argue (absurdly) that such ideas have an inbuilt affinity with racist or exterminist doctrines. Rather, it is to show that moral relativism if taken seriously can offer no defence against obnoxious creeds just so long as there is (or once was) a 'language-game', 'discourse' or cultural 'form of life' wherein they enjoyed some measure of communal assent. At the limit this produces what Hillis Miller might describe as an 'aporia' between different linguistic codes, but what must otherwise appear a kind of self-imposed moral paralysis brought about by adherence to the relativist dogma in its most extreme (and insupportable) form.

Only thus can one explain Lyotard's attitude in the face of right-wing 'revisionist' arguments like that of Robert Faurisson, namely, that since no witnesses survive who can vouch directly for what happened inside the gas-chambers at Auschwitz, therefore the historical record is mute on this point and we should treat all talk of the Holocaust as – so far as we can possibly know – a conspiracy devised to denigrate the Nazis and promote the Zionist cause.[116] The most obvious response to such sophistries would be to point out their manifestly absurd major premise, their wilful disregard for other (massively documented) sources of knowledge, and the presence of a blatant motivating interest, or crudely propagandist intent, which explains both their flouting of the factual-historical rules of evidence and their utterly unprincipled ethical stance. For Lyotard, however, such arguments are beside the point, assuming as they do that Faurisson is playing by the same evidential or ethical rules, or that opponents have the right to arraign his 'discourse' from a standpoint of assuredly superior probity and truth. By so doing, Lyotard maintains, they commit an injustice, a suppression of the 'differend', which deprives their case of any genuine claim to rectify Faurisson's similar breach of ethico-discursive responsibility.

This seems to me a very clear (and shocking) example of what can go wrong when moral relativism is joined to an extreme version of the incommensurability-thesis derived from post-structuralist and other theoretical sources. For the result of such thinking is to level the difference between truth and falsehood, good and bad faith, respect for other people's honestly-argued convictions and an attitude of all-purpose sceptical doubt which admits any viewpoint – however ill-founded, prejudicial or malign – as entitled to a hearing *on its own terms of argument* and *according to its own internal criteria*. That Lyotard claims to arrive at this position through a reading of Kant is among the greatest ironies thrown up by the current counter-enlightenment trend. Thus it was left to postmodernists and adepts of the deconstructive-textualist turn to grant the sublime such absolute pride of place that ethics could be viewed as a purely linguistic predicament, a product of the 'structural interference' between constative and performative (or grammatical and rhetorical) codes. 'An ethical judgment,' Miller writes, 'is always a baseless positing, always unjust and unjustified, therefore always liable to be displaced by another momentarily stronger or more persuasive but equally baseless positing of a different code of ethics' (Miller, p. 55). And for de Man likewise, 'ethics has nothing to do with the will (thwarted or free) of a subject, nor *a fortiori*, with the relationship between subjects. . . . The ethical category is imperative (i.e., a category rather than a value) to the extent that it is linguistic and not subjective'.[117] In which case we can only be dupes of a naive (subject-centred) epistemology and ethics if we think – like Kant – that moral judgements are a matter of principled reflection on the issues confronted by rational agents in a context of real-world deliberative choice. By displacing the focus of attention from the Second to the Third *Critique*, and by treating the sublime (rather than the beautiful) as the cardinal link between Kantian aesthetics and ethics, these theorists would effectively revoke the whole legacy of enlightened critical thought.

Such readings have little to commend them beyond the appeal to a post-modern ethos (or a generalized hermeneutics of suspicion) which counsels a stoic acquiescence in the fact of our confinement to the prison-house of language. Thus if Miller sees nothing in Kant but 'gulfs' or 'chasms' – the deconstructive equivalent of Lyotard's radical 'heterogeneity' – this results not so much from the inherent liabilities of Kantian thought but from his own (Miller's) determined effort to discover such textualist aporias at every turn. No doubt it is the case, as every commentator has to acknowledge, that Kant is very far from resolving these issues in a straightforward perspicuous manner. But to treat them, like Miller, on an *a priori* principle of radical undecidability is about the least helpful of all approaches to an 'ethics of reading' which purportedly respects the letter of the Kantian text.

This is why I have taken O'Neill's book as a salutary reminder of the paths not pursued – indeed, summarily closed off – by proponents of the current revisionist line. The relevant issues can be summarized as follows.

1) The deconstructionists are right *up to a point* in maintaining that Kant's arguments are in some sense 'radically' metaphorical. That is to say, he relies on certain 'literary' figures of thought (catachresis, allegory, hypotyposis, narrative parables etc.) in order to articulate the relations that hold – for instance – between pure and practical reason, determinate concepts and reflective ideas, or judgement in its aesthetic and ethical modes. But this offers no pretext for a version of Kant that treats his whole enterprise as a tissue of ungrounded rhetorical tropes devoid of all reference to questions of veridical knowledge or real-world moral agency. On the contrary, Kant's metaphors derive their meaning – their operative force – from a conception of practical reason that is developed throughout the three *Critiques*, and which moreover finds its fullest (ethico-political) justification in those supposedly peripheral

texts that address themselves to issues of government, collective morality, progress, 'perpetual peace', international law, and kindred themes. For in ethics as in the cognitive disciplines metaphors may serve as a means to articulate hypotheses (or regulative ideas) whose claims are verified or justified through the process of reasoned critical enquiry. At any rate the burden of proof lies with the sceptics to show just why – by what implacable order of linguistic necessity – we are constrained to elevate the 'law of the text' over any appeal to the interests of truth and morally accountable judgement.

2) The antifoundationalists are right, again up to a point, in maintaining that truth-claims are always couched in a language that carries certain culture-specific assumptions and knowledge-constitutive interests. But this gives no warrant for the sceptical conclusion that such claims can appeal to nothing more than a localized consensus view of what is 'good in the way of belief'. For if, as Kant holds, 'practical uses of reason are more fundamental than theoretical uses of reason', then it follows that thinking must necessarily be guided by regulative maxims – or principles of conduct in argument and action – whose relevance extends beyond the limits of any given cultural community. In O'Neill's words:

> It is in choosing how to act, to understand and to interpret, that we embody or flout the only principles that we could have reason to think of as principles of reason. It is also in thinking, communicating and acting that we discover that the most basic of these must enable us to accommodate the fact of our plurality and our lack (or at least ignorance) of any preestablished harmony between the modes of thought employed by different parties to a plurality. It is also in thinking, communicating and acting that we discover that we must discipline tendencies to rely on strategies of acting in ways that make others' adoption of like strategies impossible. (p. 27)

This brings out the crucial difference between pragmatism (including its postmodern or textualist variants) and what Habermas terms 'transcendental pragmatics', that is to say, the appeal to a *sensus communis* that sustains the possibility of critical debate across otherwise non-negotiable divergences of language, culture, and belief.[118] It also points a way beyond Lyotard's ethics of radical incommensurability, his idea that justice can only consist in a willing-ness to suspend all preconceived notions of truth, reason or principle in order to respect the irreducible plurality (the differend) that marks all such disputes. For this argument – along with its disabling relativist consequences – will appear simply untenable if one takes O'Neill's point about the shared human interest in attaining an enlightened community of thought and judgement wherein those disputes would at least be open to constructive dialogical exchange.

3) The revisionists are justified in their claim that the third *Critique* (or

Kant's arguments concerning the role and modalities of aesthetic judgement)
must be seen as providing some crucial links between the otherwise uncoordinated realms of sensuous intuition and conceptual understanding, or
practical reason (morality) and its analogues in the socio-political sphere.
Hence, for example, Kant's much-discussed recourse to the 'productive
imagination' as a mediating figure whereby to negotiate such problematic
points of transition. But again, these theorists go far beyond anything warranted
by the Kantian text when they relegate the beautiful (the realm of enlightened
consensus-judgement) to a distinctly subordinate role, and promote the
sublime – the figure of disjunction, radical alterity, 'gulfs', 'chasms' etc. – to
an eminent position where it works to disarticulate the entire doctrine of the
faculties. The main source of such readings, as I have said, is Heidegger's
overtly revisionist account in *Kant and the Problem of Metaphysics*. Their effect is
to aestheticize the character of ethical judgement to the point where, as in
Heidegger, language (and especially the language of the poets) becomes the
only touchstone of authenticity, of a thinking attuned to long-lost sources of
primordial wisdom and truth.[119] According to Miller it was Kant's 'recoil'
from this Heideggerian insight – his refusal to acknowledge 'the founding
power of the transcendental imagination' – which drove him to embrace the
delusory idea that moral law might find its justification in the Categorical
Imperative or the maxims of practical reason.

Here again it is worth citing O'Neill at length since her argument runs
precisely contrary to the Heidegger-Miller account.

> Human beings can receive a manifold of intuition, subject to the structural
> constraints of the forms of intuition. They can synthesize this manifold using
> empirical concepts in accordance with the categories of the understanding.
> However, they can deploy the categories in complete acts of judgment only if
> they adopt and follow certain Ideas of reason or maxims to organize this
> judging. . . . [Thus] the complex capacities that we call sensibility and under-
> standing are not usable without 'Ideas of reason', that is, without the adoption of
> maxims to regulate the use of these capacities in thinking and acting. An
> account of human knowledge will be systematically indeterminate unless these
> maxims are identified and vindicated. (p. 19)

O'Neill introduces what she takes to be a fairly straightforward piece of
summary exposition with the apologetic comment that '[this] story is familiar
to all of Kant's readers'. But no matter how familiar it has carried little weight
with readers like Lyotard and Miller. For these theorists are resolved to exploit
the full potential of Heidegger's presumed 'insight' by interpreting Kant
against himself, viewing him as a kind of errant precursor, one who lacked the
courage of his own most crucial discovery, namely the 'founding power' of
imagination in its sublime aspect.

Kant might well have 'recoiled' had he foreseen this strong-revisionist account of the productive imagination and its sovereign role *vis-à-vis* the faculties of cognitive understanding and practical reason. In fact the turn was taken much further back with Fichte's drastic solution to the Kantian antinomies, his treatment of the subject as an absolute, autonomous, world-creating ego whose privilege it was to 'posit' all the objects of its own thought and perception.[120] This idealist strain carries over into de Man's and Miller's talk of language as likewise exerting a radically 'positional' force, a self-acting power that effectively subverts all our commonplace (humanly-accountable) ideas of meaning, intention, moral agency, and truth. Hence those passages in de Man's late work — notably the essays on Nietzsche, Benjamin and Shelley — where he denies that language is ultimately a 'human' phenomenon, and proposes in stead that we should regard it as a force-field of conflicting rhetorical and grammatical codes, 'quasi-automatic' signifying structures whose complexity far exceeds the grasp of any naive (intentionalist or anthropocentric) account.[121]

Fichte is clearly one of the major sources for this most extreme version of the current revolt against 'humanism' in whatever ethical, linguistic or epistemological form. But it is also part of a wider development whose origins and history Stanley Rosen has recently set out to describe.[122] In brief, such ideas are the end-result of a counter-enlightenment impulse which began with the move to historicize (or relativize) Kant's categories of judgement, continued with the turn toward hermeneutic models of philosophy as depth-interpretation, and finished by assimilating every sphere of thought — epistemology, history, ethics, politics — to a linguistic (or textualist) paradigm. And so it comes about that a thinker like Lyotard can presume to revoke the whole enterprise of enlightenment critique through a reading of Kant that exploits the sublime as a limit-point of rational, truth-seeking discourse, a figure of the ultimate 'undecidability' (or the differend between cognitive and ethical language-games) which that enterprise supposedly strove to repress. The linguistic turn can take many forms, from Rorty's liberal-ironist 'vocabularies' of private self-perfection to de Man's relentlessly self-abnegating strain of deconstructive rhetoric. What they all have in common is a philosophy that finds no room for the subject — the knowing, willing and judging subject — whose demise, they argue, is irresistibly entailed by the passage to a postmodern (language-oriented) discourse of the 'human sciences'.

XI

I have argued that a great deal hangs on these seemingly specialized issues in the reception-history of Kant's thought from his own day to the present. In particular it raises the question of whether intellectuals or critical theorists should be thought of as bearing any particular responsibility in matters of a wider (ethico-political) concern. Undeniably this question has an old-fashioned ring, an air of harking back to what many would regard – in the wake of Foucault, Lyotard et al. – as an overweening notion of the intellectual's role in speaking up for truth despite or against the current self-images of the age. Of course there are risks attendant upon any such claim, among them (as Foucault never ceased to point out) the danger of fostering a class of 'universal intellectuals' whose authority, like that of Plato's philosopher-king, could always give rise to the worst, most oppressive forms of arrogant power/ knowledge. Hence Foucault's case for the 'specific intellectual', the thinker whose more modest task it is to deploy his or her specialized skills – as for instance in the genealogy of knowledge, the history of psychiatric medicine, or the emergence of disciplinary power-regimes – with the aim of resisting both a scholarly consensus and a range of real-world institutional practices.[123]

But there are three crucial points that tend to be neglected by proponents of the Foucault line who adopt his counter-enlightenment rhetoric as a matter of reflex postmodernist habit. One is that Foucault in his later essays came around to a markedly more appreciative reading of Kant than in those oft-cited pages from *The Order of Things* where the Kantian subject is summarily dismissed as a curious 'transcendental-empirical doublet', a figment of the bourgeois-humanist imaginary, one whose lineaments are soon to be erased by the incoming tide of a new (post-humanist) discourse.[124] As I argued in Chapter Two, his relationship to Kant remained intensely ambivalent, and cannot be regarded as signalling an end to Foucault's quarrel with the claims of enlightened critique. All the same these essays bear striking witness to my two remaining points. That is to say, they acknowledge that truth is indispensable to any ethics or politics worthy the name, and that 'enlightenment' itself – as an ethos, a project, or a critical orientation – offers a continuing source of resistance to power/knowledge in its hitherto instituted forms.[125] For it is a precondition of any such resistance that its argument should be staked on both the *falsehood* (or the distorting partiality) of established representations and the *injustice* (or the ethically repugnant character) of those practices whose conduct they serve to endorse. His return to Kant in these writings of his last decade – especially in the essay 'What Is Enlightenment?' – is one indication of Foucault's changing attitude with regard to questions of truth, knowledge, and ethical accountability.[126]

Let me end by quoting a pointedly relevant passage from Alan Montefiore's contribution to a recent symposium on *The Political Responsibility of Intellectuals*. 'It has by now become something of a commonplace,' he writes,

> that truth and reality are never delivered to human understanding as they are 'in themselves', so to speak, that is to say in conceptually free independence of the forms of thought of each one's own particular language, culture, society and

what may (with all due caution) be called its most general metaphysical perspectives. All the same – and this too may be seen to be a lesson of the theory of
meaning and of language – any culture whatsoever will have in one way or
another to come to terms with its own version of these fundamental distinctions.
No truth may be known as being absolute; but no-one is thereby dispensed from
the responsibility for recognizing the distinction, within his or her own context,
between relative truth and, relative to that truth, indisputable lie and illusion –
or from the further responsibility of testifying, where necessary, to it (and the art
of identifying that necessity is one of both moral and political judgment).[127]

This seems to me an exemplary statement of the questions that arise for any
reading of Kant which would seek to understand (the better to resist) his
recruitment in the service of counter-enlightenment or postmodern-textualist
creeds. For such ideas have gone along with the more widespread turn toward
consensus-based doctrines whose effect is to deny precisely those distinctions
that Montefiore thinks vital to the interests of justice and truth. That Kant's
writings are once again contested ground – as in earlier periods of intensive
ideological or socio-political debate – is a clear sign that the issues involved are
of more than narrowly academic significance. For what is at stake here, as
Montefiore argues, is 'that irreducible share of intellectual commitment that is
the ineliminable mark of the human being as such'. Any cultural fashion that
rejects such talk as old hat – or which views it as merely the hung-over
symptom of an obsolete 'enlightenment' ethos – is inescapably complicit with
the pragmatist drift toward an ethics and politics of inert consensus belief.

Getting at Truth: Genealogy, Critique and Postmodern Scepticism

Page duBois' book *Torture and Truth* is one of a number of recent studies that perceive an affinity between truth-seeking discourse and the practice of extracting secrets under bodily duress or bringing hidden knowledge to light through techniques of physical coercion.[1] The most obvious source-text is Foucault's *Discipline and Punish*, in particular its set-piece opening description of the torments visited upon the regicide Damiens as a token of feudal authority inscribed through a graphic reversal and literalization of the King's Body metaphor.[2] Nor should we suppose, in the smugness of 'enlightened' retrospect, that those barbarities have now been left far behind on the path to present-day civilized practices and values. For according to Foucault such Whiggish or progressivist notions are really just a species of self-serving fantasy, a means of ignoring the different kinds of violence – the forms of internalized discipline and constraint – that characterize our current sexual mores, social institutions, psychiatric techniques, ideas of justice, projects of penal reform etc. What we like to think of as 'progress' in these areas is in fact a history of steadily intensifying pressure, a multiplication of the strategies available for constructing the subject in accordance with societal norms and ensuring compliance with this or that mode of acceptable behaviour and belief. Such is the message everywhere implicit in Foucault's Nietzschean genealogies of power/knowledge: that truth-claims are always, inescapably bound up with the epistemic drive for mastery and control, even (or especially) where it masks behind a rhetoric of liberal-humanist values or emancipatory critique.[3]

Thus Foucault sees nothing but the history of an error – a typical 'Enlightenment' error – in the idea that we have achieved some measure of civilized change when one compares (say) the feudal spectacle of power as a kingly prerogative exerted upon the body of the hapless criminal with modern, more 'progressive' ways of thinking about crime, rehabilitation, social responsibility and so forth. What such notions serve to conceal, he argues, is the extent to which violence has been sublimated in the form of those internalized, quasi-voluntary checks and restraints that operate all the more effectively for the absence of any overt, sovereign or juridical machinery of punitive sanctions. From the Christian confessional to Freudian psychoanalysis, these discourses typically take effect by interpellating the subject into a range of conformable positions with regard to the truth – the inward or revealed truth – of his or her 'authentic' desires.[4] From our own point of view there appears a great difference between secrets extracted under bodily duress or by infliction of physical torment, and those other sorts of truth-claim (religious or secular) which emerge through the dialogue of consenting parties or the process of intersubjective exchange. But Foucault will have none of this comforting belief, convinced as he is that the various latterday discourses of power/ knowledge are merely an alternative, more efficient means of achieving compliance with the requisite norms. Indeed there is more than a hint of nostalgia for an epoch when power took the form of an overt (albeit often gruesome) display of monarchical privilege, and when as yet there existed nothing like the present-day range of subtilized discursive techniques for conjuring obedience on the part of notionally 'free' individuals. On Foucault's reading the passage from feudal to modern disciplinary regimes reveals nothing more than the exchange of one tyranny for another, the replacement of a violence that took the most public or spectacular forms – and was thus always liable to provoke some kind of localized popular backlash – with a violence that worked through modes of inward subjection or identification, and whose effects could thus penetrate into every aspect of our social, political, sexual, ethical and affective lives.

Hence his rejection of the so-called 'repressive hypothesis', the idea that progress came about through a lifting of the old discursive taboos and a new-found freedom to discuss topics of a hitherto private or secret character. Far from having thrown off the shackles of 'Victorian' prudery and repression in such matters, we are now, Foucault argues, approaching a point where there is simply no escape from the compulsive need to make everything (our 'innermost' desires included) into a topic for the various expert discourses – psychoanalysis among them – which constitute the modern disciplinary regime of 'enlightened' self-knowledge and truth. If we are seeking a metaphor for this condition then we should think of Bentham's 'Panopticon' project, his idea for a prison (and, beyond that, an entire social order) that would dispense with the clumsy apparatus of overt surveillance and control by exposing each inmate – each subject or citizen – to the universal 'gaze' of an authority whose centre is everywhere and nowhere, and whose effects are so thoroughly dispersed and internalized that nothing eludes its sovereign command. Or again, Foucault offers the Gulag Archipelago as an analogue for this present-day 'carceral' society where discipline is exerted through constant subjection to the manifold 'technologies' of power/knowledge, and where truth-claims are always already made over into new techniques for ensuring compliance with the ethos of confessional authenticity or the inward, self-monitoring vigil of the subject-presumed-to-know. Any resistance to this order will not come about through the appeal to some notional truth behind appearances, or some enlightened (e.g. Kantian or Marxist) attempt to lay bare the mechanisms of social repression and thus restore suffering humanity to a sense of its real historical vocation, its genuine emancipatory interests, or its capacity to grasp the conditions of its own enslavement and thus take the first step toward transforming those same oppressive conditions. Such ideas amount to nothing more than a form of grandiose delusion on the part of those old-style 'universal' intellectuals who cling to the belief that truth is an ultimate good, that 'reality' is in some sense there to be grasped, and that the path to enlightenment leads through stages of disciplined reflective self-knowledge.[5]

It was Kant who first set this project under way with his subject-centred doctrine of the faculties (pure reason, theoretical understanding, practical reason and aesthetic judgement) conceived as existing in a complex order of inter-articulated truth-claims with 'man' as the privileged focus of enquiry for philosophy and the human sciences at large. But according to Foucault this was just another transient episode in the sequence of shifting paradigms, language-games or orders of discursive representation which made up the history of Western thinking to date. And its epoch was already drawing to an end, its demise brought about by the advent of a new, post-humanist dispensation where language – or discourse – would henceforth constitute the horizon of intelligibility, and where the Kantian subject, that curious 'transcendental-empirical doublet', would soon appear as nothing more than a momentary 'fold' in the fabric of signs, a figure (in Foucault's famous metaphor) engraved in sand at the ocean's edge, soon to be erased by the incoming tide.[6] From this standpoint it should now be possible to grasp how the truth-claims of enlightened thought had always been shadowed by a discourse of power, a compulsion to yield up those guilty secrets – hidden desires, unacknowledged motives, prejudicial blind-spots, remnants of 'false consciousness' and so forth – which could only be revealed through their constant exposure to the undeceiving rigours of authentic self-knowledge. Any progress achieved in the passage from feudal to present-day juridical regimes was more than outweighed by the growing range of strategies, techniques and disciplinary resources for maintaining this self-imposed vigil.

Thus the story turns out much the same whether one tells it from a Kantian, a Marxist, a Freudian, or any other critical perspective that holds to some notion of truth at the end of enquiry. For on Foucault's account such ideas take hold only at the point where desire becomes subject to a kind of internalized self-thwarting impulse – like the Kantian 'categorical imperative', the Marxist dialectic of 'genuine' *versus* 'false' class-consciousness, or Freud's various models of instinctual repression and control – which effectively carries on the work once performed by other, more overt and spectacular forms

of institutional power. In short, every so-called 'advance' on the path to
enlightenment, truth and self-knowledge goes along with a marked intensification of the disciplines, the various codes and interdictions by which the
subject monitors its own conformity to the ground-rules and values of civilized
discourse. And this is nowhere more apparent (Foucault believes) than in the
history of subject-centred epistemic and ethico-political critique which runs
down from Kant to the present-day defenders of a kindred philosophical faith.
What these thinkers fail to recognize is the deep affinity that exists between
the quest for truth in whatever form – religious or secular, inward or objective,
vouchsafed through authentic revelation or arrived at (supposedly) through
open debate in the 'public sphere' of uncoerced dialogical exchange – and the
workings of an ever more devious and resourceful will-to-power that enlists
such claims in order to dissimulate its own ubiquitous nature. On this view, it
is no great distance from the fire, rack and pinion of old-style inquisitorial
techniques to the Christian confessional, the psychoanalytic couch, or the
Marxist mode of interrogative thought that identifies truth with the laying-
bare of ideological illusion. And the same would apply to those thinkers –
Habermas among them – who seek to carry on the 'unfinished project of
modernity' even while acknowledging the force of recent anti-foundationalist
or discourse-oriented arguments.[7] For these theories still involve a residual
appeal to the truth-seeking subject of enlightenment discourse, a strategy
whose upshot (as Foucault sees it) is to render them complicit with that whole
bad history of oppressive monological reason.

II

If Page duBois finds problems with Foucault, it is not on account of his
anti-enlightenment polemic, his Nietzschean genealogies of power/knowledge,
or his wholesale rejection of truth and critique as possessing any kind of
emancipatory value. All this duBois takes pretty much for granted, along with
the current (postmodern or post-structuralist) doxa which holds truth to be
entirely a product of the discourses, language-games or signifying systems that
happen to prevail at this or that time. What she questions, more specifically, is
Foucault's argument in *Discipline and Punish* that power no longer operates
through those forms of 'spectacular' bodily violence that once served as a means
of disciplinary enforcement under feudal or absolutist monarchical regimes. For
it is simply not the case, duBois argues, that Western societies have managed
to dispense with such crude mechanisms of social control since the advent of
alternative, more subtle and sophisticated techniques for achieving the same
basic end. On the contrary: all the evidence points to the fact that Western
(primarily US) agencies are still very much involved in the business of exporting

methods of physical and psychological torture to various 'Third World' or client states where they are deployed in the interests of maintaining 'regional stability', hegemonic power-bloc interests etc.[8] Those who protest that such things only happen elsewhere – that they have no place in the liberal democracies of late twentieth-century Western Europe and North America – are closing their eyes to this proxy violence condoned, endorsed or actively promoted under cover of the usual 'free world' rhetoric. And despite his resolute opposition to such Whiggish meta-narratives of historical progress there is a sense in which Foucault gives support to this attitude by adopting a narrowly Eurocentric viewpoint and regarding torture (at least in its more systematic, overt or 'spectacular' forms) as a manifestation of the will-to-power under an earlier, distinctively pre-modern aspect.

Thus duBois accepts most of what Foucault has to say about the intimate link between knowledge or truth and the various kinds of disciplinary regime which have marked the passage from antiquity to the present. She is likewise in agreement with post-structuralists, postmodernists and other such scions of the new orthodoxy in viewing all talk of reason and truth as a mere self-legitimizing ruse, a rhetoric adopted to no other purpose than confirming the dominance of this or that 'discourse' in the endless struggle for mastery and power. Where she differs with these thinkers is simply in claiming that they have not pushed far enough with their sceptical assault on the modern (enlightened) self-image of the age, that is to say, the idea that we have relinquished all need for dependence on such 'primitive' technologies of power as Foucault describes in the opening pages of *Discipline and Punish*. To think in these simplified binary terms – i.e., of 'feudal' *versus* 'modern' disciplinary techniques – is to risk falling back into yet another form of smug ethnocentric prejudice. And it is also a handy means of escape from what duBois regards as the single most urgent issue for anyone confronting issues of power/knowledge in the present context of a US drive for renewed global hegemony. For there is an evident link between the placid belief that torture is somehow off the agenda for 'us' citizens of the liberal-democratic West and the equally facile notion that we nowadays inhabit a postmodern, post-enlightenment, post-imperialist world order where violence takes a subtilized discursive form and no longer involves such crude (indeed 'counter-productive') mechanisms of social control. To persist in this belief despite so much daily evidence to the contrary is either to reject that evidence outright or to interpret it in line with the fixed notion – which Foucault does little to challenge – that torture can only be viewed as an anomaly, a throwback to times when the political economy of truth had not yet evolved its present range of 'advanced' disciplinary techniques. The result of such thinking is a curious failure on the part of many self-styled 'radical' intellectuals to acknowledge what is happening in regions of the world where US-backed regimes (not to mention US-trained torturers) continue in the business of extracting truth by decidedly old-fashioned means.

DuBois makes this point with reference to the copious documentary sources – first-hand accounts, Amnesty reports, psychiatric case-histories, academic surveys etc. – which prove beyond reasonable doubt that torture is both practised and effectively condoned in many countries that fall within the present-day US sphere of influence. For 'the truth is' (as she puts it in the book's closing sentence) 'that torture still exists, it has not been eliminated in a surge of enlightened globalism, and the third world, in its complexity, multiplicity, multiple sites, has become, besides the site of torture, the spectacle of the other tortured for us' (duBois, p. 157). In this respect her case seems to me so compellingly argued that any difference of view – for instance, with regard to the politics of enlightenment or the relation between power, knowledge and truth – is likely to appear just a side-issue or a frivolous theoretical distraction.

Nevertheless duBois invites such a response by arguing that these obscene practices are so closely tied in with the concepts and categories of Western philosophical thought that one cannot understand their persistence without passing that entire tradition in critical review. Thus her book starts out with the pre-Socratics (chiefly Herakleitos and Parmenides); goes on to discuss the politics of truth, or the relationship between violence and metaphysics, as revealed in Plato's dialogues; and then proceeds to trace their supposed affinity down through the history of more or less radical questionings and transvaluations which culmimates in Heidegger and Derrida. Her argument – briefly stated – is that philosophy in the mainstream Western line of descent has been hooked on a notion of truth as privileged epistemic access, as a matter of penetrating to secrets which can only be revealed through various kinds of expert hermeneutical technique, or procedures vouchsafed to those few knowing individuals who possess the requisite degree of authentic understanding. Hence the more than metaphorical link between torture and truth: the idea (already well established by Plato's time) that such wisdom involved a strenuous attempt to seek out the causes of error and illusion, to subjugate the realm of false (bodily) appearances, and to use every means – violent means if need be – to justify philosophy's sovereign claim as the touchstone of genuine wisdom. 'That truth is unitary, that truth may finally be extracted by torture, is part of our legacy from the Greeks and, therefore, part of our idea of "truth"' (p. 5). In which case, duBois argues, we can best get a grip on the hideous fact of its continuing real-world practice by examining the ways in which torture figures as a subtext, an analogue or source of argumentative strategies for thinkers who have inherited that same bad legacy.[9]

The most striking evidence in this regard is the way that the Greeks used torture as a jointly juridical and socio-political touchstone, a means of distinguishing between free-born citizens (whose testimony was judged in open court through a process of reasoned dialogical exchange) and slaves (whose witness could only be accepted under duress, since their status dictated that they lacked the rational-discursive warrant to utter any truth save that produced by application of the due penal sanctions). Thus Aristotle states it as a matter of self-evident fact that only citizens (that is to say, adult male citizens) possess *logos*, or the prerogative of truth-telling rational discourse, whereas slaves – insofar as they lack this capacity – must be subject to some form of physical coercion in order that their testimony should count as legally valid.[10] And moreover, by an odd twist of argument, this latter kind of witness should be treated as more reliable – more probably truthful – since the slave is subject to expert techniques for establishing the facts of the case, and besides has no reason (in either sense of the word: motive or rational means) for maintaining a false or self-interested version of events. Thus 'the evidence derived from the slave's body and reported to the court, evidence from the past, is considered superior to that given freely in the court, before the jury, in the presence of the litigants' (p. 65). Of course we are inclined to regard such ideas as the product of an antiquated prejudice, a juridical code whose barbarous character reflected the clearly-marked limits of Athenian democracy, the belief that slaves were 'naturally' defined as such by their non-possession of the faculties and rights pertaining to free-born citizens. But duBois sees this as just one more instance of the standard 'enlightenment' alibi, the habit of locating some convenient other – sufficiently remote in space or time – upon whom to project our strategies of disavowal. For otherwise we should have to acknowledge that the Greek distinction between citizen and slave, along with its attendant juridical sanctions, was there at the origin of much that has passed into the discourse of present-day 'civilized' reason.

It is worth quoting duBois at length on this point since her arguments for the affinity between torture and truth depend very largely on the reconstruction of a typical Athenian court-room scene. What transpired on such occasions was a contest of rival discursive regimes, the one grounded on values of autonomy, freedom of speech, right reason, citizenly duty and so on, the other dispensing with all such constitutional safeguards and treating the slave (quite literally) as a *vessel* of truth, a witness whose integrity, whose motives or rational interests were irrelevant to the case in hand, and whose secrets could only be brought to light through a quasi-objective process of bodily experiment.[11] 'In this context,' duBois writes,

the evidence from the torture of slaves is evidence from elsewhere, from another place, another body. It is evidence from outside the community of citizens, of free men. Produced by the *basanistes*, the torturer, or by the litigant in another scene, such evidence differs radically from the testimony of free witnesses in the court. It is temporally estranged, institutionally, conventionally marked as evidence of another order; what is curious is that speakers again and again privilege it as belonging to a higher order of truth than that evidence freely offered in the presence of the jurors by present witnesses. (p. 49)

But this will seem less surprising, duBois suggests, if we appreciate the extent to which such practices conform with the idea of truth as a secret to be sought out, a secret which free-born citizens (philosophers especially) may hope to attain through the exercise of reason or the quest for authentic self-knowledge, but which others can yield up only by submitting to the rigours of juridical enquiry. Among the many kinds of evidence that point in this direction is the etymological link that duBois discerns between the language of testing for validity or truth – as borrowed from the physical sciences of the day – and the language of bodily trials undergone by due process of law.[12] Thus 'the Greeks first use the literal meaning for *basanos* of "touchstone", then metaphorize it to connote a test, then reconcretize, rematerialize it to mean once again a physical testing in torture' (p. 35). And this is clearly not an instance of random semantic drift but a figure of thought with far-reaching implications for the character and subsequent influence of Greek 'democratic' ideals. For the result of such thinking – inscribed in catachrestic metaphors (like *basanos*) for which there exists no literal or non-figurative equivalent – is to make it appear 'only natural' (or self-evident to reason) that citizens should enjoy the prerogative of free speech and uncoerced testimony, while others manifestly lack such rights and are therefore subject to physical compulsion.

This is not to say that duBois rejects the very notion of ancient Greek democracy, or that she views it – in the modish cynical fashion – as a myth invented to bolster the claims of subsequent regimes with a similar need to establish their pedigree and legitimize the practice of 'enlightened' punitive sanctions. On the contrary, she finds 'something extraordinary' in the fact that the Athenians were able to attain some measure of (albeit intermittent) popular sovereignty at a time when so many hostile forces, internal and external, conspired to prevent it. These latter included the constant threat of an anti-democratic backlash among disaffected members of the old ruling-class elite; the series of punishing wars (and occasional disastrous defeats) at the hands of other, more rigidly authoritarian or militarist regimes; the structural instability endemic to a social order where principles and practice were so often sharply at odds; and, above all, the persistence of an ethos that equated truth and virtue with an attitude of sovereign contempt for any form of genuine popular democracy. For it is here that philosophers (Socrates and Plato especially, but also Parmenides before them) managed to insinuate the notion of a truth that would somehow transcend all the mere relativities of timebound human under-standing, and would thus elevate the knower to a realm of spiritual insight above and beyond such mundane concerns. The effect of this doctrine, duBois argues, was to reinforce the worst, most retrograde aspects of Greek socio-political thought by offering a ready justification for beliefs and practices – like the citizen/slave or the male/female dichotomies – which went clean against what can elsewhere be seen as an incipient democratizing impulse.

Thus the heroes of this book are those shadowy figures (among them Herakleitos and the Sophists) who rejected the appeal to a unitary Truth which could then serve as a touchstone – a *basanos* – for maintaining differentials of wealth, privilege and power. For as duBois points out, 'the idea of equality has its own dynamic, a pressure towards the consideration of all in view as entitled to the privileges of rule by the people' (p. 125). Of the pre-Socratic 'philosophers' – and duBois uses the term, so to speak, *sous rature*, with a cautionary sense of its misleading implications – Herakleitos stands out as the thinker most willing to acknowledge the unattainability of ultimate truth and the mutable, timebound, or relative nature of all human understanding. For Parmenides, conversely, the ascent to truth involved a setting aside of all such transient concerns, a contempt for mere opinion (*doxa*) as opposed to authentic or revealed wisdom, and a similar disdain for consensus values arrived at through the open, democratic exchange of rival beliefs and viewpoints.[13] What we are given to read in the few fragments that survive of these two pre-Socratics is a contest not only over the nature of truth but also over the claim that philosophy exerts – increasingly so, as Parmenides' doctrines are taken up and reworked by thinkers like Socrates and Plato – upon the conduct of everyday ethical, social and political life. In contrast to this, as duBois argues,

> the Heraclitean truth, read within his words, fragmentary as they are, celebrating flux, time, difference, allows for an alternative model to a hidden truth. Even though Herakleitos distinguishes himself from those who do not understand, who lack his grasp of reality, for him truth is process and becoming, obtained through observation, rather than a fixed, divine and immutable truth of eternity. (p. 98)

And for the sophists also – like their present-day descendants in the pragmatist camp – there is simply no difference (no difference that makes any difference, as William James pithily put it) between 'truth' and what is currently and contingently 'good in the way of belief'. DuBois has nothing to say about James, Dewey, or Peirce; nor about the recent revival of pragmatist ideas in the 'post-philosophical' writings of Richard Rorty or the turn 'against theory' in literary and legal studies, most zealously promoted by Stanley Fish.[14] Nevertheless these thinkers can best be seen as carrying on the ancient sophistical tradition which has only acquired such a bad name, duBois indignantly asserts, through its villification at the hands of those earnest philosophical seekers-after-truth, from Socrates and Plato to the present. What

is on offer from the pragmatists, ancient and modern, is an ethos of open
dialogical exchange which sees no virtue in allowing philosophy to lord it over
the interests of straightforward communal good.

Thus in Plato's dialogue of that title the Sophist is depicted as one who, like
the slave, may *apprehend* truth without actually *possessing* it, or produce all
manner of veridical statements while failing to know (or inwardly grasp) that
whereof he so fluently speaks.[15] If we meet with this shady character, Plato
recommends,

> we should arrest him on the royal warrant of reason, report the capture, and
> hand him over to the sovereign. But if he should find some lurking place among
> the subdivisions of this art of imitation, we must follow hard upon him,
> constantly dividing the art that gives him shelter, until he is caught. (cited by
> duBois, p. 113)

Although the passage seems playful enough – a piece of witty argument at the
Sophist's expense – the joke also has a 'sinister side', an aspect that should
remind us (as duBois reads it) that 'logic and dialectic are police arts', that
philosophy is always ready to become 'a method of arrest and discipline', and
moreover that such metaphors often entail 'a dividing, a splitting, a fracturing
of the logical body, a process that resembles torture' (p. 113). And this
connection is reinforced by the kinds of argumentative technique – the various
dialectical moves, counter-moves, clinching demonstrations and so forth –
which characterize Socrates' manner of dealing with these upstart rhetoricians
and purveyors of a false, non-philosophical wisdom. Thus for instance 'the
elegkhos, "elenchus", the word most often used to describe the process of
philosophical dialectic in Plato's work, was first of all "a cross-examining,
testing, for purposes of disproof or refutation"' (p. 112). It is no great distance
from this idea of a truth that emerges through the discipline of hard-pressed
dialectical dispute to the practice of torture as the readiest means of compelling
the other – whether sophist or slave – to yield up secrets which only the
philosopher (or the enlightened citizen) can interpret at their proper worth.

Hence the famous episode in the *Meno* where Socrates seeks to demonstrate
the existence of innate or *a priori* knowledge by coaxing a previously unin-
structed slave-boy to 'discover' certain elementary truths of geometry.[16] That
he is able to elicit the right answers through a process of stage-by-stage
dialectical exchange is held up by Socrates as proof that the slave in some sense
already knows these truths and only needs the prompting of a good teacher to
draw them forth in articulate form. This would seem a fairly benign piece
of pedagogic method, a technique far removed from the kinds of coercive
discipline – the equation between 'truth' and 'torture' – that duBois thinks
endemic to any such procedure. But the main purpose of Socrates' argument

here is to show that the slave's understanding of geometry derives not so much from his new-found capacity to grasp abstract ideas as from his thinking back, under expert guidance, to a primordial knowledge that had somehow been lost or forgotten. Thus, in Plato's words: 'if the truth about reality is always in our souls, the soul must be immortal, and one must take courage and try to discover – that is, to recollect – what one doesn't happen to know, or, more correctly, remember, at the moment' (cited by duBois, p. 118). Such is the Platonic doctrine of *anamnesis*, of an 'unforgetting' that enables the soul momentarily to transcend its present mortal or timebound condition, and to recall those truths which would otherwise be lost without trace in the passage from one incarnation to the next. For it was Plato's belief – derived from Pythagoras – that the soul was reborn in successive bodily guises, and that wisdom came about through occasional glimpses of what had once been known (in some previous, more spiritual phase) but had then been obscured through the soul's descent to a lower order of bodily existence. Hence the double-negative construction of a word like *anamnesis*, suggesting on the one hand the forgetfulness to which mortal knowers are always subject, and on the other the prospect of overcoming this condition through the ministry of a wise and good teacher like Socrates. For otherwise, the argument runs, we could never learn anything at all, given that the quest for authentic knowledge requires that we already possess some criterion, some touchstone of truth whereby to distinguish the genuine from the false article. In the *Meno* Socrates claims to resolve this paradox by locating truth in a realm of primordial ideas to which we gain access – albeit intermittently – by piercing the clouds of illusion and false seeming.

Another such term is the Greek *aletheia*, likewise connoting a state of oblivion, a deprivation of knowledge or failure of inward recollection, which can only be dispelled by the bringing-to-light of a hidden or buried truth. And it is here that duBois finds a sinister reminder of the link between philosophy (as Plato conceives it) and those forms of juridical compulsion or socio-political control which shadowed the Greek experiment in a kind of limited republican democracy. For if truth is a matter of 'unforgetting' (*aletheia*), if forgetfulness results from our bodily condition or enslavement to the physical senses, and if slaves (or non-citizens) can at best 'apprehend' and never authentically 'possess' such truth, then it follows (by this self-confirming logic) that such persons should be subject to physical coercion in the interests of enlightenment, justice or truth. As duBois puts it, paraphrasing Plato: 'Life is oblivion of the vision of truth; *Lethe* is a weight. *Aletheia* is the forgetting of the body, the forgetting of untruth, the forgetting of forgetting; it is the casting off of the material, deathly, woman-born body, and ascent to the realm of pure soul' (p. 119). And of course this doctrine can very easily be turned around so as to cast the citizen-philosopher in the role of self-authorized spiritual guide, and the slave

– or any person not enjoying such privileged status – as a bodily subject whose 'truth' can only be elicited through techniques of remorseless dialectical questioning analogous to the practice of juridical torture. So it was, according to duBois, that philosophy (from Plato down) became a refuge for those who rejected the values of a nascent democratic order, and who identified 'truth' with a wisdom inaccessible to anyone outside the charmed circle of innate, *a priori* ideas.

Thus 'the torture of slaves in the Athenian legal system is consistent with the privileging of oracular truth, like the seeking of truth in the recollection of metaphysical foreknowledge' (p. 126). And philosophy invites this charge insofar as it 'denies the production of truth in time and space, producing the other who knows, the philosophical opponent as well as the slave who must be treated with violence so that truth can be dis-covered' (p. 126). It thus falls in with a range of archaic attitudes and beliefs which were already, by Socrates' time, encountering resistance in other, more progressive quarters of Greek intellectual opinion. This resistance took the form of a new rationality, an emergent discourse or public sphere of open dialogical exchange where issues could be argued out at the level of collective (though still sharply limited) participant democracy, rather than revealed through the exercise of force or the bringing-to-light of a secret knowledge buried in the depths of the soul. To the extent that he endorsed this latter conception – truth as *aletheia*, as 'unforgetting', or as an inward revelation vouchsafed to the privileged few by techniques of disciplined self-knowledge – Plato stands squarely in line with those conservative thinkers for whom democracy represented a threat to social order and a vulgar abuse of established hierarchical principles. And philosophers have carried on this bad tradition of anti-democratic thought whenever they follow Plato's lead in seeking to distinguish *epistēmē* (authentic knowledge) from *doxa* (mere opinion or popular belief), or when they elevate the values of truth, reason and critique above the everyday business of striving for agreement on matters of immediate practical concern. In short, duBois more or less concurs with the view of I. F. Stone in his polemical book *The Trial of Socrates*: that the Athenians were justified in regarding such ideas as inimical to the interests of democracy and social justice, if not in their resort to the death-sentence as a means of countering this threat.[17]

DuBois has some interesting points to make about the link between this Platonic rendering of truth as *aletheia* and earlier accounts – in Homer especially – of wisdom as the upshot of an epic quest, one that typically involved exposure to various perils and temptations, a period of sojourn in the underworld, and a final homecoming (*nostos*) when the wanderer brings back the spiritual fruits of his manifold trials and ordeals. Most striking is the close resemblance that emerges between Odysseus' conduct in face of these dangers and the philosopher's idea of truth as what results from a process of strenuous dialectical questioning on the path to authentic self-knowledge. In both cases – as duBois points out – there is an underlying metaphor which equates such truth with the struggle against forms of bodily or sensuous bewitchment, most often figured in the person of some seductive or threatening female archetype whose designs the hero is enabled to thwart through possession of the requisite male (i.e., moral and intellectual) qualities. Thus

> the hero Odysseus, in the underworld, must use his sword to defend the pit of blood from his own mother, who desires to speak with him, until he hears the prescriptions of the seer, who urges *nous*, an alert and conscious intelligence, upon him in order that he survive the trials of the journey home, the attempts of Kalypso, the 'veiler', the 'coverer', the 'concealer', to keep him immortal though hidden on her island, the attempts of Circe to bury him in the unconsciousness of an animal body, the efforts of the Cyclops to hold him in his dark cave, the desire of the Phaiakians to keep him with them in their community outside of history. Odysseus must have *nous* and *aletheia*, intelligence and unforgetting, to endure.

These themes reappear in sublimated form with the advent of philosophers like Socrates and Plato. For despite their claim to have superceded such naive, primitive or mythopoeic habits of belief, these thinkers have recourse to a similar range of propadeutic techniques for establishing the sovereignty of rational discourse and – corollary to this – the inferior, duplicitous and error-prone character of bodily or sensuous perception. Above all, it is the woman's body which becomes a mere receptacle, a passive container for truths which can only be summoned to account (or achieve articulate form) through application of the various expert hermeneutical procedures deployed by the male philosopher. For the early Greeks, as duBois says,

> it may be the case that – if the female body is analogous to the interior of the earth, the interiority housing the dead and the not-yet-living, receiving the penis like the plow readying the earth for sowing – in such circumstances the woman cannot *know* truth. Perhaps she *is* truth, goddess of unconcealment called *Aletheia*, representing the fruits of the passage between light and dark without having access to those fruits herself. As such, she is like the slave under torture, the physical space, unknowable, inaccessible to the real subject of truth, yet through which the knower must pass in order to acquire truth. (pp. 82–3)

This acute piece of commentary should ring some alarm-bells for anyone who has read Derrida's *Spurs*, or other recent texts by male philosophers musing on the delightful prospects opened up by Nietzsche's famous query: 'What if truth were a woman?'[18] For it is not hard to see how such styles of talk among (no doubt well-meaning) male feminists can engender a discourse which is still subtly marked by that same distinction between knower and known – or that idea of 'woman' as the mute locus of truth – whose genealogy duBois lays open to view.

This belief is still firmly entrenched in Aristotle's metaphysics, whatever his far-reaching differences with Socrates and Plato as regards the validity of empirical cognition, the existence of innate or *a priori* ideas, and the issue of priority between these rival paradigms. For he nonetheless takes it as self-evident that women are 'defective' creatures by comparison with men, that they lack the male attributes of reason, soul, or enlightened self-understanding, and thus that any wisdom – any genuine knowledge – to be had from them must involve the male thinker in a corresponding effort of rational reconstruction.[19] And so it has come about that philosophers from Plato and Aristotle down have tended to represent the woman's mode of knowledge as a piecemeal, scattered or mutilated mode, a privative condition – as with those tantalizing fragments that survive of the pre-Socratics – which can only be restored to wholeness and truth through the saving ministry of (masculine) scholarship and reason. 'Like the slave body that needs the supplement of the *basanos* to produce truth, the female body and the fragmentary text are both constructed as lacking.' (p. 90) And techniques abound, now as ever, for ensuring that such patently anomalous instances do little to disrupt the smooth succession of interpretive mastery and power.

Nevertheless, duBois argues, the time is now ripe for mounting a challenge to the phallocentric values and beliefs that have so far held this tradition firmly in place.

Recent literary theory has rendered the reading of the fragments of early ancient philosophers more possible, even more pleasurable. It has celebrated the fragmentary. Perhaps because of the rediscovery of Nietzsche, that eccentric philologist, work on contemporary culture has recognized the aesthetic particularity of the fragment. The very search for integrity and indivisibility in all things has been called into question by the heirs of Nietzsche, among them those feminists who see the emphasis on wholeness and integrity, on the whole body, as a strategy of scholarship that has traditionally excluded the female, who has been identified as different, heterogeneous, disturbing the integrity of the scholarly body, incomplete in herself. . . . The project of scientific textual studies has been to supply the text's lack, to reduce the fragmented, partial quality of embodied, material texts, to reject the defective text as it rejected the defective female. (pp. 94–5)

DuBois finds the same residual violence at work in those present-day schools of hermeneutic thought, inspired very largely by Heidegger, where truth is conceived as the questing-back for an authentic, primordial wisdom whose traces can still be deciphered in the language of some few poets and philosophers. Thus for Heidegger the only means of access to such truth is through a rapt, brooding style of commentary that allows language (or certain languages, notably the Greek and German) to manifest what must otherwise be hidden from view at this late – perhaps terminal – stage in the history of 'Western metaphysics'.[20] That history is conceived as a process of epochal decline, a falling-away from the Edenic state when language was the 'dwelling-house' of Being, when truth shone forth without the intercession of abstract metaphysical concepts and categories, and when poets (the pre-Socratic thinkers among them) gave voice to a wisdom as yet untouched by the corrosive spirit of Socratic rationalism. Thus Heidegger's etymopoeic play on the Greek *aletheia* – on the notion of truth as 'unconcealment', 'unhiddenness', or 'bringing-to-light' – is an index (for duBois) of the way that his thought surreptitiously repeats one of the germinal motifs of Western intellectual tradition while claiming to transform its most basic constitutive values and assumptions.[21] What Heidegger has achieved, on this reading, is not so much a wholesale revaluation of 'Western metaphysics' as a drawing-forth of the latent metaphor that has always underlain that discourse, and whose darker meaning duBois finds implicit in the equation between torture and truth.

III

It is worth pausing awhile at this stage in her argument since it brings out the odd combination of insight and blindness that runs through so much of duBois' philosophical commentary. I adopt Paul de Man's terminology here since the same point is made – albeit from a slightly different angle – in the latter's essay 'Heidegger's Exegeses of Hölderlin', a text that likewise has much to say about the kinds of appropriative violence involved in such depth-hermeneutical readings.[22] De Man shows with exemplary precision how Heidegger mistakes the sense of certain crucial passages in Hölderlin; how he reads the poet as having *actually stated* (or claimed to state) the 'essence of Being', where in fact what we find are negative or subjunctive constructions, forms of utterance which express the desire to attain such ultimate, self-present, unmediated truth, but which perforce acknowledge the sheer impossibility that this should ever be the case. What prevents it from occurring, de Man argues, is the ontological gulf that opens up between word and world, subject and object, thought (or language) and the realm of primordial intuitions to which thinking in the Heideggerian mode endlessly and vainly aspires. Literature is the most 'authentic', that is to say, the least deluded mode of understanding insofar as it exists on the far side of this commonplace phenomenalist error, this tendency to suppose that language – especially poetic language – can somehow gain access to the realm of sensuous cognition, or transcend all those hateful antinomies that plague the discourse of plain-prose reason. On the contrary, de Man asserts: it is precisely by resisting such notions – by exposing them as a form of 'aesthetic ideology', a deep-laid but nonetheless erroneous and seductive habit of thought – that poets like Hölderlin advert us to the dangers of that drive for interpretive mastery and power which lurks within 'totalizing' figures like metaphor and symbol.[23]

What Heidegger thus fails to recognize (in common with many mainstream academic interpreters of Romanticism) is the extent to which these claims are 'always already' deconstructed by the workings of a certain counter-rhetoric, an 'allegory of reading' whose salient figures are metonymy, irony and allegory itself, and which implicitly acknowledges the failure of language to attain that wished-for condition of immediate, transcendent, self-authorized truth. Nor is this merely a technical issue in the field of post-Romantic aesthetics and literary theory. For according to de Man there is a close affinity – particularly close in Heidegger's case – between, on the one hand, this hermeneutic drive which assimilates language to the order of sensuous perception or revealed truth, and on the other that will to 'aestheticize politics' whose expression all too readily takes the form of mystified proto-nationalist creeds and ideologies. So it was that Heidegger regarded only two languages (the ancient Greek and modern German) as sufficiently authentic or possessed of adequate spiritual resources to serve as a vehicle for truth's unveiling through the kind of 'fundamental ontology' that would think its way back through and beyond the inherited conceptual baggage of 'Western metaphysics'. This belief went along with a profound contempt for the values of Enlightenment reason and critique, values that were, or that sought to become, wholly cosmopolitan in character, and whose truth-claims rested on their presumed appeal to the widest generality of human interests in the 'public sphere' of informed rational debate. To Heidegger's way of thinking that tradition appeared nothing more than the history of an error, one that had its origin much further back, in Plato's abandonment of the pre-Socratic *aletheia* for an epistemic doctrine of truth conceived as idea, as theory, correspondence or adequate representation. Following Nietzsche, and followed in turn by Foucault and the avatars of post-structuralism, Heidegger envisaged an imminent end to such notions, a wholesale 'transvaluation of values' that would unseat the subject (the knowing, willing and judging subject of Kantian discourse), and would thus restore language to its rightful preeminence as the authentic voice of Being and truth. But in so doing – as de Man sees it – he fell prey to a form of national-aestheticist appropriative thought which identified such truth with the sovereign claim of *one particular* language, supposedly marked out by its privileged relation to the ancient Greek sources of wisdom.[24]

Hence Heidegger's misreading of those passages in Hölderlin, brought about not so much by mere lack of attention to the sacrosanct 'words on the page', but rather by a single-minded will to reveal what those words *must mean* in accordance with Heidegger's overriding interpretive aim. It would be wrong, therefore, to treat them as 'mistakes' in the sense of that term which properly applies in the case of interpreters or scholar-critics who simply do not read with adequate care and attention. On the contrary: these are symptomatic *errors* whose source lies deep within the governing premises of Heidegger's entire philosophical project, and which thus require something more than an effort of localized corrective exegesis. What they reveal is a characteristic alternating pattern of 'blindness and insight', a pattern whereby the critical reader – or the deconstructionist alert to such signs of non-coincidence between meaning and intent – may in turn arrive at a better understanding of the interests at stake in this exemplary scene of misprision, or the kinds of aberration that typically result when a strong revisionist like Heidegger sets about interpreting a poet like Hölderlin. At this level of thought, de Man contends, there may be more truth to be gained from a reading that demonstrably *gets the text wrong* – that elides certain pointedly modal constructions, or mistakes (say) a subjunctive for a declarative utterance – than from readings whose show of *à la lettre* scholarly scruple goes along with an indifference to such issues of depth-hermeneutical concern. But the fact remains that Heidegger has enlisted Hölderlin's poetry in the service of a grandiose historico-philosophical theme – that of Being, its occlusion by 'Western metaphysics', and its bringing-to-light through a sustained meditation on the kinship between Greek and German source-texts – which leads him to ignore certain crucial linguistic details that would otherwise threaten to destabilize his project at source. And that project is one whose political resonance can hardly be ignored, given what we now know of Heidegger's sympathy with the National Socialist cause and his conduct as Rektor of Freiburg University in the years following Hitler's accession to power.

De Man has nothing explicit to say with regard to these matters that have lately been the subject of so much intensive factual-documentary research.[25] But his essay leaves no doubt of what de Man sees as the link between Heidegger's interpretive procedures – the strain of hermeneutic 'violence' that runs through his essays on Hölderlin, Rilke and others – and the notion of a manifest destiny which speaks through certain privileged national cultures and languages. The effects of such thinking are visible not only in the way that Heidegger misreads his texts but also in his willingness, for however short a period, to endorse the kind of mystified organicist rhetoric, the potent mythology of 'blood and soil', which played a large role in Nazi cultural propaganda. Hence de Man's seemingly extravagant claim in the essays of his last decade: that rhetorical close-reading in the deconstructive mode was the best safeguard against those forms of 'aesthetic ideology' which started out with Schiller's simplified redaction of Kantian themes, and whose upshot could be seen in Heidegger's espousal of a full-blown national-aestheticist creed. For what this history demonstrates is that 'aesthetic education by no means fails'; that on the contrary 'it succeeds too well, to the point of hiding the violence that makes it possible'.[26] And again, with reference to Schiller's *Letters on Aesthetic Education*: 'the "state" that is here being advocated is not just a state of mind or of soul, but a principle of political power and authority that has its own claim on the shape and the limits of our freedom'.[27]

We should therefore be wrong to adopt the line of least resistance taken by those commentators on the Heidegger 'affair' who acknowledge the fact of his Nazi involvement — having indeed little choice with all the evidence to hand — but who treat it as a passing aberration, a blindness brought about by moral and political naivete, but not (these apologists would have us believe) by anything integral to his thinking on matters of 'authentic', depth-hermeneutical import. In de Man's view, conversely, 'the ineffable demands the direct adherence and the blind and violent passion with which Heidegger treats his texts'.[28] What a deconstructive reading aims to demonstrate is the *resistance* that those texts may yet put up to any such mystified ontology of Being and truth, or any project, like Heidegger's, premised on the notion of a direct, unmediated access to truth vouchsafed to some privileged interpretive community or company of knowing exegetes. For there is always the risk — most evident in Heidegger's case — that the act of laying claim to such presumptive truth-telling warrant will then lead on to a wholesale mystique of linguistic or national origins, a 'jargon of authenticity' (in Adorno's phrase) with clearly-marked racial-suprematist overtones. All of which gives some point to de Man's otherwise preposterous assertion: that 'more than any other mode of inquiry . . . the linguistics of literariness is a powerful and indispensable tool in the unmasking of ideological aberrations, as well as a determining factor in accounting for their occurrence'.[29]

I have allowed myself this lengthy detour through de Man's reading of Heidegger since up to a point it runs strikingly parallel to duBois' argument in *Torture and Truth*. The resemblance should be obvious enough from what I have said about her book so far. Thus duBois — like de Man — finds reason to mistrust any notion of truth that locates it in a realm of 'deep' ontological concern, a realm to which thinkers can only gain access by some mode of authentic revelation. For this idea very easily lends itself to the purposes of a racist, sexist or caste-based social order whose maintenance involves the rigid distinction between those who can actually *know* truth as a matter of inward or spiritual possession, and those others — whether slaves, women or non-Aryans — who are denied such access by the fact of their belonging to some alien (inferior) group, and who can only bear witness to truth through techniques of physical or bodily coercion. This violence is often close to the surface in Heidegger's oracular style, as with the following passage from *Being and Time*:

Truth (uncoveredness) is something that must always first be wrested from entities. Entities get snatched out of their hiddenness. The factical uncoveredness of anything is always, as it were, a kind of *robbery*. Is it accidental that when the Greeks express themselves as to the essence of truth, they use a *privative* expression – *a-letheia*? (cited by duBois, p. 132)

DuBois' main purpose in citing this passage (along with several others to similar effect) is to bring out the irony – or the curious pattern of compulsive repetition – that attends Heidegger's claim to have transvalued the legacy of Western metaphysical thought. For that claim rests largely on his reading of Plato as the thinker who first broke away from the pre-Socratic teaching of truth as *aletheia*; who subjected it to the 'violence' of a new metaphysics, an epistemic order grounded in the notions of truth as Idea, as correspondence or accurate representation; and who thus set the course for all subsequent variations on this theme, including – as Heidegger reads it – the emergent relation between science (or technology) and the discourse of 'enlightened' reason.[30] But what looms through the language of Heidegger's strong-revisionist reading is a strain of equally 'violent' appropriative thought, a hermeneutics of enforced submission and disclosure whose will-to-power over Plato's text repeats the very gesture that Heidegger locates at the origin of Western (i.e., Platonist) metaphysics. And it does so not by reason of some short-term failure of moral or political intelligence on Heidegger's part, but as a result of his commitment to a truth-telling ethos which governs his project at every stage, and whose effect – like de Man's ubiquitous dialectic of 'blindness' and 'insight' – cannot be ascribed to any such merely contingent episode of thought.

DuBois brings these issues into focus in her brief account of Heidegger's argument as developed in the 1947 essay 'Plato's Doctrine of Truth'. The crucial text here is the well-known 'Allegory of the Cave' where Plato elaborates a series of binary oppositions – truth/falsehood, knowledge/ignorance, reason/ rhetoric, reality/appearance, adequate ideas *versus* sensuous or phenomenal perceptions etc. – by way of establishing philosophy's role as supreme dispenser of authentic wisdom and truth.[31] These oppositions are subsumed under a governing metaphor (light/darkness) which depicts us as self-condemned prisoners of the cave, our gaze averted from the Sun – the natural light of reason – and instead fixed upon the flickering play of artificial images and illusions that pass for reality among those who trust to the fallible evidence of the senses. Philosophy can lead us outside the cave insofar as it grants access to a realm of eternal 'forms' or 'ideas', a knowledge only possible on condition that we reject such forms of delusive commonsense assurance. And it is here, in this strenuous effort to wrest truth away from the domain of phenomenal cognition, that Heidegger reads the advent of a new epistemology, one whose character is indelibly marked by a certain metaphysical violence, a will-to-power that was absent from the earlier (pre-Socratic) ethos of truth as *aletheia*, as the coming-to-light through a process of unforced contemplative wisdom. As duBois puts it, paraphrasing Heidegger:

> In Plato's representation of the attaining of truth, 'everything depends on the shining of the phenomenon and the possibility of its visibleness'. Notions of outward appearance, *eidos*, *idea* come to the fore. . . . Unhiddenness is thus attached to perception, to *seeing*. The *idea* becomes 'the master of *aletheia*', and '*aletheia* comes under the yoke of the *idea*'. In this shift in the notion of truth, the essence of truth is no longer the unfolding of unhiddenness, but rather resides in the essence of the idea. Truth is the correctness of the gaze, not a feature of beings themselves. And this kind of truth, truth as correctness, becomes the dominant paradigm for Western philosophy. (p. 133)

But Heidegger betrays this insight by himself resorting to a language of 'unhiddenness', of truth as the possession of those few elect spirits who can penetrate the veil of mere bodily or sensuous appearance, and thus give voice to a wisdom withheld from Plato and the metaphysicians. And there is another, more literal kind of violence that is never far away when Heidegger, like Plato, describes the process by which philosophy arrives at such truth. For it is always a matter of somehow *coercing* the subject, inducing him or her (by whatever propadeutic means) to abandon the cave, emerge into the daylight realm of 'authentic' understanding, and acknowledge their hitherto benighted condition of enslavement to a false epistemology.

Thus Heidegger's 'nostalgia' for the pre-Socratics is capable of two very different interpretations. On the one hand it is possible to take him at his word, in the manner of convinced Heideggerians, as having revealed the 'violence' implicit in Plato's allegory of the cave and offered in its place 'a meditative appreciation of truth uncovering, discovering, unconcealing itself' (p. 135). On the other one can essay a symptomatic reading which finds that violence to be still operative in Heidegger's text, despite all his overt disavowals. On this account, as duBois argues,

> Heidegger shares in the sense of the truth as something withheld, obscured in daily life, participates in the religious as opposed to the dialogical truth. . . . It is this kind of truth that resides in oracles, and even in the tortured body, not in democratic debate, in conversation. The truth is elsewhere, and must un-hide itself, or be un-hidden, forced out from secrecy. (p. 135)

In which case the apologists for Heidegger are surely mistaken when they seek to represent his period of Nazi involvement as nothing more than a contingent or 'factical' episode, one that may justify criticism on moral grounds – to the point of regarding him, in Rorty's picturesque phrase, as a 'Schwarzwald redneck' – but which scarcely impinges on his 'deeper' philosophical concerns.[32] DuBois very rightly rejects such arguments, insisting that we cannot (or should not) allow this artificial dichotomy between 'life' and 'work', and that with Heidegger the relationship is plain to see for anyone not wholly given over to the spell of his oracular pronouncements. To pretend otherwise is simply to collude in that potent mystique of Being, origins and truth which not only led Heidegger so grievously astray but played an active role in the dissemination of Nazi cultural propaganda. Moreover, it did so by exploiting those same suasive devices – *Völkisch* etymologies, techniques of subliminal suggestion, appeals to an 'authentic' pseudo-wisdom contained in the collective (racial) unconscious – which Heidegger deployed in his writings early and late.[33] Thus:

> the view of *aletheia* as discovery, as unhiddenness, as revealing, consistent as it is with the ancient practice of slave torture, with a mystical vision of the secret nature of truth, its residence elsewhere, or even its being the revelation itself – all these support an antidemocratic position, a fascination with secrecy and violence. (p. 140)

This is not to say that we should read Heidegger's work solely in terms of his Nazi involvement, a view that duBois thinks overly reductive and in any case unable to account for that work's widespread and continuing influence. But it does mean that we should attend more closely to those 'absences and commitments' in the Heideggerian project which 'gain resonance when understood in light of his acts, the "social text" within which his philosophical position was generated' (p. 139). For it then becomes evident – despite all his apologists' protestations to the contrary – that Heidegger's mystified ontology of Being and truth bears a more than contingent (and certainly more than metaphorical) relation to his period of National Socialist allegiance.[34]

IV

DuBois book seems to me both important and timely in the context of present-day critical debate. Above all, it serves as a useful reminder of the way that irrationalist doctrines can resurface in the guise of a 'radical' interpretive theory – or a strong-revionisist hermeneutic – whose appeal derives largely from its specious claim to transvalue all received or existing categories of thought. We have heard a great deal of such talk just recently, most of it from thinkers in the postmodern or post-structuralist camp who themselves follow Heidegger, wittingly or not, in their zeal to have done with such outworn 'enlightenment' notions as truth, knowledge, critique, ideology, and the subject (the 'bourgeois-humanist' subject) as imaginary locus of these and other obsolete ideas. Insofar as it recalls the specific prehistory of Heidegger's counter-enlightenment turn – its origins in a mystical cult of unreason with suspect political undertones – this book makes a welcome intervention and one that may actually help to change a few minds.

However, her argument runs into problems at those points where it tends to suggest that *any* kind of truth-seeking discourse – any project beholden to values of veridical utterance, valid understanding, or genuine knowledge as distinct from mere opinion or belief – necessarily partakes of the same bad legacy that shadows Heidegger's thinking. This is why the ancient Greek sophists figure large among the victims and heroes of duBois' narrative: victims of the ridicule – the 'enormous condescension of posterity' – inflicted upon them at hands of philosophers from Socrates and Plato down, and heroes on account of their incipient democratic stand, their refusal (*contra* the autocrats of reason) to elevate some self-proclaimed ultimate 'truth' above the conduct of everyday public debate or open participant exchange. For duBois – as likewise for current neopragmatists like Rorty and Fish – the sophists got it pretty much right, at least insofar as 'getting it right' is pragmatically redefined as a sensible desire to keep the 'cultural conversation' going and not allow truth-claims, theories or principles of whatever variety to get in the way.[35] Once acknowledge this and there will seem little point in continuing to talk in that old, self-deluding style.

Thus in Rorty's view, our last best hope as 'postmodern' intellectuals is to cultivate the private virtues (compassion, tolerance, a measure of irony with regard to our own pet beliefs) and renounce all those grandiose Enlightenment ideas of setting the world to rights. Such is Rorty's recommendation for the citizens of a 'post-philosophical' culture which has witnessed, among other things, the chronic obsolescence of Kantian or Marxist *Ideologiekritik*, the exhaustion of foundationalist paradigms (or metaphors), and the definitive collapse of any hopes once vested in the progressive or emancipatory uses of reason. Given all this we had much better make a virtue of the public/private dichotomy, and not seek vainly for some means of overcoming it by harking back to a byegone epoch when intellectuals (at least in their own estimation) still ruled the roost.

The following paragraph from his recent book *Contingency, Irony, and Solidarity* puts the message in a nutshell.

Authors like Kierkegaard, Nietzsche, Baudelaire, Proust, Heidegger and Nabokov are useful as exemplars, as illustrators of what private perfection – a self-created, autonomous human life – can be like. Authors such as Marx, Mill, Dewey, Habermas and Rawls are fellow citizens rather than exemplars. They are engaged in a shared social effort – the effort to make our institutions and practices more just and less cruel. We shall only think of these two kinds of writers as *opposed* if we think that a more comprehensive philosophical outlook would let us hold self-creation and justice, private perfection and human solidarity, in a single vision. . . . [But] there is no way in which philosophy, or any other theoretical discipline, will ever let us do that. The closest we will come to joining these two quests is to see the aim of a just and free society as letting its citizens be as privatistic, 'irrationalist', and aestheticist as they please just so long as they do it on their own time – causing no harm to others and using no resources needed by those less advantaged.[36]

Rorty sees nothing but error and delusion in the attempt to link up these disparate spheres and to argue for a politics – or a generalized 'theory' of justice, social interests, emancipatory values or whatever – that would some-how bridge the private/public dichotomy. Much better to accept that we do most good (or at any rate least harm) by acknowledging the failure of all such schemes to date and the unlikelihood that anyone is about to come up with some theory that will finally provide all the answers. Hence Rorty's pragmatist mistrust of truth-claims in any shape or form, especially those sorts of argument – characteristic of philosophers in the Kantian line of descent – which take it for granted that there *must* be some relation between the individual quest for 'enlightened' self-knowledge and the interests of social justice. For such ideas have a twofold harmful effect, on the one hand pro-moting the inflated self-image of philosophers, intellectuals, social theorists, 'vanguard' ideologues etc., and on the other giving rise to a 'principled' contempt for those values (like social solidarity and citizenly virtue) which, in Rorty's view, require no justification beyond the simple fact that they provide us with a sense of communal purpose and identity.[37] Where the theorists go wrong is in underrating the importance of shared aspirations (or consensus beliefs), and in thinking to offer some workable alternative grounded in notions of truth, reason, or emancipatory critique.

That this just cannot be done, since no such 'grounds' are available, is the lesson which Rorty finds everywhere manifest in the history of enlightened (or 'foundationalist') thinking to date. Moreover, it is a project that should not even be attempted, since the failures have a nasty habit of producing untoward real-world effects, at worst revolutionary terrors and at best the kinds of planned, interventionist policy-making that likewise constitute an unwarranted intrusion upon 'private' liberties and desires.[38] This is why Rorty welcomes what he sees as the shift from a culture misguidedly fixated on 'philosophical' ideas of reason and truth to one that finds its main source of imaginative stimulus in poets, novelists and those borderline writers – Nietzsche, Heidegger(!) and Derrida among them – who likewise exemplify the passage 'beyond' philosophy as a specialized discipline of thought. It is here that we find a range of useful 'exemplars', of more or less attractive role-models, 'illustrators' (as Rorty puts it) 'of what private perfection – a self-created, autonomous human life – can be like'. But they also remind us – writers like Orwell and Nabokov especially – of the risks that go along with any attempt to theorize or legislate for other persons (let alone for humanity in general) on the basis of one's privately-cherished tastes, principles or beliefs. If the worst thing we do is cause pain or suffering to others – which Rorty takes as the one such belief on which liberals should all agree – then the novelists have on the whole done a better job than the philosophers, theorists and culture-critics in bringing this lesson home. For it is the chief merit of imaginative literature that it tends to shy away from abstract truths and focus on the kinds of human situation – particular characters in particular contexts – that stubbornly resist such presumptive universalist claims.[39]

This is Rorty's point in the above-quoted passage where he lines up various authors on either side of the public/private dichotomy. His argument appears scrupulously even-handed in crediting the systematic thinkers – Marx, Mill, Habermas, and Rawls – with a decent share of citizenly virtues, while the others (poets, novelists and hybrids like Nietzsche and Heidegger) carry on the project of 'private' self-fashioning in a realm safely apart. But the appearance is deceptive, as so often with Rorty's use of this favourite rhetorical construction ('on the one hand . . . on the other') to disguise what is in fact a very marked preference for the second alternative. The best-known example is his opening sequence in the essay 'Philosophy as a Kind of Writing' where Rorty defines the opposition in terms of 'constructive' *versus* 'edifying' discourse.[40] On the one hand are those thinkers (Plato, Kant and company) who set out to argue a knock-down case or to offer definitive solutions to genuine, 'philosophical' problems; on the other an assortment of stylish rhetoricians – Nietzsche and Derrida among them – who proceed by scoring points off their earnest-minded colleagues and who claim nothing more (as Rorty reads them) than to give the conversation a novel twist or supply fresh metaphors in place of some old, henceforth obsolete style of talk. The former still think of philosophy as a discipline, a *Fach*, a specialized subject-area with its own specific kinds of argumentative rigour and its own range of problems requiring a degree of specialized intellectual grasp. The latter tend to view it as just one 'discourse' among others, a language-game uncommonly prone to delusions of moral and epistemological grandeur, but one which still has something to contribute so long as it gives up those old ideas and converses on a level with poetry, literary criticism, or the 'human sciences' at large.

Rorty starts out in equable fashion by presenting these alternatives as each having its own prehistory, its range of currently available options, and its own kinds of claim upon the interest of readers inclined toward one or the other persuasion. But as the essay goes on this even-handedness gives way to a clear preference for the second (deconstructive or 'post-philosophical') outlook, not least on account of what Rorty sees as its willingness to tolerate the other party – those 'serious', truth-seeking types – just so long as they do not try to hog the conversation. All the same he clearly thinks that they would do much better, or be less inclined to indulge such unfortunate habits, if they could somehow be brought around to the pragmatist viewpoint, i.e., that 'truth' is just an honorific name for what we happen to believe at the moment, and that truth-talk is only of use insofar as it lends an added measure of suasive or rhetorical appeal. For behind Rorty's arguments there is a deep suspicion that *any* such talk, whatever its supposed 'grounds' or evidential criteria, is inherently prone to generate the kinds of narrow, dogmatic, self-authorizing truth-claim that have played such a prominent role in the history of human suffering and oppression. Like duBois, he goes along with the Nietzschean-Foucauldian 'genealogy' of power/knowledge, the idea that truth is nothing more than a rhetorical place-filler, a ruse adopted by the will-to-power in its struggle to silence or marginalize opposing voices. Among philosophers, this strategy most often takes the form of pretending that arguments, principles or truth-values can be simply read off from the text in hand, as if they existed *sub specie aeternitatis* in some realm of idealized concepts and categories immune to the vagaries of 'literary' interpretation. This is why Rorty finds Derrida such a useful ally: because he constantly reminds us that philosophy is indeed just another 'kind of writing', one that makes a point of disavowing its textual, metaphorical or fictive aspects since these tend to undermine its favoured self-image as a discourse specialized in questions of ultimate truth. And the results are even more damaging, Rorty contends, when this attitude is translated into socio-political terms, as with thinkers in the high rationalist tradition (Plato, Kant and Marx among them) who presume to criticize or legislate in matters of real-world communal concern.

On this point he concurs with Popper's diagnosis in *The Open Society and its Enemies*: that any theory claiming privileged access to the 'truth' of our historical situation – as opposed to its contingent, short-term, or 'ideological' appearances – is complicit with the worst, most brutal forms of totalitarian thought-control.[41] Such ideas are profoundly anti-democratic insofar as they authorize some few thinkers – philosophers, theorists, vanguard intellectuals – to set the agenda for informed debate. Hence the natural affinity, as Rorty sees it, between pragmatism (as a 'post-philosophical' outlook very much in the native American grain) and democracy conceived as an ethos of open 'conversational' exchange where participants qualify mainly by virtue of their willingness to leave off talking about 'truth', 'reason', 'ideology' or suchlike notions, and their desire to play by the current (consensus-based) rules of the game. Hence also his distinctly double-edged attitude to thinkers like Habermas and Rawls, those whom he reads as half-way pragmatists, hoping to keep faith with the 'unfinished project of modernity' even while acknowledging the linguistic turn and the force of recent communitarian or anti-foundationalist arguments.[42] Such figures deserve credit, as he concedes in the above-cited passage, for their role as citizen-philosophers, their effort to sustain the cultural conversation at a 'public' or generalized level of address. But Rorty clearly thinks of them as still being hooked on a set of quasi-universalist ideas – truth, justice, progress, enlightenment, 'real' as opposed to 'false' (or 'ideological') interests and beliefs – which show through despite their apparent conversion to a better, less arrogant way of thinking. This is why his book has a lot more to say about the benefits of a 'private' morality which on principle eschews such large (potentially coercive) designs, and whose exemplars – poets or novelists chiefly, but also such rogue philosophers as Nietzsche and Derrida – think of 'truth' as a topic of no great interest compared with the business of providing new metaphors, language-games, or styles of creative self-description. These writers have the signal merit, in Rorty's view, of keeping the conversation open and not seeking to force their novel ideas on anyone who happens (for equally 'private' reasons of their own) to prefer some alternative language-game.

Thus by playing off (for example) Kundera against Heidegger – or just about any poet or novelist against just about any philosopher – he can point up the message over and again: that the seekers-after-truth are on balance less conducive to the communal good (more apt to impose their own pet doctrine) than the modest providers of a salutary lesson in the variety of human beliefs, interests, values and private satisfactions. For these latter have no axe to grind, no ultimate moral to impart, save the virtue of seeing around this or that topic from as many viewpoints as possible, and not giving in to the bad old desire for some ultimate God's-eye perspective. 'From Kundera's point of view,' as Rorty puts it,

> the philosopher's essentialistic approach to human affairs, his attempt to sub-stitute contemplation, dialectic, and destiny for adventure, narrative, and chance, is a disingenuous way of saying: what matters for me takes precedence over what matters for you, entitles me to ignore what matters to you, because I am in touch with something – reality – with which you are not. The novelist's rejoinder to this is: it is comical to believe that one human being is more in touch with something nonhuman than another human being. It is comical to use one's quest for the ineffable Other as an excuse for ignoring other people's quite different quests. It is comical to think that *anyone* could transcend the quest for happiness, to think that any theory could be more than a means to happiness, that there is something called Truth which transcends pleasure and pain. The novelist sees us as Voltaire saw Leibniz, as Swift saw the scientists of Laputa, and as Orwell saw the Marxist theoreticians – as comic figures. What is comic about us is that we are making ourselves unable to see things which everybody else can

see – things like increased or decreased suffering – by convincing ourselves that these things are mere 'appearances'.[43]

Of course there is nothing casual about Rorty's choice of Kundera as a spokesman for this strikingly Bakhtinian idea of the novel as a 'polyphonic' discourse-genre, a melange of narrative styles and viewpoints that cannot be reduced to any single, self-validating voice of authority and truth. Indeed one might remark that here, as so often, Rorty is hammering the pragmatist lesson home with a force and insistence that suggest some kind of performative contradiction. The message comes through with that shrewdly placed reference to Orwell and the typecast 'Marxist theoreticians': that theory always makes for dogma, conformity, and the unchecked exercise of political power, while fiction – especially Kundera's style of tricksy postmodernist narrative – resists such forms of 'monological' discourse through its openness to the sheer diversity of human values and motivating interests. If we could only get to view those truth-seeking types from a comic (or absurdist) perspective, then their ideas would rapidly fall into place as so many curious exhibits in the showcase of outworn intellectual foibles. Novelists are the best anti-philosophers since they are able to expose such *idées fixes* by attaching them to various self-deluded characters, like those who throng the pages of Dickens or Kundera, and then letting the comedy work itself out in the absence of explicit authorial comment. But philosophers can help this process along, at least to the extent that they espouse Derrida's laid-back 'textualist' line and exploit the tradition for what-ever it is worth in the way of joky anachronisms, punning etymologies, intertextual allusions and so forth. By adopting this stance – unlike their 'constructive', problem-solving, truth-fixated colleagues – they will avoid falling victim to the dangerous illusion that philosophy is the discipline uniquely equipped to dictate in matters of morality or politics.

There is much to be said – and I have said some of it elsehere – about the various problems with Rorty's attempt to cut philosophy down to size.[44] Discussion could begin with his highly partial (not to say distorted and opportunist) reading of Derrida; go on to criticize his vague notion that truth-claims come down to so many 'final vocabularies' (as opposed to *propositions* or structures of argument carried by such words in context); develop this point by remarking on the various simplified binary oppositions ('concept' *versus* 'metaphor', 'reason' *versus* 'rhetoric', 'philosophy' *versus* 'literature', 'public' *versus* 'private' etc.) which so often stand in for the work of detailed analytical argument; and then – most importantly – draw out the moral and political consequences of Rorty's rejection of truth-values (or the claims of enlightenment critique) in favour of a neopragmatist appeal to what's 'good in the way of belief'. Other commentators – Roy Bhaskar among them – have approached his work along similar critical lines, showing how it sidesteps crucial issues in the areas of epistemology, philosophy of language, history of science, ethical theory and related disciplines.[45] Rorty would of course dismiss such charges as utterly beside the point, or as evidence that his critics had not yet caught up with the new (postmodern-neopragmatist) rules of the game. But this insouciant way of heading off objections – from whatever philosophical, moral or political quarter – seems to me little more than an ingenious variant of the standard ruse by which sophists through the ages have managed to avoid being drawn into arguments that would otherwise leave them bereft of any adequate response.

For Rorty, as hardly needs saying, any talk of 'sophistry' is a useless gambit on the part of his earnest opponents since the sophists belong to that same company of rhetoricians, anti-philosophers, or straightforward honest conversationalists whose reputation he is out to redeem from the scorn heaped upon them by philosophers from Socrates down. Like duBois, he thinks that we have nothing to lose – and everything to gain from the standpoint of an open, liberal-democratic polity – by dumping all that old philosophical baggage, along with the attitude of prosecuting zeal which has given the sophists (Rorty among them) such a bad name. And he is also pretty much in agreement with duBois on the matter of truth-claims in philosophy and their relation to the various forms and techniques of coercive or manipulative power. Rorty never pushes the 'truth = torture' equation to quite such a literal extreme. But he clearly assents to the general line of argument: that these two things have often gone together, with philosophers somehow complicit in the business of imposing truths on an ignorant and credulous people, or extracting them – in yet more sinister fashion – from the bodies of subjects deemed unfit to 'know' such truths for themselves. It will then follow plausibly enough that the interests of democracy are best served by abandoning (or, better still, reversing) those various 'self-evident' orders of priority that have hitherto propped up philosophy's claims as the discourse of reason and truth. Thus social 'solidarity' will henceforth appear more important, more conducive to the communal good, than any form of *Ideologiekritik*, any dissident viewpoint that argues its case on merely 'theoretical', abstract or principled grounds.[46] And by the same token we will then come to appreciate that rhetoric (not reason) is the bottom line of liberal-democratic talk; that metaphors (not concepts) are the linguistic coin in which shared social interests typically achieve their best, most creative expression; and that belief (not truth) is the sole court of appeal in any genuinely working participant democracy. Once acknowledge all this, Rorty contends, and there will no longer be the danger of a takeover-bid by the priests, commissars or zealots of a truth known only to themselves and the privileged few.

It seems to me that the argument might better be turned around to ask how it is that postmodernism, neopragmatism and other such products of the current *Zeitgeist* have attained the status of a ironcast orthodoxy among those presumed to know. For Rorty is undoubtedly swimming with the cultural tide, despite his fondness — shared with fellow pragmatists like Stanley Fish — for making the same point over and over again, as if against a massive and well-nigh unbudgeable weight of received opinion. But it will surely be apparent to any dedicated watcher of the intellectual scene that ideas like these are nowadays so firmly entrenched among 'advanced' thinkers in the humanistic disciplines that resistance to them is mostly treated, as Rorty himself tends to treat it, in tones ranging from reproof (mild or firm) to pitying fondness.[47] Quite simply, any talk of truth, reason, valid argument, critique or other such 'Enlightenment' notions is enough to mark one out as hopelessly *derrière-garde*, or as a last-ditch defender of some obsolete creed — some totalizing 'meta-narrative', in the current jargon — whose deplorable effects are witnessed everywhere around us, and whose imminent demise must surely be welcomed by all right-thinking persons.[48] 'Dogmatic relativism' is an absurd oxymoron, a conjunction of terms that cannot make sense by any standard of logical or straightforward commonsense accountability. But it is an apt enough description for the kind of reflex response that associates truth-claims of whatever kind with the workings of a brutal and arbitrary will-to-power whose effects may be read throughout the history of man's inhumanity to man. The fierce moral fervour that accompanies such arguments — and I think here of a book like Barbara Herrnstein Smith's *Contingencies of Value* — tends to suggest that this relativist orthodoxy has its own designs on the shape and limits of our intellectual freedom, or at least a strong desire to exclude opponents from the field of acceptable consensus belief.[49] The result is that its charges very often come back like a boomerang, applying much more to the relativist party than to those whose regard for the protocols of open, reasoned, truth-seeking debate prevents them from having easy resort to such unwarranted imputations.

Catherine Belsey takes a position squarely opposed to my own when she argues for a tactical alliance of interests between feminism, post-structuralism and a postmodern attitude of sceptical mistrust toward all such oppressive ('liberal-humanist') truth-claims. 'Our present is postmodern,' she writes. That is to say,

> it participates in the crisis of epistemology which has informed western culture since the aftermath of the Second World War. Both the Holocaust and Hiroshima produced a crisis of confidence in the Enlightenment version of history as a single narrative of the progressive enfranchisement of reason and truth. Where in these hideous episodes, and where in the subsequent squaring-up of the superpowers, equipped with their apocalyptic arsenals, were reason and truth to be found? Instead, two hundred years after the Enlightenment, history was seen to be an effect of conflicting interests after all, but interests defined on all sides as absolute certainties.[50]

But the question remains: *from what critical standpoint* can we offer such judgements on the monstrous folly of the arms-race, the exterminist 'logic' of deterrence-theory, or the war-crimes and acts of mass-murder committed in the name of some ultimate, all-justifying cause – National Socialism, racial purity, 'keeping the world safe for democracy', or whatever – whose 'absolute certainty' brooks no kind of reasoned counter-argument? Of course Belsey is right to regard these doctrines, along with their peremptory claims-to-truth, as among the most perverse and destructive forms of mass-induced psycho-pathology. She is also quite justified in viewing the record of modern (post-Enlightenment) history to date as in many ways a standing reproof to any version of the Whiggish meta-narrative stance, or the facile progressivist creed which ignores all the evidence and pins its faith to the inevitable triumph of reason, democracy and truth. But there is something decidedly odd about a case which argues from the manifest fact that such principles have not been carried into practice (or that they have often been perverted beyond recognition in the process) to an attitude of downright contempt for any 'discourse' that keeps those principles in view. And the oddity is compounded by Belsey's implicit appeal to standards of judgement – to factual, argumentative, moral, historical, and socio-political criteria – which would lack all conviction were it not for their reliance on the truth-claims of enlightened critique.

There are two main sources of confusion at work in this desire to have done with reason and truth in whatever philosophical guise. The first is the claim that 'Enlightenment' thinking has somehow been responsible for those various forms of injustice, cruelty and oppression whose origin should rather be sought in the outright *rejection* of Enlightenment values, most often – as with Heidegger – in favour of a potent irrationalist mystique grounded in notions of revealed truth, of national destiny, or of language (some single, privileged language) as the bearer of 'authentic' wisdom and truth. Insofar as any chapter of intellectual history can be thought of as having pointed the way to Auschwitz, Hiroshima and kindred barbarities, it is the line of counter-enlightenment thinking which runs from Nietzsche to Heidegger and other latterday apostles of unreason, and not – as postmodernists like Lyotard would have it – the tradition they set out to attack. The second confusion, closely allied to this, is the notion of 'Enlightenment' as a monolithic creed, a set of doctrines whose rigidly prescriptive and authoritarian character lays them open to the worst, most inhuman forms of socio-political implementation. But this reading is really little more than a travesty, ignoring as it does both the sheer variety of projects and arguments subsumed under that all-purpose label, and the way that these thinkers ceaselessly worked to question, challenge or problematize their own more taken-for-granted habits of belief.[51] At the furthest point of historical disillusionment it was even possible for one like Adorno – most rigorous and consequent of modern dialecticians – to impugn what he saw as the fateful complicity between reason in its 'positive' or affirmative aspect and the forces of destruction unleashed upon mind and nature alike by an implacable 'dialectic of enlightenment'.[52] To this extent his case might seem to fall square with the charges mounted against that tradition by postmodernists, neopragmatists, Foucauldians and others. Yet it is clear to any reader of Adorno's work that he is far from rejecting the claims of critical reason, seeking as he does to contest those forms of oppressive monological thought through a mode of 'negative dialectics' that subjects every truth-claim – its own propositions included – to a vigilant process of immanent critique. Nothing could be more alien to Adorno's thinking than the kinds of irrationalist or reflex anti-Enlightenment rhetoric which currently pass for advanced wisdom in many quarters of the postmodern cultural scene.

Hence the idea – almost an article of faith for those who adopt this line – that reason is somehow inextricably bound up with the workings of a malignant power/knowledge whose effects can be resisted only by refusing any part in that whole bad legacy. Thus, in Catherine Belsey's words,

> the Enlightenment commitment to truth and reason, we can now see, has meant historically a single truth and a single rationality, which have conspired in practice to legitimate the subordination of black people, the non-Western world, women. . . . None of these groups has any political interest in clinging to the values which have consistently undervalued *them*. The plurality of the postmodern, by contrast, discredits suprematism on the part of any single group. It celebrates difference of all kinds, but divorces difference from power. Postmodernism is in all these senses the ally of feminism.[53]

On the contrary, I would argue: postmodernism can do nothing to challenge these forms of injustice and oppression since it offers no arguments, no critical resources or validating grounds for perceiving them *as* inherently unjust and oppressive. In the end all this rhetoric of 'plurality' and 'difference' comes down to just another, more radical-sounding version of Rorty's neopragmatist message, that is to say, his advice that we should cultivate the private virtues – maximize the range of aesthetic satisfactions, autonomous lifestyles, modes of individual self-fulfilment etc. – and cease the vain effort to square those virtues with a sense of our larger (public, social, ethical or political) responsibilities. Postmodernism cannot do other than promote this view insofar as it rejects the principle advanced by critical-enlightenment thinkers from Kant to Habermas: namely, that the exercise of reason in its practical (or ethico-political) aspect is such as to require our willing participation *both* as autonomous, reflective individuals *and* as members of a rational community whose interests transcend the private/public dichotomy. For it is precisely the virtue of this Kantian *sensus communis* to challenge the kinds of dogmatic or prejudicial thinking – in

Belsey's words, 'suprematism on the part of any single group' – that rests its authority on a direct appeal to the truth as vouchsafed to some racial, religious, social or other such dominant caste.

It may indeed be the case, as she argues, that 'Enlightenment' values have often been coopted in the service of some far from enlightened ends, from the pursuit of empire to those various strategies of containment applied to women, racial minorities, or dissident cultures of whatever kind. But it is just as clear – and her argument implicitly concedes as much – that these are *perversions and betrayals* of the enlightenment legacy, instances that may involve a spurious appeal to the rhetoric of truth, equality and freedom, but which 'in practice' stop far short of applying those standards in a uniform and consistent way. Nor is such consistency the product of a drive to homogenize social, cultural or gender-role differences through the enforced subjugation to a 'single truth and a single rationality' equated with the norms of Western ethnocentric or patriarchal order. On the contrary: it is only by applying these criteria – of logic, reason, and reflexive autocritique – that thought can resist the kinds of dogmatic imposition which derive their authority from a mystified resort to notions of absolute, transcendent truth. Any self-styled 'critical theory' that rejects such principles is in effect harking back to a pre-critical stage of consensus belief when truth was indeed whatever counted as such according to the dictates of this or that interest-group with the power to coerce or manipulate public opinion. In this respect, as Habermas convincingly argues, postmodernism is a retrograde cultural phenomenon which unwittingly runs into many of the dead-end antinomies encountered by thinkers in previous phases of anti-enlightenment reaction.[54] Worst of all, it embraces a thorough-going version of the Nietzschean–relativist creed according to which there is *simply no difference* between truth-claims imposed by sheer, self-authorizing fiat and truths arrived at by process of reasoned debate or open argumentative exchange.

For the effect of such thinking is to block any challenge to false or presumptive truth-claims, those which rest on a direct appeal to some ultimate source of wisdom, whether religious or secular, whose authority is placed beyond reach of counter-argument or criticism on social, political, historical or ethical grounds. Hence the persistent blind-spot in Foucault's sceptical genealogies of power/knowledge: namely, his tendency to level any distinction between the various types of social order – despotic, feudal, monarchical, liberal-democratic or whatever – all of which are treated as manifestations of that same implacable drive.[55] On the one hand this produces a marked fascination (also to be found in New Historicists like Stephen Greenblatt) with the exercise of power in its most 'spectacular', public or physically manifest forms, like the famous set-piece description from *Discipline and Punish* which I cited at the beginning of this essay.[56] Such gruesome evocations at least have the virtue – from Foucault's standpoint – of graphically displaying how power operates through mechanisms of overt subjection, surveillance and control, as distinct from those other, more 'enlightened' regimes where its workings are diffused through the various modes of sublimated power/knowledge. On the other hand it leads to an attitude of extreme scepticism with regard to those forms of self-styled progressive or emancipatory thought which propose – in the manner of critical philosophers from Kant to Habermas – that the interests of humanity are best served by exposing false or dogmatic claims-to-truth and allowing reason the maximum liberty to challenge orthodox consensual habits of belief. For Foucault, this amounts to nothing more than a piece of self-serving bourgeois-liberal ideology, a failure to perceive how the repressive apparatus has now become internalized to the point where subjects willingly consent to police their own thoughts, beliefs and desires in accordance with a new set of self-imposed disciplinary imperatives. Any Kantian notion that things are changing for the better – that, for instance, we have achieved a greater measure of humane insight in matters of sexual, psychiatric or sociological understanding – is treated by Foucault as the merest of illusions, brought about by our acceptance of the standard left-liberal or 'Enlightenment' line. Quite simply, there is no appeal to reason or truth – least of all in the human or the social sciences – which does not involve the conjoint appeal to a range of authorized 'discourses', defining both what shall count as veridical utterance and, by the same token, what must be seen as marginal, deviant, or lacking in the requisite kinds of disciplined self-knowledge. In which case (he urges) we should give up thinking in those old, self-deluding ways and learn the two main lessons of a Nietzschean–genealogical approach: firstly, that there is no 'truth' outside the force-field of contending discourses or representations, and secondly, that any kind of truth-talk is sure to perpetuate the in-place structures of authority and power.

V

Such, briefly stated, is the current *doxa* which unites the various schools of 'advanced' thinking from Foucauldian genealogy to post-structuralism, New Historicism and its British ('cultural materialist') counterpart. What is wrong with all this, as I have suggested above, is that it fails to take account of the crucial difference between truths imposed by arbitrary fiat, through presumptive access to *the Truth* as revealed to some authorized body of priests or commissars, and truth-claims advanced in the public sphere of open argumentative debate. By a curious irony, nothing could be more dogmatic – less willing to engage in debate of this kind – than the new ultra-relativist orthodoxy which allows its opponents the unenviable choice of figuring either as dupes or inquisitors, victims or agents of that will-to-power which masquerades as critical reason.

Norman Geras makes this point most effectively in his recent polemical rejoinder to Ernesto Laclau and Chantal Mouffe.[57] Geras has numerous objections to their work and to other such *soi-disant* 'post-Marxist' interventions from theorists of a broadly Foucauldian persuasion. For their aim as he sees it is to undermine every last category of socialist thought while claiming to offer a new kind of 'strategy', a politics of multiple, decentered 'discourses' which allows of no appeal to such old-fashioned notions as experience, class-interest, ideology, forces and relations of production, etc., replacing them with talk of 'subject-positions' constructed in and through the play of various (often conflicting) discursive alignments. Thus Laclau and Mouffe can go as far as to argue that there is *simply no relation* between class or gender as conceived in 'traditional' (i.e., Marxist or feminist) terms and the range of strategies that is now opened up for a 'democratic socialism' happily disabused of such 'essentialist' ideas and willing to take its chance with one or other of the discourses currently on offer. In short, there are as many subject-positions as there are points of conflict or tactical alliance within and between those shifting discursive registers. From which it follows, according to Laclau and Mouffe, that Marxism can only keep pace with these developments if it gives up its old truth-telling illusions – like that of a determinate reality beyond the realm of contending 'ideological' discourses – and accepts those discourses for what they are, the very arena of political action and choice.

Geras sees clearly what is at stake in this attempt to 'update' the categories of Marxist thought in line with the current postmodernist wisdom. More specifically, he sees how it amounts to a new kind of relativist orthodoxy, one that makes much of its 'democratic' or pluralist credentials while working to close off any possibility of reasoned counter-argument. Thus:

> Marxism and Marxists, for aspiring to cognitive objectivity, are held to lay claim to certainty, absolute knowledge, transparent access to truth and so on; whereas the theory of discourses, being (what I call) a cognitive relativism, is supposedly undogmatic, open and pluralist. . . . But, unlike faith and dogma, genuine knowledge is always provisional, subject to revision in the light of new information and evidence, needing periodically to be restructured, fallible; open therefore to 'pluralist' discussion and criticism, yet at the same time, pending possible rebuttal or revision, *knowledge* so far as we have managed to get. This aspiration, and all claims to knowledge in the sense just explained, are democratic by their nature, because they have to satisfy rules of consistency, external reference, evidence, that are accessible in principle to all, *public and accessible* – if sometimes only with difficulty – *as are the realities themselves to be known.*[58]

This seems to me a very cogent defence of objectivity and truth as the requisite criteria for any 'discourse' that seeks to make good its claims through the process of open participant debate, as opposed to the dogmatic imposition of truths known only to a privileged interpretive elite. For without such criteria – minimally those of 'consistency, external reference, evidence' etc. – there could be no gainsaying the argument that 'truth' is purely and simply what counts as such according to the current consensus-view or the authority of those with the power to enforce their own (self-interested) version thereof. The critique of scriptural revelation is perhaps the most telling instance of a progress brought about through the sustained application of exactly those enlightened truth-seeking standards, deployed – over many centuries – against sizable odds of entrenched belief and coercive institutional constraint.[59] Such thinking involved both the generalized principle that reason (not faith) was the best source of guidance in matters of intellectual conscience, and the specific endeavour to criticize false claims-to-truth in light of scholarly, historical, textual and documentary evidence.

It is ironic, to say the least, that these critical techniques grew up in close alliance to the kinds of philological enquiry which later gave rise to modern hermeneutics and the warring schools of present-day literary theory. For what has now come about is a curious reversal, a process of wholesale re-mystification, whereby the conventional lifting of truth-claims as applied to literary texts is taken as a paradigm instance of the way that 'discourses' circulate beyond all reach of factual or historical accountability. So it is that theorists like Laclau and Mouffe – along with post-structuralists, Foucauldians, New Historicists and others – can argue that 'reality' is entirely a construct of linguistic, discursive or textual representation, and can do so moreover confident in the knowledge that such claims will pass without challenge from thinkers up-to-date with the current wisdom. It is hardly surprising that Geras waxes indignant, given the way that these ideas have caught on among 'radical' theorists of various persuasion who show little grasp of their disabling political consequences. For at the end of the road these thinkers are travelling there is a choice of just two destinations, the one (after Rorty) marked 'North Atlantic postmodern bourgeois-liberal neopragmatist', or however one prefers to juggle those terms, while the other points back to a pre-modern phase of consensus-belief where issues of truth and falsehood give way to issues of authority and power. What becomes simply unthinkable, from this point of view, is the idea that reasoned argument or criticism could ever do more than provide handy psychological or rhetorical back-up for beliefs that already carry weight with a large enough proportion of the relevant 'interpretive community'.[60] In which case one might as well grasp the nettle – as Rorty does, but not (understand-ably) 'post-Marxists' like Laclau and Mouffe – and proclaim that 'ideology' is henceforth an empty notion, that consensus beliefs are all we have to go on, but that this is no cause for concern since 'we' postmodern-bourgeois liberals inhabit the best of all currently conceivable worlds.

Geras offers a fair (if scathing) account of what happens when relativism is raised into a high point of doctrine, a fixed idea that all talk of 'truth' has now been played off the field and that any opposition on reasoned argumentative grounds – in point of consistency, analytical rigour, historical grasp or whatever – signals a retreat to 'enlightenment' habits of thought. For these latterday sophists

> 'democratically' cut *everybody* off from access to what could meaningfully be called either truth or objectivity – with the single exception, dear to all relativists, of themselves. Overtly denying that there is any being-as-such, any in-itself, in terms of which competing discourses might be adjudicated, they install somewhere out of sight a secret tribunal of truth, mysterious in its ways, which allows *them* to judge here: as 'essentialist', hence *wrong about the nature of the world*; as economist, thus unable to understand the *reality* of the social; as determinist, therefore misconstruing history's *actual* openness etc.; which allows them to employ a language of external reference, of objectivity, of truth . . . which allows them that long, that tireless, that never-ending 'this is how it is' with which the relativist tells you why you cannot say 'this is how it is', thus sending knowledge and consistency to the devil.[61]

Geras's reference to the 'secret tribunal' – the dogmatic assurance that undergirds these relativist arguments despite their overt rhetoric – is of particular interest in light of what duBois has to say about the kinship between 'torture' and 'truth'. This case only holds, I would argue, for those kinds of truth-claim that shun the process of reasoned critical debate, and which stake their authority on a direct appeal to presumptive sources of revealed or self-authenticating truth. In other words, it applies well enough to the tradition which duBois traces down from its origins in ancient oracular or proto-philosophical thought, and whose avatars include not only the proponents of unquestioning religious faith but also those thinkers – Heidegger among them – who trade on a similar species of high-toned verbal mystification. For it is, as she writes, 'this ancient, traditional, religious view of truth – contested by democratic process, by selection according to lot, by mass debate in agora and assembly – that anchors philosophical practice, that of many of the pre-Socratics, that of Plato, that of his modern critic, Martin Heidegger' (duBois, p. 137). But her argument demonstrably misses the mark when duBois extends it, in the postmodern-pragmatist fashion, to cover all varieties of truth-claim save those that acknowledge their own contingent or derivative status, their ultimate reliance (according to Rorty) on the currency of in-place consensus belief. The effect of these ultra-relativist arguments is to throw thinking back to a stage of pre-critical tutelage where the only thing that counts is the trick of commanding assent through a rhetoric adapted to the purposes and interests of those with the *de facto* power to decide such matters.

This argument has a number of unfortunate consequences. One is the widespread tendency – manifest in Foucault's writing and in the work of New Historicists like Greenblatt – to treat 'power' and 'knowledge' as wholly interchangeable terms, and thereby to dismiss any index or criterion of civilized progress that involves the appeal to 'enlightened' values like reason, autonomy, or freedom of thought and speech. It is in this context that we can best understand the current fascination with the human body – most often, the body in pain or under physical duress – as a site where the various disciplinary practices (or regimes of instituted power/knowledge) are supposedly inscribed in most graphic and legible form. What these 'readings' amount to is a postmodern version of the arguments and the imagery of Hobbes's *Leviathan*, one that takes over his cynical analysis of the state as an instrument of collective self-discipline, his view of the subject as a point of intersection for various conflicting power-interests, and his use of bodily metaphors and allegories by way of enforcing this harshly 'realist' message.[62] Our contemporary theorists arrive at much the same conclusion by rejecting all ideas of autonomous judgement, of practical agency, knowledge, truth, or critique, and proclaiming that nothing can be thought outside the range of discourses or subject-positions imposed by some existing configuration of power/knowledge. All of which tends to bear out Habermas's claim: that in abandoning the 'unfinished project of modernity', these thinkers have not only renounced all warrant for criticizing false or deluded beliefs, but have also effectively reverted to an outlook predating the emergence of that same project.[63] In short, what they have taken as their operative norm – their bottom-line account of knowledge, truth and belief-formation – is precisely the kind of orthodox consensus-based polity which requires unthinking doctrinal adherence and which works to enforce such an attitude through forms of overt (or highly 'spectacular') physical coercion.

Hence the otherwise strange predilection – in Foucault and the New Historicists alike – for harrowing scenes of judicial torture or drawn-out public execution which are always recounted in a style of studious detachment, as if to emphasise the error of judging such episodes from our own, supposedly more humane or liberal viewpoint. Indeed, despite occasional protests to the contrary, there is often a sense in Foucault's writing that he wishes to reverse, not merely to suspend, those facile progressivist notions. Far from having left such barbarities behind, we have now moved on (so it appears) into a new and yet more oppressive disciplinary regime, a social order where subjects are required to monitor their own desires, dispositions and beliefs, and where the corrective applications of power/knowledge take the form of those various

'expert' discourses – psychoanalysis and the 'human sciences' among them –
whose will-to-power is disguised by a rhetoric of good-willed therapeutic
intent. All of this follows consistently enough from Foucault's five major
premises, namely: 1) the obsolescence of truth-claims in whatever 'enlightened'
or quasi-transcendental form; 2) the reduction of all such claims to so many
'discourses' indifferent with regard to veridical warrant; 3) the dispersal of the
subject – the Kantian knowing, willing and judging subject – over a range of
heterogenous 'subject-positions' likewise inscribed within this or that constitutive discourse; 4) the ubiquity of power/knowledge relations as the locus of
social and political struggle; and 5) the primacy of the body – the desiring,
suffering, subjugated body – as the site whereon those struggles are enacted in
their most direct and tangible form. Hence the tone of derisive, hard-bitten
cynicism which marks so many current pronouncements on the legacy of so-
called 'Enlightenment' thought. For, given these assumptions, there would
seem no alternative to the kind of extreme sceptical or levelling view that
perceives little difference between regimes founded on the infliction of brute
(albeit 'symbolic') physical violence and regimes which claim to transcend
or eliminate such violence through reasoned argument, civilized values,
and humane understanding. Any rejoinder that invoked those old-fashioned
('liberal-humanist') criteria would simply be met with a flat re-statement of the
standard Foucauldian line.

It is the same set of premises that duBois takes over when she treats 'truth'
and 'torture' as well-nigh synonymous terms, each of them involved in a
violent logic which requires the extraction of some occult knowledge through
various disciplinary techniques. Most often, she argues, these techniques are
caught up in a specular relationship between self and other where the other is
conceived – like the slave or the woman in ancient Greek thought – as
somehow giving access (under 'expert' guidance) to a truth beyond reach of his
or her inward, authentic, self-knowing grasp. And so it comes about, in
duBois' words, that

> a hidden truth, one that eludes the subject, must be discovered, uncovered,
> unveiled, and can always be located in the dark, in the irrational, in the
> unknown, in the other. And that truth will continue to beckon the torturer, the
> sexual abuser, who will find in the other – slave, woman, revolutionary – silent
> or not, secret or not, the receding phantasm of a truth that must be hunted
> down, extracted, torn out in torture. (p. 157)

It is a powerful indictment, especially when read in light of what duBois has to
say about the extent of such practices in our own time, very often by nominally
'Third World' agencies whose acquired expertise in these matters came
by way of US 'counter-insurgency' or psychological warfare units. As she

remarks, there is still a tendency on the part of many Western commentators to pretend that these practices only occur elsewhere, in regions of the world as yet unconverted to the values of freedom and liberal democracy. But in so doing they fall straight back into the old pattern of thought, the need to cast some other in the reassuring role of scapegoat, alien or stigmatized bearer of a dark knowledge whose import can only be assessed from 'our' more humane or enlightened standpoint. Thus:

> torture has become a global spectacle, a comfort to the so-called civilized nations, persuading them of their commitment to humanitarian values, revealing to them the continued barbarism of the other world, a world that continues to need the guidance of Europe and America, a guidance that is offered in the form of a transnational global economy controlling torture as one of the instruments of world domination. (p. 157)

Anyone who doubts the truth of such claims need only reflect on the record of US *Realpolitik* as manifest in its dealings with various dictatorial regimes in South America, South East Asia, the Gulf region and other parts of the world perceived as crucial to its geo-political or military-strategic interests. Had duBois' book been published a year or so later she could have pointed to the Gulf War, its background history and the subsequent course of events as evidence enough of US willingness to switch tactical alliances almost overnight and to back any government – no matter how brutal or repressive – just so long as it served the purpose of maintaining regional hegemony.[65] For there was, to say the least, a certain grim irony about the notion of waging war to 'liberate' a country like Kuwait, one whose subjects – or a large majority of them – can scarcely have relished the liberators' promise of a swift return to the *status quo ante*.

Nothing could more clearly illustrate duBois' point about the massive hypocrisy that often goes along with Western talk of liberal democracy, 'free world' values, and other such well-worn propaganda slogans. For what usually gets exported under cover of this high-sounding rhetoric is yet another opportune shift in the balance of power – along with the requisite weapons technology, military back-up, training in advanced methods of surveillance and control, etc. – whose aim is to secure 'stability' in the region as viewed from the Pentagon or Capitol Hill.[66] And if erstwhile 'tyrants' or 'dictators' can be thus transformed into new-found 'friends' and 'allies' – on condition (of course) that the process also works in reverse – then liberal opinion is best assuaged by regarding these turn-arounds as only to be expected when dealing with such volatile regimes and characters. Moreover, it is this same self-exculpating logic – this habit of projecting blame and guilt onto a racial or cultural 'other' conceived as lacking the basic democratic virtues – which in turn permits 'us' more civilized types to enjoy an easy conscience despite all the evidence of Western complicity, connivance or worse. Such alibis are always available, as duBois says, 'to comfort American liberals who rest contented in their view that these things could never happen here. . . . They confirm the perspective from the United States and Europe that barbarism resides else-where, in the other, that other world, unenlightened, steeped in medievalism and bloody cruelty' (p. 155). To which one can only respond by acknowledging the justice of this claim as borne out by the recent history of US strategic interventions in various 'trouble-spots' around the world. And of course there has been no shortage of well-placed apologists – media commentators, think-tank pundits, 'end-of-ideology' ideologues and the like – to justify each new shift of tactical alliance and explain how it all contributes to the aim of making the world safe for democracy.

The most prominent of these 'liberal' voices at the moment is that of Francis Fukuyama, a Rand Corporation protegé and inventor of some novel variations on the old (no longer very persuasive) line of Cold War propaganda. Fukuyama achieved instant fame on the US lecture circuit for his thesis that 'history' had effectively come to an end – not to mention 'ideology' and other such obsolete notions – with the advent of a New World Order founded on the principles of liberal democracy and free-market economics.[67] He followed this up with an article on the Gulf War ('Changed Days for Ruritania's Dictator') whose closing sentences can best be read in conjunction with the passages from duBois cited above.

A large part of the world will be populated by Iraqs and Ruritanias, and will continue to be subject to bloody struggles and revolutions. But with the exception of the Gulf, few regions will have an impact – for good or ill – on the growing part of the world that is democratic and capitalist. And it is in this part of the world that we will ultimately have to make our home.[68]

It never occurs to him to ask how far those 'bloody struggles and revolutions' have been the outcome of Western interests pursued by every available strategic and military means; what a history of betrayals and proxy or delegated violence lies behind this talk of exporting the benefits of liberal democracy; how the 'impact' is more often the reverse of what Fukuyama thinks, being experienced most keenly by those on the receiving end of US foreign policy initiatives; and finally, how the geopolitical carve-up between 'them' (the Iraqs and Ruritanias) and 'us' (or that fortunate part of the world that 'we will ultimately have to make our home') is based not so much on the limits assigned to this beneovlent sphere of interest as on the need for new enemies – or scapegoat regimes – to bolster a US economy dependent on massive and continued military spending. And so it comes about, in duBois' words, that the ancient model of truth, and slave torture as the extraction of truth, still defines the first world's relationship to third world torture. While the suffering of victims under the regimes of torturers punishes and controls the citizens of their nations, the citizens of the first world observe and deplore the spectacle of third world primitivism and barbarism. The first world contents itself with other ways of achieving truth – the so-called pluralism of mass consumerism, the 'freedom' capitalism offers to choose among an assortment of putative truths as one chooses among alternate toothpastes. But the truth is that torture still exists, it has not been eliminated in a surge of enlightened globalism, and the third world, in its complexity, multiplicity, multiple sites, has become, besides the site of torture, the spectacle of the other tortured for us. (duBois, p. 157)

It is not hard to see what nonsense this makes of the orchestrated platitudes currently on offer from Fukuyama and the feel-good ideologues of US 'liberal democracy'.

But one should also notice how duBois abruptly shifts ground, in this last and most eloquent passage of her book, from attacking truth-claims in whatever form to attacking those varieties of 'first world' postmodern scepticism that would relativize issues of truth and falsehood to the point where they resemble free-market options or items of consumer choice. In fact there is a problem in squaring this passage with her earlier praise for those heterodox thinkers – from the ancient sophists to the present-day neopragmatists – who have held out against the coercive regimen of truth, and thereby pointed the way toward achieving a genuine, open, fully participant democracy. It seems to me that this unresolved tension in her argument is perhaps best explained by considering the role of such ideas – the way that they have been taken up, exploited and put to all manner of rhetorical use – by apologists for Bush's 'New World Order' and its various associated myths. For there is, as I have argued, a complicitous relation between fashionable slogans like the 'end of ideology' or the 'end of history' – slogans whose effect is to disguise and legitimate the interests of US *Realpolitik* – and those versions of the postmodern-pragmatist creed which likewise proclaim the obsolescence of values such as truth, reason and critique, and which offer in their place a consensus-based appeal to what is currently 'good in the way of belief'.[69] This argument may start out from the liberal premise that truth-claims have all too often gone along with a notion of privileged access or superior wisdom on the part of those elect individuals with authority or power to impose their version of the truth. Hence Rorty's genial recommendation that we substitute 'solidarity' for 'objectivity', or a sense of shared (that is, 'North Atlantic postmodern bourgeois-liberal') values for the attempt to get things right from a critical standpoint which challenges the currency of consensus belief. But such arguments take on a less benign aspect if one considers how easily public opinion can be mobilized, or consensus attitudes swung, to support the kinds of thinking that find expression in Fukuyama's Gulf War article. For if truth is in the end simply what counts as such according to our present interpretive lights, then one might as well push this argument all the way – along with its geostrategic implications – and endorse whatever line of state-sponsored doublethink happens to suit the current mood of revived interventionist zeal.

Thus (in Fukuyama's words) 'any "New World Order" will not be built upon abstract principles of international law, but upon the common principles of liberal democracy and market economics'.[70] And by the same token, any local resistance or opposition to those principles will be met with a placid assurance that might is right, just so long as 'right' can be defined for all practical purposes as 'good in the way of free-market doctrine and liberal-democratic belief'. This is not to cast doubt on the good faith and decency of those – Rorty among them – who appeal to such values as the last, best hope in an age that has supposedly witnessed the collapse of 'Enlightenment' values and truth-claims. 'Consider,' Rorty asks us,

> the attitude of contemporary American liberals to the unending hopelessness and misery of the lives of the young blacks in American cities. Do we say that these people must be helped because they are our fellow human beings? We may, but it is much more persuasive, morally as well as politically, to describe them as our fellow *Americans* – to insist that it is outrageous that an *American* can live without hope.[71]

Terry Eagleton cites this passage as an epigraph to his recent book *Ideology: an introduction*, along with another sentence from Rorty which declares simply: 'On the uselessness of the notion of "ideology", see Raymond Geuss, *The Idea of a Critical Theory*'.[72] Aside from Geuss's role as an unsuspecting pawn in this exchange one can see very well why Eagleton singles out such passages for what they tell us about current neopragmatist thinking and its alignment with an updated version of the 'end of ideology' thesis. For the appeal to 'us' Americans as a bottom-line of liberal reformist concern may always turn out to have sharp limits when it comes to imagining how non-Americans – in particular those condemned to inhabit Fukuyama's 'Iraqs and Ruritanias' – can somehow be brought to appreciate the benefits on offer. If their interests are to figure at all, then this requires something more than a good-willed stretch of the terms by which present-day Americans (politicians, military strategists and think-tank pundits, as well as benign individuals like Rorty) happen to define their preferred cultural self-image. Otherwise the talk of consensus-values can very easily serve, as it did during the Gulf War, to legitimate some far-from-liberal forms of public opinion management. And from this point the way is clearly open for opportunists like George Bush, or ideologues like Fukuyama, to promote their vision of a 'New World Order' exempt from even the most basic standards of historical, moral, and political accountability.

It seems to me that such conclusions are hard to avoid if one assumes, like duBois, that a pragmatist or cultural-relativist outlook is the only defence against what she calls 'the coercive, philosophical, othering, torturing mode of seeking truth'. For according to this drastically polarized view there is no alternative – least of all a 'philosophical' alternative – that would hold out against the various forms of imposed or dogmatic truth while continuing to respect the aims and priorities of enlightened critical thought. Hence her high regard for those genuinely 'democratic' thinkers, from the ancient Greek sophists to their modern neopragmatist descendants, who have found no use for any idea of truth that supposedly transcends the limiting context, the in-place assumptions or consensus values of its own time and place. Even so one comes across occasional passages in her book which suggest that this cannot be the whole story; that democracy involves something other and more than the appeal to what is currently 'good in the way of belief'; and that any worthwhile advance in this direction will require a criticism of existing institutions which can only come about through enlightened efforts to extend the scope of informed participant exchange. Thus: 'the logic of democracy, the notion of equality and equal power among members of a community, can produce an ever-expanding definition of community' (pp. 124–5); 'the idea of democracy has its own dynamic, a pressure towards the consideration of all in view as entitled to the privileges of rule by the people' (p. 125). It is no coincidence that passages like these bring duBois much closer to Habermas's thinking – to his notion of an 'ideal speech-community' as the measure of progressive or emancipatory change – than to anything envisaged on the pragmatist account of knowledge and human interests.[73] For the upshot of any such consensus-based doctrine is to level the difference between beliefs arrived at through the process of open argumentative debate and beliefs that rest solely on unexamined prejudice, ideological persuasion, or the *force majeure* of propaganda efforts like that mounted during the Gulf War campaign.

VI

It is for this reason, I would argue, that relativist philosophies can offer no defence against arbitrary (and sometimes violent) forms of doctrinal imposition. Postmodernists typically confuse the issue by assimilating all truth-claims to that mystified idea of an inward, secret, self-validating truth which has characterized the discourse of revealed religion and whose resonance persists (as duBois rightly notes) in Heidegger's etymopoeic vagaries, his 'profound' pseudo-arguments and constant resort to an irrationalist jargon of authenticity.[74] No doubt such ideas have been the cause of great confusion, as well as giving rise – all too clearly in Heidegger's case – to some vicious abuses when translated into the realm of social and political thought. To this extent duBois is justified in urging that 'torture' and 'truth' should be seen as two aspects of that domineering drive, that will-to-power over bodies and minds, whose genealogy reaches back to the origins of Western cultural tradition. What she fails to acknowledge, except in those few brief passages, is the fact that such ideas have met resistance only through the kind of enlightened critique that challenges false or presumptive truth-claims by holding them accountable to alternative standards of historical, philosophical, and ethical truth. Insofar as Christianity has been subject to a civilizing influence – induced to give up its persecuting zeal and its demands for unquestioning doctrinal adherence – it is principally owing to these efforts of reasoned counter-argument on the part of thinkers from Erasmus to the present. And the most important factor here has been the growing awareness that truth is best arrived at not on the basis of inward conviction or self-authorized scriptural warrant, but through a process of open dialogical exchange whose criteria are those of good faith, reason, and valid argumentative grounds.

That literary theorists of a 'radical' bent should now be engaged in a wholesale campaign to denigrate such values is all the more curious given their reliance – explicit disavowals notwithstanding – on precisely the modes of critical thought which derive from that same tradition. For even when denouncing 'enlightenment' beliefs as the source of all evil and oppression, these critics (Foucauldians and post-structuralists among them) still lay claim to the kind of demythologizing role which secular intellectuals have typically played over the past two centuries and more. Where they depart from that tradition – and effectively revert to an earlier, proto-theological strain – is in their raising of 'the text' (as of language or 'discourse') to a position of undisputed eminence, and in the conjoint refusal to acknowledge any argument or truth-claim that does not abide by this textualist imperative. No doubt one source of confusion here is a simplified reading of Derrida which latches on to some of his more sweeping pronouncements as regards the Western 'metaphysics of presence', and takes him to have shown – once and for all – that any talk of truth is inescapably complicit with that age-old logocentric regime.[75] On the contrary, as he puts it in a recent essay:

> the value of truth (and all those values associated with it) is never contested or destroyed in my writings, but only reinscribed in more powerful, larger, more stratified contexts. . . . And within those contexts (that is, within relations of force that are always differential – for example, socio-political-institutional – but even beyond these determinations) that are relatively stable, sometimes apparently almost unshakable, it should be possible to invoke rules of competence, criteria of discussion and of consensus, good faith, lucidity, rigour, criticism, and pedagogy.

One could hardly wish for a plainer declaration of the gulf that separates Derrida's work from the currency of postmodern-pragmatist thought.

Paul de Man makes a similar point, and with the same kinds of misunderstanding in view, when he refutes the idea that deconstruction involves a total rejection of truth-values, or that it simply suspends all questions of veridical or argumentative warrant. Thus:

> reading is an argument . . . because it has to go against the grain of what one would want to happen in the name of what has to happen; this is the same as saying that reading is an epistemological event prior to being an ethical or aesthetic value. This does not mean that there can be a true reading, but that no reading is conceivable in which the question of its truth or falsehood is not primarily involved.[77]

Postmodernism derives much of its suasive appeal from the notion that truth-claims are *always* on the side of some ultimate, transcendent, self-authorized Truth which excludes all meanings save those vouchsafed to the guardians of orthodox thought. It is this supposition that lends plausibility to Foucault's reductive genealogies of power/knowledge, to Rorty's genial postmodern variations on the theme, and also to the link between 'torture' and 'truth' which duBois sees everywhere at work in the history of Western logocentric reason. But such arguments look much less convincing when placed in a wider philosophical and socio-cultural context. For it then becomes clear that without the benefit of those values that Derrida invokes – 'consensus, good faith, lucidity, rigour, criticism' – we should still be labouring against massive odds of doctrinal imposition and entrenched dogmatic belief. More to the point, we should possess no means by which to criticize such false or groundless beliefs and thus attain a better understanding of the forces that had worked to keep them in place.

Of course it is possible to argue, like Foucault, that 'resistance' comes about solely as a product of power/knowledge differentials; that for every 'discourse' of accredited or authorized knowledge there is a counter-discourse whose social efficacy is directly proportional to the power invested in maintaining the current institutional status quo. But this doctrine really amounts to little more than a metaphor transposed from Newtonian mechanics into the realm of the human and social sciences. That is to say, it trades on a simplified analogy between physical 'forces' and those contests of meaning, motive, authority and power that involve human agents in distinctive forms of socialized conduct and exchange. The result, as I have argued, is a drastically reductive, quasi-Hobbesian conception of power/knowledge that levels all distinctions between the various orders of state and civil society, and which perceives violence (or some sublimated image of the feudal body-in-pain) as the underlying truth of any such order, whatever its 'enlightened' or progressive self-image.

It seems to me that recent theorists have pressed too far with this oddly seductive equation between 'torture' and 'truth'. To be sure, it has yielded valuable (and cautionary) insights into the way that a certain presumptive, self-authorizing discourse of 'truth' can coexist with forms of social oppression which it serves both to disguise and to legitimate. What duBois has to say on this topic, with examples from Plato to Heidegger, gives evidence enough that such collusions have occurred and that truth-talk *per se* is no guarantee of social or political virtue. But that much should be obvious to anyone who has thought about the varieties of human self-deception and the power of false ideas to pass themselves off as the highest spiritual wisdom. Indeed, it is this supposed link between *inwardness* and truth – the idea of privileged access granted to some religious or secular elite – which has done most harm down through the history of violent or persecuting creeds. One need only reflect on the self-righteous rhetoric, the scenes of presidential soul-baring and the charade of private consciences publically aired that accompanied an episode like the Gulf War to gain some idea of what might be at stake in Derrida's deconstructive critique of 'logocentrism' and the 'metaphysics of presence'.

However there is nothing to gained – and a great deal to be lost – when postmodern theorists take this as their cue for denouncing all the values and truth-claims of Enlightenment reason. For such attitudes amount to a whole-sale retreat from one of criticism's primary tasks: that is, in Jonathan Culler's words, its function of 'combating superstition, encouraging sceptical debate about competing religions and their claims or their myths, and fighting religious dogmatism and its political consequences'.[78] Moreover it is the case, as Culler points out, that literary theory in its present-day form is very largely a product of those powerful demystifying impulses – historical scholarship, textual hermeneutics, philological enquiry, comparative source-studies, sociology of belief and so forth – whose most signal achievement was the undermining of revealed or dogmatic religion. 'At the beginning of the eighteenth century,' he writes, '[most] Protestants took the Bible to be the word of God; by the beginning of the twentieth century this belief was untenable in intellectual circles'.[79] Nowadays this historical trend has been reversed, at least among the arbiters of literary-critical fashion, to a point where (for instance) deconstruction can be annexed to the discourse of negative theology, and where the values of enlightened or secular critique are routinely dismissed as an embarrassing throwback to that bad old regime of reason, progress and truth. And so it has come about that, 'instead of leading the critique of dogmatic theologies, literary criticism is contributing to the legitimation of religious discourse'.[80]

Postmodernism has opened the way to this retreat through its regular confusion between the different orders of truth-claim, on the one hand those that trade upon notions of inward certainty, privileged access, authentic revelation and the like, and on the other hand those that contest such ideas – such presumptively self-validating pseudo-truths – by adopting alternative, more rigorous standards of critical accountability. These latter bear not the least resemblance to that composite bugbear image of Truth that post-modernists and neopragmatists offer by way of discrediting the whole enlightenment enterprise. Thus Catherine Belsey again: 'history, in each of its manifestations, was the single, unified, unproblematic, extra-textual, extra-discursive real that guaranteed our readings of the texts which constituted its cultural *expression*'.[81] But such notions of expressive realism – of truth as revealed in the fullness of time through an act of omniscient retrospective grasp – have their place only within a history of thought that runs from Hegel to various forms of latterday Hegelian *Kulturgeschichte*. Of course it will be urged on the postmodernist side that 'enlightenment' truth-claims always involve this appeal to some teleological master-plot or strong metanarrative drive; that between Kant and Hegel (or Hegel and Marx) there is little to choose save minor variations on a well-worn historicist theme.[82] To which the only possible response, as I have argued, is that this is a false reading of intellectual history, one that has given rise to some damaging confusions through its will to assimilate every kind of truth to the workings of an undifferentiated power/knowledge.

Kant was clear enough on the main point at issue: on the need to maintain a due sense of the difference between private modes of conviction and belief (e.g., those arrived at through 'authentic', inward revelation) and the public sphere of openly accountable reasons, arguments, principles and values.[83] He was likewise much aware of the dangers courted by any interest-group or creed, like the current postmodern-pragmatist trend, that set out to blur the line between these disparate orders of truth-claim, and which thus ended up by effectively endorsing a wholesale reduction of truth to what is presently and contingently 'good in the way of belief'. Hence the importance of respecting those various distinctive criteria – historical, philosophical, ethical, socio-political and so forth – which alone provide adequate standards for assessing the validity of claims put forward at the level of informed argumentative debate. Hence also Kant's warning (taken up, albeit rather ambivalently, in some of Derrida's recent texts) against the risks attendant on the habit of appealing to private conscience or inward conviction as a substitute for that process of reasoned critical enquiry whereby such claims could properly be tested in point of their truth-telling warrant.[84] Nor can this be seen as just one more manifestation of that inveterate will-to-power, or that sublimated link between torture and truth, which duBois finds responsible for so much misery, oppression and suffering. On the contrary: insofar as we can register the fact of such evils and seek to understand and to remedy their causes it is a sign of our having progressed beyond the stage of unthinking doctrinal adherence or passive consensus belief. Postmodernism amounts to a vote of no confidence in this entire tradition of enlightened philosophical, ethical and social thought. That it is presently enjoying such a widespread vogue among theorists of various political persuasion is reason enough to reexamine its relation to the dominant self-images of the age.

Notes

NOTES TO CHAPTER 1

1   Christopher Norris, *Uncritical Theory: postmodernism, intellectuals and the Gulf War* (London: Lawrence & Wishart; and Amherst, Mass.: University of Massachusetts Press, 1992).

2   Francis Fukuyama, 'The End of History', *The National Interest* (Washington D.C.), Summer, 1989. See also Fukuyama, *The End of History and the Last Man* (London: Hamish Hamilton, 1992).

3   Fukuyama, 'Changed Days for Ruritania's Dictator', *The Guardian* (London), 8 April 1991.

4   Norris, *Uncritical Theory*, p. 156.

5   See for instance Jonathan Steele, Edward Mortimer and Gareth Stedman Jones, 'The End of History?' (a discussion of Fukuyama's essay), in *Marxism Today*, November 1989, pp. 26–33.

6   See the essays collected in Stuart Hall and Martin Jacques (eds.), *New Times: the changing face of politics in the 1990s* (London: Lawrence & Wishart, 1989).

7   Stuart Hall, 'No new vision, no new votes', *New Statesman and Society*, 17 April 1992, pp. 14–15. Following extracts signalled by 'Hall' and page-number only in the text. This issue also carried a number of other 'post mortem' articles on the reasons for Labour's electoral defeat and the best way forward for British socialism.

8   See Raymond Williams, *Keywords: a vocabulary of culture and society* (London: Fontana, 1976).

9   See for instance Jean Baudrillard, *Selected Writings*, ed. Mark Poster (Cambridge: Polity Press, 1989); also *America* (London: Verso, 1988), *Fatal Strategies* (London: Pluto Press, 1989) and *Revenge of the Crystal: a Baudrillard reader* (London: Pluto Press, 1990).

10 Antonio Gramsci, *Selections from the Prison Notebooks*, ed. and trans. Quintin Hoare and Geoffrey Nowell-Smith (London: Lawrence & Wishart, 1971).

11 Terry Eagleton, *Ideology: an introduction* (London: Verso, 1991), p. 3.

12 Ibid., p. 4.

13 See for instance Peter de Bolla, *The Discourse of the Sublime: readings in history, aesthetics and the subject* (Oxford: Blackwell, 1989); Neil Hertz, *The End of the Line:*

essays on psychoanalysis and the sublime (New York: Columbia University Press, 1985); Hugh Silverman and Gary Aylesworth (eds.), *The Textual Sublime* (Albany, NY: State University of New York Press, 1990); and Slavoj Zizek, *The Sublime Object of Ideology* (London: Verso, 1990).

14 See Jean-François Lyotard, *The Differend: phrases in dispute*, trans. Georges van den Abbeele (Manchester: Manchester University Press, 1988); also *The Inhuman: reflections on time*, trans. Geoffrey Bennington and Rachel Bowlby (Cambridge: Polity Press, 1991).

15 Immanuel Kant, *Critique of Pure Reason*, trans. N. Kemp Smith (London: Macmillan, 1933); *Critique of Practical Reason*, trans. Lewis W. Beck (Indianapolis: Bobbs-Merrill, 1977); and *Critique of Judgment*, trans. J. C. Meredith (Oxford: Clarendon Press, 1978).

16 Saul Kripke, *Naming and Necessity* (Oxford: Blackwell, 1980).

17 See Lyotard, *The Differend*, p. 179.

18 Ibid., p. 19.

19 Ibid., p. 9.

20 Ibid., p. 19.

21 For a sustained and intelligent (if far from conclusive) address to these issues, see Tony Bennett, *Outside Literature* (London: Routledge, 1990); also the essays collected in Derek Attridge, Geoff Bennington and Robert Young (eds.), *Post-Structuralism and the Question of History* (Cambridge: Cambridge University Press, 1987).

22 Stephen Greenblatt, 'Resonance and Wonder', in *Learning to Curse: essays in early modern culture* (London: Routledge, 1990), pp. 161–83.

23 Lyotard, *The Differend*, p. 148.

24 Ibid., p. 13.

25 Lyotard, 'Complexity and the Sublime', in Lisa Appignanesi (ed.), *Postmodernism* (London: ICA Documents/Free Association Books, 1989), pp. 19–26; p. 23.

26 See for instance Dick Hebdige, 'The Impossible Object: towards a sociology of the sublime', *New Formations* 1 (Spring, 1987), pp. 47–76 and *Hiding in the Light: on images and things* (London: Routledge, 1988).

27 Robert Scholes, *Protocols of Reading* (New Haven: Yale University Press, 1989). For a wide-ranging treatment of these issues from a sociological and philosophical viewpoint, see Margaret Gilbert, *On Social Facts* (London: Routledge, 1989).

28 Scholes, *Protocols of Reading*, p. 91.

29 Elaine Showalter, 'Critical Cross-Dressing', *Raritan* 3, no. 2 (Fall, 1983), pp. 130–49. See also Marjorie Garber, *Vested Interests: cross-dressing and cultural anxiety* (New York and London: Routledge, 1992); Stephen Heath, *The Sexual Fix* (London: Macmillan, 1982); Mary Jacobus, 'Reading Woman (Reading)' and 'The Difference of View', in *Reading Woman: essays in feminist criticism* (New York: Columbia University Press, 1986), pp. 3–24 and 27–40; and Alice Jardine and Paul Smith (eds.), *Men in Feminism* (London: Methuen, 1987).

30 Scholes, *Protocols of Reading*, p. 92.

31 Ibid., p. 92.

32 For further discussion of this and related topics, see especially W. V. O. Quine,

Ontological Relativity' and Other Essays (New York: Columbia University Press, 1969) and Donald Davidson, *Inquiries into Truth and Interpretation* (Oxford: Clarendon Press, 1984).

33 Ferdinand de Saussure, *Course in General Linguistics*, trans. Wade Baskin (London: Fontana, 1974); also translated by Roy Harris (La Salle, Ill.: Open Court, 1986) with significant changes of terminology and detail.

34 For a vigorously-argued critique of these ideas, see Raymond Tallis, *Not Saussure* (London: Macmillan, 1988). There is also some useful commentary to be found in Jonathan Culler, *Saussure* (London: Fontana, 1976); Roy Harris, *Reading Saussure* (London: Duckworth, 1987); and David Holdcraft, *Saussure: signs, systems and arbitrariness* (Cambridge: Cambridge University Press, 1991).

35 See Jacques Lacan, *Ecrits: a selection*, trans. Alan Sheridan (London: Tavistock, 1977).

36 See for instance Hebdige, *Hiding in the Light*; Hertz, *The End of the Line*; Silverman (ed.), *The Textual Sublime*; and Zizek, *The Sublime Object of Ideology*.

37 Scholes, *Protocols of Reading*, pp. 92–3.

38 See especially Jacques Derrida, 'Afterword: toward an ethics of discussion', in *Limited Inc*, 2nd edn (Evanston, Ill.: Northwestern University Press, 1988), pp. 111–60.

39 See for instance Derrida, 'Women in the Beehive: a seminar with Jacques Derrida', in Jardine and Smith (eds.), *Men in Feminism*, pp. 189–203.

40 Scholes, p. 99.

41 William Empson, *Seven Types of Ambiguity* (Harmondsworth: Penguin, 1961).

NOTES TO CHAPTER 2

1 Michel Foucault, *The History of Sexuality*, vol. 1, *An Introduction*, trans. Robert Hurley (New York: Pantheon, 1978); *The Use of Pleasure*, trans. Robert Hurley (New York: Pantheon, 1985); *The Care of the Self*, trans. Robert Hurley (New York: Pantheon, 1986).

2 Roy Boyne, *Foucault and Derrida: the other side of reason* (London: Unwin Hyman, 1990), p. 144.

3 Foucault, *The Order of Things: an archaeology of the human sciences* (New York: Random House, 1973); *The Archaeology of Knowledge*, trans. A. Sheridan-Smith (London: Tavistock, 1972).

4 See especially the essays collected in Foucault, *Language, Counter-Memory, Practice*, trans. Donald F. Bouchard and Shierry Weber (Oxford: Blackwell, 1977).

5 Foucault, *The Order of Things*, p. 318.

6 Ibid., p. 322.

7 See especially Foucault, 'Nietzsche, Genealogy, History' and 'What Is An Author?', in Paul Rabinow (ed.), *The Foucault Reader* (Harmondsworth: Penguin, 1986), pp. 76–100, 101–20.

8 Foucault, *The Use of Pleasure*, p. 86.

9 Boyne, p. 149.

10 Ibid., pp. 149–50.

11 On this topic, see Geoffrey Galt Harpham, *The Ascetic Imperative in Culture and Criticism* (Chicago: University of Chicago Press, 1987).

12 See especially Foucault, *Power/Knowledge: selected interviews and other writings* (Brighton: Harvester, 1980) and *Discipline and Punish*, trans. Alan Sheridan (New York: Pantheon, 1978).

13 See for instance Michael Sandel, *Liberalism and the Limits of Justice* (Cambridge: Cambridge University Press, 1982); Michael Walzer, *Spheres of Justice: a defence of pluralism and equality* (Oxford: Blackwell, 1983); Walzer, *Interpretation and Social Criticism* (Cambridge, Mass.: Harvard University Press, 1987); Bernard Williams, *Ethics and the Limits of Philosophy* (London: Fontana, 1985).

14 Foucault, *The Order of Things*.

15 See especially the essays collected in Foucault, *Language, Counter-Memory, Practice*.

16 Thomas Flynn, 'Foucault as Parrhesiast: his last course at the Collège de France', in James Bernauer and David Rasmussen (eds.). *The Final Foucault* (Cambridge, Mass.: MIT Press, 1988), pp. 102–18. See also Bernauer, *Michel Foucault's Force of Flight: toward an ethics of thought* (Atlantic Highlands, NJ: Humanities Press, 1990).

17 Ibid., p. 114.

18 Ibid., p. 114.

19 Ibid., p. 114.

20 Foucault, 'The Ethic of Care for the Self as a Practice of Freedom' (interview), in *The Final Foucault*, p. 7.

21 Ibid., p. 7.

22 Williams, *Ethics and the Limits of Philosophy*.

23 Alasdair MacIntyre, *After Virtue: a study in moral theory* (London: Duckworth, 1985).

24 Walzer, *Spheres of Justice*.

25 See for instance Richard Rorty, *Contingency, Irony, and Solidarity* (Cambridge: Cambridge University Press, 1989); *Objectivity, Relativism, and Truth* (Cambridge University Press, 1991); and *Essays on Heidegger and Others* (Cambridge University Press, 1991).

26 For some ingenious variations on this postmodern-pragmatist theme, see Stanley Fish, *Doing What Comes Naturally: change, rhetoric, and the practice of theory in literary and legal studies* (Durham, N. C.: Duke University Press, 1989).

27 See Foucault, *Discipline and Punish* (op. cit.) and *The Birth of the Clinic: an archaeology of medical perception*, trans. A. Sheridan-Smith (New York: Pantheon, 1973); also *Madness and Civilization*, trans. Richard Howard (New York: Pantheon 1965).

28 Foucault, 'Nietzsche, Genealogy, History' (op. cit.).

29 Rorty, 'Moral Identity and Private Autonomy: the case of Foucault', in *Essays on Heidegger and Others*, pp. 193–8. See also Rorty, 'Foucault and Epistemology', in David Couzens Hoy (ed.), *Foucault: a critical reader* (Oxford: Blackwell, 1986), pp. 41–9.

30 See Rorty, 'The Priority of Democracy to Philosophy' and 'Postmodernist

Bourgeois Liberalism', in *Objectivity, Relativism, and Truth*, pp. 175–96; 197–202.

31 See Rorty, *Contingency, Irony, and Solidarity* and 'Heidegger, Kundera, and Dickens', in *Essays on Heidegger and Others*, pp. 66–82.

32 Rorty, 'Moral Identity and Private Autonomy', p. 194.

33 Ibid., pp. 195–6.

43 See especially Foucault, *Power/Knowledge*.

44 Rorty, 'Moral Identity and Private Autonomy', p. 198.

45 Foucault, 'The Ethic of Care for the Self as a Practice of Freedom', p. 20.

46 Rorty, 'Moral Identity and Private Autonomy', p. 198.

47 Ibid., p. 196.

48 Ibid., p. 196.

49 Ibid., p. 198.

50 See Immanuel Kant, *Critique of Pure Reason*, trans. N. Kemp Smith (London: Macmillan, 1933).

51 Ian Hacking, 'Self-Improvement', in Hoy (ed.), *Foucault: a critical reader*, pp. 235–40.

52 See for instance Charles Taylor, 'Foucault on Freedom and Truth', in Hoy (ed.), *Foucault: a critical reader* (op. cit.), p. 69–102.

53 Rorty, 'Freud and Moral Reflection', in *Essays on Heidegger and Others*, pp. 143–63; p. 155.

54 Michael Walzer, 'The Politics of Michel Foucault', in Hoy (ed.), *Foucault: a critical reader*, pp. 51–68.

55 Ibid., p. 61.

56 Ian Hacking, 'Self-Improvement', pp. 238–9.

57 Foucault, 'Polemics, Politics, and Problematizations' (interview with Paul Rabinow), trans. Lydia Davis, in Rabinow (ed.), *The Foucault Reader*, pp. 381–90; p. 388.

58 Ibid., p. 390.

59 See especially Kant, *Foundations of the Metaphysics of Morals: text and critical essays*, ed. Robert P. Wolff (Indianapolis: Bobbs–Merrill, 1969).

60 Kant, *Critique of Practical Reason*, trans. Lewis W. Beck (Indianapolis: Bobbs–Merrill, 1975).

61 For some of the best recent commentary on this and other aspects of Kantian ethics, see Onora O'Neill, *Constructions of Reason: explorations of Kant's practical philosophy* (Cambridge: Cambridge University Press, 1989).

62 See Donald Davidson, *Essays on Actions and Events* (Oxford: Oxford University Press, 1980) for a treatment of these issues in the current 'analytical' mode.

63 See Walzer, *Spheres of Justice*.

64 Walzer, 'The Politics of Michel Foucault'.

65 Foucault, 'What Is Enlightenment?', trans. Catherine Porter, in Rabinow (ed.), *The Foucault Reader*, pp. 32–50. Hereafter cited as WIE with page-number in the text. See also Kant, 'What Is Enlightenment?', in L. W. Beck (ed.), *Kant: On History* (Indianapolis: Bobbs-Merrill, 1963). For further commentary on Foucault's reading of Kant, see Jürgen Habermas, 'Taking Aim at the Heart of

the Present', Hubert L. Dreyfus and Paul Rabinow, 'What Is Maturity: Habermas and Foucault on "What is Enlightenment?"', and Ian Hacking, 'Self-Improvement', all in Hoy (ed.), *Foucault: a critical reader*.

66 See also Foucault, 'Kant on Enlightenment and Revolution', trans. Colin Gordon, *Economy and Society* 15 (February, 1986), pp. 88–96.

67 See Gilles Deleuze, *Kant's Critical Philosophy: the doctrine of the faculties*, trans. Hugh Tomlinson and Barbara Habberjam (London: Athlone Press, 1984) for an incisive treatment that takes full account of these complexities in the Kantian project of thought.

68 See for instance Jean-François Lyotard, *The Differend: phrases in dispute*, trans. Georges van den Abbeele (Manchester: Manchester University Press, 1988).

69 See especially Jürgen Habermas, *Knowledge and Human Interests*, trans. Jeremy Shapiro (London: Heinemann, 1971).

70 Kant, *Critique of Judgement*, trans. J. C. Meredith (Oxford: Oxford University Press, 1978).

71 Charles Baudelaire, 'Le peintre de la vie moderne', in F. F. Gautier (ed.), *L'Art romantique* (*Oeuvres complètes*, IV [Paris, 1923]).

72 For a differently angled though pertinent commentary on these same texts of Baudelaire, see Paul de Man, 'Literary History and Literary Modernity', in *Blindness and Insight: essays in the rhetoric of contemporary criticism* (London: Methuen, 1983), pp. 142–65.

73 On this tradition of thought, see for instance Terry Eagleton, *The Ideology of the Aesthetic* (Oxford: Basil Blackwell, 1990); Paul de Man, *The Resistance to Theory* (Manchester: Manchester University Press, 1986); Michael Sprinker, *Imaginary Relations: aesthetics and ideology in the theory of historical materialism* (London: Verso, 1987); Andrew Bowie, *Aesthetics and Subjectivity from Kant to Nietzsche* (Manchester: Manchester University Press, 1990); Tony Bennett, *Outside Literature* (London: Routledge, 1991); and Philippe Lacoue-Labarthe, *Typography: mimesis, philosophy, politics*, ed. Christopher Fynsk (Cambridge, Mass.: Harvard University Press, 1989).

74 See Lyotard, *The Differend*; also Peter de Bolla, *The Discourse of the Sublime: readings in history, aesthetics and the subject* (Oxford: Blackwell, 1989); David Carroll, *Paraaesthetics: Foucault, Lyotard, Derrida* (Methuen: London, 1987); and Slavoj Zizek, *The Sublime Object of Ideology* (London: Verso, 1989).

75 I argue this case in greater detail in Norris, *What's Wrong with Postmodernism: critical theory and the ends of philosophy* (Hemel Hempstead: Harvester–Wheatsheaf; and Baltimore: Johns Hopkins University Press, 1990) and *Uncritical Theory: postmodernism, intellectuals and the Gulf War* (London: Lawrence & Wishart, 1992). See also Alex Callinicos, *Against Postmodernism: a Marxist critique* (Cambridge: Polity, 1989); David Harvey, *The Condition of Postmodernity: an enquiry into the origins of cultural change* (Oxford: Blackwell, 1989); and John McGowan, *Postmodernism and its Critics* (Ithaca, NY.: Cornell University Press, 1991).

76 See especially Lacoue-Labarthe, *Typography*.

77 This topic is addressed most explicitly in Foucault, 'Intellectuals and Power', in *Language, Counter-Memory, Practice*, pp. 205–17.

78   On this fundamental relation between *aisthesis* and *ascesis* as a recurrent burden of Western ethical thought, see Harpham, *The Ascetic Imperative*; also his more recent book *Getting It Right: language, literature, and ethics* (Chicago: University of Chicago Press, 1992).

79   See Kant, *Political Writings*, ed. Hans Reiss (Cambridge: Cambridge University Press, 1976); also *On History*, ed. L. W. Beck and *The Conflict of the Faculties*, ed. and trans. Mary J. Gregor (New York: Abaris Books, 1979).

80   See Jürgen Habermas, *The Philosophical Discourse of Modernity: twelve lectures*, trans. Frederick Lawrence (Cambridge: Polity Press, 1987).

81   Lyotard, *The Differend*.

82   Habermas, *Knowledge and Human Interests*. For the case against Habermas's reading of Freud as argued from a post-structuralist and (purportedly) Lacanian standpoint, see Rainer Nägele, 'Freud, Habermas and the Dialectic of Enlightenment: on real and ideal discourses', *New German Critique*, 22 (1981), pp. 41–62.

83   One of the best commentaries on this aspect of Lacan's thinking can be found in David Macey, *Lacan in Contexts* (London: Verso, 1988), especially his chapter 'Philosophy and Post-Philosophy', pp. 75–120. See also Ellie Ragland-Sullivan, *Jacques Lacan and the Philosophy of Psychoanalysis* (London: Croom Helm, 1986).

84   Rorty, 'Moral Identity and Private Autonomy: the case of Foucault', p. 198.

85   Ibid., p. 198.

86   For their respective (and sharply differing) views on the role of the critical intellectual, see 'Noam Chomsky and Michel Foucault: Human Nature, Justice *versus* Power' (transcript of televised dialogue), in Fons Elders (ed.), *Reflexive Waters: the basic concerns of mankind* (London: Souvenir Press, 1974), pp. 133–97. See also Norris, *Uncritical Theory* for further discussion of the issues raised by Foucault's refusal to play the role of so-called 'universal intellectual' in the typecast Enlightenment mould.

87   Rorty, 'Freud and Moral Reflection', p. 155.

88   Jean-François Lyotard, *The Postmodern Condition: a report on knowledge*, trans. Geoff Bennington and Brian Massumi (Manchester: Manchester University Press, 1986).

89   Foucault, 'Polemics, Politics, and Problematizations', p. 388.

90   Ibid., pp. 388–9.

91   See Walzer, *Spheres of Justice* and Williams, *Ethics and the Limits of Philosophy*.

92   Clifford Geertz, *Local Knowledge* (New York: Basic Books, 1983).

93   Foucault, 'On the Genealogy of Ethics: an overview of work in progress' (interview), in Rabinow (ed.). *The Foucault Reader*, pp. 340–72; p. 350.

94   See Norris, *What's Wrong with Postmodernism*.

95   Lyotard, *The Differend*.

96   Foucault, 'On the Genealogy of Ethics', p. 350.

97   See de Man, *Blindness and Insight* for some exemplary instances of textual close-reading in this deconstructive mode.

98   Habermas, *Moral Consciousness And Communicative Action* (Cambridge: Polity Press, 1990), p. 137.

99   Geoffrey Galt Harpham, *Getting It Right*, pp. 52–3.

100 See MacIntyre, *After Virtue* and Williams, *Ethics and the Limits of Philosophy*.

101 Harpham, *Getting It Right*, p. 53.

102 Foucault, 'On the Genealogy of Ethics', p. 352.

103 David Hume, *Enquiries Concerning Human Understanding and Concerning the Principles of Morals*, eds. L. Selby-Bigge and P. Nidditch (Oxford: Oxford University Press, 1975).

104 Hume, *'Of the Standard of Taste' and Other Essays* (Indianapolis: Bobbs–Merrill, 1963); Rorty, 'Freud and Moral Reflection', p. 155.

105 Foucault, 'On the Genealogy of Ethics', p. 351.

106 Maurice Merleau-Ponty, *Adventures of the Dialectic* (Evanston: Northwestern University Press, 1973).

107 Foucault, 'On the Genealogy of Ethics', p. 351.

108 Foucault, 'Polemics, Politics, and Problematizations', p. 388.

109 Patrick Colm Hogan, *The Politics of Interpretation: ideology, professionalism, and the study of literature* (New York and London: Oxford University Press, 1990), p. 176.

110 J. Hillis Miller, *The Ethics of Reading: Kant, de Man, Eliot, Trollope, James, and Benjamin* (New York: Columbia University Press, 1987), p. 24.

111 Ibid., p. 51.

112 On the fallacies involved in this 'textualist' reading of Kantian ethics, see also H. P. Rickman, 'Making a Mess of Kant', *Philosophy and Literature*, 15, no. 2 (1991), pp. 278–85. I have attempted to distinguish Miller's from de Man's more cogent and scrupulously argued account in Norris, *Paul de Man: deconstruction and the critique of aesthetic ideology* (New York: Routledge, 1988).

113 See Norris, *The Contest of Faculties: philosophy and theory after deconstruction* (London: Methuen, 1985); *Deconstruction and the Interests of Theory* (London: Pinter Publishers & Norman, Okl.: Oklahoma University Press, 1989); and *What's Wrong with Postmodernism*.

114 See for instance David Lewis, *On the Plurality of Worlds* (Oxford: Blackwell, 1986) and Thomas Pavel, *Fictional Worlds* (Cambridge, Mass.: Harvard University Press, 1987).

115 See also Miller, 'The Search for Grounds in Literary Study', in *Theory Now and Then* (Hemel Hempstead: Harvester-Wheatsheaf, 1991), pp. 263–75.

116 The point is made most explicitly – and in various contexts of argument – in Derrida, *Margins of Philosophy*, trans. Alan Bass (Chicago: University of Chicago Press, 1982).

117 Foucault, 'Polemics, Politics, and Problematizations'.

118 Ibid., p. 388.

119 Ibid., p. 390.

120 Foucault, 'On Popular Justice: a discussion with Maoists', trans. John Mepham, in *Power/Knowledge*, pp. 1–36.

121 Jean-François Lyotard and Jean-Loup Thébaud, *Just Gaming*, trans. Wlad Godzich (Manchester: Manchester University Press, 1986).

122 Ibid., p. 68.

123 Ibid., p. 69.

124 Foucault, 'Politics and Ethics: an interview', p. 376.

125 Ibid., p. 374.

126 Ibid., p. 376.

127 Ibid., p. 377.

128 Foucault, 'Polemics, Politics, and Problematizations', pp. 388–9.

NOTES TO CHAPTER 3

1   William Empson, *Seven Types of Ambiguity*, 3rd edn, revised (Penguin: Harmondsworth, 1961). All further references given by *ST* and page-number in the text.

2   These issues are addressed from a range of philosophical standpoints in Martin Hollis and Steven Lukes (eds.), *Rationality and Relativism* (Oxford: Blackwell, 1982).

3   For his own views on the matter, see Empson, *Argufying: essays on literature and culture*, ed. John Haffenden (London: Chatto & Windus, 1987), especially the various articles and reviews gathered in the final section, 'Cultural Perspectives: ethics and aesthetics, East and West'. This volume is a splendid work of dedicated scholarship and I have been grateful to Haffenden for his efforts in bringing such a mass of often fugitive material to light.

4   See especially Donald Davidson, 'On the Very Idea of a Conceptual Scheme', in *Inquiries into Truth and Interpretation* (London: Oxford University Press, 1984), pp. 183–98.

5   Benjamin Lee Whorf, *Language, Thought and Reality*, ed. John B. Carroll (New York: Willey, 1956).

6   See W. V. O. Quine, *From a Logical Point of View* (Cambridge, Mass: Harvard University Press, 1953).

7   See for instance Paul K. Feyerabend, *Against Method: outline of an anarchist theory of knowledge* (London: New Left Books, 1975).

8   The most often-cited defence of this Wittgensteinian argument may be found in Peter Winch, *The Idea of a Social Science and its Relation to Philosophy* (London: Routledge & Kegan Paul, 1958).

9   See Christopher Norris, *Deconstruction and the Interests of Theory* (London: Pinter Publishers; and Baltimore: Johns Hopkins University Press, 1988) for an exposition and critique of these movements in contemporary cultural theory.

10 Empson, *Collected Poems* (London: Chatto & Windus, 1969).

11 See Feyerabend, *Against Method*.

12 Empson, *The Structure of Complex Words* (London: Chatto & Windus, 1951). All further references given by *CW* and page-number in the text.

13 Roland Barthes, *Critique et vérité* (Paris: Seuil, 1966).

14 I. A. Richards, *Principles of Literary Criticism* (London: Routledge & Kegan Paul, 1927).

15 See for instance W. K. Wimsatt, *The Verbal Icon: studies in the meaning of poetry* (Lexington, Kentucky: University of Kentucky Press, 1954) and Cleanth Brooks,

The Well Wrought Urn (New York: Harcourt Brace, 1947).

16 Empson, 'O Miselle Passer' (response to John Sparrow), in *Argufying*, pp. 193–202.

17 Ibid., p. 197.

18 Ibid., p. 198.

19 Ibid., p. 197.

20 See especially Sigmund Freud, *Totem and Taboo and other works* in *The Standard Edition of the Complete Psychological Works of Sigmund Freud*, vol. 13, trans. James Strachey (London: Hogarth Press, 1961 reprint).

21 Empson, *Some Versions of Pastoral* (Harmondsworth: Penguin, 1966). All further refences given by *SVP* and page-number in the text.

22 See for instance René Girard, *Violence and the Sacred*, trans. Patrick Gregory (Baltimore: Johns Hopkins University Press, 1977).

23 See Neil Hertz, 'More Lurid Figures: de Man reading Empson', in Christopher Norris and Nigel Mapp (eds.), *William Empson: the critical achievement* (Cambridge: Cambridge University Press, 1993), pp. 213–42. Also Hertz, *The End of the Line: essays on psychoanalysis and the sublime* (New York: Columbia University Press, 1983).

24 See for instance Hertz, *The End of the Line* (op. cit.); Peter de Bolla, *The Discourse of the Sublime: history, aesthetics and the subject* (Oxford: Basil Blackwell, 1989); Paul Crowther, *The Kantian Sublime: from morality to art* (Oxford: Clarendon Press, 1989); Hugh J. Silverman and Gary Aylesworth (eds.), *The Textual Sublime: deconstruction and its differences* (Albany, NY: State University of New York Press, 1990); and Jean-Francois Lyotard, *The Differend: phrases in dispute*, trans. Georges van den Abbeele (Minneapolis: University of Minnesota Press, 1988).

25 See Paul de Man, 'The Dead-End of Formalist Criticism', in *Blindness and Insight: essays in the rhetoric of contemporary criticism* (London: Methuen, 1983), pp. 229–45.

26 See especially Empson, 'Still the Strange Necessity' and 'Thy Darling in an Urn', in *Argufying*, pp. 120–8 and 282–8.

27 Empson, 'Still the Strange Necessity', p. 124.

28 Empson, 'Herbert's Quaintness', in *Argufying*, pp. 256–9; p. 257.

29 Empson, 'The Verbal Analysis', in *Argufying*, p. 108.

30 Paul Ricoeur, *Freud and Philosophy* (New Haven: Yale University Press, 1970), p. 496.

31 See Stanley Fish, *Is There a Text in this Class? the authority of interpretive communities* (Cambridge, Mass.: Harvard University Press, 1980).

32 See Raymond Williams, 'Pastoral and Counter-Pastoral', *Critical Quarterly*, vol. 10 (1968), pp. 277–90.

33 G. W. F. Hegel, *The Phenomenology of Spirit*, trans. A. V. Miller (London: Oxford University Press, 1977).

34 For a useful selection of relevant texts see David Simpson (ed.), *The Origins of Modern Critical Thought: German aesthetics and literary criticism from Lessing to Hegel* (Cambridge: Cambridge University Press, 1988).

35 Paul de Man, 'The Dead-End of Formalist Criticism', in *Blindness and Insight*. All further references given by *BI* and page-number in the text.

36 Martin Heidegger, *Poetry, Language, Thought*, trans. Albert Hofstadter (New York: Harper & Row, 1971).

37 See de Man, 'The Rhetoric of Temporality', in *Blindness and Insight*, pp. 187–228; also *The Rhetoric of Romanticism* (New York: Columbia University Press, 1984).

38 See especially de Man, *The Resistance to Theory* (Minneapolis: University of Minnesota Press, 1986).

39 Empson, 'Thy Darling in an Urn', in *Argufying*, p. 285.

40 Empson, 'The Calling Trumpets', in *Argufying*, pp. 137–41; p. 141.

41 Empson, 'Advanced Thought', in *Argufying*, pp. 516–21; p. 516.

42 For a critique of these and related notions, see Christopher Norris, *What's Wrong with Postmodernism: critical theory and the ends of philosophy* (London: Harvester–Wheatsheaf; and Baltimore: Johns Hopkins University Press, 1990).

43 Haffenden records some of Empson's (to say the least) negative remarks about Derrida, Barthes and recent French theory in his introduction to *Argufying*, pp. 51–3.

44 Raymond Williams, *Keywords: a vocabulary of culture and society* (London: Fontana, 1976).

45 Empson, 'Compacted Doctrines', *Argufying*, pp. 184–9; p. 188.

46 Ferdinand de Saussure, *Course in General Linguistics*, trans. Wade Baskin (London: Fontana, 1974).

47 See Christopher Norris, *What's Wrong with Postmodernism*; also Norris, 'Deconstruction, Naming and Necessity: some logical options', in *The Deconstructive Turn* (London: Methuen, 1983), pp. 144–62 and Norris, 'Sense, Reference and Logic: a critique of post-structuralist reason' in *The Contest of Faculties* (London: Methuen, 1985), pp. 47–69.

48 See especially Roland Barthes, *S/Z*, trans. Richard Miller (London: Jonathan Cape, 1975).

49 Leonard Bloomfield, *Language* (London: Allen & Unwin, 1935).

50 W. V. O. Quine, *Quiddities: an intermittently philosophical dictionary* (Harmondsworth: Penguin, 1987), p. 156.

51 Ibid., p. 157.

52 See especially Paul de Man, 'The Resistance to Theory' and 'The Return to Philology', in *The Resistance to Theory*, pp. 3–20 and 21–6.

53 Bertrand Russell, 'On Denoting', *Mind*, vol. 14 (1905), pp. 479–93.

54 Gottlob Frege, 'On Sense and Reference', in *Translations from the Philosophical Writings of Gottlob Frege*, eds. Max Black and P. T. Geach (Oxford: Blackwell, 1952), pp. 56–78.

55 Empson, *Milton's God*, 2nd edn. (London: Chatto & Windus, 1965), p. 30.

56 See Donald Davidson, *Inquiries into Truth and Interpretation*.

57 See Quine, *From a Logical Point of View*.

58 I. A. Richards, *Interpretation in Teaching* (New York: Harcourt Brace, 1938).

59 Plato, *Theaetetus*, trans. and ed. Robin A. R. Waterfield (Harmondsworth: Penguin, 1987); Gilbert Ryle, 'Letters and Syllables in Plato', in Ryle, *Collected Papers*, vol. 1 (London: Hutchinson, 1971), pp. 54–73.

60 See for instance Noam Chomsky, *Aspects of the Theory of Syntax* (Cambridge, Mass.: MIT Press, 1965); also Chomsky, *Current Issues in Linguistic Theory* (The Hague: Mouton, 1966).

61 See Frege, 'On Sense and Reference'.

62 See especially Noam Chomsky, *Language and Politics*, ed. C. P. Otero (Montreal: Black Rose Books, 1988).

63 Empson, *Milton's God*, p. 58.

64 See Empson, 'Orwell at the BBC', in *Argufying*, pp. 495–501.

65 C. S. Lewis, *A Preface to 'Paradise Lost'* (London and New York: Oxford University Press, 1942).

66 See especially Jürgen Habermas, *Communication and the Evolution of Society*, trans. Thomas McCarthy (London: Heinemann, 1979).

67 See for instance Michel Foucault, *Language, Counter-Memory, Practice*, eds. D. F. Bouchard and S. Simon (Oxford: Blackwell, 1977) and *Power/Knowledge*, ed. Colin Gordon (Brighton: Harvester, 1980); also H. Aram Veeser (ed.), *The New Historicism* (London: Routledge, 1989).

68 Empson, review of E. A. Burtt, *The Metaphysical Foundations of Modern Science*, reprinted in *Argufying*, pp. 530–3; p. 531.

69 See for instance Stanley Fish, *Is There a Text in this Class?*; Richard Rorty, *Consequences of Pragmatism* (Minneapolis: University of Minnesota Press, 1982); and the essays collected in W. J. T. Mitchell (ed.), *Against Theory: literary theory and the new pragmatism* (Chicago: University of Chicago Press, 1985).

70 See especially Mikhail Bakhtin, *The Dialogic Imagination*, ed. Michael Holquist, trans. Caryl Emerson and Michael Holquist (Austin: University of Texas Press, 1981).

71 See Bakhtin, *Marxism and the Philosophy of Language*, trans. L. Matejka and I. R. Titunik (New York: Seminar Press, 1973).

72 See for instance Bakhtin, *Rabelais and his World*, trans. Helene Iswolsky (Cambridge, Mass.: Harvard University Press, 1968); *Problems of Dostoevski's Poetics*, ed. and trans. Caryl Emerson (Minneapolis: University of Minnesota Press, 1984); *Speech Genres and other late essays*, ed. Caryl Emerson and Michael Holquist, trans. Vern W. McGee (Austin: University of Texas Press, 1986).

73 For some well-informed and often sharply critical commentary, see Ken Hirschkop and David Shepherd (eds.), *Bakhtin and Cultural Theory* (Manchester: Manchester University Press, 1989). Other recent studies include Katerina Clark and Michael Holquist, *Mikhail Bakhtin* (Cambridge, Mass.: MIT Press, 1984); Tzvetan Todorov, *Mikhail Bakhtin: the dialogical principle* (Manchester: Manchester University Press, 1984); David Lodge, *After Bakhtin: essays on fiction and criticism* (London: Routledge, 1990).

74 Empson, 'Compacted Doctrines', in *Argufying*, p. 184.

75 Ibid., p. 187.

76 See Habermas, *Communication and the Evolution of Society* and *The Theory of Communicative Action*, vol. 1, trans. Thomas McCarthy (London: Heinemann, 1984).

77 Habermas, *Knowledge and Human Interests*, trans. Jeremy Shapiro (London: Heinemann, 1972).

78 Habermas, *The Philosophical Discourse of Modernity: twelve lectures*, trans. Frederick Lawrence (Cambridge: Polity Press, 1987).

79   See Donald Davidson, 'What Metaphors Mean', in *Inquiries into Truth and Interpretation*, pp. 245–64.

80   Cleanth Brooks, *The Well Wrought Urn*, p. 138.

81   See Empson, 'The Hammer's Ring', 'Remembering I. A. Richards' and 'Basic English', in *Argufying*, pp. 216–31.

82   Empson, 'Basic English and Wordsworth', in *Argufying*, pp. 232–8; p. 232.

83   Ibid., p. 234.

84   Ibid., p. 238.

85   Empson, 'The Foundations of Empirical Knowledge', in *Argufying*, pp. 583–4; p. 583.

86   Ibid., p. 584.

87   Ibid., p. 584.

88   Ibid., p. 583.

89   Paul de Man, 'The Rhetoric of Temporality'.

90   See especially M. H. Abrams, *The Mirror and the Lamp: romantic theory and the critical tradition* (New York: Oxford University Press, 1953).

91   See for instance de Man, 'Phenomenality and Materiality in Kant', in Gary Shapiro and Alan Sica (eds.), *Hermeneutics: questions and prospects* (Amherst: University of Massachusetts Press, 1984).

92   De Man, 'Aesthetic Formalization: Kleist's *Uber das Marionettentheater*', in *The Rhetoric of Romanticism*, pp. 263–90.

93   Empson, 'Basic English and Wordsworth', p. 238.

94   See de Man, *Wartime Journalism, 1939–43*, eds. Werner Hamacher, Neil Hertz, and Thomas Keenan (Lincoln, Nebraska: University of Nebraska Press, 1988); also *Responses: on Paul de Man's wartime journalism*, eds. Hamacher, Hertz and Keenan (Nebraska, 1989) and Christopher Norris, *Paul de Man: deconstruction and the critique of aesthetic ideology* (New York and London: Routledge, 1988).

95   See de Man, *The Resistance to Theory*.

96   See for instance Empson, 'The Cult of Unnaturalism' and 'Literary Criticism and the Christian Revival', in *Argufying*, pp. 627–31 and 632–7; also 'Hunt the Symbol', *Times Literary Supplement*, 23 April 1964, pp. 339–41.

97   Empson, review of Maynard Mack, *'King Lear' In Our Time*, *Essays in Criticism*, vol. 17 (1967), p. 95.

98   See especially the articles and reviews collected in Empson, *Using Biography* (London: Chatto & Windus, 1984) and *Essays on Shakespeare* (Cambridge: Cambridge University Press, 1986); also 'Donne the Space Man', *Kenyon Review*, vol. 19 (1957), pp. 337–99; 'The Ancient Mariner', in *Argufying*, pp. 297–319; and the various shorter pieces on these and other authors brought together by Haffenden in *Argufying*.

99   Empson, 'Donne in the New Edition', *Critical Quarterly*, vol. 8 (1966), pp. 255–80.

100 Empson, letter in response to Roger Sale, *Hudson Review*, vol. 20 (1967), p. 538.

101 John Carey, *John Donne: life, mind, art* (London: Faber, 1981); see also Empson's review, 'There Is No Penance Due to Ignorance', *New York Review of Books*, 28 (3 December 1981), pp. 42–50.

102 Empson, 'Donne in the New Edition'.
103 Empson, 'Volpone', *Hudson Review*, vol. 21 (1969), p. 659.
104 Empson, reply to James Jensen's article 'The Construction of *Seven Types of Ambiguity'*, *Modern Language Quarterly*, vol. 27 (1966), p. 257.
105 Empson, 'Orwell's *Nineteen Eighty-Four*' (letter), *Critical Quarterly*, vol. 1 (1959), p. 159.
106 Empson, *Collected Poems* (London: Chatto & Windus, 1969), p. 110.

NOTES TO CHAPTER 4

1 J. Hillis Miller, *The Ethics of Reading: Kant, de Man, Eliot, Trollope, James, and Benjamin* (New York: Columbia University Press, 1987). Henceforth referred to as 'Miller' with page-number in the text.

2 Onora O'Neill, *Constructions of Reason: explorations of Kant's practical philosophy* (Cambridge: Cambridge University Press, 1989). Henceforth referred to as 'O'Neill' with page-number in the text. See also O'Neill, *Acting on Principle: an essay on Kantian ethics* (New York: Columbia University Press, 1975).

3 See for instance Richard Rorty, 'Philosophy as a Kind of Writing', in *Consequences of Pragmatism* (Minneapolis: University of Minnesota Press, 1982), pp. 90–109.

4 For arguments to this effect see Stanley Fish, *Doing What Comes Naturally: change, rhetoric, and the practice of theory in literary and legal studies* (Oxford: Clarendon Press, 1989); also W. J. T. Mitchell (ed.), *Against Theory: literary theory and the new pragmatism* (Chicago: University of Chicago Press, 1985).

5 See also Miller, *Theory Now and Then* (Hemel Hempstead: Harvester–Wheatsheaf, 1991).

6 This case is argued most cogently in Jacques Derrida's early work. See for instance Derrida, *'Speech and Phenomena' and Other Essays on Husserl's Theory of Signs*, trans. David B. Allison (Evanston, Ill.: Northwestern University Press, 1973) and *Edmund Husserl's 'Origin of Geometry': an introduction*, trans. John P. Leavey, Junior (Stony Brook, N. Y.: Nicolas Hays, 1978).

7 See Christopher Norris, 'Philosophy as *Not* Just a "Kind of Writing": Derrida and the claim of reason', in R.W. Dasenbrock (ed.), *Re-Drawing the Lines: analytic philosophy, deconstruction, and literary theory* (Minneapolis: University of Minnesota Press, 1989), pp. 189–203 and Rorty's response, 'Two Meanings of "Logocentrism": a reply to Norris', pp. 204–16.

8 See Ludwig Wittgenstein, *Philosophical Investigations*, trans. G. E. M. Anscombe (Oxford: Blackwell, 1953) and Gottlob Frege, 'On Sense and Reference', in Max Black and P. T. Geach (eds.), *Translations from the Philosophical Writings of Gottlob Frege* (Oxford: Blackwell, 1952), pp. 56–78; also Norris, 'Sense, Reference and Logic', in *The Contest of Faculties* (London: Methuen, 1985), pp. 47–69.

9 Paul de Man, *Allegories of Reading: figural language in Rousseau, Nietzsche, Rilke, and Proust* (New Haven: Yale University Press, 1979), p. 10.

10 See for instance Cleanth Brooks, *The Well-Wrought Urn* (New York: Harcourt Brace, 1947) and W. K. Wimsatt, *The Verbal Icon: studies in the meaning of poetry* (Lexington, KY: University of Kentucky Press, 1954).

11 Miller, 'The Search for Grounds in Literary Study', in *Theory Now and Then*, pp. 263–75; p. 271.

12 Ibid., p. 271.

13 Ibid., p. 271.

14 Thomas Nagel, *The View From Nowhere* (New York and London: Oxford University Press, 1986).

15 See the essays collected in Paul de Man, *The Resistance to Theory* (Minneapolis: University of Minnesota Press, 1986).

16 Ibid., p. 14.

17 See I. A. Richards, *Principles of Literary Criticism* (London: Paul Trench Trubner, 1924).

18 See for instance Wimsatt, *The Verbal Icon*.

19 De Man, *The Resistance to Theory*, p. 14.

20 Ibid., p. 14.

21 Ibid., p. 8.

22 Ibid., p. 15.

23 Ibid., p. 16.

24 See de Man, *Allegories of Reading*; also 'Pascal's Allegory of Persuasion', in Stephen J. Greenblatt (ed.), *Allegory and Representation* (Baltimore: Johns Hopkins University Press, 1981), pp. 1–25.

25 De Man, *The Resistance to Theory*, p. 14.

26 For a briskly-argued survey of the issues raised by this line of thought, see Jerry Fodor and Ernest Lepore, *Holism: a shopper's guide* (Oxford: Blackwell, 1992).

27 De Man, *Allegories of Reading*, pp. 79–131.

28 De Man, 'Reading (Proust)', in *Allegories of Reading*, pp. 57–78; p. 57.

29 Marcel Proust, *Du Côté de chez Swann* (Paris: Pléiade, 1954), pp. 82–8. De Man gives his own translation of the relevant passages.

30 De Man, *Allegories of Reading*, p. 67.

31 Ibid., p. 15.

32 Ibid., p. 60.

33 Ibid., p. 16.

34 Ibid., p. 60.

35 Ibid., pp. 60–2.

36 De Man, 'Reading and History', in *The Resistance to Theory*, pp. 54–72; p. 64.

37 For some perceptive commentary on this aspect of de Man's work, see Geoffrey Galt Harpham, *The Ascetic Imperative in Culture and Criticism* (Chicago: University of Chicago Press, 1987); also Minae Mizumura, 'Renunciation', in Peter Brooks, Shoshana Felman and J. Hillis Miller (eds.), *The Lesson of Paul de Man* (Yale French Studies, 69: Yale University Press, 1985), pp. 81–97.

38 De Man, *Allegories of Reading*, p. 64.

39 Ibid., p. 67.

40 Ibid., p. 71.

41 See also de Man, 'The Rhetoric of Temporality', in *Blindness and Insight: essays in the rhetoric of contemporary criticism* (London: Methuen, 1983), pp. 187–228.

42 De Man, *Allegories of Reading*, p. 10.

43 De Man, *The Resistance to Theory*, p. 13.

44 De Man, *Allegories of Reading*, p. 57.

45 Ibid., p. 58.

46 See Roland Barthes, *S/Z*, trans. Richard Miller (London: Jonathan Cape, 1975) for a dazzling exposition of what has since become the stock-in-trade jargon of much post-structuralist literary theory.

47 See Perry Anderson, *In the Tracks of Historical Materialism* (London: Verso, 1983).

48 Ferdinand de Saussure, *Course in General Linguistics*, trans. Wade Baskin (London: Fontana, 1974).

49 See for instance Perry Anderson (op. cit.); Roy Bhaskar, *Reclaiming Reality: a critical introduction to modern philosophy* (London: Verso, 1989); Terry Eagleton, *Ideology: an introduction* (London: Verso, 1991); Christopher Norris, *Deconstruction and the Interests of Theory* (London: Pinter Publishers, 1988) and *What's Wrong with Postmodernism* (Hemel Hempstead: Harvester-Wheatsheaf, 1991); Raymond Tallis, *Not Saussure* (London: Macmillan, 1988) and *In Defence of Realism* (London: Edward Arnold, 1988).

50 For further discussion see Norris, *The Contest of Faculties, Deconstruction and the Interests of Theory*, and *What's Wrong with Postmodernism*.

51 See Fish, *Doing What Comes Naturally* and Rorty, *Contingency, Irony, and Solidarity* (Cambridge: Cambridge University Press, 1989).

52 Sir Philip Sidney, 'An Apology for Poetry', in D. J. Enright and Ernst de Chickera (eds.), *English Critical Texts* (London: Oxford University Press, 1962), pp. 3–49; p. 31; Roland Barthes, *S/Z*.

53 See for instance David Lewis, *On the Plurality of Worlds* (Oxford: Blackwell, 1986) and Thomas Pavel, *Fictional Worlds* (Harvard, Mass.: Harvard University Press, 1987); also John R. Searle, 'The Logical Status of Fictional Discourse', in *Expression and Meaning: studies in the theory of speech-acts* (Cambridge: Cambridge University Press, 1979), pp. 58–75 and – taking issue with Searle – Richard Rorty, 'Is There a Problem about Fictional Discourse?', in *Consequences of Pragmatism*, pp. 110–38.

54 See de Man, 'Phenomenality and Materiality in Kant', in Gary Shapiro and Alan Sica (eds.), *Hermeneutics: questions and prospects* (Amherst: University of Massachusetts Press, 1984), pp. 121–44 and 'Hegel on the Sublime', in Mark Krupnick (ed.), *Displacement: Derrida and after* (Bloomington, Indiana: Indiana University Press, 1983), pp. 139–53; also de Man, 'Pascal's Allegory of Persuasion' and his reading of Locke and Kant in 'The Epistemology of Metaphor', *Critical Inquiry*, vol. 5, no. 1 (Fall, 1978), pp. 13–30.

55 Immanuel Kant, *Critique of Practical Reason*, trans. Lewis White Beck (Indianapolis: Bobbs–Merrill, 1977) and *Foundations of the Metaphysics of Morals*, trans. L. W. Beck (Indianapolis: Bobbs–Merrill, 1978), p. 19ff.

56 Kant, *Critique of Pure Reason*, trans. Norman Kemp Smith (London: Macmillan, 1933), pp. 171–2.

57 See Frege, 'On Sense and Reference' and Bertrand Russell, *An Enquiry into Meaning and Truth* (London: Allen & Unwin, 1940).

58 De Man, 'Excuses (*Confessions*)', in *Allegories of Reading*, pp. 278–301.

59 Ibid., p. 299.

60 Ibid., p. 280.

61 Ibid., p. 293.

62 See Jean-Jacques Rousseau, *Confessions* (London: E. J. Dent, 1931), pp. 74–7.

63 De Man, *Allegories of Reading*, pp. 285–6.

64 Ibid., p. 285.

65 Ibid., p. 280.

66 See especially Jacques Derrida, *Dissemination*, trans. Barbara Johnson (London: Athlone Press, 1981) and *Margins of Philosophy*, trans. Alan Bass (Brighton: Harvester, 1982).

67 See Brooks, *The Well-Wrought Urn* and Wimsatt, *The Verbal Icon*.

68 De Man, *The Resistance to Theory*, pp. 18–19.

69 Ibid., p. 14.

70 See for instance Alasdair MacIntyre, *After Virtue: a study in moral theory* (London: Duckworth, 1981); Michael Walzer, *Spheres of Justice* (Oxford: Blackwell, 1983) and *Interpretation and Social Criticism* (Cambridge, Mass.: Harvard University Press, 1987); and Bernard Williams, *Ethics and the Limits of Philosophy* (London: Fontana, 1985).

71 See Richard Rorty, *Consequences of Pragmatism*.

72 Miller is here taking a lead from de Man, who in turn makes the point through a deliberate misquotation of Heidegger: '*Die Sprache verspricht (sich)*: to the extent that it is necessarily misleading, language just as necessarily conveys the promise of its own truth'. See de Man, *Allegories of Reading*, p. 277. Miller's reading is challenged on various points by H. P. Rickman in his article 'Making a Mess of Kant', *Philosophy and Literature*, vol. 5, no. 2 (October 1991), pp. 278–85.

73 Kant, *Foundations of the Metaphysics of Morals*, pp. 22–3. Cited by Miller, p. 31.

74 See for instance Peter Winch, *Ethics and Action* (London: Routledge & Kegan Paul, 1972).

75 See Winch, Walzer and Williams (op. cit.); also Clifford Geertz, 'Blurred Genres: the reconfiguration of social thought' and 'Common Sense as a Cultural System', in *Local Knowledge: new essays on interpretive anthropology* (New York: Basic Books, 1989), pp. 19–35 and 73–93.

76 See for instance Rorty, 'The Priority of Democracy to Philosophy' and 'Postmodernist Bourgeois Liberalism', in *Objectivity, Relativism, and Truth* (Cambridge: Cambridge University Press, 1991), pp. 175–96 and 197–202.

77 It should be noted that other recent commentators have offered some sharply differing assessments. See for instance Giles Gunn, *Thinking Across the American Grain: ideology, intellect, and the new pragmatism* (Chicago: University of Chicago Press, 1992); Cornel West, *The American Evasion of Philosophy: a genealogy of pragmatism* (Chicago: University of Chicago Press, 1987); and Robert B. Westbrook, *John Dewey and American Democracy* (Ithaca and London: Cornell University Press, 1991). See also Christopher Norris, *Uncritical Theory: postmodernism, intellectuals and the Gulf War* (London: Lawrence & Wishart, 1992) for a reading that contrasts this current neopragmatist drift with the far more robust attitudes adopted by James, Dewey and Peirce.

78 For an argument to this effect see Charles Altieri, 'Wittgenstein on

Consciousness and Language: a challenge to Derridean theory', *Modern Language Notes*, vol. 91 (1976), pp. 1, 397–423.

79 See Jean-François Lyotard, *The Postmodern Condition*, trans. Geoff Bennington and Brian Massumi (Manchester: University of Manchester Press, 1986) and *The Differend: phrases in dispute*, trans. Georges van den Abbeele (Manchester: Manchester University Press, 1988).

80 See especially Lyotard, *The Inhuman: reflections on time*, trans. Geoff Bennington and Rachel Bowlby (Cambridge: Polity Press, 1991). See also Peter de Bolla, *The Discourse of the Sublime: readings in history, aesthetics and the subject* (Oxford: Blackwell, 1989); Paul Crowther, *The Kantian Sublime: from morality to art* (Oxford: Clarendon Press, 1989); Neil Hertz, *The End of the Line: essays on psychoanalysis and the sublime* (New York: Columbia University Press, 1985); Hugh Silverman and Gary Aylesworth (eds.), *The Textual Sublime* (Albany, NY: State University of New York Press, 1990); Thomas Weiskel, *The Romantic Sublime: studies in the structure and psychology of transcendence* (Baltimore: Johns Hopkins University Press, 1976); Slavoj Zizek, *The Sublime Object of Ideology* (London: Verso, 1990).

81 Saul Kripke, *Wittgenstein on R̄ules and Private Language* (Cambridge, Mass.: Harvard University Press, 1982).

82 De Man, *The Resistance to Theory*, p. 13.

83 See also Henry Staten, *Wittgenstein and Derrida* (Lincoln, Neb. and London: University of Nebraska Press, 1984).

84 Winch, *Ethics and Action*, p. 55.

85 Ibid., p. 154.

86 De Man, *The Resistance to Theory*, p. 19.

87 See for instance some of the essays collected in Lindsay Waters and Wlad Godzich (eds.), *Reading de Man Reading* (Minneapolis: University of Minnesota Press, 1989); also Norris, *Paul de Man: deconstruction and the critique of aesthetic ideology* (New York: Routledge, 1988).

88 De Man, *Allegories of Reading*, p. 131.

89 For a wide-ranging and judicious account of these developments, see Joseph Margolis, *Pragmatism Without Foundations* (Oxford: Blackwell, 1986) and *Texts Without Referents: reconciling science and narrative* (Blackwell, 1989).

90 Jürgen Habermas, *The Philosophical Discourse of Modernity: twelve lectures*, trans. Frederick Lawrence (Cambridge: Polity Press, 1987).

91 See for instance Richard Rorty, *Philosophy and the Mirror of Nature* (Oxford: Blackwell, 1980).

92 Most of these texts are collected in Hans Reiss (ed.), *Kant's Political Writings* (Cambridge: Cambridge University Press, 1970) and L. W. Beck, R. E. Anchor and E. L. Fackenham (eds.), *Kant: On History* (Indianapolis: Bobbs–Merrill, 1963).

93 See especially Hayden White, *Tropics of Discourse* (Baltimore: Johns Hopkins University Press, 1978) and *The Content of the Form* (Johns Hopkins U. P., 1988). The issue is taken up from a variety of theoretical standpoints in Derek Attridge, Geoff Bennington and Robert Young (eds.), *Post-Structuralism and the Question of History* (Cambridge: Cambridge University Press, 1987).

94 I discuss this interdisciplinary trend – and the dangers of an undifferentiating

'textualist' approach – in Norris, *What's Wrong With Postmodernism*. See also Tony Bennett, *Outside Literature* (London: Routledge, 1991).

95   See for instance Tallis, *Not Saussure* and *In Defence of Realism*; also Gregory Currie, *The Nature of Fiction* (Cambridge: Cambridge University Press, 1990) and Cristopher Nash, *World-Games: the tradition of anti-realist revolt* (London: Routledge, 1987).

96   See Pavel, *Fictional Worlds* and Lewis, *The Plurality of Worlds*.

97   See for instance David E. Cooper, *Metaphor* (Oxford: Blackwell, 1986); Eva Feder Kittay, *Metaphor: its cognitive force and linguistic structure* (Oxford: Clarendon Press, 1987); David S. Miall (ed.), *Metaphor: problems and perspectives* (Brighton: Harvester, 1982); Andrew Ortony (ed.), *Metaphor and Thought* (Cambridge: Cambridge University Press, 1979) and Sheldon Sacks (ed.), *On Metaphor* (Chicago: University of Chicago Press, 1979). On the role of metaphor in scientific theory-formation, see also Ian Hacking, *Representing and Intervening* (Cambridge: Cambridge University Press, 1983) and Dominique Lecourt, *Marxism and Epistemology: Bachelard, Canguilhem and Foucault*, trans. Ben Brewster (London: New Left Books, 1975).

98   Kant, *Critique of Pure Reason*, p. vii.

99   Ibid., p. 766.

100 Gilles Deleuze and Félix Guattari, *A Thousand Plateaus*, trans. Brian Massumi (Minneapolis: University of Minnesota Press, 1987).

101 See Jürgen Habermas, *Communication and the Evolution of Society*, trans. Thomas McCarthy (London: Heinemann, 1979) and *The Theory of Communicative Action*, trans. McCarthy (two vols, Boston: Beacon Press, 1984 and 1989).

102 Kant, *Critique of Judgment*, trans. J. C. Meredith (Oxford: Clarendon Press, 1978), p. 293.

103 See especially Stanley Fish, *Doing What Comes Naturally* and *Is There a Text in This Class? The authority of interpretive communities* (Cambridge, Mass.: Harvard University Press, 1980).

104 Jean-Paul Sartre, 'Existentialism Is a Humanism', in Walter Kaufmann (ed.), *Existentialism from Dostoevsky to Sartre* (Cleveland: World Publishing, 1956), pp. 287–311.

105 Franz Kafka, 'Before the Law', *Wedding Preparations in the Country and Other Stories*, trans. Willa and Edwin Muir (Harmondsworth: Penguin, 1978). This parable reappears as an episode in Kafka's *The Trial*. See also Jacques Derrida, 'Before the Law', in Derrida, *Acts of Literature*, ed. Derek Attridge (New York and London: Routledge, 1992), pp. 181–220.

106 Martin Heidegger, *Kant and the Problem of Metaphysics*, trans. James S. Churchill (Bloomington, Indiana: Indiana University Press, 1962).

107 Lyotard, *The Differend*.

108 See Donald Davidson, 'On the Very Idea of a Conceptual Scheme', in *Inquiries Into Truth and Interpretation* (Oxford: Clarendon Press, 1984), pp. 183–98.

109 Hilary Putnam, *Realism and Reason* (Cambridge: Cambridge University Press, 1983), p. 237.

110 See Rorty, 'The Priority of Democracy to Philosophy' and 'Postmodernist Bourgeois Liberalism'.

111 See for instance Francis Fukuyama, *The End of History and the Last Man* (London: Hamish Hamilton, 1992); also my discussion of this postmodern 'end-of-ideology' rhetoric in Norris, *Uncritical Theory*, pp. 155–8 and *passim*. There is a common point of origin for much of this thinking – French and North American alike – in Alexander Kojève's celebrated course of lectures on Hegel, delivered in Paris during the early 1940s. See Kojève, *Introduction to the Reading of Hegel*, ed. Allan Bloom, trans. James H. Nichols (Ithaca and London: Cornell University Press, 1980).

112 Bernard Williams, *Morality: an introduction to ethics* (Cambridge: Cambridge University Press, 1972), p. 34.

113 Richard Freadman and Seumas Miller, *Re-Thinking Theory: a critique of contemporary literary theory and an alternative account* (Cambridge: Cambridge University Press, 1992).

114 Ibid., p. 64.

115 Ibid., p. 63.

116 See Lyotard, *The Differend*, in particular pp. 3–4, 14, 18–19, 32–3.

117 De Man, *Allegories of Reading*, p. 206.

118 See Habermas, *Communication and the Evolution of Society* and *The Theory of Communicative Action*; also Habermas, *Moral Consciousness and Communicative Action* (Cambridge: Polity Press, 1990).

119 See especially Martin Heidegger, *Poetry, Language, Thought*, trans. Albert Hofstadter (New York: Harper & Row, 1977).

120 J. G. Fichte, *The Science of Knowledge*, ed. and trans. P. Heath and J. Lachs (Cambridge: Cambridge University Press, 1982). For a detailed account of this chapter in the history of ideas, see Frederick C. Beiser, *The Fate of Reason: German philosophy from Kant to Fichte* (Cambridge, Mass.: Harvard University Press, 1987).

121 See de Man, *Allegories of Reading*; also 'Walter Benjamin's "The Task of the Translator"', in *The Resistance to Theory*, pp. 73–93 and 'Shelley Disfigured', in de Man, *The Rhetoric of Romanticism* (New York: Columbia University Press, 1984), pp. 93–123. De Man's only extended discussion of Fichte occurs in a late essay entitled 'The Concept of Irony', to be published in the forthcoming volume *Aesthetic Ideology*, edited by Andrzej Warminski.

122 Stanley Rosen, *Hermeneutics as Politics* (New York: Oxford University Press, 1987).

123 See especially Michel Foucault, *Power/Knowledge: selected interviews and other writings, 1972–7* (Brighton: Harvester, 1980).

124 Foucault, *The Order of Things: an archaeology of the human sciences* (New York: Random House, 1973), pp. 318–43.

125 See the later writings and interviews collected in Paul Rabinow (ed.), *The Foucault Reader* (Harmondsworth: Penguin, 1984).

126 Foucault, 'What Is Enlightenment?', in *The Foucault Reader*, pp. 32–50.

127 Alan Montefiore, 'The Political Responsibility of Intellectuals', in Ian MacLean, Alan Montefiore and Peter Winch (eds.), *The Political Responsibility of Intellectuals* (Cambridge: Cambridge University Press, 1990), pp. 201–28; pp. 225–6.

NOTES TO CHAPTER 5

1 Page duBois, *Torture and Truth* (New York and London: Routledge, 1991). All further references to this volume given by page-number only in the text. For other recent work of related interest, see for instance Elaine Scarry, *The Body in Pain: the making and unmaking of the world* (New York: Oxford University Press, 1985); Barbara Harlow, *Resistance Literature* (London: Methuen, 1987); and Barbara J. Eckstein, *The Language of Fiction in a World of Pain: reading politics as paradox* (Philadelphia: University of Pennsylvania Press, 1990).

2 Michel Foucault, *Discipline and Punish: the birth of the prison*, trans. Alan Sheridan (London: Allen Lane, 1977).

3 See especially Foucault, *Language, Counter-Memory, Practice*, ed. D. F. Bouchard and Sherry Simon (Oxford: Blackwell, 1977).

4 See Foucault, *The History of Sexuality*, vol. 1, trans. Robert Hurley, (New York: Vintage Books, 1980).

5 This argument is pursued at various points in Foucault, *Power/Knowledge: selected interviews and other writings*, ed. Colin Gordon (Brighton: Harvester, 1980).

6 See Foucault, *The Order of Things: an archaeology of the human sciences* (London: Tavistock, 1970).

7 Jürgen Habermas, *The Philosophical Discourse of Modernity: twelve lectures*, trans. Frederick Lawrence (Cambridge: Polity Press, 1988).

8 See for instance Noam Chomsky, *The Culture of Terrorism* (Boston: South End Press, 1978).

9 See also William Twining and Barrie Paskins, 'Torture and Philosophy', in *Proceedings of the Aristotelian Society*, vol. 52 (1978), pp. 143–94.

10 Aristotle, *Politics*, ed. W. D. Ross (London: Oxford University Press, 1957).

11 See Gregory Vlastos, 'Slavery in Plato's Thought', in *Platonic Studies* (New Jersey: Princeton University Press, 1973), pp. 147–63.

12 Thus for instance Pindar: 'Gold and a straight mind show what they are on the touchstone' (cited by duBois, p. 14).

13 See the texts of Herakleitos and Parmenides collected in Jonathan Barnes (ed.), *Early Greek Philosophy* (Harmondsworth: Penguin, 1987).

14 See for instance Stanley Fish, *Doing What Comes Naturally: change, rhetoric, and the practice of theory in literary and legal studies* (Oxford: Clarendon Press, 1989).

15 Plato, *Sophist*, in *Works*, vol. 1, trans. J. Burnet (London: Oxford University Press, 1903).

16 Plato, *Meno*, trans. W. K. C. Guthrie (New York: Bobbs–Merrill, 1971).

17 I. F. Stone, *The Trial of Socrates* (New York: Anchor Books, 1989).

18 Jacques Derrida, *Spurs: Nietzsche's styles*, trans. Barbara Harlow (Chicago: University of Chicago Press, 1979). See also Rosi Braidotti, 'The Becoming-Woman of Philosophy: Derrida', in *Patterns of Dissonance: a study of women in contemporary philosophy* (Cambridge: Polity Press, 1991), pp. 98–108.

19 Aristotle, *Politics*.

20 See especially Martin Heidegger, *Poetry, Language and Thought*, trans. Albert Hofstadter (New York: Harper & Row, 1971); also *What Is Called Thinking*,

trans. J. Glenn Gray (New York: Harper & Row, 1972).

21 See Heidegger, 'The Origin of the Work of Art' and 'Poetically Man Dwells . . .', in *Poetry, Language and Thought*.

22 Paul de Man, 'Heidegger's Exegeses of Hölderlin', in *Blindness and Insight: essays in the rhetoric of contemporary criticism* (London: Routledge, 1983), pp. 246–66.

23 See de Man, 'The Rhetoric of Temporality', in *Blindness and Insight*, pp. 187–228.

24 See also Philippe Lacoue-Labarthe, *Heidegger, Art and Politics*, trans. Chris Turner (Oxford: Blackwell, 1990).

25 See for instance Viktor Farias, *Heidegger et le Nazisme* (Paris: Verdier, 1987).

26 De Man, 'Aesthetic Formalization: Kleist's *Uber das Marionnettentheater*, in *The Rhetoric of Romanticism* (New York: Columbia University Press, 1984), pp. 263–90; p. 265.

27 Ibid., p. 264.

28 De Man, 'Heidegger's Exegeses of Hölderlin', p. 263.

29 De Man, *The Resistance to Theory* (Minneapolis: University of Minnesota Press, 1986), p. 19.

30 See for instance Heidegger, *The Question Concerning Technology and other essays*, trans. William Lovitt (New York: Harper & Row, 1977).

31 Plato, *The Republic*, trans. H. D. P. Lee (Harmondsworth: Penguin, 1955), pp. 278–86.

32 Rorty, review of Viktor Farias, *Heidegger et le Nazisme*, *The London Review of Books*, 3 September 1987. See also Rorty, *Essays on Heidegger and Others* (Cambridge: Cambridge University Press, 1991).

33 See Christopher Norris, 'Settling Accounts: Heidegger, de Man and the ends of philosophy', in *What's Wrong with Postmodernism: critical theory and the ends of philosophy* (London: Harvester and Baltimore: Johns Hopkins University Press, 1990), pp. 222–83.

34 For a different and subtly nuanced reading of the relevant texts, see Jacques Derrida, *De l'esprit: Heidegger et la question* (Paris: Galilée, 1987).

35 See for instance Rorty, *Consequences of Pragmatism* (Minneapolis: University of Minnesota Press, 1982) and *Contingency, Irony, and Solidarity* (Cambridge: Cambridge University Press, 1989).

36 Rorty, *Contingency, Irony, and Solidarity*, p. 19.

37 See Rorty, 'Solidarity or Objectivity?', 'The Priority of Democracy to Philosophy', and 'Postmodern Bourgeois Liberalism', in *Objectivity, Relativism, and Truth* (Cambridge: Cambridge University Press, 1991), pp. 21–34, 175–96 and 197–202.

38 See especially Rorty, 'The Priority of Democracy to Philosophy'.

39 See for instance Rorty, 'Heidegger, Kundera, and Dickens', in *Essays on Heidegger and Others*, pp. 66–82.

40 Rorty, 'Philosophy as a Kind of Writing', in *Consequences of Pragmatism*, pp. 89–109. See also Norris, 'Philosophy as *Not* just a "Kind of Writing": Derrida and the claim of reason' and Rorty, 'Two Meanings of "Logocentrism": a reply to Norris', in Reed Way Dasenbrock (ed.), *Re-Drawing the Lines: analytic philosophy,*

deconstruction, and literary theory (Minneapolis: University of Minnesota Press, 1989), pp. 189–203 and 204–16.

41 Karl Popper, *The Open Society and its Enemies* (2 vols, London: Routledge & Kegan Paul, 1966).

42 Habermas, *The Philosophical Discourse of Modernity*.

43 Rorty, 'Heidegger, Kundera, and Dickens', p. 74.

44 See Norris, 'Philosophy as *Not* just a "Kind of Writing"' and *What's Wrong with Postmodernism*.

45 See especially Roy Bhaskar, *Philosophy and the Idea of Freedom* (Oxford: Blackwell, 1991).

46 Rorty, 'Solidarity or Objectivity?'.

47 See for instance the essays collected in W. J. T. Mitchell (ed.), *Against Theory: literary theory and the new pragmatism* (Chicago: University of Chicago Press, 1985).

48 The most commonly cited source of these ideas is Jean-François Lyotard, *The Postmodern Condition: a report on knowledge*, trans. Geoff Bennington and Brian Massumi (Minneapolis: University of Minnesota Press, 1986).

49 Barbara Herrnstein Smith, *Contingencies of Value: alternative perspectives for critical theory* (Cambridge, Mass.: Harvard University Press, 1988).

50 Catherine Belsey, 'Afterword: a Future for Materialist Feminist Criticism?', in Valerie Wayne (ed.), *The Matter of Difference: materialist feminist criticism of Shakespeare* (Hemel Hempstead: Harvester–Wheatsheaf, 1991), pp. 257–70; pp. 262–3.

51 See for instance Peter Gay, *The Enlightenment: an interpretation* (2 vols, London: Routledge & Kegan Paul, 1967 and 1973).

52 T. W. Adorno, *Minima Moralia: reflections from a damaged life*, trans. E. F. N. Jephcott (London: New Left Books, 1974); also T. W. Adorno and Max Horkheimer, *Dialectic of Enlightenment* (London: Verso, 1979).

53 Belsey, 'Afterword: a Future for Materialist Feminist Criticism?', p. 262.

54 Habermas, *The Philosophical Discourse of Modernity*.

55 On this levelling or undifferentiating tendency in Foucault's work, see Michael Walzer, 'The Politics of Michel Foucault', in David C. Hoy (ed.), *Foucault: a critical reader* (Oxford: Blackwell, 1986), pp. 51–68.

56 See Foucault, *Discipline and Punish*; also various passages in Stephen Greenblatt, *Shakespearean Negotiations: the circulation of social energy in Renaissance England* (Oxford: Clarendon Press, 1988) and Greenblatt, *Learning to Curse: essays in early modern culture* (London: Routledge, 1990). I should mention that duBois is more alert to this danger – often courted by Foucault and the New Historicists – of coming to regard such scenes of 'spectacular' human agony as further material for set-piece textualist treatment. In this connection, see Scarry, *The Body in Pain*, especially chapter one, 'The Structure of Torture: the conversion of real pain into the fiction of power' (pp. 27–59).

57 Norman Geras, *Discourses of Extremity: radical ethics and post-Marxist extravagances* (London: Verso, 1990); Ernesto Laclau and Chantal Mouffe, *Hegemony and Socialist Strategy: towards a radical democratic politics* (London: Verso, 1985).

58 Geras, *Discourses of Extremity*, p. 162.

59 In this connection see Christopher Norris, *Spinoza and the Origins of Modern Critical Theory* (Oxford: Blackwell, 1991).

60 See Fish, *Doing What Comes Naturally*.

61 Geras, *Discourses of Extremity*, p. 163.

62 Thomas Hobbes, *Leviathan* (London: Dent, 1978).

63 Habermas, *The Philosophical Discourse of Modernity*.

64 See especially Foucault, *The History of Sexuality* and *Power/Knowledge*.

65 For some relevant background history, see Christopher Hitchens, 'Realpolitik in the Gulf', *New Left Review*, 186 (March/April, 1991), pp. 89–101.

66 See for instance Edward S. Herman and Noam Chomsky, *Manufacturing Consent: the political economy of the mass media* (New York: Pantheon Books, 1988).

67 Francis Fukuyama, 'The End of History', *The National Interest* (Washington), Summer 1989.

68 Fukuyama, 'Changed Days for Ruritania's Dictator', *The Guardian*, 8 April 1991, p. 19.

69 See Rorty, *Contingency, Irony, and Solidarity* and Fish, *Doing What Comes Naturally*.

70 Fukuyama, 'Changed Days for Ruritania's Dictator' (op. cit.)

71 Rorty, *Contingency, Irony, and Solidarity*, p. 113.

72 Terry Eagleton, *Ideology: an introduction* (London: Verso, 1991), p. ix.

73 See for instance Habermas, *The Theory of Communicative Action*, vol. 1, trans. Thomas MacCarthy (London: Heinemann, 1984).

74 This aspect of Heidegger's philosophy is most tellingly criticized by Adorno in *The Jargon of Authenticity*, trans. K. Tarnowski and F. Will (London: Routledge & Kegan Paul, 1973).

75 See Norris, 'Limited Think: how not to read Derrida', in *What's Wrong with Postmodernism*, pp. 134–63.

76 Derrida, 'Afterword' to *Limited Inc* (2nd edn., Evanston: Northwestern University Press, 1989), p. 146.

77 Paul de Man, Foreword to Carol Jacobs, *The Dissimulating Harmony* (Baltimore: Johns Hopkins University Press, 1978), p. viii.

78 Jonathan Culler, *Framing the Sign: criticism and its institutions* (Oxford: Blackwell, 1988), p. 78.

79 Ibid., p. 79.

80 Ibid., p. 79.

81 Catherine Belsey, 'Making Histories Then and Now', in *Uses of History: Marxism, postmodernism and the Renaissance*, ed. Francis Barker (Manchester: Manchester University Press, 1991), pp. 24–46; p. 26.

82 See for instance Lyotard, *The Postmodern Condition*.

83 See especially Kant, *Political Writings*, ed. H. Reiss (Cambridge: Cambridge University Press, 1973) and *On History*, ed. L. W. Beck (New York: Bobbs–Merrill, 1963).

84 Derrida, 'Of an Apocalyptic Tone Recently Adopted in Philosophy', trans. John P. Leavey, *The Oxford Literary Review*, vol. 6, no. 2 (1984), pp. 3–37.

Index of Names